KB054837

# 주한미군지위협정(SOFA)

# 서명 및 발효 7

# 주한미군지위협정(SOFA)

# 서명 및 발효 7

한국학술정보

# | 머리말

미국은 오래전부터 우리나라 외교에 있어서 가장 긴밀하고 실질적인 우호 · 협력관계를 맺어 온 나라다. 6 · 25전쟁 정전 협정이 체결된 후 북한의 재침을 막기 위한 대책으로서 1953년 11월 한미 상호방위조약이 체결되었다. 이는 미군이 한국에 주둔하는 법적 근거였고, 그렇게 주둔하게 된 미군의 시설, 구역, 사업, 용역, 출입국, 통관과 관세, 재판권 등 포괄적인 법적 지위를 규정하는 것이 바로 주한미군지위협정(SOFA)이다. 그러나 이와 관련한 협상은 계속된 난항을 겪으며 한미 상호방위조약이 체결로부터 10년이 훌쩍 넘은 1967년이 돼서야 정식 발효에 이를 수 있었다. 그럼에도 당시 미군 범죄에 대한 한국의 재판권은 심한 제약을 받았으며, 1980년대 후반 민주화 운동과 함께 미군 범죄 문제가 사회적 이슈로 떠오르자 협정을 개정해야 한다는 목소리가 커지게 되었다. 이에 1991년 2월 주한미군지위협정 1차 개정이 진행되었고, 이후에도 여러 사건이 발생하며 2001년 4월 2차 개정이 진행되어 현재에 이르고 있다.

본 총서는 외교부에서 작성하여 최근 공개한 주한미군지위협정(SOFA) 관련 자료를 담고 있다. 1953년 한미 상호방위조약 체결 이후부터 1967년 발효가 이뤄지기까지의 자료와 더불어, 이후 한미 합동위원회을 비롯해 민 · 형사재판권, 시설, 노무, 교통 등 각 분과위원회의 회의록과 운영 자료, 한국인 고용인 문제와 관련한 자료, 기타 관련 분쟁 자료 등을 포함해 총 42권으로 구성되었다. 전체 분량은 약 2만 2천여 쪽에 이른다.

2024년 3월

한국학술정보(주)

## | 일러두기

· 본 총서에 실린 자료는 2022년 4월과 2023년 4월에 각각 공개한 외교문서 4,827권, 76만 여 쪽 가운데 일부를 발췌한 것이다.

· 각 권의 제목과 순서는 공개된 원본을 최대한 반영하였으나, 주제에 따라 일부는 적절히 변경하였다.

· 원본 자료는 A4 판형에 맞게 축소하거나 원본 비율을 유지한 채 A4 페이지 안에 삽입하였다. 또한 현재 시점에선 공개되지 않아 '공란'이란 표기만 있는 페이지 역시 그대로 실었다.

· 외교부가 공개한 문서 각 권의 첫 페이지에는 '정리 보존 문서 목록'이란 이름으로 기록물 종류, 일자, 명칭, 간단한 내용 등의 정보가 수록되어 있으며, 이를 기준으로 0001번부터 번호가 매겨져 있다. 이는 삭제하지 않고 총서에 그대로 수록하였다.

· 보고서 내용에 관한 더 자세한 정보가 필요하다면, 외교부가 온라인상에 제공하는 『대한민국 외교사료요약집』 1991년과 1992년 자료를 참조할 수 있다.

# | 차례

머리말 4
일러두기 5

한 · 미국 간의 상호방위조약 제4조에 의한 시설과 구역 및 한국에서의 미국군대의 지위에 관한 협정(SOFA) 전59권. 1966.7.9 서울에서 서명 : 1967.2.9 발효(조약 232호) (V.20 실무교섭회의, 제32-37차, 1963.10-12월) 7

한 · 미국 간의 상호방위조약 제4조에 의한 시설과 구역 및 한국에서의 미국군대의 지위에 관한 협정(SOFA) 전59권. 1966.7.9 서울에서 서명 : 1967.2.9 발효(조약 232호) (V.21 실무교섭회의, 제38-44차, 1964.1-2월) 267

## 정/리/보/존/문/서/목/록

| 기록물종류 | 문서-일반공문서철 | 등록번호 | 918<br>9591 | 등록일자 | 2006-07-27 |
|---|---|---|---|---|---|
| 분류번호 | 741.12 | 국가코드 | US | 주제 | |
| 문서철명 | 한.미국 간의 상호방위조약 제4조에 의한 시설과 구역 및 한국에서의 미국군대의 지위에 관한 협정 (SOFA) 전59권. 1966.7.9 서울에서 서명 : 1967.2.9 발효 (조약 232호) *원본 | | | | |
| 생산과 | 미주과/조약과 | 생산년도 | 1952 - 1967 | 보존기간 | 영구 |
| 담당과(그룹) | 조약 | 조약 | 서가번호 | -- | |
| 참조분류 | | | | | |
| 권차명 | V.20 실무교섭회의, 제32-37차, 1963.10-12월 | | | | |
| 내용목차 | 1. 제32차 회의, 10.4 (p.2~35)<br>2. 제33차 회의, 10.18 (p.36~66)<br>3. 제34차 회의, 10.30 (p.67~106)<br>4. 제35차 회의, 11.14 (p.107~182)<br>5. 제36차 회의, 12.5 (p.146~182)<br>6. 제37차 회의, 12.27 (p.183~230)<br><br>* 일지 :<br>1953.8.7 이승만 대통령-Dulles 미국 국무장관 공동성명<br>- 상호방위조약 발효 후 군대지위협정 교섭 약속<br>1954.12.2 정부, 주한 UN군의 관세업무협정 체결 제의<br>1955.1월, 5월 미국, 제의 거절<br>1955.4.28 정부, 군대지위협정 제의 (한국측 초안 제시)<br>1957.9.10 Hurter 미국 국무차관 방한 시 각서 수교 (한국측 제의 수락 요구)<br>1957.11.13, 26 정부, 개별 협정의 단계적 체결 제의<br>1958.9.18 Dawling 주한미국대사, 형사재판관할권 협정 제외 조건으로 행정협정 체결 의사 전달<br>1960.3.10 정부, 토지, 시설협정의 우선적 체결 강력 요구<br>1961.4.10 장면 국무총리-McConaughy 주한미국대사 공동성명으로 교섭 개시 합의<br>1961.4.15, 4.25 제1, 2차 한.미국 교섭회의 (서울)<br>1962.3.12 정부, 교섭 재개 촉구 공한 송부<br>1962.5.14 Burger 주한미국대사, 최규하 장관 면담 시 형사재판관할권 문제 제기 않는 조건으로 교섭 재개 통고<br>1962.9.6 한.미국 간 공동성명 발표 (9월 중 교섭 재개 합의)<br>1962.9.20~ 1965.6.7 제1-81차 실무 교섭회의 (서울)<br>1966.7.8 제82차 실무 교섭회의 (서울)<br>1966.7.9 서명<br>1967.2.9 발효 (조약 232호) | | | | | |

마/이/크/로/필/름/사/항

| 촬영연도 | *롤 번호 | 화일 번호 | 후레임 번호 | 보관함 번호 |
|---|---|---|---|---|
| 2006-11-22 | I-06-0068 | 05 | 1-230 | |

0001

1. 제32차 회의, 10.4

0002

# 기 안 용 지

| 자 체 통 제 | 3등서기관 강 상 황 | 기안처 | 미 주 과 강석재 | 전화번호 | 근거서류접수일자 |
|---|---|---|---|---|---|
| | 과장 | 국장 | 차관 | 장관 | |
| 관계관 서 명 | | | | | |

| 기 안 년월일 | 1963. 10. 1 | 시 행 년월일 | | 보 존 년 한 | | 정 서 | 기 장 |
|---|---|---|---|---|---|---|---|
| 분 류 기 호 | 외정미 | 전 체 통 제 | | 종결 | | | |
| 경 유 수 신 참 조 | 건 의 | | | 발 신 | | | |
| 제 목 | 제32차 주둔군지위협정 체결교섭회의에 임할 우리측 입장 | | | | | | |

10월 4일에 개최될 제32차 주둔군지위협정체결 한미간교섭회의에서는 토지시설( A. B 및 C 조항) 및 군계약자에 관한 문제를 토의할 예정인바, 이에 관련하여 우리측 교섭실무자는 9월 26일 회합을 갖고 제32차 회의에서 취할 우리측 태도를 별첨과 같이 결정하였아오니 재가하여 주시기 바랍니다.

유첨: 제32차 주둔군지위협정체결교섭회의에 임할 우리측 태도, 끝.

보통문서로 재분류(1966. 12. 31)

1966, 12, 31에 예고문에 의거 일반문서로 재분류됨

승인서식 1-1-3 (11-00900 03) (195mm×265mm16절지)

32次

0003

1. 토지시설

가. 미국측은 토지시설 A 조 1 (a)항에 있어서 토지 및 시설의 사용은 합동위원회를 통한 양국정부의 협정으로 체결할 것을 규정하고 있는바(우리측 안에서는 " arrangements "로 하고있음) 토지시설의 사용권을 허용함에 있어서 더 확실한 문서상의 기록을 위하여 미국측 용어대로 "agreements "로 함이 타당하다고 사료되므로 이를 수락하기로 하며 또한 후단에서 규정하고 있는 토지시설의 정의 문장에 포함되어 있는 " Wherever located "라는 용어도 수락하기로 한다.

나. 미국측은 제31차 교섭회의에서 A 조 1 (b )항에 대한 대안으로서 미국군대의 토지시설은 본 협정 발효시 사용하고 있는 토지시설 뿐만 아니라 미국군대가 토지시설을 한국정부에 반환할때에 재 사용권리를 보유하고 반환한 토지시설도 포함하도록 규정하고 아울러 그러한 토지시설에 대한 기록을 합동위원회가 유지한다고 규정하고 있는바 우리측은 현재 한국정부에 반환된 토지시설 가운데 수원, 여의도, 대구 및 수영비행장등은 미공군이 재 사용권을 보유하고 반환한 사실이 있으며 또한 토지시설에 대한 기록도 이미 쌍방이 95 %나 완료하고 우리정부에 그 결과가 통보되고 있는점에 비추어 미국측 대안을 수락하기로 한다.

다. 미국측은 제31차 교섭회의에서 미국측 초안 B 조 1 항의 "비상시에 토지시설부근에 있어서 필요한 조치를 취할수 있다" 라는 규정을 합의 의사록에 삽입토록 하며 이에 대한 대안을 수교하였는바 우리측은 이를 수락하기로 함.

라. 원상회복문제에 관한 우리측 초안 13항은 (미국측 초안 C 조1항) 원칙적으로 미군의 원상회복의무를 면제하나 단지 미군의 사용으로 막심한 파손을 입은 사유재산에 대해서는 우리정부

0004

요청에 의하여 원상회복 또는 이에 대한 보상에 관하여 충분한 고려를 하도록 규정하고 있는바, 미국측은 보상문제는 본 협정과 별개의 문제로서 고려할수 없다는 입장을 취하고 있으므로 우리측은 이 문제를 당분간 보류하기로 한다.

마. 가동설비 소유권 및 처분문제에 관한 미국측 초안 C 조 2항은 우리측 초안에 규정되어 있지 않는바 이러한 설비가 미국정부의 재산이며 따라서 한국외로 철거할수 있다함은 당연한 것으로서 우리측은 조약에서 규정할 필요가 없으므로 계속 삭제할 것을 주장하고 (만일, 미국측이 끝까지 규정할것을 주장하면 합의의사록에 삽입토록 하며) 대신 토지시설 개량에 대한 우리정부의 보상의무면제에 관한 우리측 초안 14항중 " supplies or any other materials "만을 삭제한 우리측 원안을 미측 초안 C 조 2항으로 대치하도록 제의한다.

2. 군계약자

가. 군계약자의 한국법에 대한 복속원측에 관한 미국측 초안 1항 (우리측 초안1항에 해당)에 있어서 미국측 초안은 우리측초안에 삽입되어 있는 " organized under the laws of the United States "라는 구절과 " who are ordinarily resident in the United States "라는 용어를 삭제하고 계약을 체결할수 있는 법인이나 군계약자 및 그 고용원을 제3국인 까지 확대시킬수 있도록 규정하고 있는바 우리측은 동 구절의 삽입을 계속 주장하고 미국측의 입장을 듣기로 한다.

나. 군계약자에 대한 재산의 보유,사용 및 이전에 관련한 조세 면제 규정인 미국측 초안 6항(우리측 초안 5항에 해당)에 있는 " other business in Korea "라는 용어는 "제1절에서 말하고 있는 계약수행이외의 기타 영업행위"라는 양해 밑에서 수락하기로 한다.

0005

다. 소득세 및 법인세에 관한 미국측 초안 7항(우리측 초안 6항에 해당)은 우리측 초안에서 규정하고 있지 않는 한국외의 원천으로부터 나온 소득에 대한 과세 면제와 그러한 군계약자들이 한국에 체류하는 기간은 한국의 조세부과를 목적으로 한 거주기간으로 간주하지 않는다 라고 규정하고 있는바 이를 미국측 안대로 수락하기로 한다.

라. 미국측이 제의한 군계약자 조항에 대한 합의 의사록은 군계약자가 군대 이외의 미국기관(예, 미대사관 및 유솜)과의 계약을 수행하는 경우에도 본 계약자 조항의 적용에서 제외되지 않음을 규정하고 있는바 우리측은 소득세의 면제를 배제하고저 "except paragraph 7 "이라는 구절을 삽입토록 계속 주장한다.

마. 우리측 7항은 대한민국 내에서 저지른 우리 법률에 의하여 처벌 할 수 있는 범죄에 관한 군계약자들에 대한 대한민국의 재판관할권을 규정하고 있는바 미국측은 동 8 항에서 이에 관한 안을 아직 제시하지 않았으므로 군계약자들에 대한 재판관할권에 관한 미국측 안의 제시를 요구한다.

일반문서로 재분류(1966. 12.31.)

1966, 12. 31.에 예고문에 의거 일반문서로 재분류됨

0006

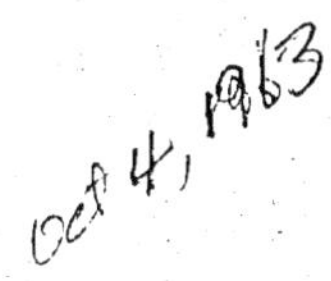

ARTICLE

1. Each Party waives all its claims against the other Party for damage to any property owned by it and used by its land, sea or air armed forces, if such damage:

(a) was caused by a member or an employee of the armed forces of the other Party in the performance of his official duties; or

(b) arose from the use of any vehicle, vessel or aircraft owned by the other Party and used by its armed forces, provided either that the vehicle, vessel or aircraft causing the damage was being used for official purposes, or that the damage was caused to property being so used.

Claims by one Party against the other Party for maritime salvage shall be waived provided that the vessel or cargo salvaged was owned by a Party and being used by its armed forces for official purposes.

2. In the case of damage caused or arising as stated in paragraph 1 to other property owned by a Party:

(a) each Party waives its claim up to the amount of $1400 or its equivalent in Korean currency at the rate of exchange provided for in the Agreed Minute to Article ___ at the time the claim is filed.

(b) claims in excess of the amount stated in subparagraph (a) shall be settled by the Party against which the claim is made in accordance with its domestic law.

3. For the purpose of paragraphs 1 and 2 of this Article, the expression "owned by a Party" in the case of a vessel includes a vessel on bare boat charter to that Party or requisitioned by it on bare boat charter terms or seized by it in prize (except to the extent that the risk of loss or liability is borne by some other person than such Party).

0007

4. Each Party waives all its claims against the other Party for injury or death suffered by any member of its armed forces while such member was engaged in the performance of his official duties.

5. Claims (other than contractual claims) arising out of acts or omissions of members or employees of the United States armed forces done in the performance of official duty, or out of any other act, omission or occurrence for which the United States armed forces are legally responsible, and causing damage in the Republic of Korea to third parties other than the two Governments shall be processed and settled in accordance with the applicable provisions of United States law. The United States Government shall entertain other non-contractual claims against members of the United States armed forces or of the civilian component and may offer an *ex gratia* payment in such cases and in such amount as is determined by the appropriate United States authorities.

6. (a) A member or employee of the United States armed forces shall not be afforded immunity from the jurisdiction of the civil courts of Korea except: (1) in a matter arising out of acts or omissions done in the performance of official duty; or (2) in respect to any claim where there has been payment in full satisfaction of the claim.

(b) In the case of any private movable property, excluding that in use by the United States armed forces, which is subject to compulsory execution under Korean law, and is within the facilities and areas in use by the United States armed forces, the United States authorities shall, upon the request of the Korean courts, render all assistance within their power to see that such property is turned over to the Korean authorities.

7. The authorities of the United States and Korea shall cooperate in the procurement of evidence for a fair disposition of claims under this Article.

0008

8. Paragraphs 2 and 5 of this Article shall apply only to claims arising incident to noncombat activities.

9. For the purposes of this Article, each Party shall have the right to determine whether a member or employee of its armed forces was engaged in the performance of official duties and whether property owned by it was being used by its armed forces for official purposes.

10. For the purposes of this Article, members of the Korean Augmentation to the United States Army (KATUSA) shall be considered as members of the United States armed forces, and members of the Korean Service Corps (KSC) shall be considered as employees of the armed forces of the Republic of Korea.

11. The provisions of this Article shall not apply to any claims which arose before the entry into force of this Agreement.

0009

ARTICLE

Health and Sanitation

Consistent with the right of the United States to furnish medical support for its armed forces, civilian component and their dependents, matters of mutual concern pertaining to the control and prevention of diseases and the coordination of other public health, medical, sanitation, and veterinary services shall be resolved by the authorities of the two Governments in the Joint Committee established under Article_____ .

0010

Article

Local Procurement

1. The United States may contract for any supplies or construction work to be furnished or undertaken in the Republic of Korea for purposes of, or authorized by, this Agreement, without restriction as to choice of supplier or person who does the construction work. Such supplies or construction work may, upon agreement between the appropriate authorities of the two Governments, also be procured through the Government of the Republic of Korea.

2. Materials, supplies, equipment and services which are required from local sources for the maintenance of the United States armed forces and the procurement of which may have an adverse effect on the economy of the Republic of Korea shall be procured in coordination with, and, when desirable, through or with the assistance of, the competent authorities of the Republic of Korea.

3. Materials, supplies, equipment and services procured for official purposes in the Republic of Korea by the United States armed forces, including their authorized procurement agencies, or procured for ultimate use by the United States armed forces shall be exempt from the following Korean taxes upon appropriate certification by the United States armed forces:

(a) Commodity tax;

(b) Traffic tax;

(c) Petroleum tax;

(d) Electricity and gas tax;

(e) Business tax.

0011

With respect to any present or future Korean taxes not specifically referred to in this Article which might be found to constitute a significant and readily identifiable part of the gross purchase price of materials, supplies, equipment and services procured by the United States armed forces, or for ultimate use by such forces, the two Governments will agree upon a procedure for granting such exemption or relief therefrom as is consistent with the purpose of this Article.

4. Neither members of the United States armed forces, civilian component, nor their dependents, shall by reason of this Article enjoy any exemption from taxes or similar charges relating to personal purchases of goods and services in the Republic of Korea chargeable under Korean legislation.

5. Except as such disposal may be authorized by the United States and Korean authorities in accordance with mutually agreed conditions, goods purchased in the Republic of Korea exempt from the taxes referred to in paragraph 3, shall not be disposed of in the Republic of Korea to persons not entitled to purchase such goods exempt from such tax.

AGREED MINUTES

1. The United States armed forces will furnish the Korean authorities with appropriate information as far in advance as practicable on anticipated major changes in their procurement program in the Republic of Korea.

2. The problem of a satisfactory settlement of difficulties with respect to procurement contracts arising out of differences between Korean and United States economic laws and business practices will be studied by the Joint Committee or other appropriate persons. representatives

0012

3. The procedures for securing exemptions from taxation on purchases of goods for ultimate use by the United States armed forces will be as follows:

(a) Upon appropriate certification by the United States armed forces that materials, supplies and equipment consigned to or destined for such forces, are to be used, or wholly or partially used up, under the supervision of such forces, exclusively in the execution of contracts for the construction, maintenance or operation of the facilities and areas referred to in Article or for the support of the forces therein, or are ultimately to be incorporated into articles or facilities used by such forces, an authorized representative of such forces shall take delivery of such materials, supplies and equipment directly from manufacturers thereof. In such circumstances the collection of taxes referred to in Article , paragraph 3, shall be held in abeyance.

(b) The receipt of such materials, supplies and equipment in the facilities and areas shall be confirmed by an authorized agent of the United States armed forces to the Korean authorities.

(c) Collection of the taxes on such materials, supplies and equipment shall be held in abeyance until

(1) The United States armed forces confirm and certify the quantity or degree of consumption of the above referred to materials, supplies and equipment, or

(2) The United States armed forces confirm and certify the amount of the above referred to materials, supplies, and equipment which have been incorporated into articles or facilities used by the United States armed forces.

0013

(d) Materials, supplies, and equipment certified under (c) (1) or (2) shall be exempt from taxes referred to in Article , paragraph 3, insofar as the price thereof is paid out of United States Government appropriations or out of funds contributed by the Government of the the Republic of Korea for disbursement by the United States.

U.S.-JAP.
XI-조-

0014

# 기 안 용 지

| 자체 통제 | | 기안처 | 미주과 강석재 | 전화번호 | 근거서류접수일자 |
|---|---|---|---|---|---|
| | 과장 | 국장 | | 차관 | 장관 |
| 관계관 서명 | 조약과장 | | | | |
| 기안 년월일 | 63. 10.8 | 시행 년월일 | 1963.10.11 | 보존 년한 | 정서기장 |
| 분류 기호 | 외정미 722.2- | 전체 통제 | | | |
| 경유 수신 참조 | 국가재건 최고회의 의장 (참조: 외무국방 위원장) 내각수반 | | | 발신 | 장관 |
| 제목 | 주둔군 지위협정 체결을 위한 제 32차 교섭회의 보고 | | | | |

1963. 10. 4 일 하오 2시부터 3:15 분까지 외무부 장관 회의실에서 개최된 제 32차 주둔군 지위협정 체결 교섭회의에서 토의된 내용을 별첨과 같이 보고합니다.

유첨: 제 32차 교섭회의 보고서 2/1 부. 끝.

1963.10.11 외무부

1966,12.31에 예고문에 의거 일반문서로 재분류됨

승인서식 1—1—3 (11—00900—03) (195mm×265mm16절지)

0015

외 무 부

외정미 722.2- 1963. 10. 11

수 신 : 국가재건 최고회의 의장

참 조 : 외무국방위원장

제 목 : 주둔군 지위협정 체결을 위한 제 32 차 교섭회의 보고

1963. 10. 4 일 하오 2시부터 3:15분까지 외무부장관 회의실에서 개최된 제 32 차 주둔군 지위협정 체결교섭 회의에서 토의된 내용을 별첨과 같이 보고합니다.

유 첨 : 제32차 교섭회의보고서 2 부., 끝.

외 무 부 장 관 김 용 식

0016

제 32 차

한미간 주둔군 지위협정 체결실무자 회의

보 고 서

1. 일 시 : 1963. 10. 4 일 하오 2시부터 3시 15분까지

2. 장 소 : 외무부 장관 회의실

3. 참석자 : 한국측 :

| | |
|---|---|
| 황 호 을 | (외무부 정무국장) |
| 신 관 섭 | (재무부 세관국장) |
| 구 충 회 | (외무부 미주과장) |
| 신 정 섭 | (외무부 조약과장) |
| 이 남 구 | (국방부 군무과장) |
| 주 문 기 | (법무부 법무과장) |
| 강 석 재 | (외무부 2등서기관) |
| 조 광 제 | (외무부 2등서기관) |

미국측 : 교섭대표단 전원

4. 토의사항 :

가. 토지시설

1) 미국측 초안 A 조 1 (a) 항에 있어서 우리측은 "토지시설에 관한 협정은 합동위원회를 통하여 양국정부에 의하여 체결한다" 라는 구정에 있어서 미국측 용어 agreements (우리측은 arrangements) 를 수락하고 또한 토지시설의 정의에 관한 문장에 있는 미국측 초안의 용어 "wherever located, used" 는 우리측 초안의 용어 "necessary to" 와 실질적으로 같은 뜻을 의미한다는 양해하에 수락하였음. 63-1-154

2) 협정 발효시의 토지시설에 대한 미국측 초안 A 조 1(a) (우리측 초안 3항) 의 대안에 대하여 우리측은 미국측이 이미 대한민국정부에 반환한 토지시설가운데 수원 혹은 여의도 비행장등과 같은 미군의 재사용 권리를 보유하고 반환한 토지시설도 포함할것에 동의하였으며 또한 미군이 사용중인 토지시설에 대한 측량은 미국측이 설명한대로 현재 95%가 완료되었으며

0017

63-1-21 (4)

미3.로 108-6 (4)

0018

나머지 5 %에 대한 측량도 불원 완료될 것이라는 점을 고려하고 만약 미군과 우리국방부 당국에서 실시한 측량의 결과에 있어서 상당한 차이가 있을 경우에는 한미합동으로 그 토지시설에 대한 재 측량을 한다는 양해(미국측은 이에 동의함)하에 미국측 대안을 수락하였음.

3) 미국측은 이미 합의를 본 미국측 초안 A 조 4( b )항의 "합동위원회는 미군대가 제한된 기간동안 사용할 토지시설에 관하여 그러한 토지시설에 관한 협정에서 본 협정 조항이 적용될 범위를 명시한다" 라는 규정을 실질적인 내용에 차이를 갖어오지 않고 편의상 표현을"...... 본 협정 조항이 적용되지 않을 범위를 명시한다"로 할 것을 제의하여 왔는바 검토후 차기 회의에서 우리측 입장을 알리기로 함.

4) 미국측이 수교한 미국측 초안 B 조에 대한 "미군대는 비상시에 토지시설 부근에 있어서 그들의 안전과 통제를 위하여 필요한 조치를 취하도록 허용하는데 합의한다"라는 합의 의사록에 대하여 우리측은 그러한 조치는 "한국 국민의 생명과 재산을 부당하게 저해하지 않는 범위내에서"라는 양해하에 수락할 것을 제의한바 미국측은 동 양해에 동의함으로서 미국측 안에 합의하였다. 이로서 토지시설내에서 취할 조치에 관한 미국측 초안 B 조는 완전 합의에 도달하였다.

5) 미국측은 미국측 초안 C 조(우리측 초안 13조)에 관하여 우리측 초안 13항 후단은 사유재산의 막심한 파괴에 대한 보상에 관한 것으로 C 조와 무관하며 오히려 전반적 보상문제에 관한 D 조와 관계가 있으므로 삭제할 것을 요구하고 또한 우리측이 미국측 초안 C 조 2항을 합의 의사록으로 넣도록 요구한데 대하여 고려하겠다고 제의하였는바 우리측은 토지시설 전반에 걸친 보상문제에 관한 조항에 합의 할때까지 우리측 초안 13항 후단을 삭제할수 없다고 답변함.

6) 토지시설 보상에 관한 미국측 초안 D 조(우리측 초안 4 및 5항)에 관하여 양측은 그 입장에 하등 변경이 없으므로 보상에 관한 문제 토의를 연기하기로 함.

63-1-155

0019

~~0018~~

0020

나. 군 계약자

1) 군계약자의 정의에 관한 미국측 초안 1항 (우리측 초안 1항)에 있어서 우리측은 제 3국인 계약자에 대한 적용을 배제하기위하여 "미국법에 의하여 조직된 법인체를 포함한 자연인과 그 고용자로서 미국에 통상 거주하는자" 다 규정하고 있는데 이에 대하여 미국측은 좀더 연구할때까지 토의를 연기하자고 제의하였음.

2) 군계약자에 대한 면제 및 특혜부여 조항에 관하여 우리측은 군계약자에 적용될 차량등록 및 면허는 미군대 구성원 군속 및 그가족에 적용되는 똑같은 혜택을 줄수 없다고 계속 주장하였음. 미국측은 좀더 연구하여 보겠다고 하고 군계약자의 사유 차량과 회사차량간에 구별을 둘것인지를 문의하여 왔는바 우리측은 하등 구별을 둘것을 고려치 않고 있다고 답변하였음. 미국측은 계속 차량등록 및 운전 면허에 관한 한국 법률은 일본 법율과 상당히 차이가 있다고 지적하고 군계약자에 적용될 한국법에 의한 세금, 등록 수수료 보험 혹은 수입차량 대수에 대한 제한 여부등을 문의하여 왔으나 차기회의에서 답변하겠다고 하였음.

3) 군계약자의 동산의 소유, 사용 및 이전에 대한 조세면제 규정인 미국측 초안 6항 (우리측 초안 5항) 에 있어서 우리측은 "other business in Korea " 라는 용어는 "미국군대와의 계약 수행외의 사업" 이라는 양해하에 수락하기를 제의하였으며 미국측은 동양해에 동의하였다.

4) 군계약자의 소득세 및 법인세 면제에 관한 미국측 초안 7항 (우리측 초안 6항) 에는 한국외의 원천으로부터 나오는 소득세에 대한 면세를 규정하고 있는바 우리측은 이에 동의하여 미국측 초안 7항을 수락하였음.

5) 우리측 7항은 한국내에서 범한 한국법률에 의하여 처벌될 성질의 범죄에 대한 재판 관할권을 규정하고 있으며 이에 관련한 미국측 초안 8항을 조속히 제시하도록 요구하였음.

63-1-156

0021 ~~0019~~

63-1-25

기.물 108-6

0022

6) 미국측은 합의 의사록에서 군계약자가 미국군대외의 기관과의 계약을 체결하는 경우에도 본 조항의 적용으로부터 배제되지 않을것을 요구하고 있으나 우리측은 미대사관 혹은 USOM 과의 계약의 경우 그러한 계약자의 사용은 국제법에 의거한 그러한 기구가 가지는 지위, 면제 혹은 특권에 따를것이나 동계약의 수행에서 나오는 군계약자에 대한 소득세의 면제는 전혀 별개의 문제임으로 군계약자 조항중 소득세 면제에 관한 규정은 적용될수 없다는 입장을 계속 주장하였으며 미국측은 이에 관여 더욱 고려해 보겠다는 답변이 있었음.

5. 중요합의 사항 :

토지시설내에서 취할 제반 조치에 관한 미국측 초안 B 조에 완전 합의 함.

6. 기타 사항 :

차기회의일자 : 1963. 10. 18 하오 2시

차기회의의제 : 차기회의까지 양측수석대표간에 합의된 사항.

63-1-159

63-1-25 (4)

미국 108-6 (4)

0024

October 4

1. Mr. Hwang opened the meeting by welcoming back to the negotiating table Col. Fuller and Mr. Fleck, both of whom had been absent on leave.

Facilities and Areas

2. Mr. Hwang then opened the substantive discussion by reviewing previous discussion of Paragraph 1 of Article "A" dealing with facilities and areas. He reminded the negotiators that they had not resolved the remaining differences in language between the U.S. draft and the Korean draft. The Korean negotiators had given careful study to the two drafts and were now prepared to accept the U.S. draft of Paragraph 1 (a). They did so with the specific understanding that the words "wherever located, used" in the third sentence of the U.S. draft have substantially the same meaning as the words "necessary to" in the Korean draft. Mr. Habib assented to this understanding and agreement was reached on paragraph 1 (a).

3. With regard to paragraph 1 (b), Mr. Hwang said that the Korean side understood the U.S. side to have said that a survey of existing areas and facilities currently is being conducted by the U.S. armed forces ~~was 95% completed, and that the remaining 5% would be finished in due course~~ and will be completed about (10) October 1964. About 95% of the results of this survey to date have been furnished to the ROK government. Pointing out that a similar survey was being conducted concurrently by the ROK armed forces, he said that the results of the two surveys should be identical. If there were any significant differences in the results of the two surveys, the Korean negotiators believed a joint survey should be made with regard to the facility or area in question. With the understanding that this would be done, the Korean side accepted the revised paragraph 1 (b) which had been tabled by the U.S. side at the previous meeting.

4. Mr. Habib replied that the U.S. negotiators had always been of the view that adjustments of the kind referred to by Mr. Hwang should be made

0025

through the Joint Committee. Full agreement having been reached on the text of Paragraph 1, it was noted that agreement had previously been reached on Paragraphs 2, 3, and 4 of this Article.

5. Mr. Habib stated that the U.S. side wished to propose a slight change in paragraph 4 (b). This paragraph refers to facilities and areas which are to be used by the U.S. armed forces for only limited periods of time. As it now reads, it provides that the Joint Committee shall decide the extent to which the SOFA shall apply to these facilities and areas. The U.S. side wished to make a slight change in method but not in principle by inserting the word "not", so that the language would read "the extent to which the provisions of this Agreement shall not apply". Mr. Habib pointed out that this change would make the task of the Joint Committee much simpler, since it would not be necessary for the Joint Committee to list all of the provisions of the SOFA which would apply to any given facility or area but only those provisions which would not apply.

6. Mr. Habib asked the negotiators to consider the case of a specific area which the U.S. armed forces proposed to occupy for a limited period of time. If such occupation was acceptable to the ROK Government, the Joint Committee would then draw up a special agreement applicable to that specific area. This procedure would be followed in every case of a limited occupancy facility. It would be much simpler for the Joint Committee to specify in each such case only those provisions of the SOFA which would not apply. The proposed change in language would not alter the requirement that the Joint Committee draw up a special agreement; it would merely simplify the Committee's task in drawing up the agreement. The change would in no way alter the understanding already reached by the negotiators with regard to this paragraph.

0026

7. Mr. Hwang replied that the change proposed by the U.S. negotiators did not appear to alter the substance of the paragraph. The Korean side would consider the matter and give its views at the next meeting.

8. Turning to draft Article "B" dealing with facilities and areas, Mr. Hwang recalled that at the previous meeting the U.S. side had tabled a proposed Agreed Minute in lieu of the second sentence of paragraph 1 of the U.S. draft. The Korean negotiators had suggested the addition at the end of the second sentence of the phrase "within the extent that Korean nationals and their property are not unduly impaired". With the understanding that the substance of this phrase will be respected by the U.S. armed forces, Mr. Hwang continued, the Korean negotiators agreed to paragraph 1 of the U.S. draft and to the Agreed Minute. Paragraphs 2 and 3 of the U.S. draft having been agreed upon previously, it was noted that complete agreement had now been reached on the text of Article "B".

9. Turning to draft Article "C" dealing with facilities and areas, Mr. Hwang recalled that the Korean negotiators had proposed to add to paragraph 1 of the U.S. draft the last sentence of paragraph 13 of the Korean draft. They had also proposed that paragraph 2 of the U.S. draft be deleted or converted into an Agreed Minute.

10. Mr. Habib stated that the U.S. negotiators had consistently opposed payment of compensation. Furthermore, the question of compensation should not properly enter into this article, inasmuch as the question of compensation is the subject of the next article. Therefore, the U.S. side proposed the deletion of the last sentence of paragraph 13 of the ROK draft from this article. The U.S. side, he added, is favorably inclined to consider conversion of paragraph 2 of the U.S. draft into an Agreed Minute but has not yet received approval from Washington.

11. Mr. Hwang agreed that the last sentence of paragraph 13 of the ROK draft related to the following article. However, the ROK side would reserve its

0027

position on deletion of the sentence until agreement was reached on draft Article "D", which deals with the subject of compensation.

12. Mr. Habib stated that the U.S. side would state its views concerning the new paragraph 2 proposed by the ROK side following the receipt of the views of the U.S. Government.

13. Mr. Habib then sought the agreement of the ROK side to the division of the facilities and areas portion of the SOFA into various separate articles, as in the U.S. draft. Mr. Hwang replied that the Korean negotiators had agreed, as a matter of convenience, to discuss the various items as separate articles, as in the U.S. draft. However, the Korean side preferred to defer final decision on this matter until negotiation of substantive matters had been completed.

14. Each side then indicated that its position with regard to the question of compensation had not changed and it was agreed to defer further consideration of U.S. draft Article "D" and paragraphs 4 and 5 of the Korean draft article.

<u>Invited Contractors</u>

15. Mr. Hwang stated that the drafts dealing with invited contractors had been discussed at many meetings and that each side knew the position of the other. With regard to paragraph 1, the difference in positions lay in the definition of invited contractors. He said the Korean position had not changed.

16. Mr. Habib stated that the U.S. side understood the Korean position. He said the U.S. side was in the process of studying this paragraph to determine which provisions were absolutely necessary to the performance of the mission of the U.S. forces. He suggested deferment of further discussion of this paragraph until completion of the study.

0028

17. The Korean side agreed to defer discussion of paragraph 1. Mr. Hwang noted that paragraph 2 of the U.S. draft had previously been agreed upon. He then requested the U.S. side to reconsider subparagraph (i) of the revised paragraph 3 of the U.S. draft.

18. Mr. Habib stated that since agreement had been reached on the article dealing with the licensing (and registration) of motor vehicles subsequent to the last discussion of the article dealing with invited contractors, the Korean side should now find subparagraph (i) acceptable.

19. Mr. Hwang stated that the Korean position had not changed and that the Korean negotiators considered contractors to be in a different category from those to whom the provisions of the article on licensing and registration of motor vehicles would apply. He said that contractors would be permitted to ~~import~~ register vehicles and obtain drivers licenses under the same conditions as ordinary aliens.

20. Mr. Habib ~~said the U.S. side wished to xxxxxxxxxxxxxxxx fxxxxx consider this matter further. He~~ asked if the Korean side made any distinction between personally-owned vehicles and vehicles owned by the contracting companies. Mr. Hwang replied that no distinction was envisaged.

21. Mr. Habib stated that while the Korean negotiators appeared to be basing their position on the provisions of the Japanese SOFA, the provisions of Korean law were quite different from those of Japanese law in regard to these matters. He was sure that the Korean negotiators did not wish to create difficulties. He then asked the Korean negotiators a series of questions regarding the application of Korean law to the invited contractors' vehicles with respect to: taxation, registration fees, insurance requirements, and whether or not there would be a limitation imposed on the number of such vehicles. Mr. Hwang stated that the Korean side would state its position with regard to these points at the next meeting

0029

22. Mr. Hwang stated that the Korean side had generally agreed to paragraph 6 of the U.S. draft, except for the phrase "other business in Korea". He said the Korean side was now prepared to agree to paragraph 6 of the U.S. draft, with the understanding that the phrase "other business in Korea" refers to business other than that conducted under contract with the U.S. armed forces. Mr. Habib stated that this understanding was correct and agreement was thereupon reached on paragraph 6.

23. Mr. Hwang stated that the only outstanding point of difference between paragraph 7 of the U.S. draft and paragraph 6 of the Korean draft was the sentence in the U.S. draft providing for exemption from taxation on income derived outside of Korea. He said the Korean side had not included such a provision in its draft because it had not been thought necessary. The Korean side agreed to paragraph 7 of the U.S. draft.

24. Mr. Hwang noted that paragraph 7 of the Korean draft related to criminal jurisdiction over contractors. He said the Korean side assumed that the missing paragraph 8 of the U.S. draft dealt with the same subject. The Korean side hoped that the U.S. side would table this missing paragraph as soon as possible. Mr. Habib confirmed Mr. Hwang's assumption concerning the subject matter of paragraph 8 and said that it would be tabled as soon as possible.

25. Mr. Habib recalled that the Korean side had asked what U.S. organizations other than the U.S. armed forces would let contracts to invited contractors. He said the U.S. Operations Mission and the U.S. Embassy were the only organizations other than the U.S. armed forces which might utilize the services of invited contractors.

26. Mr. Hwang stated that he understood that the use of such contractors by the Embassy and USOM would be respectively based on the status, immunities and privileges accorded between diplomatic organizations under international law and practice and on those accorded USOM under the pertinent agreement between the governments of the ROK and the U.S. However, exempting the contractors from payment of taxes on [illegible] from contracts with these two organizations

0030

was quite another matter. Therefore, the Korean side proposed that the provisions of paragraph 7 be excluded from the application of the Agreed Minute. If that were done, the Korean side would accept the Agreed Minute. Mr. Habib replied that the U.S. side would study this matter further.

27. It was [illegible] agreed to hold the next meeting on October 18 at 2:00 p.m.

JOINT SUMMARY RECORD OF THE 32ND SESSION

October 4, 1963

1. Time and Place: 2:00 to 3:15 p.m. October 4, 1963 at the Foreign Minister's Conference Room

| 미주과 | 양고재 | 담 당 | 과 장 | 국 장 | 특별보좌관 | 차 관 | 장 관 |
|---|---|---|---|---|---|---|---|

2. Attendants:

ROK Side:

| | |
|---|---|
| Mr. Whang, Ho Eul | Director<br>Bureau of Political Affairs<br>Ministry of Foreign Affairs |
| Mr. Shin, Kwan Sup | Director<br>Bureau of Customs Duty<br>Ministry of Finance |
| Mr. Koo, Choong Whay | Chief, America Section<br>Ministry of Foreign Affairs |
| Col. Lee, Nam Koo | Chief, Military Affairs Section<br>Ministry of National Defense |
| Mr. Chu, Mun Ki | Chief, Legal Affairs Section<br>Ministry of Justice |
| Mr. Shin, Jung Sup | Chief, Treaty Section<br>Ministry of Foreign Affairs |
| Mr. Kang, Suk Jae | 2nd Secretary<br>Ministry of Foreign Affairs |
| Mr. Cho, Kwang Jae | 2nd Secretary<br>Ministry of Foreign Affairs |

U.S. Side:

| | |
|---|---|
| Mr. Philip C. Habib | Counselor for Political Affairs<br>American Embassy |
| Brig. Gen. G.G.O'Connor | Deputy Chief of Staff<br>8th U.S. Army |
| Col. Howard Smigelor | Deputy Chief of Staff<br>8th U.S. Army |
| Mr. Benjamin A. Fleck | First Secretary<br>American Embassy |
| Col. L. J. Fuller | Staff Judge Advocate<br>United Nations Command |
| Capt. R. M. Brownlie | Assistant Chief of Staff<br>USN/K |
| Mr. James Sartorius | 2nd Secretary<br>American Embassy |
| Mr. Robert A. Lewis | 2nd Secretary and Consul<br>American Embassy |

0032

| | |
|---|---|
| Mr. Robert A. Kinney | J-5<br>8th U.S. Army |
| Maj. Robert D. Peckham | Staff Officer, JAG<br>8th U.S. Army |

1. Mr. Whang opened the meeting by welcoming back to the negotiating table Col. Fuller and Mr. Fleck, both of whom had been absent on leave.

Facilities and Areas

2. Mr. Whang then opened the substantive discussion by reviewing previous discussion of Paragraph 1 of Article "A" dealing with facilities and areas. He reminded the negotiators that they had not resolved the remaining differences in language between the U.S. draft and the Korean draft. The Korean negotiators had given careful study to the two drafts and were now prepared to accept the U.S. draft of Paragraph 1(a). They did so with the specific understanding that the words "wherever located, used" in the third sentence of the U.S. draft have substantially the same meaning as the words "necessary to" in the Korean draft. Mr. Habib assented to this understanding and agreement was reached on paragraph 1(a).

3. With regard to paragraph 1 (b), Mr. Whang said that the Korean side understood the U.S. side to have said that a survey of existing areas and facilities currently is being conducted by the U.S. armed forces and will be completed about 10 October 1964. About 95% of the results of this survey to date have been furnished to the ROK Government. Pointing out that a similar survey was being conducted concurrently by the ROK armed forces, he said that the results of the two surveys should be identical. If there were any significant differences in the results of the two surveys, the Korean negotiators

0033

believed a joint survey should be made with regard to the facility or area in question. With the understanding that this would be done, the Korean side accepted the revised paragraph 1(b) which had been tabled by the U.S. side at the previous meeting.

4. Mr. Habib replied that the U.S. negotiators had always been of the view that adjustments of the kind referred to by Mr. Whang should be made through the Joint Committee. Full agreement having been reached on the text of Paragraph 1, it was noted that agreement had previously been reached on Paragraphs 2, 3, and 4 of this Article.

5. Mr. Habib stated that the U.S. side wished to propose a slight change in paragraph 4(b). This paragraph refers to facilities and areas which are to be used by the U.S. armed forces for only limited periods of time. As it now reads, it provides that the Joint Committee shall decide the extent to which the SOFA shall apply to these facilities and areas. The U.S. side wished to make a slight change in method but not in principle by inserting the word "not", so that the language would read "the extent to which the provisions of this Agreement shall not apply". Mr. Habib pointed out that this change would make the task of the Joint Committee much simpler, since it would not be necessary for the Joint Committee to list all of the provisions of the SOFA which would apply to any given facility or area but only those provisions which would not apply.

6. Mr. Habib asked the negotiators to consider the case of a specific area which the U.S. armed forces proposed to occupy for a limited period of time. If such occupation was

0034

acceptable to the ROK Government, the Joint Committee would then draw up a special agreement applicable to that specific area. This procedure would be followed in every case of a limited occupancy facility. It would be much simpler for the Joint Committee to specify in each such case only those provisions of the SOFA which would not apply. The proposed change in language would not alter the requirement that the Joint Committee draw up a special agreement; it would merely simplify the Committee's task in drawing up the agreement. The change would in no way alter the understanding already reached by the negotiators with regard to this paragraph.

7. Mr. Whang replied that the change proposed by the U.S. negotiators did not appear to alter the substance of the paragraph. The Korean side would consider the matter and give its views at the next meeting.

8. Turning to draft Article "B" dealing with facilities and areas, Mr. Whang recalled that at the previous meeting the U.S. side had tabled a proposed Agreed Minute in lieu of the second sentence of paragraph 1 of the U.S. draft. The Korean negotiators had suggested the addition at the end of the second sentence of the phrase "within the extent that Korean nationals and their property are not unduly impaired". With the understanding that the substance of this phrase will be respected by the U.S. armed forces, Mr. Whang continued, the Korean negotiators agreed to paragraph 1 of the U.S. draft and to the Agreed Minute. Paragraphs 2 and 3 of the U.S. draft having been agreed upon previously, it was noted that complete agreement had now been reached on the text of Article "B".

9. Turning to draft Article "C" dealing with facilities and areas, Mr. Whang recalled that the Korean negotiators had proposed to add to paragraph 1 of the U.S. draft the

last sentence of paragraph 13 of the Korean draft. They had also propósed that paragraph 2 of the U.S. draft be deleted or converted into an Agreed Minute.

10. Mr. Habib stated that the U.S. negotiators had consistently opposed payment of compensation. Furthermore, the question of compensation should not properly enter into this article, inasmuch as the question of compensation is the subject of the next article. Therefore, the U.S. side proposed the deletion of the last sentence of paragraph 13 of the ROK draft from this article. The U.S. side, he added, is favorably inclined to consider conversion of paragraph 2 of the U.S. draft into an Agreed Minute but has not yet received approval from Washington.

11. Mr. Whang agreed that the last sentence of paragrph 13 of the ROK draft related to the following article. However, the ROK side would reserve its position on deletion of the sentence until agreement was reached on draft Article "D", which deals with the subject of compensation.

12. Mr. Habib stated that the U.S. side would state its views concerning the new paragraph 2 proposed by the ROK side following the receipt of the views of the U.S. Government.

13. Mr. Habib then sought the agreement of the ROK side to the division of the facilities and areas portion of the SOFA into various separate articles, as in the U.S. draft. Mr. Whang replied that the Korean negotiators had agreed, as a matter of convenience, to discuss the various items as separate articles, as in the U.S. draft. However, the Korean side preferred to defer final decision on this matter until negotiation of substantive matters had been completed.

14. Each side then indicated that its position with regard to the question of compensation had not changed and it was agreed to defer further consideration of U.S. draft Article "D" and paragraphs 4 and 5 of the Korean draft article.

0036

Invited Contractors

15. Mr. Whang stated that the drafts dealing with invited contractors had been discussed at many meetings and that each side knew the position of the other. With regard to paragraph 1, the difference in positions lay in the definition of invited contractors. He said the Korean position had not changed.

16. Mr. Habib stated that the U.S. side understood the Korean position. He said the U.S. side was in the process of studying this paragraph to determine which provisions were absolutely necessary to the performance of the mission of the U.S. forces. He suggested deferment of further discussion of this paragraph until completion of the study.

17. The Korean side agreed to defer discussion of paragraph 1. Mr. Whang noted that paragraph 2 of the U.S. draft had previously been agreed upon. He then requested the U.S. side to reconsider subparagraph (i) of the revised paragraph 3 of the U.S. draft.

18. Mr. Habib stated that since agreement had been reached on the article dealing with the licensing and registration of motor vehicles subsequent to the last discussion of the article dealing with invited contractors, the Korean side should now find subparagraph (i) acceptable.

19. Mr. Whang stated that the Korean position had not changed and that the Korean negotiators considered contractors to be in a different category from those to whom the provisions of the article on licensing and registration of motor vehicles would apply. He said that contractors would be permitted to register vehicles and obtain driver licences under the same conditions as ordinary aliens.

20. Mr. Habib asked if the Korean side made any distinction between personally-owned vehicles and vehicles owned by the contracting companies. Mr. Whang replied that no distinction was envisaged.

0037

21. Mr. Habib stated that while the Korean negotiators appeared to be basing their position on the provisions of the Japanese SOFA, the provisions of Korean law were quite different from those of Japanese law in regard to these matters. He was sure that the Korean negotiators did not wish to create difficulties. He then asked the Korean negotiators a series of questions regarding the application of Korean law to the invited contractors' vehicles with respect to: taxation, registration fees, insurance requirements, and whether or not there would be a limitation imposed on the number of such vehicles. Mr. Whang stated that the Korean side would state its position with regard to these points at the next meeting.

22. Mr. Whang stated that the Korean side had generally agreed to paragraph 6 of the U.S. draft, except for the phrase "other business in Korea". He said the Korean side was now prepared to agree to paragraph 6 of the U.S. draft, with the understanding that the phrase "other business in Korea" refers to business other than that conducted under contract with the U.S. armed forces. Mr. Habib stated that this understanding was correct and agreement was there-upon reached on paragraph 6.

23. Mr. Whang stated that the only outstanding point of difference between paragraph 7 of the U.S. draft and paragraph 6 of the Korean draft was the sentence in the U.S. draft providing for exemption from taxation on income derived outside of Korea. He said the Korean side had not included such a provision in its draft because it had not been thought necessary. The Korean side agreed to paragraph 7 of the U.S. draft.

0038

24. Mr. Whang noted that paragraph 7 of the Korean draft related to criminal jurisdiction over contractors. He said the Korean side assumed that the missing paragraph 8 of the U.S. draft dealt with the same subject. The Korean side hoped that the U.S. side would table this minning paragraph as soon as possible. Mr. Habib confirmed Mr. Whang's assumption concerning the subject matter of paragraph 8 and said that it would be tabled as soon as possible.

25. Mr. Habib recalled that the Korean side had asked what U.S. organizations other than the U.S. armed forces would let contracts to invited contractors. He said the U.S. Operations Mission and the U.S. Embassy were the only organizations other than the U.S. armed forces which might utilize the services of invited contractors.

26. Mr. Whang stated that he understood that the use of such contractors by the Embassy and USOM would be based respectively,on the status, immunities and privileges accorded diplomatic organizations under international law and practice and on those accorded USOM under the pertinent agreement between the two governments of the ROK and the U.S.A. However, exempting the contractors from payment of taxes on income derived from contracts with these two organizations was quite another matter, Therefore, the Korean side proposed that the provisions of paragraph 7 be excluded from the application of the Agreed Minute. If that were done, the Korean side would accept the Agreed Minute. Mr. Habib replied that the U.S. side would study this matter further.

27. It was agreed to hold the next meeting on October 18 at 2:00 p.m.

2. 제33차 회의, 10.18

0040

# 기 안 용 지

| 자체 통제 | | 기안처 | 미주과 강석재 | 전화번호 | 근거서류접수일자 |
|---|---|---|---|---|---|
| 1147 | | 과장 | 국장 | 차관 | 장관 |
| 관계관 서명 | | | | | |
| 기안 년월일 | 1963.10.17 | 시행 년월일 | | 보존 년한 | 정서 기장 |
| 분류 기호 | 외정미 | 전체 통제 | | 총결 | |
| 경유 수신 참조 | 건 의 | | | 발신 | |
| 제목 | 제33차 주둔군지위협정 체결교섭회의에 임할 우리측 입장 | | | | |

10월 18일에 개최될 제33차 주둔군지위협정체결 한미간교섭회의에서는 토지시설, 군계약자 및 조세문제를 토의할 예정인바, 이에 관련하여 우리측 교섭실무자는 10월 14일 회합을 갖고 제33차 회의에서 취할 우리측 태도를 별첨과 같이 결정하였아오니 재가하여 주시기 바랍니다.

유첨: 제33차 주둔군지위협정체결교섭회의에 임할 우리측 태도, 끝.

보통문서로 재분류(1966.12.31)

승인양식 1—1—3 (1112—040—016—018) (190mm×260mm16절지)

0041

토지시설

가. 미국측 초안A 조 4(b)항에 있어서 미국측이 제의한 용어의 변경은 합동위원회가 제한된 기간을 위하여 사용할 토지시설에 관한 협정에서 명시할 사항을 실질적으로 변경하는 것이 아님으로 미국측이 제의한 대로 " ....the extent to which the provisions of this Agreement shall not apply "로 변경하는 것을 수락하기로 한다.

나. 가동설비 소유권 및 처분문제에 관한 미국측 초안 C 조 2항은 계속 삭제하거나 그렇지 않으면 합의의사록에 넣도록 하고 그 대신 토지시설개량에 대한 우리정부의 보상의무면제를 규정한 우리측 초안 14항중 " Supplies or any other materials "이란 용어를 삭제하여 미국측 초안C 조 2항과 대치하도록 주장하며 이에 대한 미국측의 의견을 요구한다.

다. 미국측이 제32차 교섭회의에서 우리측초안 13항 후단의 "막심한 파손을 입은 사유재산에 대한 원상회복 및 보상에 관한"규정은 미국측 초안 C 조와 무관하므로 삭제하고 보상에 관한 미국측 D 조와 관련하여 해결하자고 제의한데 대하여서도 우리측 초안 13항 후단규정이 보상문제에 관련한것이기는 하나 미국측D 조에 대한 해결을 보기전에는 우리측 초안에서 삭제할수 없는바라고 우리의 반대의견을 계속 표명한다.

군계약자

가. 우리측 및 미국측 초안 1항의 군계약자에 대한 정의에 있어서 우리측은 그 범위를 "미국법에 따라 조직된 법인체를 포함한 사람과 그 고용자로서 통상 미국에 거주하는 자"로 한정시키기로 하며 이에 대한 미국측의 검토 결과를 문의한다.

나. 군계약자에 부여될 면제 및 특혜문제에 관한 미국측 초안 3항중 운전면허 및 차량등록에 관한 특혜부여 여부는 좀더 연구하고 다음 기회에 토의할 것을 제의하며 제32차 교섭회의에서 미국측이 질문한바 있는 군 계약자에 적용될 자동차세, 등록수수료 , 보험문제 및 자동차 대수에 대한 제한여부에 관한 사항도 역시 미국측이 재기하지 않는 한 보류한다.

0042

미국측이 제기한 사항은 현행 한국법에 의거하면 아래와 같다.

(1) 자동차 세:

자동차에 대한 세금은 지방세로서 다음과 같다.

(ㄱ) 취득세 : 처음 취득했을 경우에 부가하는 것으로 세액은 시가의 100분지 2임.

(ㄴ) 자동차세: 년 4회로 분할 납입하며 서울 및 부산에서의 세액은 년 16만원임 (지방세법—1961. 12. 8 법률 827호 및 개정법률 1962.12.29 법률 1243호 제 127조)

(2) 등록수수료:(교통부 육운국 기술과)

신규등록 1,000원

변경등록, 이전등록, 등록이관, 말소등록 각 500원

등록원본 등본 및 초본 각 250원

(3) 검사 수수료(서울시 차량과 소관)

신규등록 500원

계속검사 400원

(4) 보험(교통부 공로과 및 재무부 소관)

외국인 차량의 보험가입은 국내법에 따라야 하나 현행 법령에 의해 강제되어 있지 않고 교통부장관에 위임되고 있다. 현재 외국인은 외국보험회사에 가입하고 있는 실정이나 이 외국보험회사가 재무부 장관의 정식 인가를 받지 않고 있으므로 앞으로 외국보험회사의 영업을 인가해주거나 혹은 한국 자동차 보험회사에 가입을 강제하는 입법 조치가 요청된다고 본다.

(5) 자동차 수입대수에 대한 제한:

군계약자의 업무수행이나 혹은 가족단위로 보아 필요한 적절한 대수 까지 인정하며 부당한 제한으로 불편을 야기케 할 의도는 없다.

다. 미국측이 상금 제시하지 않고 있는 군계약자에 대한 대한민국의 재판관할권에 관한 안 (우리측 초안 7항에 해당)을 조속 제시할것을 요구한다.

라. 미국측이 제안한 군계약자 조항에 대한 합의의사록에 관하여 우리측이 소득세 면제의 적용을 배제하기 위하여 추가적 용어 " except paragraph 7 "을 제의한데 대한 미국측의 견해를 듣기로 한다.

0043

조세

가. 미국측 초안 2항의 둘째번 문장은 대한민국외의 원천에서 나오는 소득에 대한 조세면제를 규정한 것으로서 우리측 초안에서는 당연한 것으로서 규정하지 않고 합의의사록에 넣도록 주장하여 왔으나 이미 합의를 본 군계약자 조항과 같이 체제를 맞추기 위하여 미국측 안대로 수락하기로 한다.(대한민국 소득세법 1조 3항은 대한민국외의 원천에서 오는 소득세에 대한 면세를 규정하고 있음 -재무부)

나. 기타 한미양측 초안의 "Korea "와 " The Republic of Korea "및 "activities " 와 "organizations "등의 용어의 차이는 제25차 교섭회의에서 양해에 도달한대로 차후 협정문의 정비단계와 관계 비세출기관조항에서 각각 합의되는대로 조정하기로 하며 따라서 조세조항은 미측 초안에 따라 1. 2 및 3.항에 완전 합의한다.

보통문서로 재분류(1966.12.31.)

1966.12.1에 예고문에 의거 일반문서로 재분류됨

0044

# 기 안 용 지

| 자체 통제 | | 기안처 | 미주과 강석재 | 전화번호 | 근거서류접수일자 |
|---|---|---|---|---|---|
| | 과장 | 국장 | | 차관 | 장관 |
| 관계관 서명 | 조약과장 | | | | |
| 기안 년월일 | 1963.10.19 | 시행 년월일 | | 보존 년한 | 정서기장 |
| 분류 기호 | 외정미722.2 | 전체 통제 | | | |
| 경유 수신 참조 | 국가재건 최고회의 의장 (참조: 외무국방 위원장) 내각 수반 | | | 발신 | 장관 |
| 제목 | 주둔군 지위협정 체결을 위한 제33차 교섭회의 보고 | | | | |

1963년 10월 18일 하오 2시부터 3시 25분까지 외무부 장관 회의실에서 개최된 제33차 주둔군 지위협정 체결 교섭회의에서 토의된 내용을 별첨과 같이 보고합니다.

유첨: 제33차 교섭회의 보고서 2/1 부 끝

1966.12.31에 예고문에 의거 일반문서로 재분류됨

승인서식 1-1-3 (11-00000-03) (195mm×265mm16절지)

0045

제 33 차

한미간 주둔군지위협정 체결실무자 회의

보 고 서

1. 일 시: 1963. 10. 18일 하오 2시부터 3시25분까지

2. 장 소: 외무부 장관 회의실

3. 참 석 자: 한국측: 황 호 을 (외무부 정무국장)

신 관 섭 (재무부 세관국장)

구 충 회 (외무부 미주과장)

신 정 섭 (외무부 조약과장)

박 도 준중령 (국방부 군무과장)

주 문 기 (법무부 법무과장)

강 석 재 (외무부 2등서기관)

조 광 제 (외무부 2등서기관)

허 승 (외무부3등서기관)

미국측: 교섭대표단 ("제임스,사토리으스" 2등서기관 제외) 전원

4. 토의사항:

가. 토지시설

1) 미국측은 제32차회의에서 토지시설의 사용허용 및 반환에 관한 미국측 초안 A조 4(b)항의 "합동위원회는 미군대가 제한된 기간동안 사용할 토지시설에 관하여 그러한 토지시설에 관한 협정에서 본 협정조항이 적용될 범위을 명시한다"라는 규정을 "..... 본 협정조항이 적용되지 않는 범위를 명시한다"로 수정할것을 제의한데 대하여 우리측은 그러한 용어의 수정은 실질적으로 내용의 변경을 가져오는 것이 않임으로 미국측 제안을 수락하기로 하였음. 이로서 토지시설의 사용허용 및 반환에 관한 미국측 초안 A조에 대하여 완전 합의에 도달하였음.

63-1-158

나. 조세

1) 미국측 초안 2항의 둘째문장은 "한국외의 원천으로 부터 오는

0046

0047

소득에 대한 면세"를 규정하고 있는바 우리측은이미 합의를 본바있는 군 계약자조문의 면세에 관한 항을 참작하고 또한 그와 체제를 맞추기 위하여 미국측 초안을 수락하였음.

2) 조세조문에 관한 기타 항에 있어서의 " Korea "와 " the Republic of Korea " 및 " activities "와 " organizations "등의 용어의 차이에 대하여서는 지난 제25차 회의에서 양해를 본바와 같이 최종단계에 가서 조약문의 용어의 정비시와 또한 관계조문인 비세출기관 조문에서 결정되는바에 따른다는 조건하에 조세조문의 미국측 초안을 수락하기로 완전합의를 보았음.

다. 군 계약자

1) 우리측은 미국측이 제32차회의에서 군 계약자에 부여될 면제와 특혜에 관한 사항중 운전면허 및 차량등록 (미국측 초안 3( i ) )에 관한 한국법률의 적용문제와 이에 관련하여 미국측이 제기한 자동차세, 등록수수료, 보험 및 차량대수에 대한 제한여부문제에 관하여 현재 관계부처와의 검토가 끝나지 않었음으로 한국법률의 적용문제에 대한 공식 견해는 다음 회의시에 표명하겠으나 다만 현행 한국법률에 의거한다며는 미국측이 제기한 제문제는 다음과 같다고 설명하였음:

(ㄱ) 자동차세: 자동차에 대한 세금은 지방세로서 취득세와 자동차세가 있어며 취득세는 차읍 자동차를 취득했을 경우에 부가하며 그세액은 시가의 100분지 2이다. 또한 자동차세는 년 4회로 분활 납입하고 그세액은 서울 및 부산에서는 년 16만원임. 이에 관한 법률은 1961.12.8자 공고된 법률 827호 및 1962. 12. 29자 개정공포된 법률 1243호 지방세법의 제127조임.

63-1-15-9

(ㄴ) 등록수수료: 신규등록에는 1,000원 변경등록, 이전등록 등록이관 및 말소등록에는 각각 500원 등록원본의 등본 및 초본에는 각각 250원이 요하며 기타 국체소화는 신규등록에 500원 계속검사에 400원이 요한다

0048

63-1-26

미·곤 108-5

0049

(ㄷ) 보험: 외국인차량의 보험가입은 국내법에 따라야 하나 현행 법령에 의해 강제되어 있지 않고 교통부장관에 위임되고 있다. 현재외국인은 외국보험회사에 가입하고 있는 실정이나 이외국 보험회사가 재무부장관의 정식 인가를 받지 못하고 있음으로 앞으로 외국보험회사의 영업을 인가해주거나 혹은 한국자동차 보험회사에 가입을 강제하는 입법조치가 요청되며 군계약자들의 차량에 대한 보험가입문제는 이러한 문제가 결정되는 방향에 따를것이다.

(ㄹ) 자동차 수입대수에 대한 제한: 군계약자의 업무수행이나 혹은 가족단위로 보아 필요한 적절한대수까지는 인정하며 부당한 제한으로 불편을 야기케할 의도는 없다. 현재 상공부에서는 한국인에게 양도하지 않는다는 조건하에 신청하는 모든 차량수입을 허가하고 있다. 63-1-160

2) 미국측은 우리측 설명에 이어 현재 군 계약자가 사용하고 있는 차량에는 미국정부 소유차량으로 군계약자에 제공하고 있는 차량 (400 대), 계약회사의 소유차량 ( 141 대) 및 군 계약자의 사유차량 ( 13 대)등이 있는데 차량수입의 제한에 있어서 종류에 따라 구분하여 고려할것인지를 질문하여 왔는바 이에 대하여 우리측 수석대표는 그문제에 대하여서는 아직 관계부처와 협의한바 없으나 개인 견해라고 전제하면서 군 계약자에 제공된 미국정부 소유차량은 임시로 대여된것이며 소유권 자체는 미국정부에 있는것으로 보며 미국정부가 수입하고 소유하며 관리하는 차량은 면세될것으로 생각하는 바라고 말하고 관계부처와 상의한후 회답하겠다고 함. 미국측은 그러면 한국측으로서는 군 계약자가 수입할 사유차량에 대하여 제한을 할 권리를 주장하는지를 질문하였으며 이에 대하여 우리측은 군 계약자의 사유차량의 대수는 상식적인 문제이며 비단 차량뿐만 아니라 기타 일용품의 수량과 마찬가지로 일반가정에서 필요로 하는 합리적인 적당한 평균량은 제한 받지 않을 것이나 필요이상의

0050

63-1-26

미·올 10ㅂ 5

0051

수당에 대하여서는 제한해야 할것이며 군 계약회사 소유차량도 그업체의 규모, 사업 내용 및 크기에 비하여 적절하지 못하다고 판단할 경우에는 위와 같은 조건적인 제한을 할수 있는 권리를 유보한다고 본다고 답변함.

3) 미국측은 합의의사록에 관하여 한국측은 약간의 오해를 갖고 있다고 보며 이를 설명코저한다고 전제하고 미국측이 의도하고 있는바는 미군과 계약하고 있는 계약자가 미대사관이나 "유솜"과의 계약을 수행하는 경우에 이러한 계약으로 말미암아 동 계약자들이 계약자조항에서 부여된 면제나 특혜를 박탈당하지 않을 것을 바라는 것이며 미대사관이나 "유솜"과의 계약으로 부터 오는 소득에 대한 면세를 받도록 의도하는 것이 아니라고 말하였다. 미국측은 면세에 관련한 7항을 검토해줄것을 요청하면서 만약 한국측 제의대로 " except paragraph 7 "를 합의 의사록에 넣게 된다면 미대사관이나 "유솜"과 계약을 수행하게 될 경우 동 계약자가 미군대와 계약수행할 경우 가지게 되는 7항에서 규정한 모든 혜택을 박탈되게 된다고 설명하였음. 이에 대하여 우리측에서는 좀 더 연구하고 다음회의에서 계속 토의할것을 제의하였음.

5. 중요 합의 사항:

토지시설의 사용허용 및 반환에 관한 조문 및 조세에 관한 조문에 완전합의 함.

6. 기타 사항:

차기회의 일자: 1963. 10. 30 하오 2시

차기회의의제: 차기회의 까지 양측수석대표간에 합의된 사항. 끝

63-1-161



0052

63-1-26(4)

0053

October 18

1. Mr. Hwang opened the meeting by announcing that Colonel YI Nam-ku had been assigned as Chief of the Seoul Area's Military Affairs Office. He then introduced Lt. Colonel PAK Chun, ROKA, who will temporarily replace Colonel Yi on the Korean negotiating team. Mr. Habib expressed regret at the departure of Colonel Yi, who had been a member of the Korean team from the beginning, but heartily welcomed Lt. Colonel Pak to the negotiations.

Facilities and Areas

2. Taking up the first item on the agenda, Mr. Hwang stated that the Korean side had fully considered the proposal made by the U.S. side at the previous meeting to insert the word "not" before the word "apply" in the final sentence of subparagraph (b), paragraph 4, Article "A", dealing with the granting and return of facilities and areas. The Korean side accepted this insertion and full agreement was thereupon reached on the text of Article "A".

Taxation

3. With regard to the article dealing with taxation, Mr. Hwang reminded the negotiators that agreement had already been reached on the first paragraph of the U.S. draft. With respect of paragraph 2, the Korean side had previously proposed that the second sentence be deleted and its substance included in an Agreed Minute. However, inasmuch as agreement had subsequently been reached on the relevant paragraph of the article dealing with invited contractors, the Korean side now believed that for the sake of consistency the second sentence should be retained in paragraph 2. Therefore, in order that the language of this article conform with that of the contractors article, the Korean side accepted paragraph 2 of the U.S. draft, subject to later

0054

CONFIDENTIAL

resolution of the conflict between the use of the words "organizations" and "activities" in the two drafts. Mr. Habib stated that the U.S. side had been prepared to agree to the Korean side's earlier proposal to convert the second sentence of paragraph 2 into an Agreed Minute. However, the U.S. side agreed that retention of that sentence in paragraph 2 was consistent with the language in other articles and, therefore, was preferable. Subject to later decision in favor of either "organizations" or "activities", full agreement was reached on the text of the U.S. draft of this article.

## Invited Contractors

4. Turning to the article dealing with invited contractors, Mr. Habib indicated that the U.S. side would like to hear the views of the Korean side regarding subparagraph (i) of paragraph 3. In turn, the U.S. side was prepared to provide a fuller explanation of the proposed Agreed Minute, which had been the source of some misunderstanding at the previous meeting.

5. Mr. Habib referred to the series of questions asked by the U.S. side at the previous meeting concerning the applicability of Korean laws to vehicles imported into Korea by contractors and their employees. Mr. Hwang stated that the Korean side was still engaged in the process of studying with the appropriate Korean authorities the applicability of Korean laws and regulations regarding the licensing of motor vehicles to vehicles belonging to contractors. However, at this meeting he would like to provide some preliminary information concerning the relevant laws, fees and taxes.

6. Mr. Hwang stated that the relevant law is the Local Tax Law, promulgated as Law No. 827 on December 8, 1961, and amended on December 29, 1962 as Law No. 1243.

7. Mr. Hwang stated that there is an acquisition tax of 2 percent on the current value of the taxed vehicle and a vehicle tax of Won 160,000, payable in

0055

quarterly instalments.

8. Fees include an initial registration fee of Won 1,000; a renewal, transfer, and termination fees of Won 500 each; and a fee of Won 250 for obtaining a copy of an original document. Vehicle owners are also required to purchase a national savings bond in the amount of Won 500 at the time of initial registration of the vehicle and in the amount of Won 400 when each inspection of the vehicle takes place.

9. Mr. Hwang stated that insurance requirements for alien-owned vehicles should be subject to the relevant Korean law. Under the existing laws, there is no provision for compulsory enforcement of the requirement that all alien-owned vehicles be insured by a Korean insurance company. However, the matter is the responsibility of Ministry of Transportation and, therefore, at present, nearly all alien-owned vehicles are insured with foreign insurance companies. The Korean negotiators presume that However, none of these firms is officially licensed by the Ministry of Finance. A decision will have to be taken, therefore, whether to license the foreign firms or to enforce the requirement that all insurance be issued by Korean firms. A decision in favor of the latter course would require further legislation.

10. Mr. Hwang stated that with regard to the question of the U.S. side whether or not the Korean side was thinking of imposing a limitation on the number of vehicles to be imported by the contractors, the answer was that the Koreans had no intention of causing any inconvenience. They were ready to admit a reasonable number of vehicles for the performance of duty by the contractors and the convenience of their families. He pointed out that the present practice of the Ministry of Commerce is to impose no limitation on the number of vehicles imported, provided that no imported vehicle is transferred to persons

0056

not authorized to import vehicles.

11. Mr. Habib pointed out that there are three types of vehicles operated by the invited contractors: (a) those vehicles which are owned by the U.S. armed forces and which are furnished to the contractors for the use of the latter in carrying out their contracts; (b) those vehicles which are owned by the contractors; and (c) those vehicles which are owned by individual employees of the contractors. Mr. Habib pointed out that there are currently very few vehicles in category (c). He asked whether the Korean side intended to make any differentiation in the application of Korean laws and regulations to these three types of vehicles.

12. Mr. Hwang replied that this matter had not yet been discussed with the Ministries concerned. He asked for clarification of the type of vehicle furnished to the contractors by the U.S. armed forces. Major Peckham replied that a primary factor determining the type of vehicle is the geography of the site where the contract is to be carried out. In remote sites, such as mountain tops, army trucks and jeeps are made available to the contractors, inasmuch as normal civilian-type vehicles would be unable to traverse the rugged terrain.

13. Mr. Hwang expressed his personal opinion that ownership of army trucks and jeeps made available to the contractors would remain with the United States Government. However, the Korean side would discuss this question with the Ministries concerned and would comment further at a later meeting.

14. Mr. Habib then informed the Korean side that contractors currently were operating over 400 U.S. Government-owned vehicles, 141 contractor-owned vehicles, and 13 privately-owned vehicles.

15. Mr. Hwang asked if there were any difference between the types of vehicles owned by contractors and those which were privately-owned. Mr. Habib replied that the contractor-owned vehicles consisted primarily of panel trucks

and pickup trucks.

16. Mr. Habib then asked if the Korean side were thinking of insisting on the right to impose a limitation on the number of vehicles to be imported by the contractors. Mr. Hwang replied that it was a question of common sense and that so long as the quantities of vehicles imported were normal, there would be no intention by the Korean authorities to impose any limitation. He said that if one employee imported ten privately-owned automobiles, that would be considered excessive. Mr. Habib stated that not only would the U.S. armed forces agree that the example cited by Mr. Hwang was excessive - they would not permit such importation to take place.

17. In response to Mr. Habib's question whether the Korean side was speaking only of privately-owned vehicles, Mr. Hwang stated that limitations would also be imposed on contractor-owned vehicles and that determination of the number of vehicles to be imported by any one contractor would depend upon the nature of the contract which was being carried out. Mr. Habib agreed that the number of vehicles needed by a contractor for the performance of a contract would depend upon the nature of the contract. He said the U.S. side would await the Korean side's explanation at a later meeting of the latter's views regarding the applicability of Korean laws and regulations to vehicles operated by invited contractors and their employees.

18. Mr. Habib said the U.S. side wished to clear up the misunderstanding which had apparently occurred at the previous meeting regarding the sense of the Agreed Minute proposed in the U.S. draft. He said that the purpose of this Agreed Minute is to provide that contractors who may perform work for the Embassy or USOM in addition to the work which they perform for the U.S. armed forces, shall not be barred from the benefits of this article because they perform this additional work.

0058

The Korean side apparently had interpreted this Agreed Minute to convey upon the contractors involved the benefits of this article for this additional work. This is not a correct interpretation of the Agreed Minute. Mr. Habib asked the Korean side to study paragraph 7 of the U.S. draft, particularly the first sentence, which is qualified by the final clause "in connection with the construction, maintenance or operation of any of the facilities or areas covered by this agreement." He said the Korean side apparently believed that the Agreed Minute would provide exemption from payment of taxes on work performed by a contractor for the Embassy or USOM. This is not a correct interpretation of the Agreed Minute, which is intended solely to prevent a contractor from losing the benefits of this article for work performed in connection with ... facilities or areas covered by this agreement.

19. Mr. Habib pointed out that acceptance of the Korean proposal to add the phrase "except for paragraph 7" to the Agreed Minute would deprive a contractor performing work for the Embassy or USOM of all the benefits of paragraph 7 with regard to work which that contractor was performing for the U.S. armed forces. Mr. Habib added that at the present time there is no contractor who is performing work for the Embassy and USOM in addition to his work for the U.S. armed forces, although in the past the Vinnell Corporation had performed some additional work for USOM. He urged the Korean side to reconsider its proposed addition to the Agreed Minute, in the light of the explanation just given of the intent of the Agreed Minute. Mr. Hwang stated that the Korean side would take this matter under further consideration and give its views at a later date.

20. It was agreed to hold the next meeting on October 30 at 2:00 p.m.

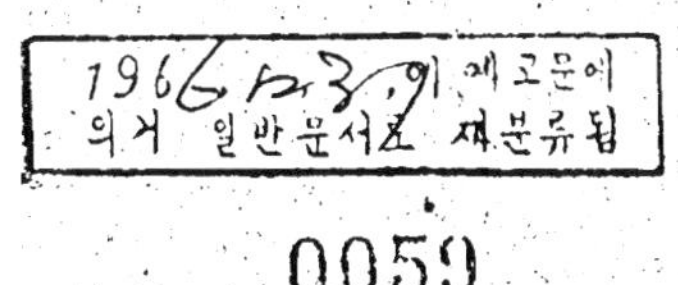

## JOINT SUMMARY RECORD OF THE 33RD SESSION

October 18, 1963

1. Time and Place: 2:00 to 3:25 p.m. October 18, 1963 at the Foreign Minister's Conference Room.

| 미주과 | 양고재 | 담 당 | 과 장 | 국 장 | 특별보좌관 | 차 관 | 장 관 |
|---|---|---|---|---|---|---|---|

2. Attendants:

ROK Side:

| | |
|---|---|
| Mr. Whang, Ho Eul | Director<br>Bureau of Political Affairs<br>Ministry of Foreign Affairs |
| Mr. Shin, Kwan Sup | Director<br>Bureau of Customs Duty<br>Ministry of Finance |
| Mr. Koo, Choong Whay | Chief, America Section<br>Ministry of Foreign Affairs |
| Mr. Chu, Mun Ki | Chief, Legal Affairs Section<br>Ministry of Justice |
| Lt. Col. Do Joon Pak | Military Affairs Section<br>Ministry of National Defense |
| Mr. Shin, Jung Sup | Chief, Treaty Section<br>Ministry of Foreign Affairs |
| Mr. Kang, Suk Jae | 2nd Secretary<br>Ministry of Foreign Affairs |
| Mr. Cho, Kwang Jae | 2nd Secretary<br>Ministry of Foreign Affairs |
| Mr. Huh, Sung | 3rd Secretary<br>Ministry of Foreign Affairs |

U.S. Side:

| | |
|---|---|
| Mr. Philip C. Habib | Counselor for Political Affairs<br>American Embassy |
| Brig. Gen. G.G. O'Connor | Deputy Chief of Staff<br>8th U.S. Army |
| Col. Howard Smigelor | Deputy Chief of Staff<br>8th U.S. Army |
| Mr. Benjamin A. Fleck | First Secretary<br>American Embassy |
| Col. L. J. Fuller | Staff Judge Advocate<br>United Nations Command |
| Capt. R. M. Brownlie | Assistant Chief of Staff<br>USN/K |
| Mr. Robert A. Lewis | 2nd Secretary and Consul<br>American Embassy |

0060

| | |
|---|---|
| Mr. Robert A. Kinney | J-5<br>8th U.S. Army |
| Maj. Robert D. Peckham | Staff Officer, JAG<br>8th U.S. Army |
| Mr. Kenneth Campen | Interpreter |

1. Mr. Whang opened the meeting by announcing that Colonel Lee Nam-koo had been assigned as Chief of the Seoul Area's Military Affairs Office. He then introduced Lt. Colonel Pak Do-joon, ROKA, who will temporarily replace Colonel Lee on the Korean negotiating team. Mr. Habib expressed regret at the departure of Colonel Lee, who had been a member of the Korean team from the beginning, but heartily welcomed Lt. Colonel Pak to the negotiations.

Facilities and Areas

2. Taking up the first item on the agenda, Mr. Whang stated that the Korean side had fully considered the proposal made by the U.S. side at the previous meeting to insert the word "not" before the word "apply" in the final sentence of subparagraph (b), paragraph 4, Article "A", dealing with the granting and return of facilities and areas. The Korean side accepted this insertion and full agreement was thereupon reached on the text of Article "A".

Taxation

3. With regard to the article dealing with taxation, Mr. Whang reminded the negotiators that agreement had already been reached on the first paragraph of the U.S. draft. With respect of paragraph 2, the Korean side had previously proposed that the second sentence be deleted and its substance included in an Agreed Minute. However, inasmuch as agreement had subsequently been reached on the relevant paragraph of the article dealing with invited

0061

contractors, the Korean side now believed that for the sake of consistency the second sentence should be retained in paragraph 2. Therefore, in order that the language of this article conform with that of the contractors article, the Korean side accepted paragraph 2 of the U.S. draft, subject to later resolution of the conflict between the use of the words "organizations" and "activities" in the two drafts. Mr. Habib stated that the U.S. side had been prepared to agree to the Korean side's earlier proposal to convert the second sentence of paragraph 2 into an Agreed Minute. However, the U.S. side agreed that retention of that sentence in paragraph 2 was consistent with the language in other articles and, therefore, was preferable. Subject to later decision in favor of either "organizations" or "activities", full agreement was reached on the text of the U.S. draft of this article.

Invited Contractors

4. Turning to the article dealing with invited contractors, Mr. Habib indicated that the U.S. side would like to hear the views of the Korean side regarding subparagraph (i) of paragraph 3. In turn, the U.S. side was prepared to provide a fuller explanation of the proposed Agreed Minute, which had been the source of some misunderstanding at the previous meeting.

5. Mr. Habib referred to the series of questions asked by the U.S. side at the previous meeting concerning the applicability of Korean laws to vehicles imported into Korea by contractors and their employees. Mr. Whang stated that the Korean side was still engaged in the process of studying with the appropriate Korean authorities the applicability of Korean laws and regulations regarding the

0062

licensing of motor vehicles to vehicles belonging to contractors. However, at this meeting he would like to provide some preliminary information concerning the relevant laws, fees and taxes.

6. Mr. Whang stated that the relevant law is the Local Taxes Law, promulgated as Law No. 827 on December 8, 1961, and amended on December 29, 1962 as Law No. 1243.

7. Mr. Whang stated that there is an acquisition tax of 2 percent on the current value of the taxed vehicle and a vehicle tax of Won 160,000, payable in quarterly instalments.

8. Fees include an initial registration fee of Won 1,000; a renewal, transfer, and termination fees of Won 500 each; and a fee of Won 250 for obtaining a copy of an original document. Vehicle owners are also required to purchase a national savings bond in the amount of Won 500 at the time of initial registration of the vehicle and in the amount of Won 400 when each inspection of the vehicle takes place.

9. Mr. Whang stated that insurance requirements for alien-owned vehicles should be subject to the relevant Korean law. Under the existing laws, there is no provision for compulsory enforcement of the requirement that all alien-owned vehicles be insured by a Korean insurance company. However, the matter is the responsibility of the Ministry of Transportation and, therefore, is left to that Ministry's discretion. The Korean negotiators presume that at present, nearly all alien-owned vehicles are insured with foreign insurance companies. However, none of these firms is officially licensed by the Ministry of Finance. A decision will have to be taken, therefore, whether to license

0063

the foreign firms or to enforce the requirement that all insurance be issued by Korean firms. A decision in favor of the latter course would require further legislation.

10. Mr. Whang stated that with regard to the question of the U.S. side whether or not the Korean side was thinking of imposing a limitation on the number of vehicles to be imported by the contractors, the answer was that the Koreans had no intention of causing any inconvenience. They were ready to admit a reasonable number of vehicles for the performance of duty by the contractors and the convenience of their families. He pointed out that the present practice of the Ministry of Commerce is to impose no limitation on the number of vehicles imported, provided that no imported vehicle is transferred to persons not authorized to import vehicles.

11. Mr. Habib pointed out that there are three types of vehicles operated by the invited contractors: (a) those vehicles which are owned by the U.S. armed forces and which are furnished to the contractors for the use of the latter in carrying out their contracts; (b) those vehicles which are owned by the contractors; and (c) those vehicles which are owned by individual employees of the contractors. Mr. Habib pointed out that there are currently very few vehicles in category (c). He asked whether the Korean side intended to make any differentiation in the application of Koean laws and regulations to these three types of vehicles.

12. Mr. Whang replied that this matter had not yet been discussed with the Ministries concerned. He asked for clarification of the type of vehicle furnished to the contractors by the U.S. armed forces. Major Peckham replied that a primary factor determining the type of vehicle is

0064

the geography of the site where the contract is to be carried out. In remote sites, such as mountain tops, army trucks and jeeps are made available to the contractors, inasmuch as normal civilian-type vehicles would be unable to traverse the rugged terrain.

13. Mr. Whang expressed his personal opinion that ownership of army trucks and jeeps made available to the contractors would remain with the United States Government. However, the Korean side would discuss this question with the Ministries concerned and would comment further at a later meeting.

14. Mr. Habib then informed the Korean side that contractors currently were operating over 400 U.S. Government-owned vehicles, 141 contractor-owned vehicles, and 13 privately-owned vehicles.

15. Mr. Whang asked if there were any difference between the types of vehicles owned by contractors and those which were privately-owned. Mr. Habib replied that the contractor-owned vehicles consisted primarily of panel trucks and pickup trucks.

16. Mr. Habib then asked if the Korean side were thinking of insisting on the right to impose a limitation on the number of vehicles to be imported by the contractors. Mr. Whang replied that it was a question of common sense and that so long as the quantities of vehicles imported were normal, there would be no intention by the Korean authorities to impose any limitation. He said that if one employee imported ten privately-owned automobiles, that would be considered excessive. Mr. Habib stated that not only would the U.S. armed forces agree that the example cited by Mr. Whang was excessive - they would not permit such importation to take place.

0065

17. In response to Mr. Habib's question whether the Korean side was speaking only of privately-owned vehicles, Mr. Whang stated that limitations would also be imposed on contractor-owned vehicles and that determination of the number of vehicles to be imported by any one contractor would depend upon the nature of the contract which was being carried out. Mr. Habib agreed that the number of vehicles needed by a contractor for the performance of a contract would depend upon the nature of the contract. He said the U.S. side would await the Korean side's explanation at a later meeting of the latter's views regarding the applicability of Korean laws and regulations to vehicles operated by invited contractors and their employees.

18. Mr. Habib said the U.S. side wished to clear up the misunderstanding which had apparently occurred at the previous meeting regarding the sense of the Agreed Minute proposed in the U.S. draft. He said that the purpose of this Agreed Minute is to provide that contractors who may perform work for the Embassy or USOM in addition to the work which they perform for the U.S. armed forces, shall not be barred from the benefits of this article because they perform this additional work. The Korean side apparently had interpreted this Agreed Minute to convey upon the contractors involved the benefits of this article for this additional work. This is not a correct interpretation of the Agreed Minute. Mr. Habib asked the Korean side to study paragraph 7 of the U.S. draft, particularly the first sentence, which is qualified by the final clause "in connection with the construction, maintenance or operation of any of the facilities or areas covered by this agreement." He said the Korean side apparently believed that the Agreed Minute would provide exemption from payment of taxes on work performed by a contractor for the Embassy or USOM. This is not a correct interpretation of

0066

the Agreed Minute, which is intended solely to prevent a contractor from losing the benefits of this article for work performed in connection with ... facilities or areas covered by this agreement.

19. Mr. Habib pointed out that acceptance of the Korean proposal to add the phrase "except for paragraph 7" to the Agreed Minute would deprive a contractor performing work for the Embassy or USOM of all the benefits of paragraph 7 with regard to work which that contractor was performing for the U.S. armed forces. Mr. Habib added that at the present time there is no contractor who is performing work for the Embassy and USOM in addition to his work for the U.S. armed forces, although in the past the Vinnell Corporation had performed some additional work for USOM. He urged the Korean side to reconsider its proposed addition to the Agreed Minute, in the light of the explanation just given of the intent of the Agreed Minute. Mr. Whang stated that the Korean side would take this matter under further consideration and give its views at a later date.

20. It was agreed to hold the next meeting on October 30 at 2:00 p.m.

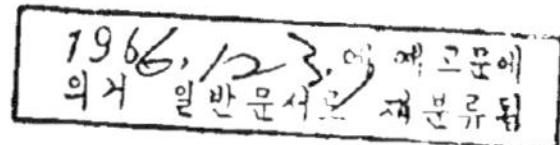

| 협 조 전 | 응 신 기 일 |
|---|---|

문서번호 외정미 442. 제 목 미주둔군지위협정 합의조문 통보

수 신: 정보국장 발 신: 정무국장 년 월 일 63.10.22 제 1 의 견

1963. 10. 4 및 1962. 10. 18 각각 개최된 제32차 및 제33차 미주둔군 지위협정 체결 한미간 실무교섭회의에서 아래 조문에 대하여 완전합의를 보았으며 합의된 조문을 별첨 송부합니다.

아 래

1. 토지시설의 사용허용 및 반환에 관한 조문 (제33차회의에서 합의)
2. 조세에 관한 조문 (제33차회의에서 합의)
3. 토지시설에 관련하여 취할 제반조치에 관한 조문 (제32차 회의에서 합의)

별첨: 합의된 조문 각 1부 끝

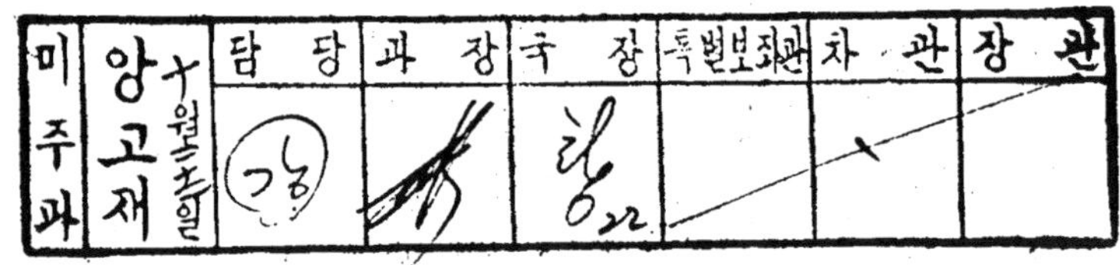

| 미주과 | 양고재 | 담 당 | 과 장 | 국 장 | 특별보좌관 | 차 관 | 장 관 |
|---|---|---|---|---|---|---|---|
| | | | | | | | |

1966.12.31.에 예고문에 의거 일반문서로 재분류

정 무 국 장 황

보통문서로 재분류(1966. 12. 31 )

승인서식 1—34 (11—13330—01) (195mm×265mm16절지)

0068

Article - <u>Taxation</u>

1. The United States armed forces shall not be subject to taxes or similar charges on property held, used or transferred by such forces in Korea.

2. Members of the United States armed forces, the civilian component, and their dependents shall not be liable to pay any Korean taxes to the Government of Korea or to any other taxing agency in Korea on income received as a result of their service with or employment by the United States armed forces, including the activities provided for in Article ___. Persons in Korea solely by reason of being members of the United States armed forces, the civilian component, or their dependents shall not be liable to apy any Korean taxes to the Government of Korea or to any taxing agency in Korea on income derived from sources outside of Korea, nor shall periods during which such persons are in Korea be considered as periods of residence or domicile in Korea for the purpose of Korean taxation. The provisions of this Article do not exempt such persons from payment of Korean taxes on income derived from Korean sources, other than those sources referred to in the first sentence of this paragraph, nor do they exempt United States citizens who claim Korean residence for United States income tax purposes from payment of Korean taxes on income.

3. Members of the United States armed forces, the civilian component, and their dependents shall be exempt from taxation in Korea on the holding, use, transfer <u>inter se</u>, or transfer by death of movable property, tangible or intangible, the presence of which in Korea is

6

0069

due solely to the temporary presence of these persons in Korea, provided that such exemption shall not apply to property held for the purpose of investment or the conduct of business in Korea or to any intangible property registered in Korea.

0070

Article - Facilities and Areas (Grant and Return of)

1. (a) The United States is granted, under Article IV of the Mutual Defense Treaty, the use of facilities and areas in the Republic of Korea. Agreements as to specific facilities and areas shall be concluded by the two Governments through the Joint Committee provided for in Article ___ of this Agreement. "Facilities and Areas" include existing furnishings, equipment and fixtures, wherever located, used in the operation of such facilities and areas.

(b) The facilities and areas of which the United States armed forces have the use at the effective date of this agreement together with those areas and facilities which the United States armed forces have returned to the Republic of Korea with the reserved right of re-entry, when these facilities and areas have been reentered by U.S. forces, shall be considered as the facilities and areas agreed upon between the two Governments in accordance with subparagraph (a) above. Records of facilities and areas of which the United States armed forces have the use or right of re-entry shall be maintained through the Joint Committee after this Agreement comes into forces.

2. At the request of either Government, the Governments of the United States and the Republic of Korea shall review such arrangements and may agree that such facilities and areas or portions thereof shall be returned to the Republic of Korea or that additional facilities and areas may be provided.

3. The facilities and areas used by the United States shall be returned to the Republic of Korea under such conditions as may be agreed through the Joint

0071

Committee whenever they are no longer needed for the purposes of this Agreement and the United States agrees to keep the needs for facilities and areas under continual observation with a view toward such return.

4. (a) When facilities and areas are temporarily not being used and the Government of the Republic of Korea is so advised, the Government of the Republic of Korea may make, or permit Korean nationals to make, interim use of such facilities and areas provided that it is agreed between the two Governments through the Joint Committee that such use would not be harmful to the purposes for which the facilities and areas are normally used by the United States armed forces.

(b) With respect to facilities and areas which are to be used by United States armed forces for limited periods of time, the Joint Committee shall specify in the agreements covering such facilities and areas the extent to which the provisions of this Agreement shall not apply.

0072

Article - Facilities and Areas (Measures taken in)

1. Within the facilities and areas, the United States may take all the measures necessary for their establishment, operation, safeguarding and control. In order to provide access for the United States armed forces to the facilities and areas for their support, safeguarding and control, the Government of the Republic of Korea shall, at the request of the United States armed forces and upon consultation between the two Governments through the Joint Committee, take necessary measures within the scope of applicable laws and regulations over land, territorial waters and airspace adjacent to, or in the vicinities of the facilities and areas. The United States may also take necessary measures for such purposes upon consultation between the two Governments through the Joint Committee.

2. (a) The United States agrees not to take the measures referred to in paragraph 1 in such a manner as to interfere unnecessarily with navigation, aviation, communication, or land travel to or from or within the territories of the Republic of Korea.

(b) All questions relating to telecommunications including radio frequencies for electromagnetic radiating devices, or like matters, shall continue to be resolved expeditiously in the utmost spirit of coordination and cooperation by arrangement between the designated communications authorities of the two Governments.

(c) The Government of the Republic of Korea shall, within the scope of applicable laws, regulations and

0073

agreements, take all reasonable measures to avoid or eliminate interference with electromagnetic radiation sensitive devices, telecommunications devices, or other apparatus required by the United States armed forces.

3. Operations in the facilities and areas in use by the United States armed forces shall be carried on with due regard for the public safety.

<u>Agreed Minute</u>

It is agreed that in the event of an emergency, the United States armed forces shall be authorized to take such measures in the vicinity of the areas and facilities as may be necessary to provide for their safeguarding and control.

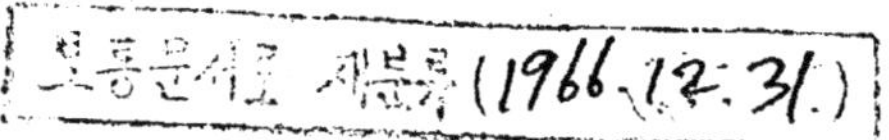




0071

3. 제34차 회의, 10.30

0075

# 기 안 용 지

| 자체 통제 | | 기안처 | 미주과 강석재 | 전화번호 | 근거서류접수일자 |
|---|---|---|---|---|---|

| | | 과장 | 국장 | 차관 | 장관 |
|---|---|---|---|---|---|
| | | (서명) | (서명) | (서명) | (서명) |

| 관계관 서명 | |
|---|---|

| 기안 년월일 | 1963. 10. 29 | 시행 년월일 | | 보존 년한 | | 정서 | 기장 |
|---|---|---|---|---|---|---|---|
| 분류 기호 | 외정미 | 전체 통제 | | 종결 | | | |

| 경유 수신 참조 | 건의 | 발신 | |
|---|---|---|---|
| 제목 | 제34차 주둔군지위협정체결교섭회의에 임할 우리측입장 | | |

10월 30일에 개최될 제34차 주둔군지위협정체결한미간 교섭회의에서는 항공통제 및 항해보조시설, 관세업무, 군사우편, 공익물 및 용역문제를 토의하고 협정개정에 관한 초안을 수교하기로 되어 있는바, 이에 관하여 우리측 교섭실무자는 10월 28일 회합을 갖고 제34차 회의에서 취할 우리측 태도를 별첨과 같이 결정하였아오니 재가하여 주시기 바랍니다.

유첨: 제34차 주둔군지위협정체결교섭회의에 임할 우리측 태도. 끝.

1966.12.31에 예고문에 의거 일반문서로 재분류됨

일반문서로 재분류(1966. 12. 31)

승인양식 1-1-3 (1112-040-016-018) (190mm×260mm16절지)

0076

1. 항공통제 및 항해보조시설

가. 우리측 초안 (1)항은 모든 민간 및 군사항공통제뿐만 아니라 통신제도도 양국 정부의 긴밀한 협조하에 발전시키도록 규정하였던바, 미국측은 통신에 관한 사항은 별도 토지시설조항에서 규제하기를 원하였으며 따라서 (1)항에 관한 토의를 보류하여 왔었다. 양측은 이미 토지시설에 관한 B 조항의 2(a)(b)및(c)항에서 통신에 관하여 상세히 규정하고 합의를 보았으므로 우리측은 우리측 초안에서 "and Communications systems "이란 용어를 삭제하기로 한다. 동 용어를 삭제하면 양측초안은 실질적인 내용의 차이가 없으며 다만 용어에 있어서 우리측은 " between the two Governments "가 첨가되어 있고 또한 미국측 초안의 " necessary for the operation of this Agreement" 대신에 " necessary for mutual security interests " 로 되어 있음. 우리측은 우리초안에 미국측이 합의하여 줄 것을 제의하고 미국측이 이에 응하지 않을 경우에는 미국측 안을 수락한다.

나. 미국측 초안 (2)항은 선박 및 항공기를 위한 보조시설의 설치와 유지를 미국측에 허용할 것을 규정하는 것인바 이러한 보조시설의 설치는 "토지시설 조문 제1절에서 규정한 절차에 의거한다" 라는 미국측이 제시한 합의 의사록과 함께 수락한다. 둘째문장에 있어서 " 그러한 항해보조시설은 한국에서 사용하는 제도에 대체적으로 일치하여야 한다"라는 규정에서 미국측 초안의 용어 " generally "는 미군대가 사용하는 통신기재중 어떤것은 한국의 현행 항해보조시설제도하에서 실질적으로 사용할수 없다는 점을 고려하여 수락한다. 셋째 문장은 그러한 보조시설을 설치하였을 경우 그 위치와 특징을 상호 통보할 것을 규정하고 또한 그러한 시설을 변경할 경우 "가능하면" 사전에 통고할 것을 규정하고 있는바, 그러한 보조시설이 긴급히 필요한 비상시나 임시로 보조시설을 설치할 필요가 있는 전투 훈련등의 경우가 있을것을 고려하여 미국측의 "where practicable "이란 용어를 수락한다.

0077

2. 관세업무

가. 미국측 초안 제2항의 비세출자금기관에 관한 용어를 "organizations "로 할 것인지 혹은 미국측이 수정제의한 "activities "로 할 것인지에 대하여서는 아직 관계부처와의 결정에 도달하지 않었으므로 당분간 보류할 것을 요구한다.

나. 미국측 초안 3항의 서문에 관하여 " charges "는 정부가 부가하는 각종 공과금만을 말하며 민간업자가 부가하는 창고료, 하역료 기타 통관업자 수수료를 말하는 것이 아니라는점을 명백히 하고 미국측 안대로 수락한다.

다. 차량 및 부속품 수입에 관한 미국측 초안 3(a)항에 관하여 우리측은 19차 회의에서 한국에 도착후 6개월내에 도입한 차량은 관세를 면제하며 부속품에 대해서는 시간적 제한을 두지 않겠다고 제의한데 대하여 미국측의 의견을 문의한다.

라. 세관검사 면제대상규정인 미국측 초안 (5)항에 있어서 우리측은 계속 (ㄱ) 단체 (unit )로서 입국하는 자에 한하여 세관검사 면제를 부여토록 주장하고 (ㄴ) 사용우편물에 대해서는 세관검사를 실시하며 단지 official mail 만을 면제하도록 주장한다. 우리측은 이미 미국측 초안 3( c )에서 군사우체국을 통하여 한국으로 우송되는 사용을 위한 적절한 량의 개인용품 및 가사도구등의 면세를 인정하였는 만큼 세관검사는 적절한 량의 여부를 확인하기 위하여 필요하다는 입장을 취한다.
(ㄷ) 군사화물중에서 비세출기관에 탁송되는 물품은 세관검사 면제대상에서 제외하도록 계속 주장한다.

마. 관세업무 조항에 대한 합의 의사록에 있어서

(1) 제 2 항 문장의 " free of duty " 다음에 "reasonable quantities of "라는 구절을 삽입토록 계속 주장하며 본 합의 의사록 (2)항이 관계하고 있는 미국측 초안 3(c)항에 동 구절이 있음을 상기하도록

0078

미국측에 설명한다.

(2) 합의 의사록 (3)항의 " and their non-appropriated fund organizations provided for in Article.......... " 은 우리측이 미국측 초안 5(c)항에 관하여 비세출 자금기관을 제외하도록 제의한바와 같이 " but excluding their non-appropriated fund organizations...."로 수정하던지 또는 완전히 삭제할 것을 주장한다.

3. 군사우편시설

가. 미국측 초안 (2)항은 통상,해외에서 그러한 특권이 부여된 미국 정부관리 및 그 가족들도 군사우편 시설을 사용할수 있도록 규정하고 있는바 양측 대표는 제19차 회의에서 이 규정은 예외적인 것으로 합의 의사록에 넣도록 하는데 합의하였으며 그 내용에 대해서는 밀접한 관련이 있는 관세 업무조항 중 세관검사 면제규정의 5(b)항에 대한 합의를 본 후 최종적 결정을 하도록 합의하였는바 우리측은 "and their dependents "를 삭제할 것을 요구하며 단약 미국측이 전기 관세조항 5(b)에 있어서 우리측 요구대로 사용 우편물에 대한 세관검사를 수락할 경우에는 미국측 안대로 합의하기로 한다.

4. 공익물

가. 공익물에 관한 미국측 초안 3(a)는 우리측이 24차 회의에서 제의한대로 만약 미국측이 공익물 및 용역의 정의에 관한 둘째문장에서 " however produced "라는 용어를 삭제할것에 동의한다면 "whether publicly or privately owned "라는 구절을 삭제하고 "which are "라는 구절 다음에 " owned "라는 용어를 삽입하며 "political subdivisions "대신에 " local administrative subdivisions " 라는 구절을 삽입하고 또한 미국측이 새로 제안한 3(a)항의 셋째 및 넷째문장을 수락할 것임을 설명하고 이에 대한 미국측의 의견을 문의한다.

0079

나. 미국측 초안 3(b )은 비상시 작전상의 필요가 있을시 대한민국은 공익물 및 용역의 제공을 보장하기 위한 조치를 취할 것을 규정하고 있는바 그 비상작전상의 요구가 일방적인 통고로 인정될 것이 아니라 우리 정부가 그 요구가 적절하고 인정할 만한 것이라 ( reasonable and justifiable ) 합의할 경우라야 한다고 주장하며 그러한 내용으로 문장을 수정하여 이를 합의의사록에 넣도록 주장한다.

다. 미국측 초안 4항에 대하여는 이에 해당하는 우리측 초안 2(a )항과 관련하여 약간의 오해가 있었다고 보며 그 오해는 (ㄱ) 미국측 초안 4항은 단지 본 협정에서 일어나는 금전거래에 적용될 청산조치만을 규정하고 있는 반면 우리측 초안은 철도운송, 전기 및 수도등 공익물 및 용역은 현재 8군이 교통부운수국, 한국전력회사 및 서울시 수도국과 각각 계약을 체결하고 요금을 청산하고 있는 거와 같이 앞으로도 8군과 한국정부 및 정부기관간의 특별한 조치에 따라 할 것을 규정하고 있다. (ㄴ) 미국측 초안에 의하면 새로운 청산조치를 위하여 양국 정부가 별도 교섭을 필요로 하는 인상이 있으며 (ㄷ) 또한 미국측 초안은 전기 한바와 같은 철도 운송, 전기 및 수도등에 관한 현행 양국간의 조치에 대한 언급이 없는바 이러한 점에 관한 미국측의 의견을 묻기로 한다.

라. 합의 의사록 (1)항에 있어서 우리측이 24차 회의에서 "... shall be the subject of prior consultation in the joint Committee " 대신에 "... shall, at the Joint Committee, be notified within 15 days after the effective date of such a change" 라는 구절과 대치하자고제의한데 대하여 미국측의 의견을 묻기로 한다.

마. 합의 의사록 (2)항은 1958.12.18 자 한미양국이 체결한 공익물에 관한 청구권 청산협정의 효력을 존속시키도록 한 규정이며 우리측 초안 2(b)와 관련된 것인바 우리측은 공익물에 관한 청구권 청산협정 외에 기타 현존하는 제반 조치도 계속 유효하도록 규정하고 있으므로 실질적인 차이가 없으며 우리측 안이 오히려 더욱 포괄적이라고 생각한다고 주장하고 미국측의

0080

의견을 묻기로 한다.

5. 협정 개정

본 협정의 개정에 관한 초안을 교환토록 되어 있는바 우리측은 별첨과 같은 안을 수교하기로 함.

보통문서로 재분류(1966.12.31.)

1966.12.31.에 예고문에 의거 일반문서로 재분류됨

0081

Article ____(Revision)____

Either Government may at any time request the revision of any article of this Agreement, in which case the two Governments shall enter into negotiation through diplomatic channels.



0082

APO 관계 檢擧現況

서울 稅關

| 검거 日字 | 63.8.6 | 9.12 | 9.14 | 9.17 | 9.19 | 10.1 | 10.26 |
|---|---|---|---|---|---|---|---|
| 國籍 | 한국 | 美國 | 美國 | 국제결혼 | 국제결혼 | 한국 | 美國 |
| 職業 | 미군 部隊 從業員 | 무직 | " | " | " | 미군 部隊 從業員 | 무직 |
| 人員 | 1명 | 2 | 1 | 1 | 1 | 1 | 1 |
| 검거 場所 | 議政府 | 서울 | " | " | " | 坡州 | 서울 |
| 市価 | 101,100 | 400,000.- | 53,600.- | 170,000.- | 200,000. | 80,000.- | 2,723,960.- |
| 押收 品目 | 鹿茸 10句 外 2種 | 카메라 4개 외 4종 | 口紅 外 26종 | 鹿茸 2斤半 外 3종 | 로렉스 시계 外 8종 | 밍크오바코트 外 6종 | 鹿茸 21.3kg 外 16종 |

※ 件數 7件
人員 8名
市価計 3,728,660.원

승인서식 1—1—2 (11—00900—02) (195mm×265mm16절지)

0083

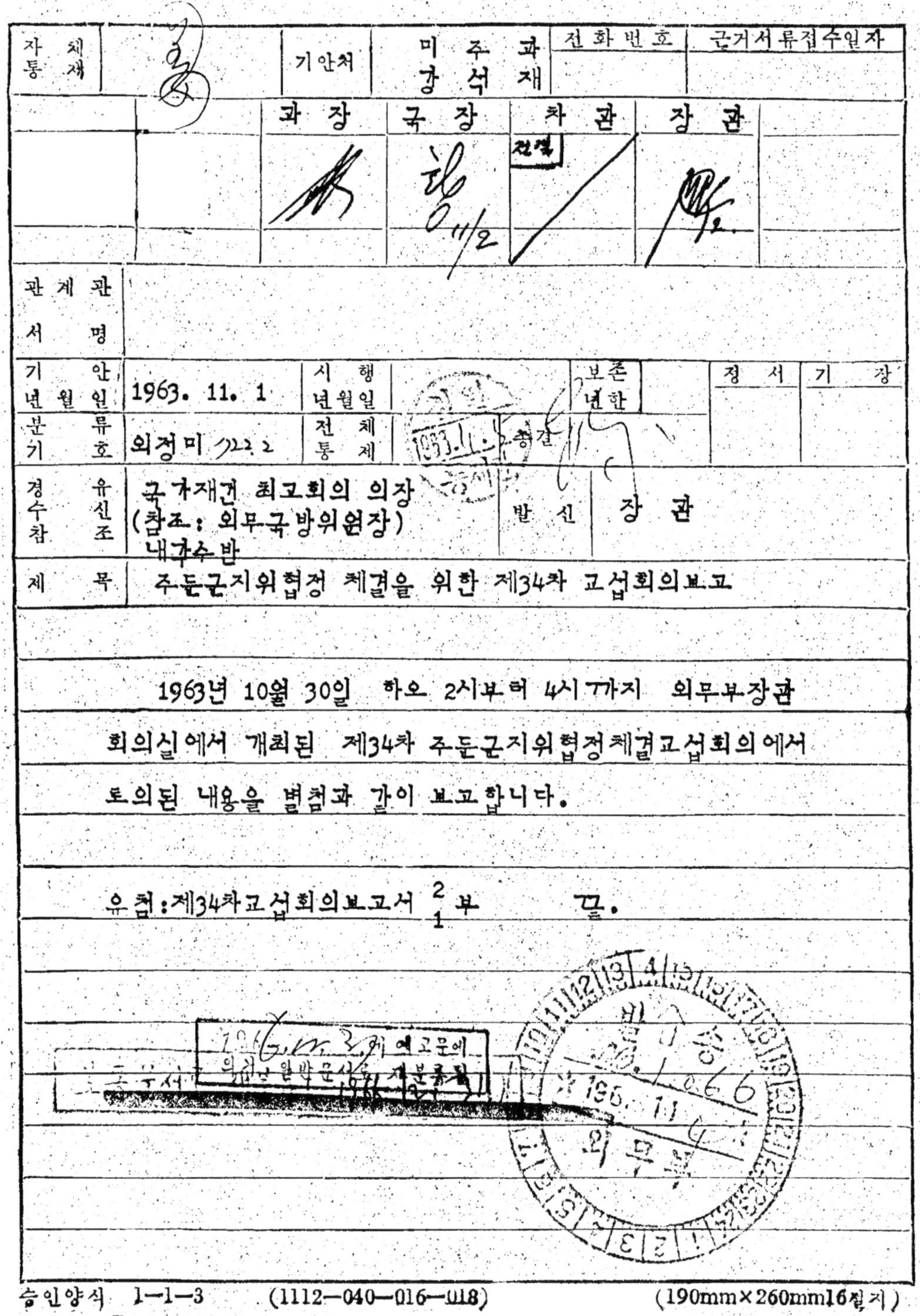

# 기 안 용 지

| 자 체<br>통 제 | | 기안처 | 미 주 과<br>강 석 재 | 전화번호 | 근거서류접수일자 |
|---|---|---|---|---|---|
| | 과 장 | 국 장 | 차 관 | 장 관 | |
| 관계관<br>서 명 | | | | | |
| 기 안<br>년월일 | 1963. 11. 1 | 시 행<br>년월일 | | 보존<br>년한 | 정 서 기 장 |
| 분 류<br>기 호 | 외정미 722.2 | 전 체<br>통 제 | | | |
| 경 유<br>수 신<br>참 조 | 국가재건 최고회의 의장<br>(참조: 외무국방위원장)<br>내각수반 | | 발 신 | 장 관 | |
| 제 목 | 주둔군지위협정 체결을 위한 제34차 교섭회의보고 | | | | |

1963년 10월 30일 하오 2시부터 4시까지 외무부장관 회의실에서 개최된 제34차 주둔군지위협정체결교섭회의에서 토의된 내용을 별첨과 같이 보고합니다.

유첨: 제34차교섭회의보고서 2/1 부 끝.

1966.12.31 예고문에 의거 일반문서로 재분류됨

승인양식 1-1-3 (1112-040-016-018) (190mm×260mm16절지)

0084

외 무 부

외정미 722.2 1963. 11. 4

수 신 : 국가재건 최고회의 의장

참 조 : 외무국방위원장

제 목 : 주둔군지위협정 체결을 위한 제34차 교섭회의 보고

1963년 10월 30일 하오 2시부터 4시까지 외무부장관 회의실에서 개최된 제34차 주둔군지위협정체결교섭회의에서 토의된 내용을 별첨과 같이 보고합니다.

유 첨 : 제34차교섭회의보고서 2부. 끝.

외 무 부 장 관 김 용 식

0085

제 34 차

한미간 주둔군지위협정 체결실무자 회의

보 고 서

1. 일 시 : 1963 년 10 월 30 일 하오 2시부터 4시 7까지

2. 장 소 : 외무부 장관 회의실

3. 참 석 자 : 한국측 : 황 호 을 ( 외무부 정무국장)

신 관 섭 ( 재무부 세관국장)

구 충 회 ( 외무부 미주과장)

신 정 섭 ( 외무부 조약과장)

박 도 준 중령(국방부 군무과)

주 문 기 ( 법무부 법무과장)

강 석 재 ( 외무부2등서기관)

이 경 빈 ( 외무부3등서기관)

미국측 : 교섭대표단 전원

4. 토의사항

가. 항공통제 및 항해보조시설

(1) 우리측 초안 (1)항은 민간 및 군사항공통제뿐만 아니라 통신제도도 양국정부간의 긴밀한 협조하에 발전시키도록 규정하고 있는바 우리측은 통신에 관한 사항을 이미 토지시설 조항 중에서 별도 규정하였으므로 " and communications systems "라는 용어를 삭제하기로 동의하고 기타 용어상 미국측 초안은 " for the operation of this Agreement "로 되어 있고 우리측 초안은 " for mutual security interests"로 되어 있는 차이는 주둔군지위협정의 모든 조항이 양국의 안전보장을 목적으로 하고 있다는 양해하에 미국측 초안의 용어를 수락하였다.

(2) 미국측 초안 2 항의 첫재 문장은 선박 및 항공기를 위한 보조시설의 설치와 유지를 미국측에 허용할 것을 규정하는 것인바 그러한 보조시설의 설치는 미국측이 제의한 "토지시설 조문 제 1 절에서 규정한 절차에 의거



63-1-162

0086

05-1-29(4)

미국,문 108-4 (4)

0087

한다"라는 합의 의사록과 함께 수락하였다.

(3) 미국측 초안 (2)항의 둘째 문장은 "그러한 항해보조시설은 한국에서 사용하는 제도에 일치할것"을 규정하고 있는바 미군이 사용하고 있는 통신기재중 어떤종류는 우리나라의 현행 항해 보조시설제도하에서 실제로 사용할수 없는 사정을 고려하여 미국측 초안의 "대체적으로"( generally ) 라는 용어를 수락하기로 하였다.

(4) 미국측 초안 (2)항의 셋째문장은 "그러한 보조시설 설치시의 그 위치 및 특징에 관한 상호 통보와 그러한 시설을 변경할 경우 사전 통고할것" 을 규정하는 것인바 비상시나 혹은 전투훈련시에는 그러한 보조시설의 설치가 긴급히 필요할 경우가 있으며 사전통고가 반드시 가능하지 못할것이라는 점을 고려하여 미국측 초안에 있는 "가능할 경우"( where practicable )이란 용어를 수락하였다. 이로서 양측 실무교섭자는 항공통제 및 항해 보조시설에 관한 조문을 미국측 초안과 그 합의의사록에 완전 합의하였다.

나. 관세 업무

(1) 미국측 초안 2항(우리측 초안 (2)항에 해당)은 미군대의 공적 사용과 군대구성원, 군속 및 가족의 사용을 위하여 도입되는 모든 물자, 보급품 및 장비와 또한 궁극적으로 미군대가 사용하는 시설에 통합될 그러한 물자의 무세도입을 규정하고 있으며 본항중 아직 미합의된 점은 비세출자금기관을 " organizations "로 할것인지 혹은 " activities "로 할것인지에 대한 점인바 우리측은 이 문제에 대한 결정을 (비세출자금기관 조항 토의시까지) 보류하도록 요구하였음.

(2) 미국측은 이 문제에 대한 토의보류를 수락하나 그러한 용어의 차이는 본질적인 변경을 의미하는 것이 아니라고 강조하고 또한 미국측 초안 (2)항과 (5)항 및 합의 의사록에 나타나 있는 "공인 조달기관과 __조에서 규정한 비세출자금기관을 포함한"( including their authorized procurement agencies and their non-appropriated fund organizations ..... ) 라는 구절을 괄호로 포함시키고 있는것은 그 조직과 활동이 좀 다르기는 하나 그러한 기구가 미국군대구성의 일부이며 그 테두리내에 포함되어야 하기 때문이며 미국 정규군대와 구분되는 별도의 조직체가 아니라고 거듭 강조하였다.

67-1-163

0088

63-1-29

미일 108-4

0089

(3) 우리측은 면세통관의 대상을 규정하는 미국측 초안 (3)항 서문에 있어서 " charges "라는 용어는 우리정부가 부가하는 각종 공과금만을 말하며 민간업자가 부가하는 창고료, 하역료 또는 통관업자 수수료 등을 포함하는 것이 아니라는 점을 명백히 한후 미국측 초안을 수락하였다.

(4) 차량 및 부속품의 면세에 관한 미국측 초안 3(b )항에 관하여 우리측은 제19차 회의에서 제의한 대로 한국에 도착한후 6개월내에 도입한 차량은 관세를 면제하고 부속품에 대해서는 그러한 시간적 제한을 두지 않겠다는 입장을 계속 취했는바 미국측은 여기서 문제가 되는 것은 원측적으로 관세를 면제하느냐 혹은 하지 않느냐의 문제이지 어떠한 기간을 설정하여 면세여부를 달리 규정할 성질의 것이 아니라고 말하고 군 구성원 및 군속에 의하여 사용을 목적으로 도입하는 차량은 면세되어야 한다고 강조하였음.

(5) 세관검사 면제대상규정인 미국측 초안 (5)항 (우리측 초안(5)항)에 있어서

ㄱ) 우리측은 "부대"( unit )로서 입국하는자에 한하여 세관검사를 면제하도록 주장하였으나 미국측은 현재 한국에 나와있는 미군은 교체나 휴가차 출입국 할시 부대로서 행동하는 것이 아니고 사실상 개인 단위로 취해지고 있다고 설명하고 따라서 군 구성원에 대한 세관검사는 면제되어야 한다는 입장을 취하고 있다.

ㄴ) 우리측은 공용 우편물만을 세관검사를 면제하고 기타 사용 우편물은 검사를 하여야 한다고 주장하고 그 이유로서 과거 극소수의 비양심적인 사람들이 군사우편시설을 사용할수 있는 특권을 악 이용하여 수입금지품을 반입하는 예가 있었다고 지적하였다. 미국측은 그러한 사례가 있었는지 모르나 검사를 함으로서 남용을 방지할수 있다는 기대를 가지기 어려우며 오히려 그러한 행정적인 조치는 우편의 지연이나 혼동을 야기케 하는것외에 별다른 효과가 없다고 말하고 그러나 한국측이 염려하고 있는바를 참작하여 " under official postal seal "라는 구절을 첨가하자고 제의하였다. 우리측은 동 구절이 의미하는바에 대하여 미국측에 문의하였으나 실질적인 차이가 없으므로 계속 사용 우편물에 대한 검사할 권한을 규정함으로서 남용

63-1-164

0090

63-1-27 미묘 108-4

0091

자들의 유혹을 배제하고 사전방지를 효과적으로 할수 있다고 주장하였다. 미국측은 사선에 대한 검사도 하고저 하는지 우리의 의도를 탁진해 왔는데 대하여 우리는 사선에 대한 검사는 우리 헌법상 금지되고 있는바이며 우리측이 관심을 갖고 있는것은 우편소포에 대한 검사이라고 답변하였다. 양측은 이 문제에 대하여 계속 토의하였는바 미국측은 우리의 의도를 양해한후 고려하겠다고 약속함.

ㄷ) 우리측은 군사화물중 비세출기관에 탁송되는 물품에 대해서는 세관검사를 해야한다고 주장하였는바 미국측은 비세출기관이 미국군대 구성과 별도의 것으로 구분될수 없다는 입장을 되풀이 하고 이 문제의 토의를 보류함.

(6) 미국측이 제안한 관세 업무조항에 관한 합의 의사록 (2)항 문장에 있어서 우리측은 " free of duty "다음에 reasonable quantities of "라는 구절을 삽입토록 계속 주장하였는바 미국측은 본 합의 의사록에 관계하는 관세 업무조문 초안 3(c)항에 "적절한 양" 이란 규정이 있음으로 여기서 다시 규제할 필요가 없다는 입장을 취하였음.

(7) 합의 의사록 (3)항에 관하여 우리측은 군사화물의 정의에서 비세출자금기관에 탁송된 물품을 제외할 것을 계속 주장하였으나 미국측은 본 합의 의사록이 관계하는 5(c)항에서와 같은 입장을 취하고 이 문제에 대한 토의를 보류하였음.

다. 협정개정조항 초안 교환

양측 실무교섭자는 협정 개정에 관한 별첨과 같은 초안을 교환하였다.

5. 중요합의사항

항공통제 및 항해보조시설에 관한 조문에 완전합의함.

6. 기타 사항

63-1-165

차기회의 일자 : 1963 년 11 월 14 일 하오 2 시

차기회의 의제 : 차기회의 까지 양측수석대표간에 합의된 사항.

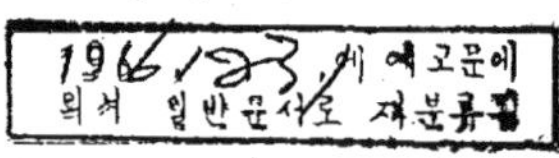


0092

63-1-27(4)　　　미국문 108-4 (4)

0093

October 30, 1963

1. Mr. Hwang opened the meeting by introducing Mr. YI Chong-bin, of the Treaty Section of the Foreign Ministry, who has been designated a member of the Korean negotiating team replacing Mr. HO Sung. Mr. Habib welcomed Mr. Yi to the negotiations.

Air Traffic Control and Navigational Aids

2. Taking up the draft article dealing with air traffic control and navigational aids, Mr. Hwang commented that paragraph 1 of the Korean draft included a reference to communications systems. In view of the fact that paragraph 2 (b) of Facilities and Areas Article "B", the text of which had already been agreed to, provides for arrangements regarding communications systems, the Korean side now agreed to the deletion of the reference to communications systems from the Air Traffic Control article. With this change, there remained no difference in substance between the two drafts of paragraph 1. However, the Korean draft referred to coordination "between the two governments" and spoke of "mutual security interests". Since there was no real difference in substance, he urged the U.S. side to agree to the Korean draft.

3. Mr. Habib replied that the U.S. negotiators were under the impression that fundamental agreement had previously been reached on the U.S. draft, subject only to agreement on Facilities and Areas Article "B", which had subsequently been reached, as Mr. Hwang had just pointed out. The language of the U.S. draft is intended to relate this article to the Status of Forces Agreement as a whole, which in turn is related to the Mutual Defense Treaty. The SOFA itself, therefore, is related to our mutual security interests and there is no need to repeat in each article this fundamental concept. In the Preamble, which has already been agreed to, there is specific reference to the Mutual Defense Treaty and the desire of both governments to strengthen "the

0094

close bonds of mutual interest". Inasmuch as anything done under the provisions of the SOFA will be done for mutual security interests, there is no need to make such a specific reference in this article when it has not been included in other articles.

4. Mr. Hwang replied that the wording contained in the Korean draft appeared in some other status of forces agreements. However, the Korean side agreed that this Agreement as a whole will be based on the mutual security interests of the two governments. With this understanding, the Korean side accepted the text of paragraph 1 of the U.S. draft.

5. Turning to paragraph 2, Mr. Hwang stated that the chief difference in the two drafts lay in the use of the words "in territorial waters adjacent thereto or in the vicinity thereof" in the Korean draft, while the U.S. draft used the words "throughout the Republic of Korea and in the territorial waters thereof". Inasmuch as the U.S. draft, provides in the Agreed Minute that installation of navigational aids should be in accordance with the procedure established under paragraph 1 of Facilities and Areas Article "A", the Korean side accepted the first sentence of the U.S. draft, and the accompanying Agreed Minute.

6. Referring to the use of the word "generally" in the second sentence of paragraph 2 of the U.S. draft, Mr. Hwang stated that the Korean side accepted this sentence, inasmuch as certain U.S. systems are somewhat different from systems being used by the ROK Government.

7. In view of the possibility of the establishment of temporary or emergency navigational aids, Mr. Hwang stated that the Korean side accepted the third sentence of the U.S. draft, which provides for mutual notification of positions and characteristics of navigational aids which have been established and advance notification "where practicable" before making any changes or establishing additional aids.

8. It was noted that full agreement had thereupon been reached on the text of this article, subject to possible later editorial changes of a

0095

stylistic nature.

Customs

9. Taking up the Customs Article, Mr. Hwang suggested that the negotiators defer discussion of the unresolved question of whether to use the word "activities" or the word "organizations", since the Korean negotiators had not yet reached full agreement with the Ministries concerned. He asked whether the U.S. side had any comments to make regarding other points at issue in paragraph 2 of the article.

10. Mr. Habib replied that in this paragraph and elsewhere in the article there existed a difference of opinion regarding the inclusion of authorized procurement agencies and their non-appropriated fund activities. The U.S. side had already proposed that the references to them in the U.S. draft be placed in parentheses to emphasize the fact that they form an integral part of the U.S. armed forces. What the Korean side was suggesting, by omitting activities from the provisions of the article, was that the U.S. armed forces should penalize themselves merely because of the organizational and administrative framework under which the armed forces operate. This framework superficially appears to set these agencies apart, whereas in actual fact they are an integral part of the armed forces. This is the only fundamental difference of opinion remaining with regard to paragraph 2.

11. Mr. Hwang stated that the Korean side would consider the explanation given by Mr. Habib and would be prepared to discuss this issue as soon as agreement was reached with the appropriate ministries.

12. Mr. Hwang noted that the introductory section of paragraph 3 had already been agreed upon, with the understanding that the word "charges" does not refer to charges by civilian firms, such as unloading charges, storage charges, and charges by customs brokers. Mr. Habib agreed with this understanding.

13. Noting that subparagraphs (c) had already been agreed upon,

0096

Mr. Hwang stated that at the 19th negotiating meeting, the Korean side had proposed that subparagraph (b) be modified by providing for a 6-month exemption from payment of duty on imported vehicles, with no time limitation on the importation of spare parts.

14. Mr. Habib replied that the U.S. negotiators continued to be reluctant to agree to the imposition of any time limit on the importation of duty-free vehicles. At previous meetings, the Korean negotiators had indicated a willingness to recognize problems arising out of delays in shipment and other causes of late arrival of vehicles. The basic issue is whether members of the U.S. armed forces should be expected to pay customs duty on normally available personal property. The establishment of a time limit does not answer this basic question.

15. Mr. Hwang replied that the point made by Mr. Habib required further consideration by the Korean negotiators.

16. Turning to paragraph 5, Mr. Hwang noted that the Korean side had previously suggested the substitution of the word "units" for the word "members" in subparagraph (a) of the U.S. draft. Mr. Habib replied that it was a fact that, in general, the members of the U.S. armed forces entered Korea as individuals and not as members of units. Therefore, the change proposed by the Korean negotiators would not be an accurate description of the actual process of entry and exit. The rotation of personnel and the granting of leave are both accomplished on an individual basis. Mr. Hwang took note of Mr. Habib's explanation and proposed that further discussion be postponed until a later meeting.

17. Taking up subparagraph (b), Mr. Hwang noted that the Korean negotiators had previously proposed the insertion of the word "official" before the word "mail", to provide for exemption from customs

0097

inspection of only official mail. He pointed out that agreement had already been reached on paragraph 3(c), which provides for duty-free entry of "reasonable quantities" of personal effects and household goods mailed through U.S. military post offices. Therefore, provisions should be made in paragraph 5(b) for inspection of personal mail to insure that only reasonable quantities of such goods were being imported through the mail channel.

18. Mr. Habib replied that this article was not intended to include provisions for verification of violations. The U.S. armed forces do not wish to misuse the military postal channels and are prepared to see, through the use of proper controls, that such channels are not misused. The right of inspection, even if granted to Korean customs authorities, would not give them adequate control over violations. Attempts to keep records of each soldier's personal mail would be an administrative nightmare which could not possibly be carried out, except perhaps at the cost of extended delays in the delivery of mail which would be unreasonable. Misuse of the mail channel is a disciplinary matter, which is covered in other portions of the Status of Forces Agreement. In order to meet the psychological needs of the Korean side and to form the basis of compromise, the U.S. side proposed the addition of the phrase "under official postal seal". Stating that the U.S. side did not wish to confuse the Korean negotiators, Mr. Habib explained that most mail addressed to members of the U.S. armed forces (including personal mail) arrives in Korea under official postal seal.

19. In response to Mr. Hwang's request for a fuller explanation, Mr. Habib stated that there is a small seal on each incoming container of mail which identifies the contents of that container as mail within official U.S. postal channels. Mr. Hwang stated that the term "official documents under official seal" was understood. He asked whether any difference existed between mail under official postal seal and ordinary mail.

0098

20. Mr. Habib replied that the major portion of the mail being discussed was personal mail. He said the U.S. negotiators were trying to provide language which would make this provision of the article more palatable to the Korean negotiators. The Korean proposal for customs inspection of mail could not be carried out in a practical or administratively sound manner. It would result in delay and interference with the delivery of mail which would be unwarranted. He asked if the Korean negotiators were proposing to station a customs officer at every battalion and regimental military post office. The Korean proposal would only create confusion and was not the proper way to control violations. An alternative method of carrying out the Korean proposal would be to open the incoming mail at the ports of entry. This also would result in confusion and delays in delivery. In the end, the right of inspection would never be exercised. If the U.S. negotiators thought that the proposal had a useful purpose, they would agree, even though the implementation proved to be cumbersome. However, the Korean proposal does not protect either the ROK Government or the U.S. armed forces against violations.

21. Mr. Hwang stated that the Korean negotiators by no means intended to delay or confuse delivery of mail to the U.S. armed forces. In the past, unauthorized goods had been imported through military postal channels. The Korean authorities, therefore, wished to maintain preventive measures but these were not intended to confuse or delay the delivery of mail. He said the Korean negotiators had photographs of cases in which the military postal channels had been misused. In the past, the Korean authorities have not had the opportunity to examine mail passing through these channels and they suspected that there had been unauthorized importation of goods. The adoption of this provision in the SOFA might itself prove to be an effective preventive measure.

0099

22. Mr. Habib replied that the question of policing the use of the mails was a disciplinary matter. This was true also of misuse of privileges with regard to post exchanges, commissaries, and similar activities. The photographs in the possession of the Korean negotiators were probably taken in conjunction with the U.S. authorities, since there was close cooperation between the U.S. military police and the Korean police.

23. Mr. Hwang stated that the Korean negotiators realized that the bulk of the incoming mail was from the families in the United States of the members of the U.S. armed forces. However, some dishonest persons had abused this privilege and the Korean negotiators desired, through this provision of the SOFA, to warn them that military postal channels can not be abused. He said they had parcels primarily in mind. They did not propose to send customs inspectors to every battalion and regimental post office, since this would exceed the personnel resources of the Customs Bureau. What they were proposing was to station customs inspectors at the ports and airports to make spot checks of incoming parcels. The U.S. negotiators had explained that misconduct would be discovered through joint action by Korean and U.S. police and the violators arrested and disciplined. However, since the misconduct was carried out in secret, it would be impossible to uncover all offenders. Therefore, there should be some means by which to give a psychological warning to offenders that their misdeeds may be discovered and punished.

24. Mr. Habib stated that he gathered from Mr. Hwang's remarks that it was the intention of the Korean negotiators that letter mail should not be inspected and that they were interested primarily in inspecting non-

0100

letter mail.

25. Mr. Hwang replied that under the provisions of the ROK Constitution, personal letters are sacrosanct, the personal letters of the members of the ROK armed forces are not inspected. Therefore, the Korean authorities could not think of examining letter mail of members of the U.S. armed forces.

26. Mr. Habib stated that letter mail is known in the United States as "first class mail". He said the U.S. negotiators would consider the statements made by Mr. Hwang and would discuss this matter further at a later meeting. He said he gathered that if suitable language could be found to exempt letter mail from customs inspection the Korean negotiators would look upon it favorably.

27. Turning to subparagraph (c), Mr. Hwang noted that at a previous meeting, the Korean negotiators had proposed the deletion from the U.S. draft of the phrase "and their non-appropriated fund organizations provided for in Article ___". Mr. Habib replied that these activities form an integral part of the U.S. armed forces and should be so described, not only in this suparagraph but throughout the article.

28. Mr. Hwang stated that in paragraph 2 it had been agreed in principle that equipment and supplies imported by these organizations may be imported free of duty. In this subparagraph, the Korean negotiators wished to provide only that such imports be subject to customs inspection. Mr. Habib replied that Agreed Minute #1 limits such importations to "the extent reasonably required". There was no reason to examine what are, in the U.S. view, official cargoes. If questions arose, the Joint Committee could be asked to look into the matter. In view of the tone of the article, the U.S. negotiators were not prepared to agree to examination of official military cargoes.

29. Mr. Hwang stated that the Korean negotiators would reply to

0101

this statement at the next meeting. He noted that agreement had previously been reached on paragraphs 6, 7, 8, and 9.

Revision of the Agreement

30. At this point, it was agreed to adjourn the meeting. Before adjourning, the two sides exchanged drafts of the article providing for Revision of the Agreement.

31. The next meeting was scheduled for November 14 at 2:00 p.m.

JOINT SUMMARY RECORD OF THE 34TH SESSION

November 7, 1963

1. Time and Place: 2:00 to 4:00 p.m. October 30, 1963 at the Foreign Minister's Conference Room

2. Attendants:

ROK Side:

| | |
|---|---|
| Mr. Whang, Ho Eul | Director<br>Bureau of Political Affairs<br>Ministry of Foreign Affairs |
| Mr. Shin, Kwan Sup | Director<br>Bureau of Customs Duty<br>Ministry of Finance |
| Mr. Koo, Choong Whay | Chief, America Section<br>Ministry of Foreign Affairs |
| Mr. Chu, Mun Ki | Chief, Legal Affairs Section<br>Ministry of Justice |
| Lt. Col. Do Joon Pak | Military Affairs Section<br>Ministry of National Defense |
| Mr. Shin, Jung Sup | Chief, Treaty Section<br>Ministry of Foreign Affairs |
| Mr. Kang, Suk Jae | 2nd Secretary<br>Ministry of Foreign Affairs |
| Mr. Lee, Chung Bin | 3rd Secretary<br>Ministry of Foreign Affairs |

U.S. Side:

| | |
|---|---|
| Mr. Philip C. Habib | Counselor for Political Affairs |
| Brig. Gen. G. G. O'Connor | Deputy Chief of Staff<br>8th U.S. Army |
| Col. Howard Smigelor | Deputy Chief of Staff<br>8th U.S. Army |
| Mr. Banjamin A. Fleck | First Secretary<br>American Embassy |
| Col. L.J. Fuller | Staff Judge Advocate<br>United Nations Command |
| Capt. R. M. Brownlie | Assistant Chief of Staff<br>USN/K |
| Mr. James Sartorius | 2nd Secretary<br>American Embassy |
| Mr. Robert A. Lewis | 2nd Secretary and Consul<br>American Embassy |

0103

| | |
|---|---|
| 8 Mr. Robert A. Kinney | J-5<br>8th U.S. Army |
| 10 Maj. Robert D. Peckham | Staff Officer, JAG<br>8th U.S. Army |
| 11 Mr. Kenneth Campen | Interpreter |

1. Mr. Whang opened the meeting by introducing Mr. YI Chong-bin, of the Treaty Section of the Foreign Ministry, who has been designated a member of the Korean negotiating team replacing Mr. Ho Sung. Mr. Habib welcomed Mr. Yi to the negotiations.

Air Traffic Control and Navigational Aids

2. Taking up the draft article dealing with air traffic control and navigational aids, Mr. Whang commented that paragraph 1 of the Korean draft included a reference to communications systems. In view of the fact that paragraph 2 (b) of Facilities and Areas Article "B", the text of which had already been agreed to, provides for arrangements regarding communications systems, the Korean side now agreed to the deletion of the reference to communications systems from the Air Traffic Control article. With this change, there remained no difference in substance between the two drafts of paragraph 1. However, the Korean draft referred to coordination "between the two governments" and spoke of "mutual security interests". Since there was no real difference in substance, he urged the U.S. side to agree to the Korean draft.

3. Mr. Habib replied that the U.S. negotiators were under the impression that fundamental agreement had previously been reached on the U.S. draft, subject only to agreement on Facilities and Areas Article "B", which had subsequently been reached as Mr. Whang had just pointed out. The language of the U.S. draft is intended to relate this article to the Status of Forces Agreement as a whole, which in turn is related to the Mutual Defense Treaty. The SOFA itself,

0104

therefore, is related to our mutual security interests and there is no need to repeat in each article this fundamental concept. In the Preamble, which has already been agreed to, there is specific reference to the Mutual Defense Treaty and the desire of both governments to strengthen "the close bonds of mutual interest". Inasmuch as anything done under the provisions of the SOFA will be done for mutual security interests, there is no need to make such a specific reference in this article when it has not been included in other articles.

4. Mr. Whang replied that the wording contained in the Korean draft appeared in some other status of forces agreements. However, the Korean side agreed that this Agreement as a whole will be based on the mutual security interests of the two governments. With this understanding, the Korean side accepted the text of paragraph 1 of the U.S. draft.

5. Turning to paragraph 2, Mr. Whang stated that the chief difference in the two drafts lay in the use of the words "in territorial waters adjacent thereto or in the vicinity thereof" in the Korean draft, while the U.S. draft used the words "throughout the Republic of Korea and in the territorial waters thereof". Inasmuch as the U.S. draft, in the Agreed Minute, provides that installation of navigational aids should be in accordance with the procedures established under paragraph 1 of Facilities and Areas Article "A", the Korean side accepted the first sentence of the U.S. draft and the accompanying Agreed Minute.

6. Referring to the use of the word "generally" in the second sentence of paragraph 2 of the U.S. draft, Mr. Whant stated that the Korean side accepted this sentence, inasmuch as certain U.S. systems are somewhat different from systems being used by the ROK Government.

0105

7. In view of the possibility of the establishment of temporary or emergency navigational aids, Mr. Whang stated that the Korean side accepted the third sentence of the U.S. draft, which provides for mutual notification of positions and characteristics of navigational aids which have been established and advance notification "where practicable" before making any changes or establishing additional aids.

8. It was noted that full agreement had thereupon been reached on the text of this article, subject to possible later editorial changes of a stylistic nature.

Customs

9. Taking up the Customs Article, Mr. Whang suggested that the negotiators defer discussion of the unresolved question of whether to use the word "activities" or the word "organizations", since the Korean negotiators had not yet reached full agreement with the Ministries concerned. He asked whether the U.S. side had any comments to make regarding other points at issue in paragraph 2 of the article.

10. Mr. Habib replied that in this paragraph and elsewhere in the article there existed a difference of opinion regarding the inclusion of references to the U.S. armed forces authorized procurement agencies and their non-appropriated fund activities. The U.S. side had already proposed that the references to them in the U.S. draft be placed in parentheses to emphasize the fact that they form an integral part of the U.S. armed forces. What the Korean side was suggesting, by omitting activities from the provisions of the article, was that the U.S. armed forces should penalize themselves merely because of the organizational and administrative framework under which the armed forces operate. This framework superficially appears to set these

0106

agencies apart, whereas in actual fact they are an integral part of the armed forces. This is the only fundamental difference of opinion remaining with regard to paragraph 2.

11. Mr. Whang stated that the Korean side would consider the explanation given by Mr. Habib and would be prepared to discuss this issue as soon as agreement was reached with the appropriate ministries.

12. Mr. Whang noted that the introductory section of paragraph 3 had already been agreed upon, with the understanding that the word "charges" does not refer to charges by civilian firms, such as unloading charges, storage charges, and charges by customs brokers. Mr. Habib agreed with this understanding.

13. Noting that subparagraphs (a) and (c) had already been agreed upon, Mr. Whang stated that at the 19th negotiating meeting, the Korean side had proposed that subparagraph (b) be modified by providing for a 6-month exemption from payment of duty on imported vehicles, with no timelimitation on the importation of spare parts.

14. Mr. Habib replied that the U.S. negotiators continued to be reluctant to agree to the imposition of any time limit on the importation of duty-free vehicles. At previous meetings, the Korean negotiators had indicated a willingness to recognize problems arising out of delays in shipment and other causes of late arrival of vehicles. The basic issue is whether members of the U.S. armed forces should be expected to pay customs duty on normally available personal property. The establishment of a time limit does not answer this basic question.

15. Mr. Whang replied that the point made by Mr. Habib required further consideration by the Korean negotiators.

16. Turning to paragraph 5, Mr. Whang noted that the Korean side had previously suggested the substitution of the word "units" for the word "members" in subparagraph (a) of the U.S. draft. Mr. Habib replied that it was a fact that, in general, the members of the U.S. armed forces entered Korea as individuals and not as members of units. Therefore, the change proposed by the Korean negotiators would not be an accurate description of the actual process of entry and exit. The rotation of personnel and the granting of leave are both accomplished on an individual basis. Mr. Whang took note of Mr. Habib's explanation and proposed that further discussion be postponed until a later meeting.

17. Taking up subparagraph (b), Mr. Whang noted that the Korean negotiators had previously proposed the insertion of the word "official" before the word "mail", so as to provide for exemption from customs inspection of only official mail. He pointed out that agreement had already been reached on paragraph 3 (c), which provides for duty-free entry of "reasonable quantities" of personal effects and household goods mailed through U.S. military post offices. Therefore, provision should be made in paragraph 5(b) for inspection of personal mail to insure that only reasonable quantities of such goods were being imported through the mail channel.

18. Mr. Habib replied that this article was not intended to include provisions for verification of violations. The U.S. armed forces do not wish to misuse the military postal channels and are prepared to see, through the use of proper controls, that such channels are not misused. The right of inspection, even if granted to Korean customs authorities, would not give them adequate control over violations. Attempts to keep records of each soldier's personal mail would be an administrative nightmare which could not possibly be carried out, except perhaps at the cost of extended delays

0108

in the delivery of mail which would be unreasonable. Misuse of the mail channel is a disciplinary matter, which is covered in other portions of the Status of Forces Agreement. In order to meet the psychological needs of the Korean side and to form the basis of compromise, the U.S. side proposed the addition of the phrase "under official postal seal". Stating that the U.S. side did not wish to confuse the Korean regotiators, Mr. Habib explained that nost mail addressed to members of the U.S. armed forces, including personal mail, arrives in Korea under official postal seal.

19. In response to Mr. Whang's request for a fuller explanation, Mr. Habib stated that there is a small seal on each incoming container of mail which identifies the contents of that container as mail within official U.S. postal channels. Mr. Whang stated that the term "official documents under official seal" was understood. He asked whether any difference existed between mail under official postal seal and ordinary mail.

20. Mr. Habib replied that the major portion of the mail being discussed was personal mail. He said the U.S. negotiators were trying to provide language which would make this provision of the article more palatable to the Korean negotiators. The Korean proposal for customs inspection of mail could not be carried out in a practical or administratively sound manner. It would result in delay and interference with the delivery of mail which would be unwarranted. He asked if the Korean negotiators were proposing to station a customs officer at every battalion and regimental military post office. The Korean proposal would only create confusion and was not the proper way to control violations. An alternative method of carrying out the Korean proposal would be to open the incoming mail at the ports of entry. This also would result in confusion and delays in delivery. In the end, the right of inspection would never be exercised. If the U.S.

0109

negotiators thought that the proposal had a useful purpose, they would agree, even though the implementation proved to be cumbersome. However, the Korean proposal does not protect either the ROK Government or the U.S. armed forces against violations.

21. Mr. Whang stated that the Korean negotiators by no means intended to delay or confuse delivery of mail to the U.S. armed forces. In the past, unauthorized goods had been imported through military postal channels. The Korean authorities, therefore, wished to maintain preventive measures but these were not intended to confuse or delay the delivery of mail. He said the Korean negotiators had photographs of cases in which the military postal channels had been misused. In the past, the Korean authorities have not had the opportunity to examine mail passing through these channels and they suspected that there had been unauthorized importation of goods. The adoption of this provision in the SOFA might itself prove to be an effective preventive measure.

22. Mr. Habib replied that the question of policing the use of the mails was a disciplinary matter. This was true also of misuse of privileges with regard to post exchanges, commissaries, and similar activities. The photographs in the possession of the Korean negotiators were probably taken in conjunction with the U.S. authorities, since there was close cooperation between the U.S. military police and the Korean police.

23. Mr. Whang stated that the Korean negotiators realized that the bulk of the incoming mail was from the families in the United States of the members of the U.S. armed forces. However, some dishonest persons had abused this privilege and the Korean negotiators desired, through this provision of the SOFA, to warn them that military postal channels can not be abused. He said they had parcels primarily in mind.

0110

They did not propose to send customs inspectors to every battalion and regimental post office, since this would exceed the personnel resources of the Customs Bureau. What they were proposing was to station customs inspectors at the ports and airports to make spot checks of incoming parcels. The U.S. negotiators had explained that misconduct would be discovered through joint action by Korean and U.S. police and the violators arrested and disciplined. However, since the misconduct was carried out in secret, it would be impossible to uncover all offenders. Therefore, there should be some means by which to give a psychological warning to offenders that their misdeeds may be discovered and punished.

24. Mr. Habib stated that he gathered from Mr. Whang's remarks that it was the intention of the Korean negotiators that letter mail should not be inspected and that they were interested primarily in inspecting non-letter mail.

25. Mr. Whang replied that under the provisions of the ROK Constitution, personal letters are sacrosanct and accordingly the secrecy of the personal letters of Korean nationals is protected. The Korean authorities, therefore, could not think of examining letter mail of members of the U.S. armed forces.

26. Mr. Habib stated that letter mail is known in the United States as "first class mail". He said he gathered that if suitable language could be found to exempt letter mail from customs inspection the Korean negotiators would look upon it favorably. He said the U.S. negotiators would consider the statements made by Mr. Whang and would discuss this matter further at a later meeting.

27. Turning to subparagraph (c), Mr. Whang noted that at a previous meeting, the Korean negotiators had proposed the deletion from the U.S. draft of the phrase "and their non-appropriated fund organizations provided for in Article--".

0111

Mr. Habib replied that these activities form an integral part of the U.S. armed forces and should be so described, not only in this subparagraph but throughout the article.

28. Mr. Whang stated that in paragraph 2 it had been agreed in principle that equipment and supplies imported by these organizations may be imported free of duty. In this subparagraph, the Korean negotiators wished to provide only that such imports be subject to customs inspection. Mr. Habib replied that Agreed Minute #1 limits such importations to "the extent reasonably required". There was no reason to examine what are, in the U.S. view, official cargoes. If questions arose, the Joint Committee could be asked to look into the matter. In view of the tone of the article, the U.S. negotiaotrs were not prepared to agree to examination of official military cargoes.

29. Mr. Whang stated that the Korean negotiators would reply to this statement at the next meeting. He noted that agreement had previously been reached on paragraphs 6,7,8, and 9.

Revision of the Agreement

30. At this point, it was agreed to adjourn the meeting. Before adjourning, the two sides exchanged drafts of the article providing for Revision of the Agreement.

31. The next meeting was scheduled for November 14 at 2:00 p.m.

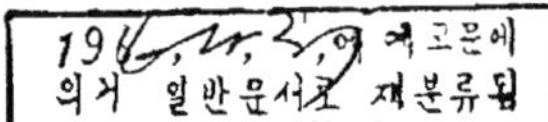

0112

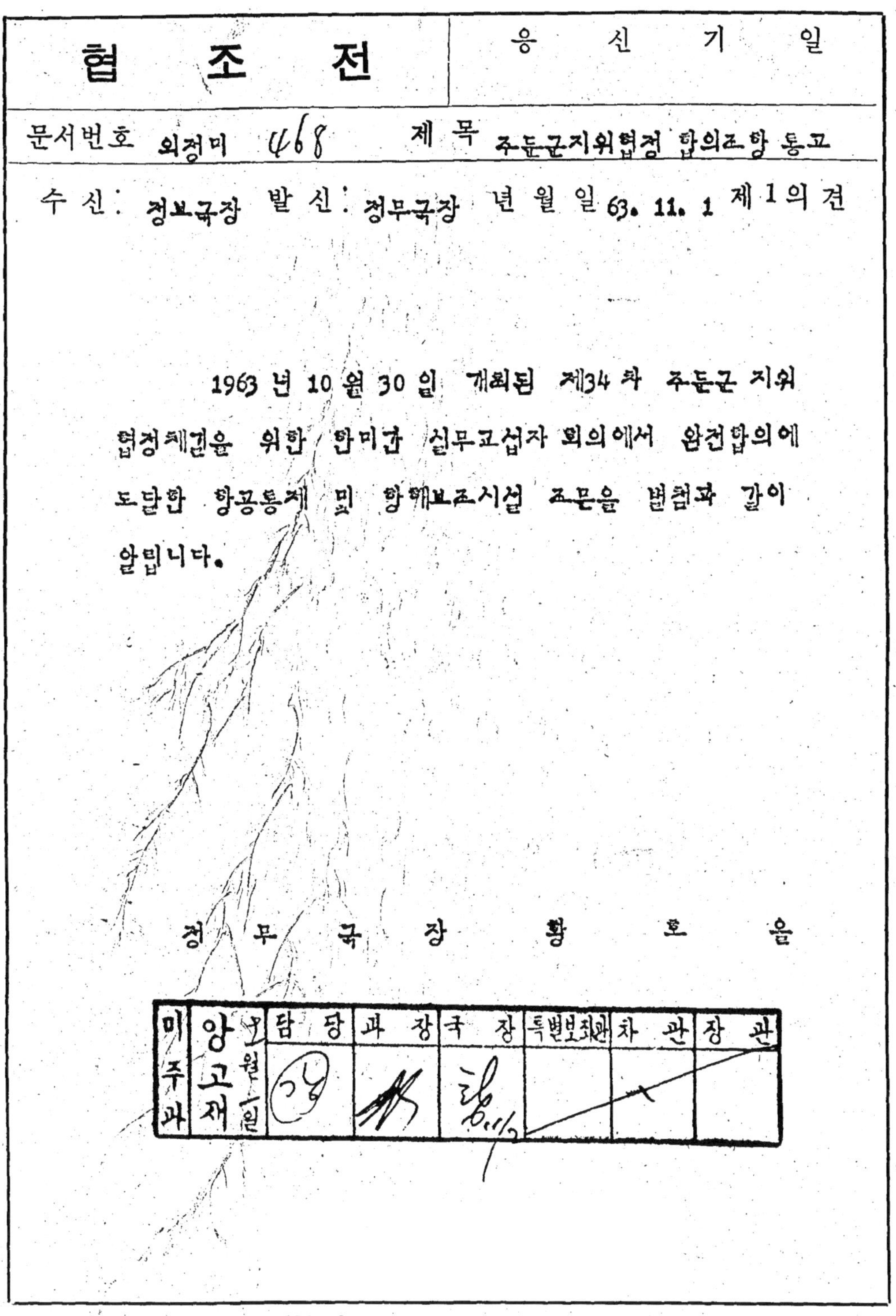

# 협 조 전

응 신 기 일

문서번호 외정미 468 제 목 주둔군지위협정 합의조항 통고

수 신: 정보국장 발 신: 정무국장 년 월 일 63. 11. 1 제 1 의 견

1963 년 10 월 30 일 개최된 제34 차 주둔군 지위 협정체결을 위한 한미간 실무교섭자 회의에서 완전합의에 도달한 항공통제 및 항해보조시설 조문을 별첨과 같이 알립니다.

정 무 국 장 황 호 을

| 미주과 | 안고재 | 담 당 | 과 장 | 국 장 | 특별보좌관 | 차 관 | 장 관 |
|---|---|---|---|---|---|---|---|
| | 월 일 | | | | | | |

승인서식 1—34 (11—13330—01) (195mm×265mm16절지)

0113

Article

1. All civil and military air traffic control shall be developed in close coordination and shall be integrated to the extent necessary for the operation of this Agreement. Procedures, and any subsequent changes thereto, necessary to effect this coordination and integration will be established by arrangement between the appropriate authorities of the two Governments.

2. The United States is authorized to establish, construct and maintain aids to navigation for vessels and aircraft, both visual and electronic as required, throughout the Republic of Korea and in the territorial waters thereof. Such navigation aids shall conform generally to the system in use in Korea. The United States and Korean authorities which have established navigation aids shall duly notify each other of their positions and characteristics and shall give advance notification where practicable before making any changes in them or establishing additional navigation aids.

Agreed Minute

Installation by the United States Armed Forces of permanent navigational aids for vessels and aircraft outside of areas and facilities in use by the United States Armed Forces will be effected in accordance with the procedures established under paragraph 1 of Article ____.

0114

(2)

# 미주둔군 지위 협정 체결 교섭 계획

(박승치 […])

1. 현 황 :

한미 양국은 1962년 9월 6일 주둔군지위협정체결을 위한 교섭재개에 합의하고 제1차 한미간 실무자 교섭회의를 1962년 9월 20일 개최하였으며 1963년 10월 30일 현재 34차에 걸친 교섭회의를 거듭하였고 상당한 진전을 보았다.

2. 진전상황 :

실무자 교섭회의는 먼저 협정에 포함될 중요조항으로 29개(1개항목추가) 항목을 채택하고 한미양국의 현존하는 우호 및 유대관계를 더욱 증진시키며 아울러 양국에 만족스러운 협정을 체결코저 진지한 교섭을 전개하여 왔는바 교섭진전현황은 다음과 같다.

가. 완전 합의에 도달한 조항 (12개)

협정 서문

용어의 정의

항공통제 및 항해보조시설

합동위원회

출입국 관리

선박 및 항공기의 기착

예비병의 소집 및 훈련

기상업무

차량 및 운전면허

접수국 법규존중

조세

위생 및 보건조치

나. 토의중에 있는 조항 (12개)

토지시설

관세업무



0115

공익물 및 용역

근로

군사우편

미군인 가족 및 재산의 안전

외환관리

비세출자금 기관

청구권

현지조달

군계약자

협정의 개정사항

다. 미토의 조항 (5 개)

형사재판관할권

계약상의 분쟁

노무

협정의 비준, 발효 및 시행사항

협정의 유효기간 및 만료사항

3. 교섭상의 애로 :

가. 전기한 29 개 조항중 완전합의에 도달한 12개 조항을 제외하면 앞으로 교섭대상 조항으로 17개 조항이 남아 있는바 그중 토지시설, 청구권 및 형사재판관할권 조항은 양국 입장의 근본적인 대립으로 난제로 예상되며 실무자 교섭회의에서 양국 입장의 접근을 계속 시도할 것이나, 교섭귀추에 따라서는 최종단계에 가서 실무교섭회의와는 별도의 타개책을 강구하도록 조치할수 있는 것으로 고려됨.

나. 전기한 3개조항의 난제외의 기타 미합의 조항은 대체로 순조로히 합의에 도달할수 있으나 다만 한미간에 체결되고 있는 잉여 재산처분협정(1958.10.1 공포), 공익물에 관한 청구권 청산협정(1958.12.18 공포) 및 경제기술원조 협정(1961.2.8 공포)등 기존협정에서 이미 합의된 표현 및 내용과 본협정체결을 위한 우리측 주장과의 사이에 존재하는 지엽적인 기술적 사항의 차이로 인하여 교섭상 난점이 있으며 동 차이점의 조종을 위하여

0116

상당한 시간이 소요될 것으로 예상됨.

다. 한미간 주둔군지위협정 체결을 위한 실무자 교섭은 1962 년 9월 20일 개시된 이래 약 1년 1개월의 기간이 경과하였는바 원래 정부간 교섭이란 상대방 국가의 동의를 요건으로 비로서 성공적인 교섭을 기대할수 있으며 또한 한미간 공동성명서에서 지적한바와 같이 어떠한 주둔군지위협정도 복잡한 문제를 내포하고 있는고로 교섭은 상당한 시일을 요하며, 미국측 안을 일방적으로 수리한다면 별문제 없겠으나, 우리의 제반실정을 유리하게 반영하여 실리적인 협정을 체결코저 한다면 실무교섭자로서 협정의 조기 체결에만 급급한 나머지 국가이익에 불리한 결과를 초래케하는 일이 없도록 신중을 기할것이 요청된다. 미국이 나토제국과 체결한 협정도 약 2 년이란 기간이 소용되었으며 중국과의 교섭도 1957년 이래 6 년간 계속하고 있으나 상금 교섭이 완료하지 못하고 있으며, 미.비간의 기지협정개정도 아직 답보 상태에 있는 점을 고려할때 한미간 실무교섭회의는 짧은 기간에 상당한 성과를 거두었다고 할수 있으므로 교섭상 시간적 제약에 구애됨이 없이 가급적 조속히 전기한 난제와 아울러 제반 애로점을 원만히 해결하고 보다 유리한 협정을 체결하도록 할것이 요망된다.

4. 교섭계획 :

우리측 실무교섭자는 전기한 애로점을 충분히 고려하여 계속 성실과 열의로서 교섭에 임하여 가능한 한 조속한 협정체결이 요망되는 현실적인 요청에 부응할수 있도록 다음과 같은 교섭계획에 의하여 적극 추진하고저 한다.

가. 미로의 5개조항에 대한 양측 초안을 연내로 교환토록 추진한다.

나. 합의에 이루지 못한 17개 조항은 1964년 3월말까지에는 합의에 도달하도록 교섭을 적극 추진한다.

다. 1964년 3월말까지 현재 난제로 예상되는 토지시설, 청구권 및 형사재판관할권문제에 관하여 실무자 교섭회의에서 합의에 도달치 못할 경우에는 양국 정부의 고위층에 의한 타개책을 모색하도록 하여 조속한 시일에 협정체결을 이룩할수 있도록 교섭을 완결한다.





0117

## 미 주둔군 지위협정 체결 교섭개황

1. 정부는 5.16혁명후 주한미국군대 지위에 관한 협정체결을 위하여 미국측에 강력한 교섭을 꾸준히 전개한 결과 드디어 1962년 9월 6일 한미양국은 실무자교섭회의를 재개하는데 합의하였다. 한미간 실무자교섭회의는 1962년 9월 20일 제1차 회의를 개최한후 1963년 10월 30일 현재 34차에 걸친 회의를 거듭하였다.

2. 어떠한 주둔군 지위협정도 1962년 9월 6일 한미 공동성명서에서 지적한바와 같이 광범위하고도 복잡한 문제들을 내포하는 까닭으로 교섭은 상당한 시간이 요한다고 보는바 한미간 실무자회의는 양국간에 현존하는 우호관계와 유대를 더욱 공고히하고 상호 만족스러운 협정을 체결하기 위하여 열의와 성의로서 회의에 임하고 있으며 현재 교섭은 상당한 진전을 보고있다.

3. 실무자교섭회의에서는 먼저 협정에 포함될 중요조항을 채택하고 진지한 교섭을 계속하고 왔는바 1963년 10월 30일 현재 그중 약 반수에 달하는 조항에 대해서는 양측의 완전합의에 도달하였으며 남어지 조항도 에 있어서도 상당한 합의의 진전을 보았으므로 양측입장을 접근시키며 지엽적인 기술적 사항을 조정하면 머지 않아 합의에 도달할수 있을 것으로 전망된다.

4. 한미간 실무자교섭회의가 개최된후 약 1년 1개월의 기간이 경과하였지만 미국이 나토제국과 체결한 협정도 약 2년이란 기간이 소요되었고 중국과의 교섭도 1957년 이래 6년간이나 계속하고 있으나 상금 교섭이 완료하지 못하고 있으며 미.비간의 기지협정 개정도 아직 답보상태에 있다는점을 고려할때 한미간 실무교섭회의는 짧은 기간에 상당한 성과를 거두었다고 할수 있다. 우리실무자로서는 우리의 제반실정을 유리하게 반영시며 실리적인 협정을 체결하고저 교섭에 심중을 기하고 있으며 협정의 조기체결에만 급급한 남어지 국가 이익에 불리한 결과를 초래하는 일이 없도록 만전을 기하고 있는 반면 또한 가능한 조속히 협정이 체결되기를 희구하는 현실적인 요청에 부응하여 교섭의 성공적인 완결에 온갖 노력을 경주하고 있다.

0118

4. 제35차 회의, 11.14

0119

# 기 안 용 지

| 자체 통제 | | 기안처 | 미주과 강석재 | 전화번호 | 근거서류접수일자 |
|---|---|---|---|---|---|
| | 과장 | 국장 | 차관 | 자관 | |
| 관계관 서명 | | | | | |
| 기안 년월일 | 1963. 11. 13 | 시행 년월일 | | 보존 년한 | 정서기장 |
| 분류 기호 | | 전체 통제 | 종결 | | |
| 경유 수신 참조 | 건 의 | | 발신 | | |
| 제목 | 제 35차 주둔군지위협정체결교섭회의에 임할 우리측 입장 | | | | |

11월 14일에 개최될 제 35차 주둔군지위협정 체결 한미간 교섭회의에서는 관세업무, 군사우편, 공익물및 용역과 협정의 개정에 관한 조항을 토의하도록 예정되고 있는바 이에 관하여 우리측 교섭 실무자는 11월 12일 회합을 갖고 제 35차 회의에서 취할 우리측 태도를 별첨과 같이 결정하였아오니 재가하여 주시기 바랍니다.

유첨: 제35차 주둔군지위협정체결교섭회의에 임할 우리측 태도, 끝

보통문서로 재분류 (1966, 12, 31)

1966. 12. 31 에 예고문에 의거 일반문서로 재분류됨

승인서식 1-1-3 (11-00000-03) (195mm×265mm16절지)

0120

1. 관세업무

가. 우편물 검사면제에 관한 미국측 초안 5(b)항에 대하여 지난 34 차 회의에서 우리측은 군사 우편계통을 통하여 들어오는 우편물중 공용 및 사용 서한에 대해서는 검사를 면제할 것이나 소포에 대해서는 세관당국이 검사할 권한이 허용되어야 한다고 우리의 입장을 명백히 하였던바, 미국측은 이 문제를 재고하여 우리의 요구를 충족시킬수 있는 방안을 모색하겠다고 약속하였는바 이에 대한 견해를 묻기로 한다.

나. 만약 미국측이 전기한 5(b)항에 관한 우리측이 요구한대로 소포에 대한 검사권한을 인정하여 줄 경우에는 (ㄱ) 미국측 초안 2항의 비세출자금 기관에 관한 용어를 미국측이 제의한대로 " activities "로 할것에 동의하며 또한 (ㄴ) 미국측 초안 3(b)항의 차량 및 부속품의 무세수입에 관하여 시간적 제한을 가하지 않고 미국측 초안을 수락하기로 한다.

다. 세관검사 면제대상 규정에 관한 미측 초안 5(a)항은 미군대 구성원( members )에 대한 세관 검사를 면제하도록 규정하고 있는데 대하여 우리측안은 부대( units )로 입국할 경우에만 검사를 면제하도록 규정하고 있다. 우리측은 (ㄱ) 미일 협정에도 units 로 규정되어 있음을 지적하고,

(ㄴ) 비록 그렇게 규정하드래도 구성원에 대하여 꼭 검사를 실시할 의도는 없으며 종전회의시 미측에서 설명한바와 같이 현재 일본 정부에서는 구성원에 대하여 실제로 검사를 면제해 주고 있다는 점을 고려하여 우리측도 대부분의 경우 그와 같이 검사를 면제할 용의가 있으며,

(ㄷ) 검사를 할수 있는 권한을 보유하되 실제로 검사를 면제해 주는 것과 전혀 검사할 권한이 없다는 것과는 근본적인 차이가 있으며,

(ㄹ) 특히 이러한 문제에 관하여 우리국민들이 보여 주고 있는 지대한 관심을 고려할때 협정상에서 반드시 units 로 입국할 경우에만 세관검사를 면제하도록 규정하여야겠다는 것이 우리측 입장이라고 주장한다.

라. 미국측 초안 5(c)항 및 이에 관련된 합의 의사록(3)은 "군사화물"에 대한 세관검사 면제와 또한 "군사화물"에는 공인된 조달기관 및 비세출자금기관에 탁송되는 모든 물품까지도 포함하는 것으로 규정하고

0121

있는바 우리측은 (ㄱ) 관세조문 2항에서 이러한 물품들에 대한 무세통관을 허용하고 있으며 (ㄴ) 또한 비세출자금기관에 탁송되는 담배. 술. 화장품 등과 같은 물품은 성질상 군사 화물로 간주할수 없으며 (ㄷ) 어떠한 종류의 물품이 얼마만큼 들어오며 부당할 경우에는 이 문제를 미측에 제기할수 있는 길을 갖게 위해서도 검사만용할 권한이 부여되어야 한다고 주장한다.

마. 도착일부터 6개월내에는 개인용품 및 가사도구를 무세로 수입할수 있다고 규정하는 미측이 제출한 합의 의사록(2)에 관하여 우리측은 동 합의 의사록이 관계하고 있는 관세 업무조항의 3(a)항에 있어서"적절한 량" ( reasonable quantities )으로 제한되어 있음을 밝히고 그러한 양해에서 합의 의사록에 " reasonable quantities of "라는 구절을 삽입토록 하자는 종래의 제의를 철회한다고 하고 미국측 안대로 수락하기로 한다.

2. 군사우편시설

가. 미국측 초안 (2)항은 통상해외에서 그러한 특권이 부여된 미국정부 관리 및 그 가족들도 군사우편 시설을 사용할수 있도록 규정하고 있는바, 양측 대표는 제19차 회의에서 이 규정은 예외적인 것으로 합의 의사록에 넣도록 하는데 합의하였으며 그 내용에 대해서는 밀접한 관련이 있는 관세업무 조항 중 세관검사 면제규정의 5(b )항에 대한 합의를본후최종적 결정을 하도록 합의하였는바 우리측은 " and their dependents "를 삭제할 것을 요구하며 만약 미국측이 전기 관세조항 5(b )에 있어서 우리측 요구대로 사용 우편물에 대한 세관검사를 수락할 경우에는 미국측 안대로 합의하기로 한다.

3. 공익물 및 용역

가. 공익물에 관한 미국측 초안 3(a )에 있어서 우리측은

(ㄱ) 공익물 및 용역의 정의에 관한 둘째문장에 있는 "however produced "라는 구절을 "Utilities Claims Settlement Agreement 의 개정 가능성을 배제하는 것이 아니며 만약 개정될시에는 그 개정에 따라 이 용어도 수정될수 있다는 점을 유보하고 수락하며 ,

(ㄴ) 또한 미국측이 제의한대로 " whether publicly or

0122

privately owned "라는 구절을 삭제하고 " which are "라는 구절 다음에 " owned "라는 말을 삽입하며,

(ㄷ) " political subdivisions "대신에 " local administrative subdivisions "라는 구절로 대치하도록 하며,

(ㄹ) 미국측이 수정제안한 3(a)항의 셋째 및 넷째 문장을 수락하도록 한다. 따라서 미국측 조안 3(a)의 첫째 문장은 다음과 같다.

The United States armed forces shall have the use of all utilities and services which are owned, controlled or regulated by the Government of the Republic of Korea or local administrative subdivisions thereof.

나. 미국측 조안 3(b)항 둘째 문장은 비상시 작전상의 필요가 있을 시 대한민국은 공익물 및 용역의 제공을 보장하기 위한 조치를 취할것을 규정하는바 우리측은 그러한 비상작전상의 요구가 일방적인 통고로 인정될것이 아니라 우리정부가 적절하다 인정할만한 것이라야 한다는 점을 회의 기록에 명백히 남기고 동 규정을 합의 의사록에 넣도록 주장한다.

다. 미국측 조안 4항에 대하여는 이에 해당하는 우리측 조안 2(a)항과 관련하여 약간의 오해가 있었다고 보며 그 오해는 (ㄱ) 미국측 조안 4 항은 단지 본 협정에서 일어나는 금전거래에 적용될 청산조치만을 규정하고 있는 반면 우리측 조안은 철도운송, 전기 및 수도 등 공익물 및 용역은 현재 8군이 교통부 육운국, 한국전력회사 및 서울시 수도국과 각각 계약을 체결하고 요금을 청산하고 있는 거와 같이 앞으로도 8군과 한국정부 및 정부기관간의 특별한 조치에 따라 할 것을 규정하고 있다. (ㄴ) 미국측 조안에 의하면 새로운 청산조치를 위하여 양국 정부가 별도 교섭을 필요로 하는 인상이 있으며 (ㄷ) 또한 미국측 조안을 전기 한바와 같은 철도 운송, 전기 및 수도등에 관한 현행 양국간의 조치에 대한 언급이 없는바 이러한 점에 관한 미국측의 의견을 묻기로 한다. 만약 미국측이 공익물사용에 관한 전기한 조치가 계속 유효하다는데 동의한다면 미국측 조안 4항을 수락하되 현존 조치에 대해서는 미국측 합의 의사록(2)에 포함시키거나 혹은 우리측 조안 2(b)항을

0123

수락토록 하여야 할것이라고 주장한다.

라. 합의 의사록 (1)항에 있어서 우리측이 24차 회의에서 "...shall be the subject of prior consultation in the joint Committee" 대신에 "... shall, at the Joint Committee, be notified within 15 days after the effective date of such a change " 라는 구절과 대치하자고 제의한데 대하여 미국측의 의견을 묻기로 한다.

마. 합의 의사록 (2)항은 1958.12.18 자 한미양국이 체결한 공익물에 관한 청구권 청산협정의 효력을 존속시키도록 한 규정이며 우리측 조안2(b ) 와 관련된 것인바 우리측은 공익물에 관한 청구권 청산협정외에 기타 현존하는 제반 조치도 계속 유효하도록 규정하고 있으므로 실질적인 차이가 없으며 우리측 안이 오히려 더욱 포괄적임으로 우리측 안을 수락해 줄 것을 요구한다.

4. 조약의 개정

협정 개정을 위한 교섭에 있어서 우리측 조안은 외교계통을 통할 것을 규정하고 있으나 미국측은 " 적절한 계통"( appropriate channels ) 을 통하도록 규정하고 있다. 우리측은 기타 용어의 차이에 대한 것은 미국측의 용어대로 수락할수 있으나 협정의 개정을 위한 교섭은 역시 협정을 체결한 양 정부의 당국과 비등한 권한을 가진 당국간에 협의되는 것이 합리적이며 적절하다고 인정함으로 우리측 조안의 용어대로 diplomatic channels 로 할 것에 수락하기를 요구한다.

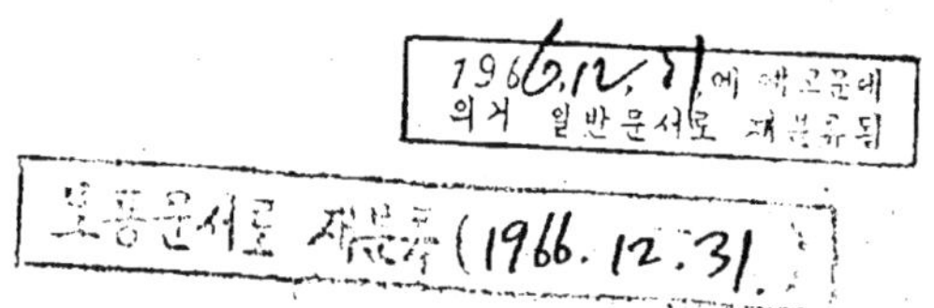


0124

# 기 안 용 지

| 자체 통제 | 외무사무관 강상왕 | 기안처 | 미주과 강석재 | 전화번호 | 근거서류접수일자 |
|---|---|---|---|---|---|
| | 과장 | 국장 | 차관 | 장관 | |
| | | 18 | 전결 | 18 | |
| 관계관 서명 | | | | | |
| 기안 년월일 | 1963. 11.16 | 시행 년월일 | | 보존 년한 | 정서기장 |
| 분류 기호 | 외정미722.2 | 전체 통제 | 검열 1963.11.17 통제관 | | |
| 경유 수신 참조 | 국가재건 최고회의 의장 (참조: 외무국방 위원장) 내각 수반 | | | 발신 | 장관 |
| 제목 | 주둔군지위협정 체결을 위한 제 35차 교섭회의 보고 | | | | |

1963 년 11 월 14 일 하오 2 시부터 4 시 30분까지 외무부 장관회의실에서 개최된 제 35 차 주둔군지위협정 체결교섭회의에서 토의된 내용을 별첨과 같이 보고합니다.

유첨: 제 35 차 교섭회의보고서 2/1 부. 끝.

1966.12.31에 예고문에 의거 일반문서로 재분류됨

승인서식 1-1-3 (11-00300-03) (195mm×265mm16절지)

0125

외 무 부

외정미 722.2 1963. 11. 19.

수 신 : 국가재건 최고회의 의장

참 조 : 외무국방위원장

제 목 : 주둔군지위협정 체결을 위한 제35차 교섭회의 보고

1963 년 11 월 14 일 하오 2시부터 4시30분까지 외무부 장관회의실에서 개최된 제35 차 주둔군지위협정 체결교섭회의에서 토의된 내용을 별첨과 같이 보고합니다.

유첨: 제35차 교섭회의 보고서 2 부, 끝.

외 무 부 장 관 김 용 식

0126

제 35 차

한미간 주둔군지위협정 체결실무자 회의

보 고 서

1. 일 시 : 1963 년 11 월 14 일 하오 2 시부터 4 시 30분까지

2. 장 소 : 외무부 장관 회의실

3. 참석자 : 한국측 : 황 호 을 ( 외무부 정무국장)

신 관 섭 ( 재무부 세관국장)

구 충 회 ( 외무부 미주과장)

박 도 준 중령(국방부 군무과)

주 문 기 ( 법무부 법무과장)

강 석 재 ( 외무부2등서기관)

이 정 빈 ( 외무부3등서기관)

미국측: 수석대표 "하비브" 참사관 및 "사토리오스" 2등서기관을 제외한 교섭대표 전원(수석대표로 "오코나"준장이 참석함)

4. 토의사항 :

가. 세관업무

(1) 우리측은 먼저 우편물 검사 면제에 관한 미국측 초안 5(b)항에 대한 토의를 제의하고 군사우편계통을 통하여 들어오는 우편물중 공용 및 사용서한에 대한 검사는 면제할 것이나 소포에 대해서는 우리 세관 당국이 검사할 권리를 가져야 한다고 주장하고 이에 관한 미국측의 견해를 요구하였던바, 미국측은 출입국 항구에 들어오는 모든 우편물은 봉인된 부대로 들어와서 직접 개봉하지 않고 한국에 분산되어 있는 17개 주요 군사우편국에서 비로서 개봉된다. 여기서 우편물은 적은 보자기에 싸여 32개의 우편물 "디스트리뷰숀.센타"로 송달되며 여기서 다시 부대로 배달되면 우편장교가 검열한다. 이러한 제도하에 미군의 군사우편당국은 항상 군사우편시설사용의 특권을 남용하는 자가 있으면 적발하여 처벌하고 있으며 1963년에 들어와서 약 60명의 사람이 그 특권을

63-1-166

0127

63-1-28 (6) 미주·문 108-3 (6)

0128

박탈당한바 있다. 우편물을 공항이나 항구에서 검열한다면 지연과 혼란을 야기케 할 우려가 있으며 행정적인 애로가 많으며 미군 군사우편 당국에서도 권리 남용을 방지하도록 감시와 관리를 항상하고 있음으로 미국측이 제34차 회의에서 제안한 대로 즉 "mail in the United States military postal channels under official postal seal "로 수락하여 주기를 바란다고 말하였다.

(2) 우리측은 계속 이 문제에 관하여 미국측의 제도로 보아 직접 출입국 항구나 공항에서 소포에 대한 검열을 하기 곤란하다면 17개소의 주요 군사우편국이나 혹은 32개소의 "디스트리뷰숀.센타"에서 검사하게 하여 세관업무의 질서 확립과 남용자에 대한 경고와 효과적인 예방조치를 기할수 있도록 소포에 대한 검사 권한을 가져야 한다고 주장하고 만약 미국측이 이 문제에 대한 우리측 입장을 수락한다면 기타 연관된 문제에 대하여 양보할 용이도 있음으로 우리측 입장을 수락하여 미합의문제를 조속 해결토록 하자고 거듭 촉구하였는바, 미국측은 재고하여 보겠다고 답변하였다.

(3) 군사화물에 관한 미국측 초안 5(c)와 이에 관련된 합의의사록 (3)에 관하여 우리측은 관세조문 (2)항에서 이미 이러한 물품에 대한 무세통관을 허용하고 있으며 또한 비세출자금기관에 탁송되는 담배,술 및 화장품과 같은 물품은 성질상 군사화물로 간주할수 없는 만큼 만약 이러한 물품이 부당하게 많이 반입될 경우 그러한 물품이 암시장에서 거래될 우려성도 있는바, 미측에 그 부당성을 제기하여 시정을 요구해야 할 문제임으로 어떠한 물품이 얼마만큼 반입되고 있는지를 파악하기 위해서 검사만은 실시할 권한이 허용되어야 한다고 주장하였다. 미국측은 "피.엑스"에서 물품을 판매하는것은 "레이숀.카드"제에 의하여 매인당 구매할수 있는 량이 한정되어 있으며 또한 적절한 감시와 감독을 실시하고 남용방지에 효과적인 방지책을 다하고 있다. 비록 검사를 하드래도 얼만큼이 적절한 량인지를 판단키 어려우며 더욱 비세출자금기관이란 세출자금기관인 미국군대와 명칭이 좀 다르다 뿐이지 미국 군대 조직의 일부에 지나지 않으며 비세출자금기관이 반입한 물품도 일반군사화물과 똑같이 중요한 만큼 이를 구별하여 검사케 할수없다고 답변하였다.

63-1-167

0129

03-1-28

미·분108-3

0130

(4) 우리측은 계속 미국측이 우편물 검사에 관한 미국측 초안5(b) 항과 군사화물에 관한 5(c)항에 있어서 우리측 입장에 양보하여 준다면 우리측도 관세조문 (2)항에 있어서 비세출자금기관에 관한 용어를 " activities " 로 하며 또한 3(b)항의 차량 및 부속품의 무세통관문제도 시간적 제한을 하지 않고 미국측 안을 수락할 용이가 있으므로 재고하여 주도록 요청하였음.

(5) 세관검사 면제규정의 하나인 미국측 초안 5(a)항에 대하여 우리측은 부대( units )에 대한 검사 면제를 규정한다 하드래도 반드시 구성원 ( members )에 대한 검사를 실시할 의도는 없으며 실제로 대부분의 경우 구성원에 대한 검사를 면제할 용이가 있음으로 우리측 제안을 수락하여 주도록 주장하였다. 미국측은 한국에 출입하는 미군들은 부대로 행동하지 않고 개인적으로 이동하고 있는 점을 고려하여 구성원에 대한 검사 면제를 고려하여 달라고 답변하여 왔음. 우리측은 이 문제에 관련하여 검사를 할수있는 권한을 보유하되, 실제로 검사를 면제해 주는 것과 전혀 검사할 권한이 없는것과는 근본적인 차이가 있음으로 협정문에서는 부대에 대한 검사면제만을 규정하도록 미국측의 재고를 부탁하였다.

나. 군사우편시설

미국측 초안 (2)항은 통상해외에서 그러한 특권이 부여된 미국정부관리 및 그 가족들도 군사우편을 사용할수 있도록 규정하고 있는바, 양측 대표는 제 19차 회의에서 이 규정은 예외적인 것임으로 합의 의사록에 넣도록 합의된바 있다. 우리측은 이규정의 내용에 있어서 " and their dependents "를 삭제하기를 요구하고 동시에 대안으로서 만약 미국측이 관세조문중 우편물검사에 관한 5(b)항에 대하여 우리측 요구를 수락해 준다면 미국측 안대로 받아들일 용의가 있다는 입장을 밝혔던바, 미국측은 우편물 검사에 관한 5(b)항이 합의되지 않었으므로 더 이상 언급할 것이 없다고 답변하였다.

다. 공익물 및 용역

63-1-168

(1) 공익물 및 용역에 관한 미국측 초안 3(a)항의 둘재 문장에 있어서 우리측은 " however produced "라는 구절을 동 구절이 사용된 공익물에 관한 청구권 청산 협정의 개정 가능성을 배제하는 것이 아니며

0131

63-1-28 미.문 108-3

0132

만약 동 협정이 개정될 경우에는 동 구절도 이에 따라 수정될수 있다는 유보하에 받아들이 겠다고 하였는바 미국측은 우리측의 유보조건을 검토한후 답변하겠다고 함.

(2) 우리측은 공익물 및 용역에 관한 미국측 초안 3(a )항의 첫째 문장에 있어서 미국측이 제의한 대로 " whether publicly or privately owned "라는 구절을 삭제하고 대신 " which are "구절 다음에 "owned " 라는 단어를 삽입하며 " local administrative subdivisions " 로서 " political subdivisions "라는 구절에 대치할 것에 동의하였으며 아울러 미국측이 새로 수정 제안한 3(a )항의 셋째 및 넷째 문장을 수락하였다.

(3) 비상시 작전상의 필요가 있을때 공익물 및 용역의 제공 보장을 규정하는 미국측 초안 3(b )항의 둘째 문장에 관하여 우리측은 그러한 비상시 작전상의 필요가 일방적인 통고로 인정될 것이 아니라 우리정부로서 그 필요성이 적절하다고 인정할만하다고 인정할때에 공익물 및 용역의 제공을 보장할 조치를 한다는 점을 명백히 기록상에 남기고 동 규정을 합의 의사록에 넣도록 한다면 수락할 의사가 있다고 표명하였던바 미국측은 우리의 양해 사항을 고려하겠다고 답변함.

(4) 미국측 초안 (4)항과 이에 해당하는 우리측 초안 2(a )항에 관하여 우리측은 양측안 간에 약간의 오해가 있는듯 하다고 전제하고 (ㄱ) 미국측 안은 단지 금전거래에 적용될 청산조치만을 규정하고 있는 반면 우리측 초안은 철도운송, 전기 및 수도등의 이용에 관하여 현재 8군이 교통부, 한국전력회사 및 서울시와 각각 계약을 체결하고 있는바와 같이 앞으로도 8군과 한국정부간에 체결될 그와 같은 조치에 따를것을 규정하고 있으며 (ㄴ) 미국측 초안에 의하면 청산조치를 위하여 양국 정부가 별도 새로운 교섭을 필요로 하는 인상을 주며 (ㄷ) 또한 미국측은 전기한 현행조치에 대한 언급이 없는바 앞으로 그와 같은 계약에 의한 현행조치는 어떻게 될것인지 질문하고 만약 미국측이 그와 같은 현행조치가 계속 유효할 것이라는 점에 동의한다면 미국측 합의 의사록 (2)나 우리측 초안2(b ) 항에 포함시켜 규정하도록 하자고 주장하였던바 미국측은 공익물 및 용역 사용에 관한 현행 사정을 설명하여 준데 대하여 감사하고 미국측으로서는 그러한 현행조치가

63-1-16P

0133

63-1-28

미·문 108-3

0134

계속 유효할 것이기 때문에 언급하지 않았으나 우리측 2( a)항에는 용어상 만족하지 않는것이 있기 때문에 합당한 용어를 고려하도록 해 보겠다는 답변을 하였음.

(5) 합의 의사록 (1)에 관하여 제24차 회의에서 우리측은 공익물 및 용역제공의 우선 순위 및 요금의 변경이 있을 경우에는 사전 협의를 하지 않고 그러한 변경이 있은 후 15일간내에 통고하기로 하자고 제의한데 대하여 미국측의 견해를 문의하였던바 미국측은 이 문제가 중요하여 또한 일반 사용자와 다른 만큼 사전 협의를 해야한다고 주장하고 그러나 사전협의가 반드시 미국측의 동의를 필요로 하는 것은 아니라고 답변하였다. 우리측은 계속 미국측은 우선 순위나 요금에 있어서 우리정부기관이 받는 대우 보다 불리한 대우를 받지 않을 것이며 또한 그러한 문제에 변경이 있을시는 양국에 다 같이 중요한 문제이며 특히 한국 경제에 지대한 영향을 미치게 될 것임으로 한국정부로서 신중을 기할 것이며 양국간에 사전 협의가 있을 것으로 양해한다. 그러나 협정상 사전협의를 규정한다면 의무적이 되므로 사후 통고로 할 것을 제의하오니 재고하여 줄것을 요청하였던바 미국측은 이 문제를 더 연구한후 다음기회에 토의하도록 하자고 제의하였다.

(6) 미국측 합 의 의사록 (2)항은1958.12.18 자 한미 양국이 체결한 공익물에 관한 청구권 청산협정의 효력을 존속시킬것을 규정하고 있는바 우리측은 동 협정뿐만 아니라 공익물 사용에 관한 제반 현존 조치도 함께 포함시켜야 할 것이므로 우리측 초안 2( b)가 더욱 포괄적이므로 우리측 안을 수락하여 주기를 재차 요구하였던바 미국측은 이 문제를 재고하여 다음 회의에서 계속 토의할 것을 제의하였다.

다. 협정의 개정

63-1-170

협정 개정에 관한 조문에 있어서 우리측은 "article " 및 " negotiations "란 용어는 미국측 안대로 수락할수 있으나 개정을 위한 교섭은 역시 협정을 체결한 양 정부의 당국과 비등한 권한을 가진 당국간에 협의되는 것이 합리적이며 적절하다고 인정함으로 " diplomatic "계통으로 할 것을 수락하도록 요구하였다. 미국측은 " appropriate "라는 용어는 매우 광범위하며 외교계통도 포함할수 있다고 주장하고 또한 합동위원회나

0135

63-1-28

미.울 108-3

0136

혹은 전쟁 발발시에는현지 군사령관과 한국정부간의 교섭도 고려할수 있는 것이므로 "적절한 계통"이란 용어를 채택할 것을 바라며 또한 교섭은 누가하던지 양국정부에 의하여 최종적으로 승인되어야 하지 않겠는가고 반문하였다. 우리측은 우리의 입장을 되풀이 하고 "외교계통"으로 할 것을 계속 주장하였으나 양측은 이 문제를 좀더 고려하여 다시 토의하기로 합의 보았다.

5. 중요합의사항:

없 음.

6. 기타 사항 :

차기회의 일자 : 1963 년 12 월 3 일 하오 2 시

차기회의 의제 : 차기회의까지 양측 수석 대표간에 합의된 사항.

63-1-28 (10)

미정·문 108-3 (6)

0138

Customs

1. Mr. Hwang opened the meeting by suggesting resumption of discussion of paragraph 5 of the Customs Article but asked if the U.S. side cared to make any comments on paragraphs 1, 2, 3, or 4. Gen. O'Connor replied that the U.S. side had no further comment to make ~~at that time~~ regarding those paragraphs. However, it might be useful to review the remaining points of difference. Full agreement had already been reached on paragraphs 1 and 4. Regarding paragraph 2 there were still two points at issue. First, it had still not been decided ~~whereas~~ whether to use the word "organizations" or the word "activities" in this paragraph and in paragraph 5 (c) and Agreed Minutes 1 and 3. Secondly, the Korean side had suggested the deletion of (references to) the U.S. armed forces' ~~authorized procurement agencies and their~~ non-appropriated fund activities from this paragraph, while the U.S. side had proposed placing the references to these agencies and activities in parentheses in order to emphasize the fact that they form an integral part of the U.S. armed forces. Although agreement had been reached on subparagraphs (a) and (c) of paragraph 3, ~~there~~ the substance of subparagraph (b) was still in dispute.

2. With regard to paragraph 5(b), Mr. Hwang noted that the Korean side had stated that there was no intention on the part of the Korean authorities to inspect official mail or private letters addressed to members of the U.S. armed forces by members of their families in the United States. However, the Korean side desired to have the paragraph so worded that it would give the Korean authorities the right to ~~of~~ inspect ~~ion~~ parcel mail.

3. General O'Connor replied that at the previous negotiating meeting, the Korean side had stated that unauthorized goods had been imported into the Republic of Korea through military postal channels. The Korean side had emphasized that the Korean authorities did not wish to inspect first class mail or to delay or confuse delivery of parcel mail. However, the Korean side had expressed the view that the

0139

inclusion in the SOFA of a provision authorizing the inspection of parcel mail by ROK customs authorities might prove to be an effective preventive measure to check abuses of the military postal channels. The Korean side had stated that they did not propose to send customs inspectors to every battalion or regimental post office but rather to station customs inspectors at ports and airports to spot-check incoming parcels.

4. In view of these statements by the Korean side, General O'Connor continued, he wished to give a more detailed explanation of how the military postal system operates. U.S. military mail arrives in Korea in large metal containers, eight feet by six feet by seven feet in dimensions, or a total of approximately 330 cubic feet each. These sealed containers are not opened at the port of entry but are sent directly to one of the 17 main military post offices which are located in various parts of the Republic of Korea. These containers are opened at one of these main military post offices and the mail is then distributed in sealed mail sacks to 32 unit distribution ~~points~~ centers. It is at these unit distribution ~~points~~ centers where effective surveillance of parcels received by an individual addressee can be maintained. U.S. military postal authorities at these individual postal units are continuously on the lookout for any abuse or violation of postal or customs regulations. Thus far in 1963, a total of 60 individuals have been denied further use of APO mails in Korea because they were found to have abused their APO privileges. Stern punitive action will be taken against any other personnel who may be discovered abusing their APO privileges.

5. As indicated by the foregoing explanation, General O'Connor continued, it would be very complicated, if not impossible, to maintain surveillance of parcels at ports of entry. Attempts to maintain surveillance at these points would be an administrative nightmare which could only result in extended delays and confusion and probable damage to the goods as the result of inadequate repacking.

0140

U.S. military postal authorities are aggressively implementing a program designed to eliminate any abuses in the APO system as they may arise. This surveillance program focuses on the point of parcel distribution, at the end of the line, where unusual or repeated shipments of parcels to individuals can be easily spotted and the violators punished. This is a practical program that works, whereas the proposed program of spot inspection at ports of entry would be impracticable. Therefore, the U.S. side continued to propose acceptance of the following language for paragraph 5(b): "Official documents under official seal and mail in United States military postal channels under official postal seal".

6. Mr. Hwang thanked General O'Connor for his explanation and stated that the Korean side now understood that the mail was not opened at ports of entry but only at the 17 main military post offices and the 32 unit distribution centers. He said the Korean side would study the matter and explore the possibility of sending Korean customs inspectors to the post offices and unit distribution centers. He said the Korean authorities had no intention of causing unnecessary confusion or delays. However, since there had been in the past quite a few abuses, the Korean side wished to give a warning to prospective violators and make apprehension and punishment possible. To that end, Korean customs inspectors should be given the authority to inspect the parcel mail.

7. General O'Connor stated that the U.S authorities believed the present inspection system to be effective. He said the U.S. military postal authorities take a special look at packages mailed to members of the U.S. armed forces from Hong Kong and Japan. The U.S. side was of the opinion that the proposals set forth by the Korean side would create confusion and delay the delivery of the mail.

8. Mr. Hwang said the Korean authorities were grateful for the actions taken by the U.S. military authorities in preventing abuses. However, the SOFA must provide for an orderly admin[illegible]orean customs regulations. He said the Korean

0141

side was prepared to agree to the U.S. position with regard to certain other points at issue in this article if the U.S. side would accept the Korean position with regard to paragraph 5 (b). General O'Connor replied that the U.S. side would take the Korean position under further consideration.

9. Turning to paragraph 5 (c), Mr. Hwang stated that the Korean side continued to desire the deletion of the reference to non-appropriated fund activities from this subparagraph. He stated that if the U.S. side were willing to agree to so limit the provisions of this subparagraph, the Korean side was prepared to agree to use the word "activities" instead of the word "organizations" throughout the article. Furthermore, if the U.S. side agreed to the Korean position regarding subparagraphs (b) and (c) of paragraph 5, the Korean side would not only agree to use of the word "activities" but would also agree to the U.S. text of paragraph 3(b). General O'Connor replied that the U.S. side could not change its position with regard to paragraph 5 (c) because cargoes assigned to authorized procurement agencies and their non-appropriated fund activities are military cargoes.

10. Reverting to paragraph 5(a), Mr. Hwang urged the U.S. side to accept the ROK text. He said that use of the word "units", as proposed by the Korean side, did not mean that the Korean authorities intended to conduct a customs examination of every individual member of the U.S. armed forces entering or leaving the Republic of Korea. He said the intention was to grant exemptions from such examination in almost every case. However, the ROK authorities wanted the SOFA to grant them the right of inspection, even though they did not intend to inspect in every case in actual practice. He further stated that there is a fundamental difference between the granting of exemptions from inspection while reserving the right to inspect and not reserving any right to inspect at all. General O'Connor replied by reiterating the fact that members of the U.S. armed forces enter and leave the Republic of Korea as individual members of the armed forces and not as members of units. He said the U.S. side would take the Korean position under consideration.

0142

11. Returning to paragraph 5(c), Mr. Hwang pointed out that in this subparagraph and Agreed Minute 3, according to the U.S. draft, "all cargo" includes cargo assigned to non-appropriated fund organizations. In paragraph 2, it has already been spelled out that such imports shall be permitted entry free of customs duty. However, cigarettes, tobacco, and similar items consigned to non-appropriated fund organizations, cannot be construed as military cargo. The Korean authorities wish to have an idea of the types of cargo and the quantities shipped so that they can discuss unusual shipments with the U.S. authorities. Therefore, they wish to exclude cargo consigned to non-appropriated fund organizations from the provisions of this subparagraph.

12. General O'Connor replied that since the Korean side had already agreed that such cargo should be admitted free of customs duty, the U.S. side failed to see the point of conducting customs examination of such cargo. He pointed out the difficulty of differentiating between certain types of rations issued directly by the armed forces and goods sold in the post exchanges. He said the proper time to deal with infractions is when the goods are sold or disposed of illegally in the Republic of Korea. He pointed out that the inclusion of non-appropriated fund cargo as military cargo is not a situation peculiar to Korea but is U.S. military practice.

13. Mr. Hwang stated that while it was true that agreement had been reached on importation of these goods duty-free under the provisions of paragraph 2, importation of such goods in excess of consumption needs could result in their sale on the black market. Therefore, the Korean customs authorities should be in a position to know the quantities of such goods actually imported.

14. General O'Connor replied that control over the sale of goods imported by non-appropriated fund activities is maintained through rationing of purchases at the post exchanges. He displayed a sample ration card and pointed out that the sale of such items as soap, soft drinks, and stockings is strictly rationed. With regard to items which are imported in bulk, he pointed out that adequate supplies must be maintained in the pipe line and that it would be difficult for persons not in supply operations to know what constitutes a "reasonable quantity". He added that the rationing system is under

0143

continuing review. Mr. Hwang stated that this question had been fully discussed and suggested that both sides give further consideration to the other side's position.

Military Post Offices

15. Turning to the article on Military Post Offices, Mr. Hwang recalled that at the 19th negotiating meeting, the both sides had agreed to convert paragraph 2 of the U.S. draft into an Agreed Minute. Final agreement on this article must await agreement on the text of paragraph 5(b) of the Customs Article. Mr. Hwang proposed deletion of the words "and their dependents" from paragraph 2 (or the Agreed Minute) and as an alternative he further proposed that the Korean side would then be prepared to agree to the (retention of the words "and their dependents" in) paragraph 2 if the U.S. side would agree to the Korean position regarding paragraph 5(b) of the Customs Article. General O'Connor indicated that the U.S. side would respond when this article is taken up again, after agreement on paragraph 5(b) of the Customs article.

Utilities and Services

16. Taking up the drafts regarding Utilities and Services, Mr. Hwang recalled that the U.S. side had proposed in the first sentence the deletion of the phrase "whether publicly or privately owned", the insertion of the word "owned" before the word "controlled", and the substitution of the phrase "local administrative subdivisions" for the phrase "political subdivisions". Mr. Hwang stated that the Korean side accepted the U.S. draft of the first sentence with the proposed changes.

17. Recalling that the Korean side had proposed the deletion of the phrase "however produced" from the second sentence of the U.S. draft, Mr. Hwang asked for comment by the U.S. side. Colonel Fuller replied that this phrase was included in the Utilities and Claims Settlement Agreement and had been included in the first Korean draft of this article. The U.S. side was unable to understand why the Korean side now wished to delete the phrase from this article.

18. Mr. Hwang replied that inasmuch as the phrase "however produced" was contained in the Utilities and Claims Settlement Agreement, the Korean side agreed to its

0144

inclusion in this article of the SOFA, with the reservation that subsequent revision of the Utilities and Claims Settlement Agreement was not precluded and that if such revision should result in the elimination of the phrase from the latter agreement, the language of the SOFA would be changed accordingly. Colonel Fuller replied that the U.S. side would have to consider the implications of the proposed reservation by the Korean side before it could agree to the Korean side's conditional acceptance of the second sentence of paragraph 3(a) of the U.S. draft.

19. Mr. Hwang stated that the Korean side accepted the revised third and fourth sentences of the U.S. draft. If the U.S. would agree to the Korean reservation with regard to the second sentence, full agreement could be reached on paragraph 3(a) of the U.S. draft.

20. Passing on to paragraph 3(b) of the U.S. draft, Mr. Hwang noted that the first sentence had been agreed to and that the original second sentence had been deleted. With regard to the original third sentence, now the second sentence of this paragraph, which deals with emergency operating needs of the U.S. armed forces, the needs in question should be those which the ROK Government recognizes to be reasonable and justifiable. Mr. Hwang stated that the Korean side would like to have the record clearly show that the ROK Government must also agree that emergency operating needs exist before it will take measures to assure provision of utilities and services necessary to meet these needs. He said the Korean side would prefer to transfer the substance of this sentence to an Agreed Minute.

21. In response to Colonel Fuller's request for clarification, Mr. Hwang stated that the Korean side understood this provision to mean that when an emergency operating need arises, the U.S. armed forces will notify the ROK Government. However, the Korean side held that the ROK Government, after receiving such notification, must agree that such a need exists before taking action. In other words, the Korean side could not agree to a provision which would provide for unilateral determination by the U.S. armed forces that an emergency operating need existed. The

0145

Korean side also wished to move the entire sentence to an Agreed Minute. Colonel Fuller replied that the U.S. side would take these proposals under consideration.

22. Mr. Hwang stated that some misunderstanding appeared to have arisen regarding paragraph 4 of the U.S. draft and paragraph 2 of the Korean draft. He said that Mr. Ku would explain the views of the Korean side. Mr. Ku stated that the U.S. draft provided only for accounting arrangements, whereas the Korean draft specifically provided that specific arrangements entered into by the U.S. armed forces for the use of and payments for utilities and services would continue in effect. Such arrangements include those contracts already in effect with the Seoul City Water Supply, the Korean Electric Company, and the national railways. The U.S. draft gives the impression that the two governments must enter into arrangements in addition to the SOFA in order to continue such financial transactions in the future. And there is no mention in the U.S. draft of existing arrangements for such transactions. Assuming that the U.S. side agrees that existing arrangements should continue after the SOFA enters into force, it is necessary to say so in the Agreement. This could be done either in an Agreed Minute or by agreement on paragraph 2(b) of the Korean draft.

23. Colonel Fuller replied that the U.S. side believed that the existing arrangements would continue in effect after the SOFA came into force. The U.S. draft paragraph 4 was intended to provide only for the establishment of an accounting system. The U.S. side would give further consideration to paragraph 2 of the ROK draft but it appeared that some changes of language would be desirable. For instance, the ROK draft used the phrase "public utilities", which is not used elsewhere in the article. In fact, it had already been agreed to delete the phrase "whether publicly or privately owned".

24. Mr. Ku replied that the misunderstanding referred to earlier by Mr. Hwang had been cleared up and the Korean side was hopeful that appropriate and mutually acceptable language could be found. The Korean side would take under consideration Colonel Fuller's explanation. Colonel Fuller stated that paragraph

0146

4 of the U.S. draft was originally intended to refer to paragraphs 1 and 2 of the U.S. draft article, as well as paragraph 3.) It was difficult to split the article into two separate articles, as the Korean side had suggested, ~~and~~ since ~~[illegible]~~ would create a somewhat awkward situation with regard to paragraph 4. Mr. Ku replied that the decision whether to have a separate utilities and services article could be made at a later date.

25. Turning to the Agreed Minutes ~~[illegible]~~ in the U.S. draft, Mr. ~~[illegible]~~ Ku noted that at the 24th meeting, it had been agreed to delete the phrase "increase in utility or service" from Agreed Minute #1. He added that the Korean side had proposed a further change in this Minute which would replace the reference to prior consultation with a provision for notification to the U.S. armed forces within fifteen days after the effective date of any change in priority or rates.

26. Colonel Fuller stated that it made a great difference whether the U.S. armed forces were consulted before a change was effected or notified afterwards. ~~[illegible]~~ Any change in rates was so important a matter for the armed forces that they should be consulted beforehand. Mr. Ku replied that this was an important matter for both governments. The impact of any change in rates on the Korean economy and the people in general was enormous. In the past, there had ~~always~~ usually been ~~mutual~~ consultation on all matters of mutual concern ~~before any change was effected~~. Such an important matter must be profoundly studied before any change was implemented. There would ~~undoubtedly~~ possibly be discussion ~~[illegible]~~ by the Joint Committee. In any case, the final decision would be communicated to the U.S. authorities.

27. Colonel Fuller pointed out that prior consultation does not necessarily imply prior agreement. The U.S. side believed that use of these utilities and services by the U.S. armed forces was somewhat different than use by private users in Korea. It was so important a matter for the armed forces that they should be consulted about any pending change, not merely notified after the change was put into effect.,

0147

28. Mr. Ku stated that the treatment accorded the U.S. armed forces in this regard has always been equal to, or better than, that accorded to agencies of the ROK Government. Proposed changes will be considered from every angle with all prudence. The U.S. forces would continue to receive favorable consideration. Mr. Hwang stated that he wished to supplement Mr. Ku's remarks. He said the Korean side did not intend to exclude prior consultation. Since any change would have a profound effect on both the Korean economy and the U.S. armed forces, prior consultation would be held with the armed forces. However, the Korean side did not believe that this provision of the SOFA should make prior consultation obligatory. Colonel Fuller remarked that perhaps more suitable language could be found after both sides had given this matter further consideration.

29. Regarding Agreed Minute #2 in the U.S. draft, Mr. Ku stated that the Korean side intended that existing arrangements should be continued, including those falling under the provisions of the Utilities and Claims Settlement Agreement. Colonel Fuller stated that the U.S. side had the same intention. He asked what the Korean side was proposing with regard to Agreed Minute #2. Mr. Ku replied that the Korean side accepted the substance of Agreed Minute #2. However, they proposed that some specific mention should be made of existing arrangements, either in this Agreed Minute or in a separate Minute.

agreed to accept the words "any Article" and "negotiations" as used in the U.S draft article. However the Korean side

Revision of the Agreement

30. Turning to the drafts of the article dealing with revision of the Agreement, Mr. Hwang stated that the Korean side believed the term "diplomatic channels" in the Korean draft to be better than the term "appropriate channels" in the U.S. draft, since ~~the Agreement itself was being negotiated through diplomatic channels~~. it is quite logical to assume that negotiations for revision of any agreement should also be entered into by the same authorities which have originally negotiated the agreement. General O'Connor replied that the term "appropriate" was broader and therefore included the term "diplomatic" but was not restricted to the latter. He pointed out that there

0148

might be occasions on which channels other than diplomatic channels might be more appropriate. In response to Mr. Hwang's query, General O'Connor stated that the Joint Committee itself might be the appropriate body to negotiate revision, or in time of war diplomatic channels might not be available, in which case the U.S. military commander might be the appropriate authority on the U.S. side to negotiate revision. Mr. Hwang stated that the Joint Committee was intended only to settle disputes, not to negotiate changes in the Agreement. Even if diplomatic channels were not available in wartime, the U.S. Government would be the party with which the ROK Government would negotiate revisions. General O'Connor observed that no matter who did the negotiating, any revisions would have to be approved by the two governments. It was agreed to give further consideration to this matter.

31. It was agreed to hold the next meeting on December 3 at 2:00 p.m.



0149

JOINT SUMMARY RECORD OF THE 35TH SESSION

November 23, 1963

1. Time and Place: 2:00 to 4:30 p.m. November 14, 1963 at the Foreign Minister's Conference Room

| 미주과 | 강석재 | 담 당 | 과 장 | 국 장 | 특별보좌관 | 차 관 | 장 관 |
|---|---|---|---|---|---|---|---|

2. Attendants:

ROK Side:

| | |
|---|---|
| Mr. Whang, Ho Eul | Director<br>Bureau of Political Affairs<br>Ministry of Foreign Affairs |
| Mr. Shin, Kwan Sup | Director<br>Bureau of Customs Duty<br>Ministry of Finance |
| Mr. Koo, Choong Whay | Chief, America Section<br>Ministry of Foreign Affairs |
| Mr. Chu, Mun Ki | Chief, Legal Affairs Section<br>Ministry of Justice |
| Lt. Col. Do Joon Pak | Military Affairs Section<br>Ministry of National Defense |
| Mr. Kang, Suk Jae (Rapporteur and Interpreter) | 2nd Secretary<br>Ministry of Foreign Affairs |
| Mr. Lee, Chung Bin | 3rd Secretary<br>Ministry of Foreign Affairs |

U.S. Side:

| | |
|---|---|
| Brig. Gen. G. G. O'Connor | Deputy Chief of Staff<br>8th U.S. Army |
| Col. Howard Smigelor | Deputy Chief of Staff<br>8th U.S. Army |
| Mr. Benhamin A. Fleck (Rapporteur and Press Officer) | First Secretary<br>American Embassy |
| Col. L. J. Fuller | Staff Judge Advocate<br>United Nations Command |
| Capt. R. M. Brownlie | Assistant Chief of Staff<br>USN/K |
| Mr. Robert A. Lewis | 2nd Secretary and Consul<br>American Embassy |
| Mr. Robert A. Kinney | J-5<br>8th U.S. Army |
| Maj. Robert D. Packham | Staff Officer, JAG<br>8th U.S. Army |

0150

Discussions

Customs

1. Mr. Whang opened the meeting by suggesting resumption of discussion of paragraph 5 of the Customs Article but asked if the U.S. side cared to make any comments on paragraph 1, 2, 3, or 4. Gen. O'Connor replied that the U.S. side had no further comment to make regarding those paragraphs. However, it might be useful to review the remaining points of difference. Full agreement had already been reached on paragraphs 1 and 4. Regarding paragraph 2 there were still two points at issue. First, it had still not been decided whether to use the word "organizations" or the word "activities" in this paragraph and in paragraph 5(c) and Agreed Minutes 1 and 3. Secondly, the Korean side had suggested the deletion of references to the U.S. armed forces'non-appropriated fund activities from this paragraph, while the U.S. side had proposed placing the references to these agencies and activities in parentheses in order to emphasize the fact that they form an integral part of the U.S. armed forces. Although agreement had been reached on subparagraphs (a) and (c) of paragraph 3, the substance of subparagraph (b) was still in dispute.

2. With regard to paragraph 5(b), Mr. Whang noted that the Korean side had stated that there was no intention on the part of the Korean authorities to inspect official mail or private letters addressed to members of the U.S. armed forces by members of their families in the United States. However, the Korean side desired to have the paragraph so worded that it would give the Korean authorities the right to inspect parcel mail.

3. General O'Connor replied that at the previous negotiating meeting, the Korean side had stated that un-

0151

authorized goods had been imported into the Republic of Korea through military postal channels. The Korean side had emphasized that the Korean authorities did not wish to inspect first class mail or to delay or confuse delivery of parcel mail. However, the Korean side had expressed the view that the inclusion in the SOFA of a provision authorizing the inspection of parcel mail by ROK customs authorities might prove to be an effective preventive measure to check abuses of the military postal channels. The Korean side had stated that they did not propose to send customs inspectors to every battalion or regimental post office but rather to station customs inspectors at ports and airports to spot-check incoming parcels.

4. In veiw of the these statements by the Korean side, General O'Connor continued, he wished to give a more detailed explanation of how the military postal system operates. U.S. military mail arrives in Korea in large metal containers, eight feet by six feet by seven feet in demensions, or a total of approximately 330 cubic feet each. These sealed containers are not opened at the port of entry but are sent directly to one of the 17 main military post offices which are located in various parts of the Republic of Korea. These containers are opened at one of these main military post offices and the mail is then distributed in sealed mail sacks to 32 unit distribution centers. It is at these unit distribution centers where effective surveillance of parcels received by an individual addressee can be maintained. U.S. military postal authorities at these individual postal units are continuously on the lookout for any abuse or violation of postal or customs regulations. Thus far in 1963, a total of 60 individuals have been denied further use of APO mails

0153

in Korea because they were found to have abused their APO privileges. Stern punitive action will be taken against any other personnel who may be discovered abusing their APO privileges.

5. As indicated by the foregoing explanation, General O'Connor continued, it would be very complicated, if not impossible, to maintain surveillance of parcels at ports of entry. Attempts to maintain surveillance at these points would be an administrative nightmare which could only result in extended delays and confusion and probable damage to the goods as the result of inadequate repacking. U.S. military postal authorities are aggressively implementing a program designed to eliminate any abuses in the APO system as they may arise. This surveillance program focuses on the point of parcel distribution, at the end of the line, where unusual or repeated shipments of parcels to individuals can be easily spotted and the violators punished. This is a practical program that works, whereas the proposed program of spot inspection at ports of entry would be impracticable. Therefore, the U.S. side continued to propose acceptance of the following language for paragraph 5(b): "Official documents under official seal and mail in United States military postal channels under official postal seal".

6. Mr. Whang thanked General O'Connor for his explanation and stated that the Korean side now understood that the mail was not opened at ports of entry but only at the 17 main military post offices and the 32 unit distribution centers. He said the Korean side would study the matter and explore the possibility of sending Korean customs inspectors to the post offices and unit distribution centers. He said the Korean authorities had no

0153

intention of causing unnecessary confusion or delays. However, since there had been in the past quite a few abuses, the Korean side wished to give a warning to prospective violators and make apprehension and punishment possible. To that end, Korean customs inspectors should be given the authority to inspect the parcel mail.

7. General O'Connor stated that the U.S. authorities believed the present inspection system to be effective. He said the U.S. military postal authorities take a special look at packages mailed to members of the U.S. armed forces from Hong Kong and Japan. The U.S. side was of the opinion that the proposals set forth by the Korean side would creat confusion and delay the delivery of the mail.

8. Mr. Whang said the Korean authorities were grateful for the actions taken by the U.S. military authorities in preventing abuses. However, the SOFA must provide for an orderly administration of Korean customs regulations. He said the Korean side was prepared to agree to the U.S. position with regard to certain other points at issue in this article if the U.S. side would accept the Korean position with regard to paragraph 5(b). General O'Connor replied that the U.S. side would take the Korean position under further consideration.

9. Turning to paragraph 5 (c), Mr. Whang stated that the Korean side continued to desire the deletion of the reference to non-appropriated fund activities from this subparagraph. He stated that if the U.S. side were willing to agree to so limit the provisions of this subparagraph, the Korean side was prepared to agree to use the word "activities" instead of the word "organizations" throughout

0154

the article. Furthermore,if the U.S. side agreed to the Korean position regarding subparagraphs (b) and (c) of paragraph 5, the Korean side would not only agree to use of the word "activities" but would also agree to the U.S. text of paragraph 3(b). General O'Connor replied that the U.S. side would not change its position with regard to paragraph 5(c) because cargoes assigned to authorized procurement agencies and their non-appropriated fund activities are military cargoes.

10. Reverting to paragraph 5(a), Mr. Whang urged the U.S. side to accept the ROK text. He said that use of the word "units", as proposed by the Korean side, did not mean that the Korean authorities intended to conduct a customs examination of every individual member of the U.S. armed forces entering or leaving the Republic of Korea. He said the intention was to grant exemptions from such examination in almost every case. However, the ROK authorities wanted the SOFA to grant them the right of inspection, even though they did not intent to inspect in every case in actual practice. He further stated that there is a fundamental idfference between the granting of exemptions from inspection while retaining the right to inspect and not retaining any right to inspect at all. General O'Connor replied by reiterating the fact that members of the U.S. armed forces enter and leave the Republic of Korea as individual members of the armed forces and not as members of units. He said the U.S. side would take the Korean position under further consideration.

11. Returning to paragraph 5(c), Mr. Whang pointed out that in this subpragraph and Agreed Minute 3, according to the U.S. draft, "all cargo" includes cargo assigned to non-appropriated fund organizations. In paragraph 2, it has already been spelled out that such imports shall be

0155

permitted entry free of customs duty. However, cirgarettes, tobacco, and similar items consigned to non-appropriated fund organizations, cannot be construed as military cargo. The Korean authorities wish to have an idea of the types of cargo and the quantities shipped so that they can discuss unusual shipments with the U.S. authorities. Therefore, they wish to exclude cargo consigned to non-appropriated fund organizations from the provisions of this subparagraph.

12. General O'Connor replied that since the Korean side had already agreed that such cargo should be admitted free of customs duty, the U.S. side failed to see the point of conducting customs examination of such cargo. He pointed out the difficulty of differentiating between certain types of rations issued directly by the armed forces and good sold in the post exchanges. He said the proper time to deal with infractions is when the goods are sold or disposed of illegally in the Republic of Korea. He pointed out that the inclusion of non-appropriated fund cargo as military cargo is not a situation peculiar to Korea but is worldwide U.S. military practice.

13. Mr. Whang stated that while it was true that agreement had been reached on importation of these goods duty-free under the provisions of paragraph 2, importation of such goods in excess of consumption needs could result in their sale on the black market. Therefore, the Korean customs authorities should be in a position to know the quantities of such goods actually imported.

14. General O'Connor replied that control over the sale of goods imported by non-appropriated fund activities is maintained through rationing of purchases at the post exchanges. He displayed a sample ration card and pointed

0156

out that the sale of such items as soap, soft drinks, and stockings is strictly rationed. With regard to items which are imported in bulk, he pointed out that adequate supplies must be maintained in the pipe line and that it would be difficult for individuals not in supply operations to know what constitutes a "reasonable quantity". He added that the rationing system is under continuing review. Mr. Whang stated that this question had been fully discussed and suggested that both sides give further consideration to the other side's position.

Military Post Offices

15. Turning to the article on Military Post Offices, Mr. Whang recalled that at the 19th negotiating meeting, the both sides had agreed to convert paragraph 2 of the U.S. draft into an Agreed Minute. Final agreement on this article must await agreement on the text of paragraph 5(b) of the Customs Article. Mr. Whang proposed deletion of the words "and their dependents" from paragraph 2 (or the Agreed Minute) and as an altérnative he further proposed if the U.S. side would agree to the Korean position regarding paragraph 5(b) of the Customs Article, the Korean side would then be prepared to agree to the retention of the word " and their dependents" in paragraph 2. General O'Connor indicated that the U.S. side would respond when thise Article is taken up again, after Agreement on paragraph 5(b) of the Customs Article.

Utilities and Services

16. Taking up the drafts regarding Utilities and Services, Mr. Whang recalled that the U.S. side had proposed in the first sentence the deletion of the phrase "whether publicly or privately owned", the insertion of the word "owned" before the word "controlled", and the substitution of the phrase "local administrative subdivisions" for the phrase "political subdivisions". Mr. Whang stated

0157

that the Korean side accepted the U.S. draft of the first sentence with the proposed changes.

17. Recalling that the Korean side had proposed the deletion of the phrase "however produced" from the second sentence of the U.S. draft, Mr. Whang asked for comment by the U.S. side. Colonel Fuller replied that this phrase was included in the Utilities and Claims Settlement Agreement and had been included in the first Korean draft of this article. The U.S. side was unable to understand why the Korean side now wished to delete the phrase from this article.

18. Mr. Whang replied that inasmuch as the phrase "however produced" was contained in the Utilities and Claims Settlement Agreement, the Korean side agreed to its inclusion in this article of the SOFA, with the reservation that subsequent revision of the Utilities and Claims Settlement was not preculded and that if such revision should result in the elimination of the phrase from the latter agreement, the language of the SOFA would be changed accordingly. Colonel Fuller replied that the U.S. side would have to consider the implications of the proposed reservation by the Korean side before it could agree to the Korean side's conditional acceptance of the second sentence of paragraph 3(a) of the U.S. draft.

19. Mr. Whang stated that the Korean side accepted the revised third and fourth sentences of the U.S. draft. If the U.S. would agree to the Korean reservation with regard to the second sentence, full agreement could be reached on paragraph 3(a) of the U.S. draft.

20. Passing on to paragraph 3(b) of the U.S.draft, Mr. Whang noted that the first sentence had been agreed to and that the original second sentence had been deleted.

0158

With regard to the original third sentence, now the second sentence of this paragraph, which deals with emergency operating needs of the U.S. armed forces, the needs in question should be those which the ROK Government recognizes to be reasonable and justifiable. Mr. Whang stated that the Korean side would like to have the record clearly show that the ROK Government must also agree that emergency operating needs exist before it will take measures to assure provision of utilities and services necessary to meet these needs. He said the Korean side would prefer to transfer the substance of this sentence to an Agreed Minute.

21. In response to Colonel Fuller's request for clarification, Mr. Whang stated that the Korean side understood this provision to mean that when an emergency operating need arises, the U.S. armed forces will notify the ROK Government. However, the Korean side held that the ROK Government, after receiving such notification, must agree that such a need exists before taking action. In other words, the Korean side could not agree to a provision which would provide for unilateral determination by the U.S. armed forces that an emergency operating need existed. The Korean side also wished to move the netire sentence to an Agreed Minute. Colonel Fuller replied that the U.S. side would take these proposal under consideration.

22. Mr. Whang stated that some misunderstanding appeared to have arisen regarding paragraph 4 of the U.S. draft and paragraph 2 of the Korean draft. He said that Mr. Ku explain the views of the Korean side. Mr. Ku stated that the U.S. draft provided only for accounting arrangements, whereas the Korean draft specifically provided that specific arrangements entered into by the U.S. armed forces for the use of, and payments for, utilities and services would continue in effect. Such arrangements include those contracts

0159

already in effect with the Seoul City Water Supply, the Korean Electric Company, and the national railways. The U.S. draft gives the impression that the two governments must enter into arrangements in addition to the SOFA in order to continue such financial transactions in the future. And there is no mention in the U.S. draft of existing arrangements for such transactions. Assuming that the U.S. side agrees that existing arrangements should continue after the SOFA enters into force, it is necessary to say so in the Agreement. This could be done either in an Agreed Minute or by agreement on paragraph 2(b) of the Korean draft.

23. Colonel Fuller replied that the U.S. side believed that the existing arrangements would continue in effect after the SOFA came into force. The U.S. draft of paragraph 4 was intended to provide only for the establishment of an accounting system. The U.S. side would give further consideration to paragraph 2 of the ROK draft but it appeared that some changes of language would be desirable. For instance, the ROK draft used the phrase "public utilities", which is not used elsewhere in the article. In fact, it had already been agreed to delete the phrase "whether publicly or privately owned".

24. Mr. Ku replied that the misunderstanding referred to earlier by Mr. Whang had been cleared up and the Korean side was hopeful that appropriate and mutually acceptable language could be found. The Korean side would take under consideration Colonel Fuller's explanation. Colonel Fuller stated that paragraph 4 of the U.S. draft was originally intended to refer to paragraphs 1 and 2 of the U.S. draft article, as well as paragraph 3. It was difficult to split the article into two separate articles, as the Korean side had suggested, since this would create

0160

a somewhat awkward situation with regard to paragraph 4. Mr. Ku replied that the decision whether to have a separate utilities and services article could be made at a later date.

25. Turning to the Agreed Minutes in the U.S. draft, Mr. Ku noted that at the 24th meeting it had been agreed to delete the phrase "increase in utility or service" from Agreed Minute #1. He added that the Korean side had proposed a further change in this Minute which would replace the reference to prior consultation with a provision for notification to the U.S. armed forces within fifteen days after the effective date of any change in priority or rates.

26. Colonel Fuller stated that it made a great difference whether the U.S. armed forces were consulted before a change was effected or notified afterwards. Any change in rates was so important a matter for the armed forces that they should be consulted beforehand. Mr. Ku replied that this was an important matter for both governments. The impact of any change in rates on the Korean economy and the people in general was enormous. In the past, there had usually been consultation on all matters of mutual concern. Such an important matter must be profoundly studied before any change was implemented. There would possibly be discussion by the Joint Committee. In any case, the final decision would be communicated to the U.S. authorities.

27. Colonel Fuller pointed out that prior consultation does not necessarily imply prior agreement. The U.S. side believed that use of these utilities and services by the U.S. armed forces was somewhat different than use by private users in Korea. It was so important a matter for the armed forces that they should be consulted

0161

about any pending change, not merely notified after the change was put into effect.

28. Mr. Ku stated that the treatment accorded the U.S. armed forces in this regard has always been equal to, or better than, that accorded to agencies of the ROK Government. Proposed changes will be considered from every angle with all prudence. The U.S. forces would continue to receive favorable consideration. Mr. Whang stated that he wished to supplement Mr. Ku's remarks. He said the Korean side did not intend to exclude prior consultation. Since any change would have a profound effect on both the Korean economy and the U.S. armed forces, prior consultation would be held with the armed forces. However, the Korean side did not believe that this provision of the SOFA should make prior consultation obligatory. Colonel Fuller remarked that perhaps more suitable language could be found after both sides had given this matter further consideration.

29. Regarding Agreed Minute #2 in the U.S. draft, Mr. Ku stated that the Korean side intended that existing arrangements should be continued, including those falling under the provisions of the Utilities and Claims Settlement Agreement. Colonel Fuller stated that the U.S. side had the same intention. He asked what the Korean side was proposing with regard to Agreed Minute #2. Mr. Ku replied that the Korean side accepted the substance of Agreed Minute#2. However, they proposed that some specific mention should be made of existing arrangements, either in this Agreed Minute or in a separate Minute.

Revision of the Agreement

30. Turning to the drafts of the article dealing with revision of the Agreement, Mr. Whang stated that the Korean side agreed to accept the words "any Article"

0162

and "negotiations" as used in the U.S. draft article. However the Korean side believed the term "diplomatic channels" in the Korean draft to be better than the term "appropriate channels" in the U.S. draft, since it is quite logical to assume that negotiations for revision of any agreement should also be entered into by the same authorities which have originally neogitated the agreement. General O'Connor replied that the term "appropriate" was broader and therefore included the term "diplomatic" but was not restricted to the latter. He pointed out that there might be occasions on which channels other than diplomatic channels might be more appropriate. In response to Mr. Whang's query, General O'Connor stated that the Joint Committee itself might be the appropriate body to negotiate revision, or in time of war diplomatic channels might not be available, in which case the U.S. military commander might be the appropriate authority on the U.S. side to negotiate revision. Mr. Whang stated the Joint Committee was intended only to settle disputes, not to negotiate changes in the Agreement. Even if diplomatic channels were not available in wartime, the U.S. Government would be the party with which the ROK Government would negotiate revisions. General O'Connor observed that no matter who did the negotiating, any revisions would have to be approved by the two governments. It was agreed to give further consideration to this matter.

31. It was agreed to hold the next meeting on December 3 at 2:00 p.m.

0163

5. 제36차 회의, 12.5

0164

# 기 안 용 지

| 자체 통제 | | 기안처 | 미주과 강석재 | 전화번호 | 근거서류접수일자 |
|---|---|---|---|---|---|

| | 과장 | 국장 | 차관 | 장관 |
|---|---|---|---|---|
| | [서명] | [서명] 3 | 대결 | [서명] |

| 관계관 서명 | |
|---|---|

| 기안 년월일 | 1963.12.2 | 시행 년월일 | | 보존 년한 | | 정서 | 기장 |
|---|---|---|---|---|---|---|---|
| 분류 기호 | | 전체 통제 | | 종결 | | | |
| 경유 수신 참조 | 건의 | | | 발신 | | | |
| 제목 | 제36차 주둔군지위협정 체결교섭회의에 임할 우리측 입장 | | | | | | |

12월 5일에 개최될 제36차 주둔군지위협정 체결 한미간 교섭 회의에서는 관세업무, 비세출자금기관 및 협정의 개정에 관한 조항을 토의하도록 예정되고 있는바 이에 관하여 우리측 교섭 실무자는 11월 29일 회합을 갖고 제36차 회의에서 취할 우리측 태도를 별첨과 같이 결정하였아오니 재가하여 주시기 바랍니다.

유첨: 제36차 주둔군지위협정체결교섭회의에 임할 우리측태도, 끝.

1966. 12. 31.에 예고문에 의거 일반문서로 재분류됨

보통문서로 재분류 (1966, 12, 31 )

승인양식 1—1—3 (1112—040—016—018) (190mm×260mm16절지)

0165

1. 관세업무

가. 관세조항중 아직 합의에 도달치 못한 미국측 초안 (2)항,3(b)항,(5)항의 a,b 및 c 항 및 합의의사록 2 및 3항에 관한 우리측의 입장은 지난 제35차 회의시에 명백히 한바 있고 미국측의 재고를 촉구한바 있으며 그후 우리측 입장에는 하등의 변동이 없다는 것을 설명하고 미국측 견해를 요구한다. 그리하여 만약 미국측이 우편물 검사면제에 관한 미국측 초안 5(b)에 있어서 우리측 요구대로 소포에 대한 검사권한을 인정하여 줄 경우에는 (ㄱ) 미국측 초안 (2)항의 비세출 자금기관에 관한 용어를 미국측이 제의한 대로 "activities "로 하고 (ㄴ) 미국측 초안 3(b)항의 차량 및 부속품의 무세수입에 시간적 제한을 가하지 않을 것이며 미국측 초안대로 수락하기로 한다.

나. 세관검사면제 대상 규정중 미국측 초안 5(a)항에 관하여 우리측이 부대( units )로 입국할 경우에만 검사를 면제하도록 주장한데 대한 미국측의 견해를 요구한다. 만약 미국측이 우리 입장을 수락치 않을 경우에는 이 문제를 우선 보류하고 군사화물에 관한 문제를 토의한다.

다. 군사화물에 대한 세관검사 면제와 공인된 조달기관 및 비세출자금 기관에 탁송되는 물품도 군사화물로 간주할 것을 규정하는 미국측 초안 5(c)항 및 합의 의사록 (3)에 관하여 우리측은 비세출자금기관에 탁송되는 물품에 대해서는 한국 세관 당국에 검사할 권한이 부여되어야 하며 또한 그러한 물품은 군사화물로 간주할수 없다고 주장하여 온데 대하여 미국측의 견해를 묻기로 하며 만약 미국측이 우리측 입장을 받아들일경우에는 우리측도 전기한 미국측 초안 5(a)항을 그대로 수락하기로 한다.

라. 미국측 합의 의사록 (2)는 도착일 부터 6개월내에는 개인용품 및 가사 도구를 무세로 수입할수 있다고 규정하고 있는데 대하여 우리측은 계속 "reasonable quantities of "라는 구절의 삽입을 주장하고 미국측의 견해를 요구한다.

0166

2. 비세출자금 기관

가. 주보, 식당, 사교크럽, 극장, 신문 기타 비세출 자금기관의 설치를 허용하고 있는 미국측 초안 (1)항에 있어서 우리측은

(1) 신문에 관해서는 별도 1(b)항에서 대한민국의 법규, 허가, 세금 기타 통제에 따라야 한다고 규정하기로 합의본바 있음으로 당연히 여기서 삭제되어야 함을 밝히고,

(2) 비세출 자금기관의 용어를 "organizations "로 혹은 "activities "로 할 것인지의 문제는 관세조문에 관한 미국측 입장에 따라 결정하기로 하며,

(3) 우리측 안은 그러한 비세출자금기관의 설치를 "미국군대가 사용하고 있는 토지시설내"로 한정하도록 규정하고 있으며 이에 관하여 제21차 회의시에 우리측은 만약 토지시설외에 임시로 주보를 운영할 경우에도 "합동위원회를 통하여 양국정부간에 합의된 장소"에 설치해야 할 것이라고 제의한바 있었음을 상기하고 이에 대한 미국측의 견해를 묻기로 한다. 그러나 만약 미국측이 관세조항의 5(c)항에 있어서 우리측 요구대로 비세출자금기관에 탁송되는 물품에 대한 검사권한을 허용해 줄 경우에는 우리측은 이문제에 관한 미국측 입장을 재고하여 주기로 한다.

나. 미국측 초안 (2)항의 첫째 문장은 비세출자금 기관에 의한 물품의 판매에는 한국세금을 부가치 않을것을 규정하고 있는바 신문판매에 관한 1(b)항으로 말미아마 제21차 회의에서 "except as provided in paragraph 1(b)"라는 구절을 삽입키로 합의본바 있고 둘째문장은 한국내에 있어서의 비세출자금기관에 의한 상품 및 보급품의 구매는 한국조세에 따라야 할것을 규정하고 있으나 " to which other purchasers of such merchandise and supplies are subject and at rates no less favorable than those imposed on other purchasers "라는 구절은 (ㄱ) 사실상 불필요하며 (ㄴ) 실제에 있어서 불리한 율의 조세를 부가하는 일이 없을 것이므로 (ㄷ) 회의기록에 동 구절의 내용을 우리측이 양해한다는 점을 명백히

0167

남기는 것으로 충분함으로 협정문의 체제상 동 구절을 삭제할것을 주장한다.

다. 미국측 초안 (4)항은 대한민국 조세법에 의하여 필요한 정보를 비세출자금기관이 한국사세당국에 제공할 것을 규정하고 있는바 우리측은 " after consultation between the representatives of the two Governments in the Joint Committee"라는 구절에 관하여 미국측이 제21차 회의시 염려를 표시한바와 같이 (ㄱ)불필요한 정보의 제공을 요구하는 일이 없을것이며 또한 (ㄴ) 대개의 경우 그러한 정보제공은 합동위원회를 통하여 요구될 것이므로 자연히과도하고 불필요한 요구가 있을수 없다고 봄으로 동 구절의 삭제를 요구하기도 한다.

라. 미군 구성원, 군속 및 가족외의 사람들에 의한 비세출자금기관의 사용허용을 규정하는 미국측 초안 (5)항에 관하여 우리측은 동 규정이 지나치게 복잡하고 또 중복된바 있으므로 이를 간결하게 규정하고 또한 성질상 합의 의사록에 넣도록 하자고 주장한다. 우리측은 그 이유로서 (ㄱ) 군계약자에 의한 비세출자금기관의 사용은 군계약자 조문의 3(ㅂ)항에서 별도 규정한바 있으며 (ㄴ) 미국 적십자 요원 및 USO 요원들에 관해서 미국측은 군사우편조문에 관한 미국측 초안 (2)항 (제19차 회의시 합의의사록으로 변경해로 합의본바 있음) 토의시 "personnel ........, ordinarily occorded such privileges abroad "라는 구절가운데에는 미국적십자 요원 및 USO 요원도 포함하는것이라 말하였으며 우리측도 그렇게 양해하고 있는 점을 상기시키고 미국측 초안 (5)항도 군사우편 조문에 대한 합의의사록과 똑같이 즉, The ~~activities~~ organizations referred to in paragraph 1 may be used by other officers ~~and~~ or personnel of the United States Government~~, and their dependents,~~ ordinarily occorded such privileges "로 규정하고 이를 합의 의사록에 넣도록 할 것을 제의한다.

3. 협정의 개정

협정개정에 관한 조문에 있어서 우리측 초안은 "외교계통"을 통하여 교섭할 것을 규정하고 있는데 반하여 미국측 초안은 "적절한 계통"을 통하여 교섭하

0168

도록 규정하고 있다. 우리측은 우리측 초안의 용어를 수탁하여 줄 것을 요구하고 만약 미국측이 계속 불응할 경우에는 협정개정을 위한 교섭은 부득이한 경우를 제외하고는 통상외교계통을 통하여 한다는 양해하에 미국측 초안의 용어를 수탁하기로 한다.

보통문서로 재분류(1966.12.31)

1966.12.31에 예고문에 의거 일반문서로 재분류됨

0169

# 기 안 용 지

| 자체 통제 | 2등서기관 강상황 | 기안처 | 미주과 강석재 | 전화번호 | 근거서류접수일자 |
|---|---|---|---|---|---|

| | | 과장 | 국장 | 차관 | 장관 | |
|---|---|---|---|---|---|---|
| | | | | 대결 | | |

| 관계관 서명 | 조약과장 |
|---|---|

| 기안 년월일 | 1963.12.7 | 시행 년월일 | | 보존 년한 | | 정서 | 기장 |
|---|---|---|---|---|---|---|---|
| 분류 기호 | 외정미722.2 | 전체 통제 | | 종결 | | | |

| 경유 수신 참조 | 국가재건 최고회의 의장 (참조: 외무국방위원장) 내각수반 | 발신 | 장관 |
|---|---|---|---|

| 제목 | 주둔군지위협정 체결을 위한 제36차 교섭회의보고 |
|---|---|

1963년 12. 5 하오 3시부터 5시까지 외무부장관회의실에서 개최된 제 36차 주둔군지위협정 체결교섭회의에서 토의된 내용을 별첨과 같이 보고합니다.

유첨: 제 36 차 교섭회의 보고서 2/1 부 끝.

1966,12.31, 에 예고문에 의거 일반문서로 재분류됨

승인양식 1-1-3 (1112-040-016-018) (190mm×260mm16절지)

0170

의 무 부

외정미 722.2 1963. 12. 10

수 신:

제 목: 주둔군 지위협정 체결을 위한 제36차 교섭회의 보고

1963년 12월 5일 하오 3시부터 5시까지 외무부 장관 회의실에서 개최된 제36차 주둔군 지위협정 체결 교섭회의에서 토의된 내용을 별첨과 같이 보고합니다.

유 첨: 제36차 교섭회의 보고서 부 끝

외 무 부 장 관 김 용 식

0171

제 36 차

한미간 주둔군 지위협정 체결실무자 회의

보 고 서

1. 일 시 : 1963 년 12 월 5 일 하오 3시부터 5시까지

2. 장 소 : 외무부 장관 회의실

3. 참석자 : 한국측 : 황 호 을 ( 외무부 정무국장 )

구 충 회 ( 외무부 미주과장 )

박 봉 진 ( 재무부 관세과장 )

주 문 기 ( 법무부 법무과장 )

김 원 길 대령(국방부 군무과장 )

오 재 희 ( 외무부 조약과장 )

강 석 재 ( 외무부 2등서기관 )

조 광 제 ( 외무부 2등서기관 )

이 정 빈 ( 외무부 3등서기관 )

미국측 : 교섭대표 전원

4. 토의사항:

63-1-172

가. 관세업무

(1) 우리측은 관세조문중 미합의된 사항에 관한 우리측 입장에 대하여 미국측의 견해를 요구하였던바, 미국측은 금차 회의에서는 관세조문중 우편물 검사에 관한 미국측 초안 5(b)항만을 토의하자고 제의하였다. 미국측은 먼저 한국측은 한국세관당국이 우편물중 서신을 제외한 소포에 대해서만 검사할 권한을 가질것을 원하고 있는 것으로 이해하고 있다고 전제하고 미국측으로서도 소포 검사 권한에 관한 한국측의 관심을 양해하는 바이나, 검사에 관련하여 문제가 되는 것은 우편물 포대가 출입국 항구나 공항에서 개봉되지 않고 밀봉된채 각 우체국으로 발송되어 비로서 개봉되므로 중앙우체국에서 검사를 한다면 우편물 배달을 지연시키는 결과를 가져 올 것인바 한국측으로서는 각 우체국마다 검사관을 파견할

0172

63-1-29 (6)　　미외문 108-2 (6)

0173

것인지 혹은 중앙우체국에서 검사할 것인지에 대하여 우리측의 의견을 요구하였다.

(2) 우리측은 당초에는 출입국공항이나 비행장에서 검사하기를 원하였으나 미국측의 우편물 송달 과정과 방법으로 미루어 보아 32 개소의 mail distribution center 에 세관관리를 파견하여 검사할 것을 구상하고 있다고 답변하고 한국측이 소포에 대한 검사 권한을 보유할 것을 주장하는 것은 소포에 대하여 일일히 검사할려는 목적이 아니고 필요할 경우에는 검사할수 있도록 권한을 보유함으로서 군사우편시설을 남용하려는 소수의 불미스러운자들에 대한 적절한 사전경고의 효과를 거둘것을 목적으로 하고 있으며 또한 권한을 보유하되 실제로 검사를 하지 않는것과 애당초 검사할 권한이 없는것과는 근본적인 차이가 있는 것이라는 점을 부가하여 말하였다.

(3) 미국측은 검사권한을 행사하는데 있어서 우편물의 배달이 지연되어서는 않되며 또한 한국측으로서는 필요할 경우에만 검사할 것이란 점을 양해하고 검사실시에 관한 세부 상항은 합동위원회에서 조정하기로 하며 소포 우편물에 대한 검사 권한을 원하고 있는 한국측 요구에 절충하기 위하여 5(b)항을 "official documents under official seal and first class mail in the United States military postal channels under official postal seal " 로 수정할 것을 제안하였다.

63-1-173

(4) 우리측은 미국측의 수정제안에 대하여 소포 우편물을 검사할 권한을 보유할지라도 우편물의 배달을 불필요하게 지연시키거나 혼란을 야기케 하지 않을 것이라 말하고 first class mail 은 서신만을 의미하며 소포는 포함되지 않는지를 문의하였던바 미국측은 소포는 통상 포함되지 않으나 경우에 따라서는 first class mail 로 송달될수도 있다고 답변하였다. 우리측은 그렇다면 first class mail 로서의 소포의 규격이나 무개에 어떠한 제한이 있는지 구체적인 자료를 제공하여 줄 것을 요구하였던바 미국측은 소포를 first class mail 로 송부한다면 막대한 요금이 필요할 것이므로 특별한 경우 아니면 이용

0174

63-1-29

예문108-2

0175

하지 않을 것으로 사료하며 규격이나 무게등에 관한 제한이 있는지에 대하여는 다음 회의에서 구체적인 것을 알려주겠다는 답변이 있었다.
우리측은 전기한 자료를 얻어 검토한 후 미국측이 제안한 수정안에 대한 우리측의 견해를 답변하기로 하였음.

나. 비세출자금기관

(1) 미국측은 토의에 들어가기 전에 먼저 비세출자금기관의 성격과 범위에 관한 일반적인 설명을 하겠다고 전제하고 한국측은 미군에 있어서 비세출자금으로 행하는 각종 활동사업을 세출자금에 의한 미국군대 활동과 구분하여 고려해야 한다는 착각을 가지고 있으나 비세출 자금기관의 활동은 군 구성원, 군속 및 그 가족을 위하여 필요 불가결한 것이며 또한 사기 왕성과 오락을 위하여 중요한 것이며 미국본토에서는 비세출자금으로 운영되고 있어며 한국과 같은 곳에서는 비록 명목은 비세출 자금기관의 활동이나 실제 자금은 세출자금으로 운영되고 있으며 미국군대가 이러한 비세출기관 활동을 하고 있는 것은 군대구성상 그러한 것임으로 한국측으로서는 유국된 오해를 없에 주기 바란다고 말하였다. 미국측은 계속하여 미국측 초안에서 가장 중요한 점은 그러한 비세출자금기관이 미국군대에 의하여"authorized and regulated "된 것임을 지적하였다. 63-1-174

(2) 우리측은 미국측의 설명에 사의를 표명하고 미국측의 말한 여러점을 잘 이해하고 있다고 말하고 호혜적인 이해를 갖고 본 조문토의에 임할것을 제의하였다. 우리측은 또한 관세조문과 관련하여 비세출자금 기관에 탁송되는 물품에 대하여 한국세관에서 검사할 권한을 가져야 한다고 주장하고 그러나 미군에 불편을 야기케 할 의도는 없으며 오직 적절한 량과 품목이 반입되고 있는지의 여부만을 확인하고저 한다고 말하였다.

(3) 미국측은 우리측 초안 4항에서 비세출자금기관의 사용을 위하여 반입하는 물품은 적절한 량으로 제한할 것을 규제하고 있으나 이러한 규정은 이미 합의본바 있는 관세조문에 관한 합의의사록 (1)에서 규제한바 있으므로 여기서 재차 되풀이 할 필요가 없다고 말하였다. 우리측은 한국측 초안의(4)항을 삭제할 것에 동의하나 관세조문에 있어서 만약

0176

63-1-29 미.도 108-2

0177

비세출자금기관에 탁송되는 물품에 대하여 한국세관당국이 검사할 권한을 허용할 것에 합의를 볼수있다면 비세출 자금기관에 관한 조문도 용의하게 합의볼수 있다고 말하였다.

(4) 미국측은 "적절한 량"으로 제한 한다는 점에 있어서는 우리측과 의견을 같이하는 바이나, 어떠한 량이 적절한 량인지를 한국정부가 결정한다는데 대해서는 찬동할수 없다고 답변하고 한국측보다 오히려 그 물품을 사용하는 미군당국이 적절한 량을 결정할수있는 입장이지만 사실상 아무도 적절한 량을 정확히 판단할수는 없는 것이라고 말하였다. 미국측은 계속하여 이 문제를 합동위원회에서 다룰수 있을지 모르나 행정적으로 복잡하며 타당치 못하다고 말하고 미국측은 미군 당국 스스로가 경제적 이유로 필요 이상의 물품을 도입하는 일이 없을 것이며 적절한 량으로 제한할것을 규정한 이상 미군당국으로서도 이를 준수할 것이니 한국측은 신의로서 이를 수락하여야 한다고 말하고 또한 통례적으로 다른 행정협정에서도 이 정도로 규정하고 있을 뿐이라고 설명하였다.

(5) 우리측은 적절한 량에 대한 결정 기준을 종래 회의에서 언급한바 있는것 처럼 미국의 일반 가정의 소비기준에 준하여 결정할수 있을 것이라 답변하고 한국측이 검사권한을 요구하는 이유는 현재 비세출자금기관의 활동을 위하여 반입된 물품들이 그 사용목적을 벗어나 한국시장에서 매매되고 있는 실정에서 부정을 방지할수 있는 방안을 마련할 것을 희구하는 까닭이라고 설명하였다. 미국측은 비단 비세출자금기관에 탁송되는 물품뿐만아니라 세출자금기관의 물품도 암시장에서 거래되고 있는데 그렇다면 세출자금기관의 물품도 검사해야 할 것이 아닌가하고 반문하여 이러한 물품들의 암시장에로의 유출은 검사만으로는 부족하며 위반자에 대한 적발 징계처분조치가 필요한 것이다. 미군당국으로서는 이러한 불법행위를 방지하기 위하여 최선의 노력을 경주하고 있으며 앞으로서 계속 노력할 것이라고 답변하였다. 63-1-175

(6) 비세출자금기관에 관한 조문토의에 들어가서 우리측은 미국측초안 1(a)항에 있는 신문에 대한 언급은 1(b)항에서 별도 규정하였기 때문에 삭제할 것을 제의하였는바 미국측은 신문발행기관의 설치와 신문판매는 별도의 것임으로 이해를 돕기위하여 그대로 둘것을 요구하였으며 우리측은 이에 동의하였다.

0178

13-1-2.

미·日 198-2

0179

(7) 비세출자금기관에 관한 용어에 있어서 미국측은 한국측이 "activities "대신에 "organizations"로 할것을 요구하는 이유를 문의하여 왔는바, 우리측은 "organizations "라는 용어가 개념상 매우 적절하나 "activities"라는 용어는 모호하고 불명확한 것이라 답변하였다. 미국측은 그렇다면 용어를 "organizations "로 할 의사가 있으나 의미상 미국측이 " activities "로 이해하고 있는 모든 활동을 뜻하며 포함해야 한다고 제의하였으며 그러한 양해하에 용어를 "organizations"로 할것에 합의 보았다.

(8) 우리측초안 (1)항은 비세출자금기관의 설치를 "미군이 사용중인 토지시설내로" 제한할것을 규정하고 있으며, 또한 제21차 회의시 우리측이 만약 토지시설이외의 장소에 임시주보등을 운영할 필요가 있을 경우에라도 합동위원회를 통하여 양국간에 합의된 장소에 설치해야 한다고 요구한데 대한 미국측의 견해를 문의하였던바 미국측은 행정상 실현키 어려움으로 개별적으로 해결하는 것이 좋겠다는 의견을 피력하고 미일 협정에 동일한 구절이 있기는 하나 사실상 필요가 없기때문에 미국측 초안에서 삭제한 것이며 이러한 문제는 필요할 경우에는 합동위원회에서 다룰수 있을것이라는 답변이 있었음. 우리측은 그러한 문제는 상호협조하에 처리할수 있을 것으로 양해하며 동구절의 삭제를 수락한다고 하였다. 우리측은 또한 우리측 초안의 "........비세출자금기관을 미군대 구성원, 군속 및 가족의 배타적 사용을 위하여...."라는 구절에서"배타적"이란 용어를 삭제할 것을 제의하여 합의보았다.

다. 협정개정

63-1-176

(1) 협정개정을 위한 교섭에 있어서 우리측 초안은 "외교계통"을 통하도록 규제하고 있는데 대하여 미국측 초안에서는 "적절한 계통"을 통하도록 규정하고 있다. 우리측은 이용어의 차이에 관하여 협정개정을 위한

0180

63-1-29 미문 108-2

0181

교섭은 부득이한 경우외에는 통상 외교계통을 통한다는 양해하에 미국측 초안의 용어에 동의할 것을 제의하였으며 양측은 이러한 양해에 합의보고 따라서 협정개정에 관한 조문에 완전 합의를 보았다.

5. 중요합의사항:

협정개정에 관한 조문에 완전 합의봄.

6. 기타 사항 :

차기회의일자 : 1963 년 12 월 19 일 하오 2 시

차기회의의제 : 차기회의 까지 양측 수석대표간에 합의된 사항.

63-1-177



0182

63-1-29(6)　　　　마이크로 108-2 (6)

0183

December 5

1. Mr. Hwang opened the meeting by introducing Mr. PAK Pong-chin, Chief of the Customs Section, Ministry of Finance, who was attending in place of Mr. SIN Kwan-sop, and two new members of the Korean negotiating team: Colonel KIM Won-kil, replacing Colonel YI Nam-ku; and Mr. O Chae-hi, newly appointed Chief of the Treaty Section, Ministry of Foreign Affairs, replacing Mr. SIN Chung-sop. Mr. Habib welcomed these gentlemen to the negotiating table on behalf of the U.S. negotiators.

Customs

2. Taking up the Customs Article, Mr. Hwang stated that it had been the subject of discussion at many previous meetings and many portions of it had been agreed upon. However, there still remained some paragraphs concerning which agreement had not yet been reached. He asked whether the U.S. side had any comment to make regarding any of these.

3. Mr. Habib replied that the U.S. side wished to confine discussion of this article at this meeting to paragraph 5(b), which relates to mail. He recalled that at the previous meeting, the Korean side had indicated a particular interest in examining parcels because of concern over the possible importation of illegal items. The Korean side had indicated that the Korean authorities had no interest in examining the personal letter mail of the U.S. troops. The U.S. side had explained the manner in which the mail arrives in Korea - in sealed containers which are sent directly from the ports of entry to individual postal units, where they are opened and the mail distributed. He recalled further that the question of how the Korean authorities proposed to implement any right of inspection also came up. The U.S. side had inquired whether the Korean authorities intended to send customs inspectors to each of the individual postal units or, alternatively, planned to open the sealed containers at the ports of entry, thus disrupting the swift and efficient

0131

distribution system now in effect. He asked the Korean side to explain how they proposed to carry out any right of inspection.

4. Mr. Hwang replied that initially the Korean authorities had intended to inspect parcels at the ports of entry. However, after hearing the explanation of how the mail is handled, given by the U.S. side at the previous meeting, the Korean authorities now realized that examination at the ports of entry would be inconvenient. They were thinking, therefore, in terms of dispatching customs inspectors to the individual postal units. However, the Korean authorities did not intend that the inspectors would examine every parcel. From the point of view of the Korean side, the important thing was that the Korean authorities be given the right of inspection. The existence of that right in the SOFA would act as a deterrent. He pointed out that there is a difference between possession of a right and not exercising it and not having the right at all.

5. Mr. Habib stated that apparently the Korean side had in mind what is known in the United States as "spot inspection" of parcels. He also understood Mr. Hwang's comments to mean that the Korean side is concerned that the distribution of mail not be held up by any system of inspection which might be established. He pointed out that the U.S. authorities felt very strongly that the mail should not pile up because of delays caused by such inspection. He said he believed Mr. Hwang's comments to indicate that the Korean side has no intention of delaying the delivery of mail. Mr. Hwang replied that this was the correct interpretation of his remarks.

6. Mr. Habib stated that, with the understanding that the Korean authorities had no intention or desire to delay the distribution of mail to the U.S. armed forces, the U.S. side was prepared to modify the language of paragraph 5(b) in the U.S. draft to read as follows:

> "5(b). Official documents under official seal and First Class mail in United States military postal channels under official postal seal;"

He added that it was also the [illegible] the U.S. negotiators that the Korean

0185

side was proposing that inspection would take place at the individual postal units and not at the ports of entry. He stated that the proposed change in language would provide to the Korean authorities a right that they would not exercise except as deemed necessary and through the exercise of which they would not interfere with the prompt delivery of mail. He said the details of administering this provision of the SOFA could be worked out by the Joint Committee.

7. Mr. Hwang stated that it was the understanding of the Korean side that: (1) there would be no inspection of official letters or personal letters; (2) Korean customs officials would have the right to inspect parcels; and (3) there would be no inspection at the ports of entry.

8. Mr. Habib said that what is known in the United States as "parcel post" is not first class mail. The great bulk of the packages come as parcel post. Mr. Hwang stated that the Korean side understood that first class mail excluded parcels and consisted only of letter mail.

9. Mr. Habib replied that this was not the case and that it is possible for parcels to be sent as first class mail, although unusual. He explained that the system described by the revised language just proposed by the U.S. side was actually the system which is in effect in Japan, although it is not spelled out specifically in the SOFA with Japan. In practice, this is the system which has evolved in Japan, through arrangements made with the Japanese authorities.

10. Mr. Hwang inquired whether there is any limitation on the size of parcels which may be included in first class mail. Mr. Habib replied that there are limitations on the size of parcels, which he did not have immediately available at the meeting but would procure for the information of the Korean side. He pointed out that there is also a very real limitation imposed by the postal rates, which are higher for first class mail than for parcel post. As a result, it is so expensive to send parcels by first class mail that very few are sent. He promised to report

0186

at a subsequent meeting on the size limitations.

11. Mr. Hwang then asked whether there was any difference in the markings which appear on the various classes of mail. Mr. Habib replied in the affirmative. Mr. Hwang stated that the Korean side would give its views on the U.S. proposal after receiving more information about size limitations and methods of marking.

Non-Appropriated Funds

12. The negotiators then turned their attention to the Article dealing with Non-Appropriated Fund Organizations. Mr. Habib said that before beginning paragraph by paragraph discussion, the U.S. side wished to make a general statement regarding the role of non-appropriated fund activities in the U.S. armed forces, in an effort to clarify the nature and scope of these activities. He pointed out that the non-appropriated fund activities are an integral and essential part of the United States armed forces worldwide and of their civilian component abroad. Although in many countries, such activities are covered by appropriated funds, in the U.S. armed forces they are carried out through the use of non-appropriated funds. This difference in structure does not in any way make the non-appropriated fund activities any less an integral part of the U.S. armed forces. Such forces are designed to promote and provide a well-rounded morale, welfare, and recreational program for the armed forces and their civilian component. The U.S. side feels sure, Mr. Habib continued, that the ROK Government agrees that such activities, which help to insure the mental and physical well being of U.S. personnel in Korea (in connection with our mutual defense of the Republic of Korea,) is in the interests of both the ROK and U.S. Governments. The U.S. side wished to point out again that the key words in paragraph 1(a) of the U.S. draft of this article are the words: "authorized and regulated by U.S. military authorities". These words should provide the necessary assurance to the ROK side that activities covered in the article include only those officially

0187

authorized and regulated by U.S. military authorities. Such activities are under the close, and continuing supervision of these authorities, just as are the appropriated fund activities. As an example, Mr. Habib called the attention of the Korean side to the case of an officers' club and a company mess. The former is a non-appropriated fund activity while the latter is an appropriated fund activity, and yet the supervision, control, and regulation is as close for one as for the other. There is nothing strange about these activities, he continued. They are normal activities to which the troops of any military force are entitled.

13. Mr. Hwang replied that as a result of Mr. Habib's explanation, the Korean side clearly understood the nature and scope of the non-appropriated fund organizations. The Korean side agreed that such organizations were very necessary for the morale and welfare of the members of the U.S. armed forces. He stated that both sides recognized and accepted the fundamental spirit and intention of this article. The Korean side, he said, was not trying to interfere with, or cause unnecessary inconvenience to, non-appropriated fund organizations. However, the Korean side had maintained that ROK customs authorities should be authorized to inspect goods imported by these organizations. This was not intended as interference in their operation. The Korean side had explained again and again that it is necessary for the Korean customs authorities to know the quantity of goods imported because of the current state of the Korean economy. The proposal that customs inspection be authorized was made not because of a lack of understanding on the part of the Korean side but because of the state of the Korean economy.

14. Mr. Habib replied that agreement had already been reached in principle that the amount of goods imported by these activities should be limited to reasonable quantities. He pointed out that the only place where this question arises in this article is in paragraph 4 of the Korean draft. The language of this paragraph is identical with the language of Agreed Minute #1 to the Customs Article, U.S. draft. The U.S. side believed that there was no point in having identical wording appear in

0188

two different articles. Since this provision appeared to be more appropriate for inclusion in the customs article, and since agreement had already been reached regarding that particular Agreed Minute, it appeared unnecessary to include this paragraph in this article.

15. Mr. Hwang replied that since the wording was duplicative, the Korean side agreed to the deletion of paragraph 4 from the Korean draft of this article.

16. Mr. Habib stated that recent discussion of the Customs Article indicated a desire on the part of the Korean authorities to inspect goods imported for the non-appropriated fund activities in order to insure that only "reasonable quantities" of such goods were imported. He said that the U.S. side was not prepared to agree that Korean authorities shall decide what constitutes a "reasonable quantity". The normal cooperative relationship prevailing between the U.S. armed forces and the Korean authorities would lead the Korean authorities to call for consultation should they wish to verify whether or not this provision of the SOFA was working. The U.S. side believed that it would be unworkable and unreasonable for the Korean authorities to attempt to determine unilaterally what are reasonable quantities. The U.S. armed forces have highly trained specialists in logistics and supply who carefully monitor the flow of military cargoes into Korea. It would be contrary to the interests and desires of the U.S. armed forces to bring in more imports than are reasonably required, for to do so would only result in uneconomical operation and supply maladjustments. The Korean side must assume that the U.S. armed forces operate these activities in good faith. The U.S. side is quite prepared to agree to a limitation in the Customs Article to "reasonable quantities". There is a mechanism provided in the SOFA to enable either side to make sure that the other side lives up to the Agreement. The U.S. side is convinced that the ROK authorities do not have sufficient personnel, the capability, or the desire to make a unilateral determination of what constitutes

0189

reasonable quantities. What both sides are trying to do is to draft an Agreement which will provide the framework which will enable each side to protect its interests. There should be no ambiguity in the language of the Agreement.

17. Mr. Hwang expressed agreement with the final point made by Mr. Habib. He said that in the view of the Korean side the determination of what consituted a reasonable quantity would be based on the annual consumption rate of the average American family, not the average Korean family. The Korean side appreciated the intention of the U.S. side to live up to the terms of Agreed Minute #1 of the Customs Article. However, goods imported for the non-appropriated fund organizations of the U.S. armed forces were actually on sale in Korean markets. This would not be the case, in the view of the Korean side, if these goods were imported in the quantities actually required. Therefore, the Korean customs authorities should be enabled to confirm that the quantity imported is limited to the amounts which are reasonably required.

18. Mr. Habib replied that the two sides appeared to be discussing two different subjects. He said the U.S. side wholeheartedly shared the desire of the Korean officials to prevent such goods from being channelled into the Korean black market. The U.S. armed forces do everything possible to help check and prevent such diversions. However, the U.S. side did not agree that the way to accomplish this objective was to permit inspection of non-appropriated fund cargoes by the Korean customs authorities. The U.S. side has agreed to include provisions in the SOFA which will allow the prevention of black marketing of these goods, as well as black marketing of appropriated fund supplies and equipment. Did the Korean side wish the right to inspect cargoes of the latter type also? Non-appropriated fund cargoes are military cargoes. Diversion of military cargoes is a criminal act. In actual fact, Mr. Habib continued, the inspection of cargoes does not prevent black marketing. There are requirements on the part of the Korean authorities as well as on the part of the U.S. armed forces to control the people engaged in black marketing.

0190

The U.S. side was just as much concerned as the Korean side but was not prepared to agree to the inclusion of provisions in the SOFA which would provide no result in terms of the objective sought. An international agreement, he continued, is a set of principles which guides the parties in the carrying out of certain functions. In this present case, the SOFA was an agreement pertaining to the presence of the U.S. armed forces in the Republic of Korea.

19. Mr. Hwang thanked Mr. Habib for this presentation of the views of the U.S. side. He said that as a result of this exchange of views, each side understood the position of the other. He suggested that the negotiators proceed with a paragraph by paragraph discussion of the article. Mr. Habib agreed.

20. Mr. Hwang noted that since newspapers were the subject of paragraph 1(b), the word "newspapers" could be deleted from the U.S. draft of paragraph 1(a). Mr. Habib disagreed, pointing out that whereas paragraph 1(b) sets up certain conditions under which a newspaper can be sold to the general public, paragraph 1(a) provides the U.S. armed forces with the right to establish the newspaper. Therefore, "newspapers" should be retained in paragraph 1(a). In this connection, Mr. Habib noted that the U.S. side agreed to the suggestion made previously by the Korean side that the words "except as provided in paragraph 1(b)" be added to the end of the first sentence of paragraph 2 of the U.S. draft. Mr. Hwang agreed.

21. Mr. Hwang noted that the matter of "activities" versus "organizations" was dependent upon resolution of this question in other articles. Mr. Habib replied that the U.S. side desired to settle this matter. He said the U.S. side still did not understand why the Korean side objected to the word "activities". Was it because this word was not used in the SOFA with Japan?

22. Mr. Hwang replied that the view of the Korean side had been made clear at the last meeting. The word "organizations" is clearer in meaning to the Korean side and seemed more appropriate. The word "activities" is ambiguous.

23. Mr. Habib stated that the U.S. side believed "activities" to be a better word. However, the U.S. side was prepared to agree to "organizations" wherever it appears in the Agreement, if it removes ambiguity in the Korean translation, with the clear understanding in the record that the Korean side agrees that the word "organizations" in the Agreement includes all non-appropriated fund functions and entities described as "activities" by the U.S. armed forces. He pointed out that there was no question that both sides were talking about the same thing. Mr. Hwang agreed to this understanding.

24. Referring to the phrase "within the facilities and areas in use by the United States armed forces" in the Korean draft of paragraph 1(a), Mr. Hwang recalled that at the 21st negotiating meeting, the Korean side had suggested that whenever it is necessary to operate a temporary exchange outside of the facilities and areas, such an exchange should be established at the place agreed upon between the two governments through the Joint Committee.

25. Mr. Habib replied that the U.S. side had considered this proposal but believed that it would establish an extra administrative burden which would not gain anything for either side. If the question ever arose, he pointed out, it could be discussed by the Joint Committee. But the adoption of this Korean proposal would not facilitate the smooth functioning of the Agreement in any way. The practical experience gained by the U.S. armed forces in the functioning of the SOFA with Japan had shown that such a provision merely imposes an extra administrative burden.

26. Mr. Hwang stated that the Korean side agreed that this provision might create an unnecessary administrative burden. The Korean side agreed to the deletion of this language, with the understanding that such matters would be raised in the Joint Committee. Mr. Habib replied that they could be raised, if the Korean side had any question; however, it was not necessary to make it a requirement. If the Korean authorities wished to raise any question of this sort in the Joint Committee

0192

they were perfectly entitled to do so. Mr. Hwang stated that with that understanding, the Korean side agreed to the deletion of the phrase "within the facilities and areas in use by the United States armed forces".

27. Mr. Hwang stated that the Korean side wished to ~~delete~~ delete the word "exclusive" from the Korean draft of paragraph 1(a), with the understanding that ~~[illegible]~~ non-appropriated fund organizations might be utilized by members of the U.S. armed forces, their dependents, and others. The use of these organizations by "others" was defined elsewhere in the Agreement. Therefore, the word "exclusive" should be deleted in this paragraph. Mr. Habib agreed. Mr. Hwang noted that discussion of this article had not been completed but suggested that the negotiators move on to discuss the Article on Revision of the Agreement. Mr. Habib agreed.

Revision of the Agreement

28. Mr. Hwang asked whether the U.S. side wished to make any comment on the only substantive difference existing in this article - the use of the word "appropriate" or the word "diplomatic".

29. Mr. Habib stated that "appropriate" is the more usual phraseology. Obviously, the channel for revision will be determined by the two governments when the occasion for revision arises.

30. Mr. Hwang stated that the Korean side agreed to the use of the word "appropriate", with the understanding that negotiations for revision will normally take place through diplomatic channels, except for unusual cases. Mr. Habib agreed with this understanding. Full agreement was thereupon reached on the text of this article.

31. The next meeting was scheduled for December 19 at 2:00 p.m.

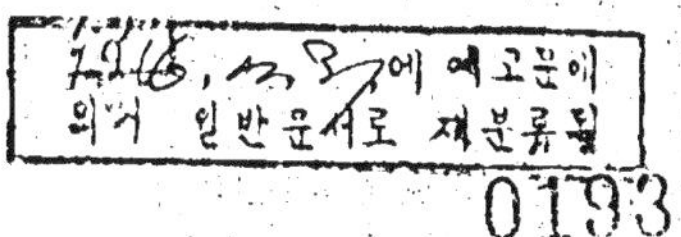


0193

JOINT SUMMARY RECORD OF THE 36TH SESSION

December 23, 1963

1. Time and Place: 3:00 to 5:00 p.m. December 5, 1963 at the Foreign Minister's Conference Room

| 미주과 | 담 당 | 과 장 | 국 장 | 특별보좌관 | 차 관 | 장 관 |
|---|---|---|---|---|---|---|
| 강고재 | | | | | | |

2. Attendants:

ROK Side:

| | |
|---|---|
| Mr. Whang Ho Eul | Director<br>Bureau of Political Affairs<br>Ministry of Foreign Affairs |
| Mr. Koo, Choong Whay | Chief, America Section<br>Ministry of Foreign Affairs |
| Mr. Park, Bong Chin | Chief, Customs Section<br>Ministry of Finance |
| Mr. Choo, Moon Ki | Chief, Legal Affairs Section<br>Ministry of Justice |
| Col. Kim, Won Kil | Chief, Military Affairs Section<br>Ministry of National Defence |
| Mr. Oh, Jae Hee | Chief, Treaty Section<br>Ministry of Foreign Affairs |
| Mr. Kang, Suk Jae (Rapporteur and interpreter) | 2nd Secretary<br>Ministry of Foreign Affairs |
| Mr. Cho, Kwang Jae | 2nd Secretary<br>Ministry of Foreign Affairs |
| Mr. Lee, Chung Bin | 3rd Secretary<br>Ministry of Foreign Affairs |

U.S. Side:

| | |
|---|---|
| Mr. Philip C. Habib | Counselor for Political Affairs<br>American Embassy |
| Brig. Gen. G. G. O'Connor | Deputy Chief of Staff<br>8th U.S. Army |
| Col. Howard Smigelor | Deputy Chief of Staff<br>8th U.S. Army |
| Mr. Benjamin A. Fleck (Rapporteur and Press Officer) | First Secretary<br>American Embassy |
| Col. L. J. Fuller | Staff Judge Advocate<br>United Nations Command |
| Capt. R. M. Brownlie | Assistant Chief of Staff<br>USN/K |

0194

| | |
|---|---|
| Mr. James Sartorius | 2nd Secretary<br>American Embassy |
| Mr. Robert A. Lewis | 2nd Secretary and Consul<br>American Embassy |
| Mr. Robert A. Kinney | J-5<br>8th U.S. Army |
| Maj. Robert D. Peckham | Staff Officer, JAG<br>8th U.S. Army |
| Mr. Kenneth Campen | Interpreter |

1. Mr. Whang opened the meeting by introducing Mr. Park Bong Chin, Chief of the Customs Section, Ministry of Finance, who was attending in place of Mr. Shin Kwan Sup, and two new members of the Korean negotiating team: Colonel Kim Won Kil, replacing Colonel Lee Nam Koo; and Mr. Oh Chae Hee, newly appointed Chief of the Treaty Section, Ministry of Foreign Affairs, replacing Mr. Shin Chung Sup. Mr. Habib welcomed these gentlemen to the negotiating table on behalf of the U.S, negotiators.

<u>Customs</u>

2. Taking up the Customs Article, Mr. Whang stated that it had been the subject of discussion at many previous meetings and many portions of it had been agreed upon. However, there still remained some paragraphs concerning which agreement had not yet been reached. He asked whether the U.S. side had any comment to make regarding any of these.

3. Mr. Habib replied that the U.S. side wished to confine duscussion of this article at this meeting to paragraph 5(b), which relates to mail. He recalled that at the previous meeting, the Korean side had indicated a particular interest in examining parcels because of concern over the possible importation of illegal items. The Korean side had indicated that the Korean authorities had no interest in examining the personal letter mail of the U.S. troops.

0195

The U.S. side had explained the manner in which the mail arrives in Korea - in sealed containers which are sent directly from the ports of entry to individual postal units, where they are opened and the mail distributed. He recalled further that the question of how the Korean authorities proposed to implement any right of inspection also came up. The U.S. side had inquired whether the Korean authorities intended to send customs inspectors to each of the individual postal units or, alternatively, planned to open the sealed containers at the ports of entry, thus disrupting the swift and efficient distribution system now in effect. He asked the Korean side to explain how they proposed to carry out any right of inspection.

4. Mr. Whang replied that initially the Korean authorities had intended to inspect parcels at the ports of entry. However, after hearing the explanation of how the mail is handled, given by the U.S. side at the previous meeting, the Korean authorities now realized that examination at the ports of entry would be inconvenient. They were thinking, therefore, in terms of dispatching customs inspectors to the individual postal units. However, the Korean authorities did not intend that the inspectors would examine every parcel. From the point of view of the Korean side, the important thing was that the Korean authorities be given the right of inspection. The existence of that right in the SOFA would act as a deterrent. He pointed out that there is a difference between possession of a right and not exercising it and not having the right at all.

5. Mr. Habib stated that apparently the Korean side had in mind what is known in the United States as "spot inspection" of parcels. He also understood Mr. Whang's comments to mean that the Korean side is concerned that the distribution of mail not be held up by any system of inspection which might be established. He pointed out that the U.S.

0196

authorities felt very strongly that the mail should not pile up because of delays caused by such inspection. He said he believed Mr. Whang's comments to indicate that the Korean side has no intention of delaying the delivery of mail. Mr. Whang replied that this was the correct interpretation of his remarks.

6. Mr. Habib stated that, with the understanding that the Korean authorities had no intention of desire to delay the distribution of mail to the U.S. armed forces, the U.S. side was prepared to modify the language of paragraph 5(b) in the U.S. draft to read as follows:

> "5(b). Official documents under official seal and First Class mail in United States military postal channels under official postal seal;"

He added that it was also the understanding of the U.S. negotiators that the Korean side was proposing that inspection would take place at the individual postal units and not at the ports of entry. He stated that the proposed change in language would provide to the Korean authorities a right that they would not exercise except as deemed necessary and through the exercise of which they would not interfere with the prompt delivery of mail. He said the details of administering this provision of the SOFA could be worked out by the Joint Committee.

7. Mr. Whang stated that it was the understanding of the Korean side that: (1) there would be no inspection of official letters or personal letters; (2) Korean customs officials would have the right to inspect parcels; and (3) there would be no inpsection at the ports of entry.

8. Mr. Habib said that what is known in the United States as "parcel post" is not first class mail. The great bulk of the packages come as parcel post. Mr. Whang stated that the Korean side understood that first class mail excluded parcles and consisted only of letter mail.

0197

9. Mr. Habib replied that this was not the case and that it is possible for parcels to be sent as first class mail, although unusual. He explained that the system described by the revised language just porposed by the U.S. side was actually the system which is in effect in Japan, although it is not spelled out specifically in the SOFA with Japan. In practice, this is the system which has evolved in Japan, through arrangements made with the Japanese authorities.

10. Mr. Whang inquired whether there is any limitation on the size of parcels which may be included in first class mail. Mr. Habib replied that there are limitations on the size of parcles, which he did not have immediately available at the meeting but would procure for the information of the Korean side. He pointed out that there is also a very real limitation imposed by the postal rates, which are higher for first class mail than for parcel post. As a result, it is so expensive to send parcels by first class mail that very few are sent. He promised to report at a subsequent meeting on the size limitations.

11. Mr. Whang then asked whether there was any difference in the markings which appear on the various classes of mail. Mr. Habib replied in the affirmative. Mr. Whang stated that the Korean side would give its views on the U.S. proposal after receiving more information about size limitations and methods of marking.

Non-Appropriated Funds

12. The negotiators then turned their attention to the Article dealing with Non-Appropriated Fund Organizations. Mr. Habib said that before beginning paragraph by paragraph discussion, the U.S. side wished to make a general statement regarding the role of non-appropriated fund activities in the U.S. armed forces, in an effort to clarify the nature

0198

and scope of these activities. He pointed out that the non-appropriated fund activities are an integral and essential part of the United States armed forces world-wide and of their civilian component abroad. Although in many countries, such activities are covered by appropriated funds, in the U.S. armed forces they are carried out through the use of non-appropriated funds. This difference in structure does not in any way make the non-appropriated fund activities any less an integral part of the U.S. armed forces. Such forces are designed to promote and provide a well-rounded morale, welfare, and recreational program for the armed forces and their civilian component.

The U.S. side feels sure, Mr. Habib continued, that the ROK Government agrees that such activities, which help to insure the mental and physical well being of U.S. personnel in Korea in connection with our mutual defense of the Republic of Korea is in the interests of both the ROK and U.S. Governments.

The U.S. side wished to point out again that the key words in paragraph 1 (a) of the U.S. draft of this article are the words : "authorized and regulated by U.S. military authorities". These words should provide the necessary assurance to the ROK side that activities covered in the article include only those officially authorized and regulated by U.S. military authorities. Such activities are under the close, and continuing supervision of these authorities, just as are the appropriated fund activities. As an example, Mr. Habib called the attention of the Korean side to the case of an officers culb and a company mess. The former is a non-appropriated fund activity while the latter is an appropriated fund activity, and yet the supervision, control, and regulation is as close for one as for the other. There is nothing strange about these activities, he continued. They are normal activities to which the troops of any military

0199

force are entitled.

13. Mr. Hwang replied that as a result of Mr. Habib's explanation, the Korean side clearly understood the nature and scope of the non-appropriated fund organizations. The Korean side agreed that such organizations were very necessary for the morale and welfare of the members of the U.S. armed forces. He stated that both sides recognized and accepted the fundamental spirit and intention of this article. The Korean side, he said, was not trying to interfere with, or cause unnecessary inconvenience to, non-appropriated fund organizations. However, the Korean side had maintained that ROK customs authorities should be authorized to inspect goods imported by these organizations. This was not intended as interference in their operation. The Korean side had explained again and again that it is necessary for the Korean customs authorities to know the quantity of goods imported because of the current state of the Korean economy. The proposal that customs inspection be authorized was made not because of a lack of understanding on the part of the Korean side but because of the state of the Korean economy.

14. Mr. Habib replied that agreement had already been reached in principle that the amount of goods imported by these activities should be limited to reasonable quantities. He pointed out that the only place where this question arises in this article is in paragraph 4 of the Korean draft. The language of this paragraph is identical with the language of Agreed Minute #1 to the Customs Article, U.S. draft. The U.S. side believed that there was no point in having identical wording appear in two different articles. Since

0200

this provision appeared to be more appropriate for inclusion in the customs article, and since agreement had already been reached regarding that particular Agreed Minute, it appeared unnecessary to include this paragraph in this article.

15. Mr. Hwang replied that since the wording was duplicative, the Korean side agreed to the deletion of paragraph 4 from the Korean draft of this article.

16. Mr. Habib stated that recent discussion of the Customs Article indicated a desire on the part of the Korean authorities to inspect goods imported for the non-appropriated fund activities in order to insure that only "reasonable quantities" of such goods were imported. He said that the U.S. side was not prepared to agree that Korean authorities shall decide what constitutes a "reasonable quantity". The normal cooperative relationship prevailing between the U.S. armed forces and the Korean authorities would lead the Korean authorities to call for consultation should they wish to verify whether or not this provision of the SOFA was working. The U.S. side believed that it would be unworkable and unreasonable for the Korean authorities to attempt to determine unilaterally what are reasonable quantities. The U.S. armed forces have highly trained specialists in logistics and supply who carefully monitor the flow of military cargoes into Korea. It would be contrary to the interests and desires of the U.S. armed forces to bring in more imports than are reasonably required, for to do so would only result in uneconomical operation and supply maladjustments. The Korean side must assume that the U.S. armed forces operate these activities in good faith. The U.S. side is quite prepared to agree to a limitation in the Customs Article to "reasonable quantities". There is a mechanism provided in the SOFA to enable either side to make sure that the

other side lives up to the Agreement. The U.S. side is convinced that the ROK authorities do not have sufficient personnel, the capability, or the desire to make a unilateral determination of what constitutes reasonable quantities. What both sides are trying to do is to draft an Agreement which will provide the framework which will enable each side to protect its interests. There should be no ambiguity in the language of the Agreement.

17. Mr. Hwang expressed agreement with the final point made by Mr. Habib. He said that in the view of the Korean side the determination of what consituted a reasonable quantity would be based on the annual consumption rate of the average American family, not the average Korean family. The Korean side appreciated the intention of the U.S. side to live up to the terms of Agreed Minute of the Customs Article. However, goods imported for the non-appropriated fund organizations of the U.S. armed forces were actually on sale in Korean markets. This would not be the case, in the view of the Korean side, if these goods were imported in the quantities actually required. Therefore, the Korean customs authorities should be enabled to confirm that the quantity imported is limited to the amounts which are reasonably required.

18. Mr. Habib replied that the two sides appeared to be discussing two different subjects. He said the U.S. side wholeheartedly shared the desire of the Korean officials to prevent such goods from being channelled into the Korean black market. The U.S. armed forces do everything possible to help check and prevent such diversions. However, the U.S. side did not agree that the way to accomplish this objective was to permit inspection of non-appropriated fund cargoes by

0202

the Korean customs authorities. The U.S. side has agreed to include provisions in the SOFA which will allow the prevention of black marketing of these goods, as well as black marketing of appropriated fund supplies and equipment. Did the Korean side wish the right to inspect cargoes of the latter type also? Non-appropriated fund cargoes are military cargoes. Diversion of military cargoes is a criminal act. In actual fact, Mr. Habib continued, the inspection of cargoes does not prevent black marketing. There are requirements on the part of the Korean authorities as well as on the part of the U.S. armed forces to control the people engaged in black marketing. The U.S. side was just as much concerned as the Korean side but was not prepared to agree to the inclusion of provisions in the SOFA which would provide no result in terms of the objective sought. An international agreement, he continued, is a set of principles which guides the parties in the carrying out of certain functions. In this present case, the SOFA was an agreement pertaining to the presence of the U.S. armed forces in the Republic of Korea.

19. Mr. Hwang thanked Mr. Habib for this presentation of the views of the U.S. side. He said that as a result of this exchange of views, each side understood the position of the other. He suggested that the negotiators proceed with a paragraph by paragraph discussion of the article. Mr. Habib agreed.

20. Mr. Hwang noted that since newspapers were the subject of paragraph 1 (b), the word "newspapers" could be deleted from the U.S. draft of paragraph 1 (a).
Mr. Habib disagreed, pointing out that whereas paragraph 1 (b) sets up certain conditions under which a newspaper can be sold to the general public, paragraph 1 (a) provides the U.S. armed forces with the right to establish the newspaper. Therefore, "newspapers" should be retained in paragraph 1 (a).

0203

In this connection, Mr. Habib noted that the U.S. side agreed to the suggestion made previously by the Korean side that the words "except as provided in paragraph 1 (b)" be added to the end of the first sentence of paragraph 2 of the U.S. draft. Mr. Hwang agreed.

21. Mr. Hwang noted that the matter of "activities" versus "organizations" was dependent upon resolution of this question in other articles. Mr. Habib replied that the U.S. side desired to settle this matter. He said the U.S. side still did not understand why the Korean side objected to the word "activities". Was it because this word was not used in the SOFA with Japan?

22. Mr. Hwang replied that the view of the Korean side had been made clear at the last meeting. The word "organizations" is clearer in meaning to the Korean side and seemed more appropriate. The word "activities" is ambiguous.

23. Mr. Habib stated that the U.S. side believed "activities" to be a better word. However, the U.S. side was prepared to agree to "organizations" wherever it appears in the Agreement, if it removes ambiguity in the Korean translation, with the clear understanding in the record that the Korean side agrees that the word "organizations" in the Agreement includes all non-appropriated fund functions and entities described as "activities" by the U.S. armed forces. He pointed out that there was no question that both sides were talking about the same thing. Mr. Hwang agreed to this understanding.

24. Referring to the phrase "within the facilities and areas in use by the United States armed forces" in the Korean draft of paragraph 1 (a), Mr. Hwang recalled that at the 21st negotiating meeting, the Korean side had suggested that whenever it is necessary to operate a temporary exchange outside of the facilities and areas, such an exchange should be established at the place agreed upon between the two

0204

governments through the Joint Committee.

25. Mr. Habib replied that the U.S. side had considered this proposal but believed that it would establish an extra administrative burden which would not gain anything for eigher side. If the question ever arose, he pointed out, it could be discussed by the Joint Committee. But the adoption of this Korean proposal would not facilitate the smooth functioning of the Agreement in any way. The practical experience gained by the U.S. armed forces in the functioning of the SOFA with Japan had shown that such a provision merely imposes an extra administrative burden.

26. Mr. Hwang stated that the Korean side agreed that this provision might create an unnecessary administrative burden. The Korean side agreeed to the deletion of this language, with the understanding that such matters would be raised in the Joint Committee. Mr. Habib replied that they could be raised, if the Korean side had any question; however it was not necessary to make it a requirement. If the Korean authorities wished to raise any question of this sort in the Joint Committee they were perfectly entitled to do so. Mr. Hwang stated that with that understanding, the Korean side agreed to the deletion of the phrase "within the facilities and areas in use by the United States armed forces."

27. Mr. Hwang stated that the Korean side wished to delete the word "exclusive" from the Korean draft of paragraph 1 (a), with the understanding that non-appropriated fund organizations might be utilized by members of the U.S. armed forces, their dependents, and others. The use of these organizations by "others" was defined elsewhere in the Agreement. Therefore, the word "exclusive" should be deleted in this paragraph . Mr. Habib agreed. Mr. Hwang noted that discussion of this article had not been completed but suggested that the negotiators move on to discuss the Article on Revision of the Agreement. Mr. Habib agreed.

0205

Revision of the Agreement

28. Mr. Hwang asked whether the U.S. side wished to make any comment on the only substantive difference existing in this article - the use of the word "appropriate" or the word " diplomatic".

29. Mr. Habib stated that "appropriate" is the more usual phraseology. Obviously, the channel for revision will be determined by the two governments when the occasion for revision arises.

30. Mr. Hwang stated that the Korean side agreed to the use of the word "appropriate", with the understanding that negotiations for revision will normally take place through diplomatic channels, except for unusual cases. Mr. Habib agreed with this understanding. Full agreement was thereupon reached on the text of this article.

31. The next meeting was scheduled for December 19 at 2:00 p.m.

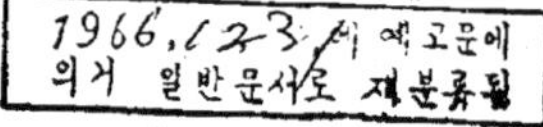

6. 제37차 회의, 12.27

0207

# 기 안 용 지

| 자 체 통 제 | | 기안처 | 미주과 강석재 | 전화번호 | 근거서류접수일자 |
|---|---|---|---|---|---|
| | 과장 | 국장 | 차관 | 장관 | |
| | 12/26 | 12/26 | | | |
| 관계관 서명 | 아주국장 (수석대표) 12/26 | | | | |
| 기안 년월일 | 1963. 12. 26 | 시행 년월일 | | 보존 년한 | 정 시 기 장 |
| 분류 기호 | | 전체 통제 | | 종결 | |
| 경유 수신 참조 | 건 의 | | | 발신 | |
| 제 목 | 제 37차 주둔군 지위협정 체결교섭회의에 임할 우리측 입장 | | | | |

12월 27일에 개최될 제37차 주둔군지위협정 체결 한미간 교섭회의에서는 비세출자금기관, 관세업무 및 군사우편에 관한 조문을 토의하도록 예정되고 있는바 이에 관하여 우리측 교섭 실무자는 12월 24일 회합을 갖고 제37차 회의에서 취할 우리측 태도를 별첨과 같이 결정하였아오니 재가하여 주시기 바랍니다.

유첨: 제37차 주둔군지위협정 체결교섭회의에 임할 우리측태도 끝

1966.12.31.에 예고문에 의거 일반문서로 재분류됨

보통문서로 재분류(1966. 12. 31)

승인서식 1-1-3 (11 00900-03) (195mm×265mm16절지)

0208

1. 비세출 자금 기관

가. 미국측 초안 (2) 항의 첫째 문장은 비세출 자금 기관에 의한 물품 혹은 용역의 판매에는 한국 세금을 부과치 않을 것을 규정하고 있는바 신문 판매에 관한 1 (b ) 항과 일치 시키기 위하여 제 21 차 회의에서 합의되고 36차에서 재확인된 " except as provided in paragraph 1 (b) " 라는 구절을 삽입 하기로 합의 본바 있다. 미국측 초안 (2) 항의 둘째 문장은 우리측 초안과 같이 한국 내에 있어서의 비세출 자금 기관에 의한 상품 및 보급품의 구매는 한국 조세에 따라야 할 것을 규정하고 있으나 " to which other purchasers of such merchandises and supplies are subject and at rates no less favorable than those imposed on other purchasers "

라는 구절을 첨가하고 있는바 이 구절은 (ㄱ) 한국 정부로서 실제에 있어서 불리한 세금을 부과할 의도가 없으며 (ㄴ) 물품 구매에 관한 한국 조세 제도는 간접 세법을 채택하고 있음으로 소비자에 따라 상위한 세율이 적용되는 일이 없으며 (ㄷ) 미일 협정에도 이러한 규정이 없으며 우리가 교섭중인 협정은 시행에 관한 세부적 사항을 합동 위원회의 조정에 맡기고 단지 원측적인 광범위한 테두리만을 규정하면 충분하다고 생각함으로 이와 같은 양해하에 동 구절을 협정 원문에서 삭제 할것을 주장한다.

나. 미국측 초안 (4) 항 및 우리측 초안 (5) 항은 비세출 자금 기관이 한국 조세법에 의하여 필요한 정보를 제공 할것을 규정하고 있는바 미국측 초안은 " after consultation between the representatives of the two Governments in the joint committee " 라는 구절을 삽입하고 있는바 (ㄱ) 대개의 경우 그러한 정보제공은 합동 위원회를 통하여 요구될것이며 (ㄴ) 또한 미국

0209

측이 제 21 차 회의시 염려를 표시한바와 같이 불필요한 정보를 요구하는 일이 없을 것임으로 동 구절을 삭제 할 것을 주장한다. 만약 미국측이 이에 응하지 않을 경우에는 " after consultation

" 을 " through consultation "

으로 변경하자는 대안을 제의한다.

다. 미국측 초안 (5)항은 미군대 구성원, 군속 및 그들의 가족외의 사람들에 의한 비세출 자금 기관의 사용 허용을 규정하고 있는바 우리측은 동 규정은 비세출 자금기관에 대한 예외적인 규정이며 또한 지나치게 복잡하고 중복되게 규정 되었다고 봄으로 (ㄱ) 첫째 이를 합의 의사록에서 규제하는 것이 더욱 적절하며 (ㄴ) 둘째 간결하게 규제할 것을 제의한다. 우리측은 본항에 관련하여 (ㄱ) 군계약자 조문 3 (d) 항에서 군계약자에 의한 비세출 자금 기관의 사용이 규제 되었음을 상기 시키고 아울러 (ㄴ) 미국측 초안의 " personnel..... ordinarily accorded such privileges " 와 또한 " such organizations 라는 구절에는 어떠한 사람들이 혹은 기관들이 포함되는지 구체적으로 열거 해 줄것을 요구한다.

2. 관세업무

가. 미군대의 공용과 군대 구성원, 군속 및 그들의 가족들의 사용을 위한 물자, 보급품 및 장비의 무세통관을 규정하는 미국측 초안 (2) 항에서 문제가 되고 있는점은 비세출 자금 기관 조문에 있어서 미국측은 우리측의 원래의 요구대로 " organizations " 로 할것에 동의한바 있음으로 본항도 역시 " organizations " 로 하여 미국측 초안을 수락하기로 한다.

나. 관세 조항중 기타 미합의 사항은 미국측 초안 3 (b) 항, 5 항의 (a) (b) 및 (c) 항과 합의 의사록 2 및 3 항인바 먼저

0210

우편물 검사 면제에 관한 5 (b) 항을 토의하기로 제의한다.

제 36 차 회의에서 미국측은 5 (b) 항을 " official documents under official seal and First Class mail in United States military postal channels under official postal seal " 로 하자는 대안을 제안 하였는바 우리측이 지난 회의에서 문의 한바와 같이 "first class mail " 에 포함될수 있는 소포에 적용되는 규격이나 표식상의 제한에 관한 미국측의 설명을 요구하기로 하고 동 설명에 따라 미국측대안에 대한 우리측의 입장을 결정하도록 한다.

다. 세관 검사 면제에 관한 규정중 5 (c) 항의 군사화물에 관한 검사 면제문제에 있어서 우리측은 이미 합의를 본 미국측 조안 (6) 항 즉 무세로 수입된 물품은 상호 합의된 조건에 의거 한미 당국에 의하여 그 처분이 허가되는 경우를 제외하고는 그러한 물품을 무세로 수입할 권한이 없는자에게 처분할수 없다는 규정에 위배하여 처분하였을 경우에는 한국 관세법에 적용을 받는다는 것을 적절한 항에 추가 규제 (또는 그와 같은 양해를 얻거나 혹은 관세조문 제 (1) 항을 그와 같이 해석할수 있다는 유보하에) 할것을 주장하고 미국측이 이 제의에 응한다면 세관 검사 면제에 관한 미국측안을 수락하도록 한다. 단 이경우 미국측 합의 의사록 3 항은 군사 화물은 공인된 조달 기관 및 비세출 자금 기관을 포함한 미군대에 탁송된 모든 화물을 망라하도록 규제하고 있음으로 5 (c) 항에있는 " including their authorized procurement agencies and their non-appropriated fund organizations provided for in Article " 란 구절을 삭제하도록 제의한다.

다. 만약 전기 (다) 와 같은 우리측 입장을 미국측이 수락 한다면 (7) 한국에 출입하는 미군대 구성원에 대한 세관검사는 미국측

0211

안대로 " members " 로 할것에 동의하여 (ㄴ) 미국측 합의 의사록 (2) 및 (3) 항도 수락하기로 한다.

마. 차량및 부속품의 무세수입에 관한 미국측 초안 3 (b ) 항에 관하여 우리측은 종래 부속품에 대해서는 시간적 제한을 가하지 않을 것이나 차량의 무세수입은 한국에 도착후 6 개월내에 수입하는 차량에 한하도록 주장하여 왔는바 만약 우편물 검사 면제 규정인 5 (b ) 항이 우리측 요구대로 만족 스럽게 해결될 경우에는 우리측은 3 (b ) 항의 차량및 부속품의 무세수입에 관하여 미국측 초안대로 수락하기로한다.

3. 군사우편

미국측 초안 (2) 항은 통상 해외에서 그러한 특권이 부여된 미국 정부 관리 및 그들의 가족들도 군사 우편 시설을 이용할수 있도록 규정하고 있는바 제 19 차 회의에서 양측은 본 규정은 예외적인 규정임으로 본문 대신에 합의 의사록에 넣도록 할것에 합의한바 있다. 우리측은 먼저 미국측 초안에 " their dependents " 란 구절을 포함시킨 이유를 묻기로 하고 미국측이 계속 동 구절의 삽입을 원할 경우에는 그들의 가족도 군사 우편을 이용할수 있다는 양해를 회의 기록에 남기도록 하고 본 문장에서는 삭제 할 것을 주장한다.

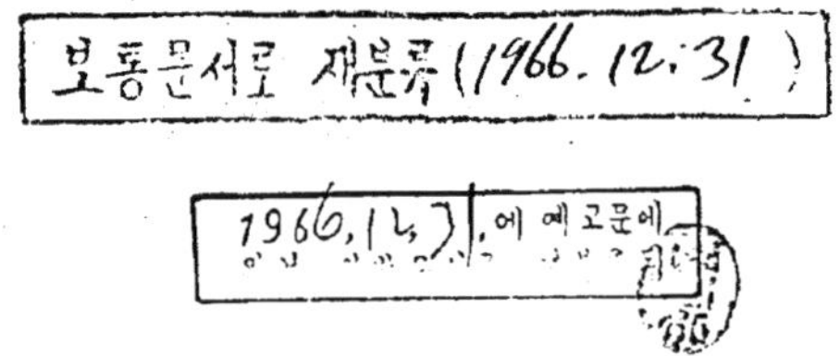


0212

## SOFA NEGOTIATION

### Agenda for the 37th Session

15:00, December 27, 1963

1. Continuation of Discussions on:
   a. Non-Appropriated Fund Organizations Article
   b. Customs Article
   c. Military Post Offices Article
2. Other Business
3. Agenda and Date of the Next Meeting
4. Press Release

0213

제이안. Dec 27, 1963.

AGREED MINUTE

The United States Armed Forces may grant the use of the organizations referred to in paragraph 1 of Article to: (a) other officers or personnel of the United States Government ordinarily accorded such privileges; (b) those other non-Korean Armed Forces in Korea under the Unified Command which receive logistical support from the United States Armed Forces, and their members; (c) those non-Korean persons whose presence in the Republic of Korea is solely for the purpose of providing contract services financed by the United States Government; (d) those organizations which are present in the Republic of Korea primarily for the benefit and service of the United States Armed Forces, such as the American Red Cross and the United Service Organizations, and their non-Korean personnel; (e) dependents of the foregoing; and (f) other persons and organizations with the express consent of the Government of the Republic of Korea.

0214

5. The activities referred to in paragraph 1 may be used by other officers or personnel of the United States Government ordinarily accorded such privileges, by non-Korean persons whose presence in Korea is solely for the purpose of providing contract services financed by the United States Government, by the dependents of the foregoing, by organizations which are present in the Republic of Korea primarily for the benefit and service of the United States armed forces personnel, such as the American Red Cross and the United Service Organizations, and by the non-Korean personnel of such organizations and their dependents.

0215

## Non-Appropriated Fund Activities Article

Suggested Paragraph 1 (b):

(b) When a newspaper authorized and regulated by the United States military authorities is sold to the general public, it shall be subject to Korean regulations, licenses, fees, taxes or similar controls so far as such circulation is concerned.

0216

ARTICLE ____

1. Persons, including corporations, their employees, and the dependents of such persons, present in Korea solely for the benefit of the United States armed forces or other armed forces in Korea under the Unified Command receiving logistical support from the United States armed forces, who are designated by the Government of the United States in accordance with the provisions of paragraph 2 below, shall, except as provided in this Article, be subject to the laws and regulations of Korea.

2. The designation referred to in paragraph 1 above shall be made upon consultation with the Government of Korea and shall be restricted to cases where open competitive bidding is not practicable due to security considerations, to the technical qualifications of the contractors involved, to the unavailability of materials or services required by United States standards, or to limitations of United States law. The designation shall be withdrawn by the Government of the United States:

(a) Upon completion of contracts with the United States for the United States armed forces or other armed forces in Korea under the Unified Command receiving ligistical support from the United States armed forces:

0217

(b) Upon proof that such persons are engaged in business activities in Korea other than those pertaining to the United States armed forces or other armed forces in Korea under the Unified Command receiving logistical support from the United States armed forces;

(c) Upon proof that such persons are engaged in practices illegal in Korea.

3. Upon certification by appropriate United States authorities as to their identity, such persons shall be accorded the following benefits of this Agreement:

(a) Rights of accession and movement, as provided for Article , paragraph 2;

(b) Entry into Korea in accordance with the provisions of Article ;

(c) The exemption from customs duties, and other such charges provided for in Article , paragraph 3, for members of the United States armed forces, the civilian component, and their dependents;

(d) If authorized by the Government of the United States, the right to use the services of the activities provided for in Article ;

(e) Those rights provided in Article , paragraph 2, for members of the United States armed forces, the civilian component, and their dependents;

0218

(f) If authorized by the Government of the United States, the right to use military payment certificates, as provided for in Article ;

(g) The use of postal facilities provided for in Article ;

(h) Those rights accorded the United States armed forces by Article , paragraph 3, relating to utilities and services;

(i) Those rights provided to members of the United States armed forces, the civilian component, and their dependents by Article , relating to driving permits and registration of vehicles;

(j) Exemption from the laws and regulations of Korea with respect to terms and conditions of employment, and licensing and registration of businesses and corporations.

4. The arrival, departure, and place of residence in Korea of such persons shall from time to time be notified by the United States armed forces to the Korean authorities.

5. Upon certification by an authorized representative of the United States armed forces, depreciable assets, except houses, held, used or transferred by such persons exclusively for the execution of contracts referred to in paragraph 1 shall not be subject to taxes or similar charges of Korea.

0219

# 기 안 용 지

| 자체 통제 | | 기안처 | 미주과 강석재 | 전화번호 | 근거서류접수일자 |
|---|---|---|---|---|---|
| | 과장 | 국장 | 차관 | 장관 | |
| 관계관 서명 | 아주국장 조약과장 | | | | |
| 기안 년월일 | 1964.1.4 | 시행 년월일 | | 보존 년한 | 정서기장 |
| 분류 기호 | 외정미 722.2 | 전체 통제 | | 종결 | |
| 경유 수신 참조 | 대통령(참조 비서실장) 국무총리 | | | 발신 | 장관 |
| 제목 | 주둔군지위협정 체결을 위한 제37차 교섭회의 보고 | | | | |

1. 1963. 12. 27 하오 2시부터 4시10분까지 외무부 회의실에서 개최된 제37차 주둔군지위협정 체결교섭회의에서 토의된 내용을 별첨과 같이 보고합니다.

2. 주둔군지위협정 체결을 위한 교섭회의 보고서는 종래 매 회의 종료후 정기적으로 외무국방위원장 참조 국가재건 최고회의 의장 (국무총리앞 공한── 내각수반) 앞으로 제출하여 왔음을 첨언 합니다.

유첨: 제37차 교섭회의 보고서 1부 끝

승인서식 1-1-3 (11-00000-03) (195mm×265mm16절지)

1966, 12, 31에 예고문에 의거 일반문서로 재분류됨

0220

외 무 부

외정미 722.2 1964. 1. 8

수 신: 대 통 령

참 조: 비 서 실 장

제 목: 주둔군지위협정 체결을 위한 제37차 교섭회의 보고

1. 1963. 12. 27 하오 2시부터 4시10분까지 외무부 회의실에서 개최된 제37차 주둔군지위협정 체결 교섭회의에서 토의된 내용을 별첨과 같이 보고합니다.

2. 주둔군지위협정 체결을 위한 교섭회의 보고서는 매 회의 종료후 정기적으로 외무국방 위원장 참조 국가재건 최고회의 의장앞으로 제출하여 왔음을 첨언합니다.

유첨: 제37차 교섭회의 보고서 1부 끝

외 무 부 장 관 정 일 권

0221

# 외 무 부

외정미 722.2　　　　　　　　　　　　1964. 1. 8

수 신: 국 무 총 리

제 목: 주둔군 지위협정 체결을 위한 제37차 교섭회의 보고

1. 1963. 12. 27. 하오2시부터 4시10분까지 외무부 회의실에서 개최된 제37차 주둔군지위협정 체결 교섭회의에서 토의된 내용을 별첨과 같이 보고합니다.

2. 주둔군지위협정 체결을 위한 교섭회의 보고서는 종전 매 회의 종료후 정기적으로 내각수반앞으로 제출하여 왔음을 첨언합니다.

유첨: 제37차 교섭회의 보고서　1부　끝

외 무 부 장 관　정 일 권

0222

제 37 차

한미간 주둔군 지위협정 체결 실무자회의

보 고 서

1. 일 시: 1963년 12월 27일 하오 2시부터 4시10분까지

2. 장 소: 외무부 장관실

3. 참석자 : 한국측: 황 호 을 (외무부 아주국장)

장 상 문 (외무부 구미국장)

구 충 회 (외무부 미주과장)

박 봉 진 (재무부 감정과장)

주 문 기 (법무부 법무과장)

김 원 길 대령 (국방부 군무과장)

오 재 히 (외무부 조약과장)

강 석 재 (외무부 외무서기관)

이 근 팔 (외무부 외무사무관)

이 정 빈 (외무부 외무사무관)

미국측: "지.지. 오크나"준장을 제외한 교섭대표 전원

4. 토의사항:

가. 비세출자금 기관

(1) 미국측 초안 (2)항의 둘째문장은 "비세출 자금기관에 의한 물품의 구매는 한국조세에 따라야 할것"을 규정하고 있는바 to which other purchasers of such merchandises and supplies are subject and at rates no less favorable than those imposed on other purchasers 라는 부대적 구절을 포함하고 있음으로 우리측은 이구절에 관하여 (ㄱ) 한국정부는 비세출자금기관에 의한 물품의 구매에 불리한 세금을 부과하지 않고 있어며 또한 앞으로도 과할 의도가 없어며 (ㄴ) 물품구매에 관한 한국의 조세제도는 간접세법을 채택하고 있기 때문에 소비자에 따라서 각각 상위한 조세율이 적용되는 일이 없으며 (ㄷ) 협정에서는 원측적인

63-1-178

0223

63-1-30(6)

미각문 108-1(6)

0224

광범위한 테두리만을 규제하고 세부적 사항은 합동 위원회의 조정에 맡기면 됨으로 동구절을 협정 원문에서 삭제할것을 주장하였다.
미국측은 한국정부가 불리한 세율을 과하지 않고 있으며 또한 차별적인 세율이 적용되는 일이 없는 간접세법을 채택하고 있다는점에 감사하고 만약 한국정부의 의도와 제도가 그렇다면 미국측의 부대적 구절을 삭제하지 않고 그대로 두는것이 좋지 않느냐고 주장하였다.

(2) 우리측은 협정에 모든 상세한 사항을 전부 규제하기는 곤란하며 세부적 사항은 합동위원회의 조정에 맡기기로 하고 원측적인 테두리만 규정하면 족하다고 생각함으로 한국정부가 차별적인 세율을 과하지 않을것이라는 양해를 기록에 남기고 동구절은 원문에서 삭제 할것을 재차 주장하였으나 미국측은 현재 실시중에 있는 한국의 조세법이 장차 변경되지 않으리라는 보장은 없으며 또한 미국측 초안의 부대적 구절이 결코 세부적 사항에 속하는 것이아니며 오히려 원측문제인 것이라고 답변하였다. 양측은 상호의 입장을 재 고려한후 다음회의에서 이문제를 계속 토의하기로 합의하였다.

(3) 미국측 초안 4항 (우리측 초안 5항에 해당) 은 비세출 자금기관이 한국 조세법에 의하여 필요한 정보를 제공하여야 할것을 규정하고 있는바 " after consultation between the representatives of the two Governments in the Joint Committee "라는 구절을 첨가하고 있음으로 이에 관하여 우리측은 (ㄱ) 대개의 경우 그러한 정보제공은 합동위원회를 통하여 요청될것이며 (ㄴ) 또한 미국측이 염려하고 있는것 처럼 불필요한 정보의 제공을 요구하지 않을것임으로 동구절을 원문에서 삭제하자고 요구하였던바 미국측은 동구절은 정보제공을 거부하는 것이 아니며 정보제공을 용의하게 하기위하여 필요하다고 본다고 답변하였다.
우리측은 그러면 " After consultation "을 "through consultation "로 변경하자고 제의하였으나 미국측은 협의라고 함은 결코 합의를 뜻하는 것이 아니라고 말하고 계속하여 그러한 견지사로서는 " upon "이나 혹은 " by "등 여러 가지 단어를

0225

67-1-17

63-1-30 미·문108-1

0226

고려할수 있으나 의미에 있어서 모두 대동소이하다고 말하였다. 우리측은 동구절을 " upon request by the Republic of Korea through the Joint Committee "란 구절로 대치하는 것이 어떠냐고 제의하였으나 양측은 이문제를 좀더 연구하여 다음회의에서 토의할것에 합의하였다.

(4) 미국측 초안 (5)항은 미국군대 구성원, 군속 및 그들의 가족외의 사람들에 의한 비세출자금기관의 사용 허용을 규정하고 있는바 우리측은 동규정은 (ㄱ) 비세출자금기관에 대한 예외적인 규정이며 (ㄴ) 또한 지나치게 복잡하고 중복되게 규정되고 있음을 지적하고 따라서 이를 합의 의사록에 간결하게 규제함이 적절하다고 주장하였다. 미국측은 이점에 관하여 미국측도 그점에 관해 고려한바 있다고 말하고동규정을 합의의사록으로 새로 수정하여 제안하는 바이라고 설명하고 별첨과 같은 합의 의사록을 수교하였다. 미국측은 새로 수교한 합의의사록은 매우 정확하고 명확히 규정되어 있어며 이에 관하여 약간의 설명을 하겠다고 전제하고 동 합의 의사록의 범주 ( b )속에는 미군으로 부터 병참지원을 받는 유엔군 사령부 소속 인원이 포함되며 범주 ( c )속에는 군 계약자외에 주한 원조기관의 계약자도 포함되며 범주 ( f )속에는 UNCURK 및 UNTAB 등과 같은 유엔 전문기구와 그간 장기간동안 관례적으로 비세출자금기관의 이용이 허용되었던 외교관, 한미재단, 몇 Scandinavian Medical Mission ~~및 International Social Service~~ 와 같은 단체들도 포함되어 있는바 이들의 비세출자금기관 이용문제는 대단히 미묘한 문제이며 미국측으로서나 한국정부로서도 신중히 다루어야 할 성질의 것임으로 이들 인원 및 단체는 한국정부의 명시적 동의가 있을 경우에 한하여 비세출자금기관의 이용이 허용될것이라는 점을 설명하였다. 우리측은 미국측의 설명에 이어 범주 ( a ) 및 ( d ) 에 포함될 사람과 기관들을 구체적으로 망라하여 줄것을 요구하였던바 미국측은 범부 ( a )속에는 대사관 및 "유 솜"의 비한국인 고용자, 무관 및 그 신분이 별도 협정에서 규제되고 있는 군사 고문단등이 포함되며 범주 ( d )에는 미국적십자 및 USO 외에 현재로서는 해당이 없으나

63-1-180

0227

63-1-30

미.문 1841

0228

장차 다른 기관이 포함될수도 있다고 답변하여 왔다. 양측은 이에 관하여 검토를 한후 다음회의에서 계속 토의할것에 합의 하였다.

나. 관세 업무

(1) 미군대의 공용과 군대구성원, 군속 및 그들의 가족들의 사용을 위한 물자, 보급품 및 장비의 무세통관을 규정하는 미국측 초안 (2)항에 관하여 우리측은 이미 비세출자금기관 조문에서 합의를 본바와 같이 본항에 나타나 있는 "비세출자금기관"의 용어도 "organizations" 로 하는데 합의한다면 미국측 초안을 수락할 용의가 있음을 제의하였던바 미국측은 우리측 제의에 동의하여 양측은 미국측 초안 (2)항에 완전 합의하였다.

(2) 우편물 세관검사 면제에 관한 5(b)항에 있어서 미국측은 제36차 회의에서 " official documents under official seal and First Class mail in United States military postal channels under official seal "로 하자는 대안을 제안하였으며 우리측은 "first class mail "범주속에 포함될 소포에 적용되는 규격 및 표식상의 제한과 차이에 관한 설명을 요구한바 있었다. 미국측은 이에 관하여 "first class mail " 로서의 소포는 무게에 있어서 70 파운드로 제한되어 있으며 등급 표식이 있고 타 우편물과는 별도 포장으로 송달되며 료금도 서신 우편물과 같이 1온수당 5 센트이다. 따라서 10파운드에 약 미화 8불이 소요되며 보통 소포료금과는 엄청난 차이가 있음으로 대개의 경우는 일반 소포로서 이용하게 될것이라는 설명이 있었다.

63-1-181

(3) 이에 관하여 미국측은 한국세관 검사당국은 (ㄱ) 출입국 항구나 공항에서 우편물 검사를 실시하지 않을 것이며 (ㄴ) first class mail "를 제외한 소포검사의 권한을 가지메 부득이 필요한 경우에만 검사를 하며 모든 우편물에 대하여 전부 검사를 실시하지 않으며 (ㄷ) 부당하게 우편물의 배달을 지연시키지 않는다는 등의 양해사항을 되풀이 하였다. 우리측은 소포검사를 32개소의 " mail distribution center "대신에 17개소의 " main military postal offices "에서 실시할것을 제의하였던바

0229

63-1-30 미·도 1081

0230

미국측은 그러한 세부사항은 합동위원회에서 조정키로 하자는 답변이 있었다.

(4) 군사화물의 세관검사에 관한 5( c )항에 있어서 우리측은 이미 합의를 본 미국측 초안 (6)항 즉 "무세로 수입된 물품은 상호 합의된 조건에 의거 한미당국에 의하여 그처분이 허가된 경우를 제외하고는 그러한 물품을 무세로 수입할 권한이 없는자에게 처분할수 없다"라는 규정에 위배하여 처분하였을 경우에는 한국 관세법의 적용을 받는다는 것을 적절한 항에 추가 규제할것을 제의하였던바 미국측은 이미 합의를 본 합의의사록 4 및 5항은 그러한 위반행위에 관하여 규제하고 있다고 지적하였다. 우리측은 허가되지 않은자에 대한 처벌은 물론이지만 그러한 물품을 허가되지 않은자에 처분한 미국인도 한국 관세법에 적용받아야한다는 점을 강조하였던바 미국측은 허가되지 않은 자에 대한 관할권은 물론 한국측에 있어며 또한 불법적인 처분을 한 사람은 본 협정에서 별도 규제하지 않는한 접수국법의 존중, 형사 재판관할권 및 미군대규칙에 적용받게 될것이라고 답변하였다.

(5) 우리측은 계속하여 합의의사록 3항은 "군사화물이란 무기나 장비뿐만 아니라 공인된 조달기관 및 비세출자금기관을 포함한 미국군대에 탁송되는 모든 화물을 의미한다"라고 상세히 규제하고 있음으로 중복을 피하기 위하여 " including their authorized procurement agencies and their non-appropriated fund organizations provided for in Article ______"
이란 구절을 삭제할것을 주장하였는바 미국측은 이에 동의하면서 다음회의까지 우리측의 제의를 고려하겠다고 답변하였다.

5. 중요 합의 사항: 없음

6. 기타 사항:

차기회의 일자: 1964년 1월 9일 하오 2시

차기회의 의제: 차기회의시까지 양측 대표간에 합의된 사항

63-1-182

1966,12,31에 예고문에 의거 일반문서로 재분류됨

0231

63-1-30

미올 1087

0232

AGREED MINUTE

The United States Armed Forces may grant the use of the organizations referred to in paragraph 1 of Article to: (a) other officers or personnel of the United States Government ordinarily accorded such privileges; (b) those other non-Korean Armed Forces in Korea under the Unified Command which receive logistical support from the United States Armed Forces, and their members; (c) those non-Korean persons whose presence in the Republic of Korea is solely for the purpose of providing contract services financed by the United States Government; (d) those organizations which are present in the Republic of Korea primarily for the benefit and service of the United States Armed Forces, such as the American Red Cross and the United Service Organizations, and their non-Korean personnel; (e) dependents of the foregoing; and (f) other persons and organizations with the express consent of the Government of the Republic of Korea.

63-1-183 (조)



0233

[illegible]-1-30(6)

미국·물 108-1 (6)

0234

STATUS OF FORCES NEGOTIATIONS: 37th Meeting

SUBJECTS: 1. Non-Appropriated Fund Organizations
2. Customs

PLACE: Ministry of Foreign Affairs

DATE: December 27, 1963

PARTICIPANTS:

| Republic of Korea | United States |
|---|---|
| HWANG Ho-ul | Philip C. Habib |
| CHANG Sang-mun | Colonel Howard G. Smigelow, USA |
| KU Chung-hwe | Captain R. M. Brownlie, USN |
| Colonel KIM Won-kil, ROKA | Colonel L. J. Fuller, USA |
| O Chae-hi | Benjamin A. Fleck |
| PAK Pong-chin | Robert A. Kinney |
| CHU Mun-ki | Robert A. Lewis |
| YI Chong-bin | James Sartorius |
| KANG Suk-che (Interpreter) | Major Robert D. Peckham, USA |
| YI Kyun-pal | Kenneth Campen (Interpreter) |

0235

2

1. Mr. Hwang opened the meeting by introducing Mr. Chang Sang-mun, newly-appointed Director of the Europe and America Bureau of the Foreign Ministry. Mr. Hwang stated that a reorganization within the Ministry had split the former Bureau of Political Affairs, of which he had been Director, into the Bureau for Europe and America and a Bureau for Asian Affairs. Mr. Hwang had been appointed Director of the Bureau of Asian Affairs; as a result, he would no longer be associated with the Status of Forces negotiations and Mr. Chang would succeed him as Chief Negotiator for the ROK Government. Mr. Hwang announced that Mr. Pak was attending the meeting in place of Mr. SIN Kwan-sup, who had another engagement. Mr. Hwang then introduced Mr. YI Kyun-pal, a Foreign Service Officer who had just returned from an assignment to the Korean Consulate General in San Francisco and had joined the staff of the America Section of the Foreign Ministry.

2. Mr. Habib welcomed Mr. Yi to the negotiations and stated that Mr. Pak was an old friend who was always welcome at the negotiating table. Mr. Habib stated that he wished to make a few remarks in connection with the change of leadership on the Korean side of the table. He said that during the period in which Mr. Hwang had served as Chief Negotiator, there had always been great frankness and honesty of discussion between the two negotiating teams. The U.S. side had a feeling of deep appreciation for Mr. Hwang's leadership. During this period, the U.S. side had consistently felt that the negotiations were a team effort, with both sides cooperating in developing a mutually satisfactory Agreement rather than battling each other.

3. Mr. Habib said that the great regret felt by the U.S. side at Mr. Hwang's departure from the negotiating table did not dampen the warmth with which they greeted Mr. Chang. When the Agreement is finally signed, the great contributions made by Messrs. Chin, Hwang, and Chang will be fully recognized. Mr. Habib pledged to Mr. Chang the fullest cooperation of the U.S. negotiators and said that they fully expected the continuation of the excellent negotiating relations which had

0236

existed to date. He said they looked forward to receiving the advice and assistance of Mr. Hwang from time to time.

4. Mr. Hwang replied that this was a significant meeting for him, inasmuch as it was the last one of 1963 and the last one in which he would participate. He thanked Mr. Habib for his kind words and said that he had found his association with the U.S. negotiators to be a very happy one. He felt honored to have had the opportunity to participate in these historic negotiations. He was also very grateful for the close friendships which had developed between himself and the U.S. negotiators. He said he would continue to be concerned with the course of the negotiations and looked forward to final agreement at the earliest possible time. The atmosphere of the negotiations had been very amicable and he was personally sad at leaving the negotiating table. However, he was glad that Mr. Chang was his successor and he felt confident that Mr. Chang would make a great contribution to the negotiations.

5. Mr. Chang stated that he felt it a personal privilege and honor to participate in the SOFA negotiations, which had been in progress for a long time. Mr. Hwang had made a great contribution to the course of the negotiations, with the cooperation of the U.S. negotiators. He said he would try to follow Mr. Hwang's example. He hoped to have the fullest cooperation of the U.S. negotiators. The presence of the U.S. armed forces in Korea was for the mutual benefit of the ROK Government and the U.S. Government and he was convinced that the negotiators could reach a mutually satisfactory Agreement.

6. Mr. Habib replied that the U.S. negotiators welcomed the spirit expressed by Mr. Chang and stated that Mr. Chang could be assured of the full cooperation of the U.S. negotiators.

Non-Appropriated Fund Organizations

0237

4

Non-Appropriated Fund Organizations

7. Turning to the first item on the agenda, Mr. Hwang stated that with regard to the article dealing with non-appropriated fund organizations, it had been agreed at the previous meeting to use the word "organizations" rather than the word "activities" throughout the article and the entire Agreement. It had also been agreed to insert the phrase "except as provided in paragraph 1(b)" at the end of the first sentence of paragraph 2 of the U.S. draft. Mr. Habib confirmed Mr. Hwang's statements.

8. Mr. Hwang stated that the second sentence of the U.S. draft of paragraph 2 was similar to the Korean draft, except that the U.S. draft contained the phrase "Korean taxes to which other purchasers of such merchandise and supplies are subject and at rates no less favorable than those imposed on other purchasers". In this connection, he said, the ROK Government has no intention of imposing taxes on these organizations at less favorable rates. The existing taxation system is one of indirect taxes and, therefore, there cannot be different rates for different purchasers. This language in the U.S. draft is therefore irrelevant. Furthermore, it does not appear in the SOFA with Japan. The Korean negotiators believe that details of this nature should be worked out by the Joint Committee. The SOFA is supposed to provide a broad framework of principles and not include details of this nature. Therefore, the Korean side suggested that this language be deleted.

9. Mr. Habib replied that the U.S. side was under the impression that the language of this paragraph had already been agreed to at previous meetings. However, the U.S. negotiators welcomed the statement by Mr. Hwang that no discriminatory tax rates exist and that the ROK Government has no intention of establishing discriminatory rates in the future. This is what the language of the U.S. draft is intended to insure. The fact that this language does not appear in the SOFA with Japan is no reason to leave it out of the Agreement under negotiation, particularly if it will spell out

0238

5

the point at issue. If the ROK Government has no intention of imposing discriminatory taxes, then it should have no objection to including this language in the Agreement. The U.S. negotiators believe its retention is desirable in order to make certain that no discriminatory taxes will be imposed.

10. Mr. Hwang replied that the Korean negotiators understood the intention of the U.S. side. However, it would be impossible to include every detail in the SOFA. The Agreement should consist of a broad framework of principles, with the details left for subsequent working out by the Joint Committee. He suggested that the language in question be deleted, with the negotiating record clearly showing the understanding of both sides that the present system of taxation is one of indirect taxation under which there are no different rates for different purchasers and the understanding that the ROK Government has no intention of imposing discriminatory taxes on the organizations covered by this article.

11. Mr. Habib replied that the U.S. negotiators agreed that the SOFA should avoid getting into details. However, the point at issue was not a detail such as the rates, levels, or methods of taxation to be imposed by the ROK Government. The point at issue was a statement of principle. The U.S. negotiators appreciated the explanation and assurances given by the Korean negotiators. The U.S. negotiators were not trying to avoid the payment of taxes by non-appropriated fund organizations but were trying to have included in the SOFA the principle that there shall be no discriminatory taxation. This is a well understood principle, on which the U.S. negotiators thought that agreement had already been reached.

12. At Mr. Hwang's suggestion, it was agreed to give further consideration to this question and discuss it further at a subsequent meeting.

13. Mr. Hwang pointed out that paragraph 4 of the U.S. draft and paragraph 5 of the Korean draft provide for the provision of tax information required by Korean legislation. Requests for such information would be made through

0239

the Joint Committee. Since no unnecessary request would be made, the Korean negotiators considered unnecessary the clause "after consultation between the representatives of the two governments in the Joint Committee" in the U.S. draft. He suggested the deletion of this language.

14. Mr. Habib replied that the language of the U.S. draft was very positive in that it bound the U.S. authorities to provide required information to the Korean authorities. The language is intended to establish the framework of a system which will enable the U.S. authorities to assist the Korean authorities through the provision of the desired information. It would enable the Joint Committee to perform a valuable function. With regard to a matter as complicated as the provision of tax information, the U.S. negotiators believe that the Agreement should indicate the manner in which the information is to be presented. The language of the U.S. draft would provide a channel for facilitating the provision of the desired information, and would bind the U.S. authorities to provide the information.

15. Mr. Hwang expressed appreciation for Mr. Habib's explanation and suggested substitution of the word "through" for the word "after". Mr. Habib said "through" would not be as good English as "after". Perhaps the Korean side meant "upon consultation". The U.S. side believed "after consultation" was the best usage. It was not intended to be a preventive device but merely a time factor. As he had already pointed out, the word "shall" would bind the U.S. authorities to provide the requested information.

16. Mr. Hwang replied that "after consultation" implies that the information will be provided only after the consultation has been completed. Therefore, the Korean side would prefer "through consultation". Mr. Habib pointed out that the U.S. negotiators wanted to provide for the opportunity for discussion of the requests in the Joint Committee. The language does not say "after agreement"; it merely says "after consultation". It was thereupon agreed to consider this matter further.

0240

17. Mr. Hwang then stated that paragraph 5 of the U.S. draft provided for use of the facilities of non-appropriated fund organizations by persons other than members of the U.S. armed forces. For this reason, it constituted an exception to the provisions of the remainder of the article. The Korean negotiators suggested, therefore, that it be converted into an Agreed Minute and be rewritten in simpler language.

18. Mr. Habib replied that the U.S. negotiators agreed that this paragraph was exceptional and also agreed to its conversion into an Agreed Minute. He said the U.S. side had given a great deal of additional consideration to this problem and had redrafted the paragraph in an effort to make the language much more specific and less susceptible to conflicting interpretations. Mr. Habib thereupon tabled a proposed Agreed Minute to be substituted for paragraph 5 of the U.S. draft and gave a brief explanation of the new language.

19. As the Korean negotiators were aware, Mr. Habib said, the presence of U.S. officials and other official and private organizations and individuals has created a unique situation in the Republic of Korea. This paragraph constitutes an attempt to meet this situation in a manner which will be mutually satisfactory. He pointed out that the right to use non-appropriated fund facilities is customarily given to other officers and personnel of the U.S. Government, as provided in item (a) of the paragraph. This is common practice worldwide and is a simple concept. The same is true of items (c) and (d), which provide for contractors and service organizations, respectively. However, the situation in Korea is a bit more complicated than usual because of the presence of non-Korean forces other than the U.S. armed forces, which receive logistical support from the latter. These forces include the Thai and Turk troops and the liaison officers of various nations assigned to the UN Command. These forces are covered by item (b).

0241

8

Inasmuch as it is impractical to try to provide such privileges for the principals and not for their dependents, the dependents of all the categories of persons covered by items (a) through (d) are covered by item (e). Item (f) would provide non-appropriated fund privileges to other entities such as the United Nations Commission for the Unification and Rehabilitation of Korea (UNCURK), the United Nations Technical Assistance Board (UNTAB), other UN agencies, non-American diplomatic personnel, certain missionary organizations, and others. The language of the paragraph provides that privileges would be extended under item (f) only "with the express consent of the Government of the Republic of Korea". Summing up, Mr. Habib stated that this paragraph provided for the extension of non-appropriated fund facilities to three general groups: (a) U.S. Government personnel ordinarily accorded such privileges; (b) those organizations and individuals who are integral parts of the U.S. armed forces; and (c) such other organizations and individuals as the ROK Government will expressly agree to.

20. Mr. Hwang stated that the Korean negotiators had suggested conversion of this paragraph to an Agreed Minute and the use of simpler and clearer language. The draft tabled by the U.S. side raised certain questions. For instance, could the U.S. negotiators enumerate those persons who would be included under item (a) and what other organizations would be included under item (d) in addition to the Red Cross and the USO?

21. Mr. Habib replied that item (a) would cover non-Korean employees of the U.S. Government in Korea, including the Embassy, USOM, USIS, the (Embassy) military attaches, and members of the various military advisory groups. At the present time, there were no organizations other than the Red Cross and the USO that would be covered by item (d). This item was so phrased to permit the inclusion of additional groups at some future time and to allow for the possibility of changes in organizational structure of the two organizations specifically named. For instance, the United Service Organi-

0242

zations are composed of several separate groups which have banded together for this particular function but conceivably might, at some future date, decide to reorganize in some other fashion. At present, he pointed out, only a handful of people would be involved under item (d). Item (f), Mr. Habib continued, was more complicated. In addition to UNCURK and UNTAB, this item would include such organizations as the Scandinavian Medical Mission (100 persons), the American-Korean Foundation, ~~Hillside House (1 person), International Social Service (2 persons)~~, and members of the diplomatic corps. Personnel of these organizations would be covered by this paragraph only with the express consent of the ROK Government. As the Korean negotiators were fully aware, this was a very delicate problem which would have to be approached cautiously and which could only be solved by the mutual efforts of the Korean and U.S. authorities.

22. Mr. Hwang stated that item (c) obviously referred to the invited contractors working for the U.S. armed forces. He asked if anyone else would be covered by this item. Mr. Habib replied that this item was intended to cover not only invited contractors of the U.S. armed forces but also contractors working for the United States Operations Mission under specific contracts. He said that no expansion in the range of such contracts was foreseen.

23. Mr. Hwang thanked Mr. Habib for his explanation of the proposed Agreed Minute. Mr. Hwang said the Korean negotiators would study the Agreed Minute and give their views at a subsequent meeting.

Customs

24. Turning to the Customs Article, Mr. Hwang stated that the Korean negotiators were prepared to accept paragraph 2 of the U.S. draft, with the understanding that the word "organizations" was to be used instead of the word "activities",

0243

as agreed upon at the previous meeting. Mr. Habib confirmed that the word "organizations" was to be used throughout the Agreement wherever the phrase "non-appropriated fund organizations" appeared. He said the U.S. side assumed that the Korean negotiators were also agreeing to the previous U.S. proposal to place in parentheses the phrase "including their authorized procurement agencies and their non-appropriated fund organizations provided for in Article ____". Mr. Hwang asked if there was any special significance to the use of parentheses in this context. Mr. Habib replied that it was being proposed solely for the sake of grammatical clarity. Mr. Hwang remarked that inasmuch as the use of parentheses did not change the substance of the paragraph, the Korean negotiators agreed to the placing of the phrase in question in parentheses.

25. Mr. Hwang remarked that agreement had not yet been reached on subparagraph (b) of paragraph 3, subparagraphs (a), (b), and (c) of paragraph 5, and Agreed Minutes 2, and 3. He suggested that the negotiators take up paragraph 5(b) for discussion, noting that at the previous meeting the Korean negotiators had requested information regarding the size and markings of parcels mailed as first class mail.

26. Mr. Habib stated that the maximum weight limitation on parcels shipped by first class mail is 70 pounds. They are marked to indicate the class of mail being used. First class mail is handled separately from other classes of mail and parcels sent by first class mail are shipped in separate mail bags and not mixed with first class letter mail. He pointed out that because of the greater cost of first class mail, the great bulk of parcels are shipped by parcel post. As an example of the cost differential, he cited the case of a 10 lb. parcel shipped by parcel post in Zone 8 (over 1800 miles). The cost of sending such a parcel would be $2.16. To ship the same parcel by first class mail would cost $8.00.

27. Mr. Hwang st[illegible] negotiators would like to have it

0244

agreed that Korean customs inspectors would function at the 17 main military post offices rather than at the 32 mail distribution centers mentioned by the U.S. negotiators at the previous meeting.

28. Mr. Habib replied that this was a detail which was not appropriate for inclusion in the SOFA but would have to be worked out by the Joint Committee. He said that the U.S. negotiators understood that if the Korean negotiators agreed to the revised text of paragraph 5(b) proposed by the U.S. negotiators at the previous meeting, it would be with the following understandings:

a. Examinations of parcels in the MPO mails in the ROK by ROK customs inspectors will be conducted so as not to damage the contents of the parcels inspected or delay delivery of the mail;

b. Such examinations will be conducted in U.S. MPO installations at designated points of mail distribution and in the presence of U.S. officials;

c. No parcel in the MPO mails will be removed from U.S. postal channels except as mutually agreed;

d. It is understood that the right of inspection will be exercised on a "spot check" basis so as not to unduly delay delivery or increase the administrative burden of the postal authorities.

With those understandings, Mr. Habib continued, the U.S. negotiators are prepared to agree to the principle of the right of the Korean authorities to inspect non-first class mail. The Korean authorities can be assured of the cooperation of the U.S. armed forces in implementing this provision of the SOFA.

29. Turning to paragraph 6, Mr. Hwang stated that although the text of this paragraph had already been agreed upon, the Korean negotiators would like to spell out the fact that disposal goods in contravention of the provisions of para-

0245

12

graph 6 shall be dealt with under Korean laws and customs regulations.

30. Mr. Habib replied by referring to Agreed Minutes #4 and #5. Colonel Fuller pointed out that obviously, if an illegal transaction occurred involving an unauthorized person, the Korean authorities would have jurisdiction over such a person. He added that in the case of any person caught disposing of goods illegally, the provisions of the Respect for Local Law Article, the Criminal Juriddiction Article, and the U.S. armed forces' regulations would apply. Any exception to the foregoing would have to be spelled out in the Agreement.

31. Turning to paragraph 5(c), Mr. Hwang pointed out that the phrase (including their authorized procurement agencies and their non-appropriated fund organizations provided for in Article ___) was included both in 5(c) and in Agreed Minute #3, which related to 5(c). The Korean negotiators believed the appearance of the phrase in both places was redundant and suggested its deletion from paragraph 5(c). Mr. Habib replied that the U.S. negotiators would take this proposal under consideration.

32. At this point the meeting was adjourned. The next meeting was scheduled for January 9, 1964 at 2:00 p.m.



0246

## JOINT SUMMARY RECORD OF THE 37TH SESSION

1. Time and Place: 2:00 to 4:10 P.M. December 27, 1963 at the Foreign Ministry's Conference Room

| 미주과 | 양고재 | 담 당 | 과 장 | 국 장 | 특별보좌관 | 차 관 | 장 관 |
|---|---|---|---|---|---|---|---|
| | | | | | | | |

2. Attendants:

ROK Side:

| | |
|---|---|
| Mr. Whang, Ho Eul | Director<br>Bureau of Asian Affairs<br>Ministry of Foreign Affairs |
| Mr. Chang, Sang Moon | Director<br>Bureau of European and American Affairs<br>Ministry of Foreign Affairs |
| Mr. Koo, Choong Whay | Chief, American Section<br>Ministry of Foreign Affairs |
| Mr. Park, Bong Chin | Chief, Customs Section<br>Ministry of Finance |
| Mr. Choo, Moon Ki | Chief, Legal Affairs Section<br>Ministry of Justice |
| Col. Kim, Won Kil | Chief, Military Affairs Section<br>Ministry of National Defence |
| Mr. Oh, Jae Hee | Chief, Treaty Section<br>Ministry of Foreign Affairs |
| Mr. Kang, Suk Jae (Rapporteur and Interpreter) | 2nd Secretary<br>Ministry of Foreign Affairs |
| Mr. Lee, Chung Bin | 3rd Secretary<br>Ministry of Foreign Affairs |
| Mr. Lee, Keun Pal | 3rd Secretary<br>Ministry of Foreign Affairs |

U.S. Side:

| | |
|---|---|
| Mr. Philip C. Habib | Counselor for Political Affairs<br>American Embassy |
| Col. Howard Smigelow | Deputy Chief of Staff<br>8th U.S. Army |
| Col. L.J. Fuller | Staff Judge Advocate<br>United Nations Command |
| Capt. R.M. Brownlie | Assistant Chief of Staff<br>USN/K |

0247

| | |
|---|---|
| Mr. Benjamin A. Fleck (Rapporteur and Press Officer) | First Secretary American Embassy |
| Mr. James Sartorius | 2nd Secretary American Embassy |
| Mr. Robert A, Lewis | 2nd Secretary and Consul American Embassy |
| Mr. Robert A, Kinney | J-5 8th U.S. Army |
| Maj. Robert D. Peckham | Staff Officer, JAG 8th U.S. Army |
| Mr. Kenneth Campen | Interpreter |

1. Mr. Whang opened the meeting by introducing Mr. Chang Sang Moon, newly appointed Director of the Europe and America Bureau of the Foreign Ministry. Mr. Whang stated that a reorganization within the Ministry had split the former Bureau of Political Affairs, of which he had been Director, into the Bureau for Europe and America and a Bureau for Asian Affairs. Mr. Whang had been appointed Director of the Bureau of Asian Affairs; as a result, he would no longer be associated with the Status of Forces negotiations and Mr. Chang would succeed him as Chief Negotiator for the ROK Government. Mr. Whang announced that Mr. Park was attending the meeting in place of Mr. Shin Kwan Sup, who had another engagement. Mr. Whang then introduced Mr. Lee Keun Pal, a Foreign Service Officer who had just returned from an assignment to the Korean Consulate General in San Francisco and had joined the staff of the American Section of the Foreign Ministry.

2. Mr. Habib welcomed Mr. Lee to the negotiations and stated that Mr. Park was an old friend who was always welcome at the negotiating table. Mr. Habib stated that he wished to make a few remarks in connection with the change of leadership on the Korean side of the table. He said that during the period in which Mr. Whang had served as Chief Negotiator, there had

0248

always been great frankness and honesty of discussion between the two negotiating team. The U.S. Side had a feeling of deep appreciation for Mr. Whang's leadership. During this period, the U.S. side had consistently felt that the negotiations were a team effort, with both sides co-operating in developing a mutually satisfactory Agreement rather than battling each other.

3. Mr. Habib said that the great regret felt by the U.S. side at Mr. Whang's departure from the negotiating table did not dampen the warmth with which they greeted Mr. Chang. When the Agreement is finally signed, the great contributions made by Messrs. Chin, Whang, and Chang will be fully recognized. Mr. Habib pledged to Mr. Chang the fullest cooperation of the U.S. negotiators and said that they fully expected the continuation of the excellent negitiating relations which had existed to date. He said they looked forward to receiving the advice and assistance of Mr. Whang from time to time.

4. Mr. Whang replied that this was a significant meeting for him, inasmuch as it was the last one of 1963 and the last one in which he would participate. He thanked Mr. Habib for his kind words and said that he had found his association with the U.S. negotiators to be a very happy one. He felt honored to have had the opportunity to participate in these historic negotiations. He was also very grateful for the close friendships which had developed between himself and the U.S. negotiators. He said he would continue to be concerned with the course of the negotiations and looked forward to final agreement at the earliest possible time. The atmosphere of the negotiations had been very amicable and he was personally sad at leaving the negotiating table. However, he was glad that Mr. Chang was his successor and he felt confident that Mr. Chang would make a great contribution to the negotiations.

0249

5. Mr. Chang stated that he felt it a personal privilege and honor to participate in the SOFA negotiations, which had been in progress for long time. Mr. Whang had made a great contribution to the course of the negotiations, with the cooperation of the U.S. negotiators. He said he would try to follow Mr. Whang's example. He hoped to have the fullest cooperation of the U.S. negotiators. The presence of the U.S. armed forces in Korea was for the mutual benefit of the ROK Government and the U.S. Government and he was convinced that the negotiators could reach a mutually satisfactory Agreement.

6. Mr. Habib replied that the U.S. negotiators welcomed the spirit expressed my Mr. Chang and stated that Mr. Chang could be assured of the full cooperation of the U.S. negotiators.

Non-Appropriated Fund Organizations

7. Turning to the first item on the agenda, Mr. Whang stated that with regard to the article dealing with non-appropriated fund organizations, it had been agreed at the previous meeting to use the word "organizations" rather than the word "activities" throughout the article and the entire Agreement. It had also been agreed to insert the phrase "except as provided in paragraph 1(b)" at the end of the first sentence of paragraph 2 of the U.S. draft. Mr. Habib confirmed Mr. Whang's statements.

8. Mr. Whang stated that the second sentence of the U.S. draft of paragraph 2 was similar to the Korean draft, except that the U.S. draft contained the phrase "Korean taxes to which other purchasers of such merchandise and supplies are subject and at rates no less favorable than those imposed on other purchasers". In this connection, he said,

0250

the ROK Government has no intention of imposing taxes on these organizations at less favorable rates. The existing taxation system is one of indirect taxes and, therefore, there cannot be different rates for different purchasers. This language in the U.S. draft is therefore irrelevant. Furthermore, it does not appear in the SOFA with Japan. The Korean negotiators believe that details of this nature should be worked out by the Joint Committee. The SOFA is supposed to provide a broad framework of principles and not to include details of this nature. Therefore, the Korean side suggested that this language be deleted.

9. Mr. Habib replied that U.S. side was under the impression that the language of this paragraph had already been agreed to at previous meetings. However, the U.S. negotiators welcomed the statement by Mr. Whang that no discriminatory tax rates exist and that the ROK Government has no intention of establishing discriminatory rates in the future. This is what the language of the U.S. draft is intended to insure. The fact that this language does not appear in the SOFA with Japan is no reason to leave it out of the Agreement under negotiation, particularly if it will spell out the point at issue. If the ROK Government has no intention of imposing discriminatory taxes, then it should have no objection to including this language in the Agreement. The U.S. negotiators believe its retention is desirable in order to make certain that no discriminatory taxes will be imposed.

10. Mr. Whang replied that the Korean negotiators understood the intention of the U.S. side. However, it would be impossible to include every detail in the SOFA. The Agreement should consist of a broad framework of

0251

principles, with the details left for subsequent working out by the Joint Committee. He suggested that the language in question be deleted, with the negotiating record clearly showing the understanding of both sides that the present system of taxation is one of indirect taxation under which there are no different rates for different purchasers and the understanding that the ROK Government has no intention of imposing discriminatory taxes on the organizations covered by this article.

11. Mr. Habib replied that the U.S. negotiators agreed that the SOFA should avoid getting into details. However, the point at issue was not a detail such as the rates, levels, or methods of taxation to be imposed by the ROK Government. The point at issue was a statement of principle. The U.S. negotiators appreciated the explanation and assurances given by the Korean negotiators. The U.S. negotiators were not trying to avoid the payment of taxes by non-appropriated fund organizations but were trying to have included in the SOFA the principle that there shall be no discriminatory taxation. This is a well understood principle, on which the U.S. negotiators thought that agreement had already been reached.

12. At Mr. Whang's suggestion, it was agreed to give further consideration to this question and discuss it further at a subsequent meeting.

13. Mr. Whang pointed out that paragraph 4 of the U.S. draft and paragraph 5 of the Korean draft provide for the provision of tax information required by Korean legislation. Requests for such information would be made through the Joint Committee. Since no unnecessary request would be made, the Korean negotiators considered unnecessary the clause "after consultation between the representatives of the two governments

0252

in the Joint Committee" in the U.S. draft. He suggested the deletion of this language.

14. Mr. Habib replied that the language of the U.S. draft was very positive in that it bound the U.S. authorities to provide required information to the Korean authorities. The language is intended to establish the framework of a system which will enable the U.S. authorities to assist the Korean authorities through the provision of the desired information. It would enable the Joint Committee to perform a valuable function. With regard to a matter as complicated as the provision of tax information, the U.S. negotiators believe that the Agreement should indicate the manner in which the information is to be presented. The language of the U.S. draft would provide a channel for facilitating the provision of the desired information, and would bind the U.S. authorities to provide the information.

15. Mr. Whang expressed appreciation for Mr. Habib's explanation and suggested substitution of the word "through" for the word "after". Mr. Habib said "through" would not be as good English as "after". Perhaps the Korean side meant "upon consultation". The U.S. side believed "after consultation" was the best usage. It was not intended to be a preventive device but merely a time factor. As he had already pointed out, the word "shall" would bind the U.S. authorities to provide the requested information.

16. Mr. Whang replied that "after consultation" implies that the information will be provided only after the consultation has been completed. Therefore, the Korean side would prefer "through consultation". Mr. Habib pointed out that the U.S. negotiators wanted to provide for the opportunity for discussion of the requests in the Joint Committee. The language does not say "after agreement";

0253

it merely says "after consultation". It was thereupon agreed to consider this matter further.

17. Mr. Whang then stated that paragraph 5 of the U.S. draft provided for use of the facilities of non-appropriated fund organizations by persons other than members of the U.S. armed forces. For this reason, it constituted an exception to the provisions of the remainder of the article. The Korean negotiators suggested, therefore, that it be converted into an Agreed Minute and be rewritten in simpler language.

18. Mr. Habib replied that the U.S. negotiators agreed that this paragraph was exceptional and also agreed to its conversion into an Agreed Minute. He said the U.S. side had given a great deal of additional consideration to this problem and had redrafted the paragraph in an effort to make the language much more specific and less susceptible to conflicting interpretations. Mr. Habib thereupon tabled a proposed Agreed Minute to be substituted for paragraph 5 of the U.S. draft and gave a brief explanation of the new language.

19. As the Korean negotiators were aware, Mr. Habib said, the presence of U.S. officials and other official and private organizations and individuals has created a unique situation in the Republic of Korea. This paragraph constitutes an attempt to meet this situation in a manner which will be mutually satisfactory. He pointed out that the right to use non-appropriated fund facilities is customarily given to other officers and personnel of the U.S. Government, as provided in item (a) of the paragraph. This is common practice worldwide and is a simple concept. The same is true of items (c) and (d), which provide for contractors

0254

and service organizations, respectively. However, the situation in Korea is a bit more complicated than usual because of the presence of non-Korean forces other than the U.S. armed forces, which receive logistical support from the latter. These forces include the Thai and Turk troops and the liaison officers of various nations assigned to the UN Command. These forces are covered by item (b). Inasmuch as it is impractical to try to provide such privileges for the principals and not for their dependents, the dependents of all the categories of persons covered by items (a) through (d) are covered by item (e). Item (f) would provide non-appropriated fund privileges to other entities such as the United Nations Commission for the Unification and Rehabilitation of Korea (UNCURK), the United Nations Technical Assistance Board (UNTAB), other UN agencies, non-American diplomatic personnel, certain missionary organizations, and others. The language of the paragraph provides that privileges would be extended under item (f) only"with the express consent of the Government of the Republic of Korea". Summing up, Mr. Habib stated that this paragraph provided for the extension of non-appropriated fund facilities to three general groups: (a) U.S. Government personnel ordinarily accorded such privileges; (b) those organizations and individuals who are integral parts of the U.S. armed forces; and (c) such other organizations and individuals as the ROK Government will expressly agree to.

20. Mr. Whang stated that the Korean negotiators had suggested conversion of this paragraph to an Agreed Minute and the use of simpler and clearer language. The draft tabled by the U.S. side raised certain questions. For instance, could the U.S. negotiators enumerate those persons

0255

who would be included under item (a) and what other organizations would be included under item (d) in addition to the Red Cross and the USO?

21. Mr. Habib replied that item (a) would cover non-Korean employees of the U.S. Government in Korea, including the Embassy, USOM, USIS, the Embassy military attaches, and members of the various military advisory groups. At the present time, there were no organizations other than the Red Cross and the USO that would be covered by item (d). This item was so phrased to permit the includion of additional groups at some future time and to allow for the possibility of changes in organizational structure of the two organizations specifically named. For instance, the United Service Organizations are composed of several separate groups which have banded together for this particular function but conceivably might, at some future date, decide to reorganize in some other fashion. At present, he pointed out, only handful of people would be involved under item (d). Item (f), Mr. Habib continued, was more complicated. In addition to UNCURK and UNTAB, this item would include such organizations as the Scandinavian Medical Mission (100 persons), the American-Korean Foundation, and members of the diplomatic corps. Personnel of these organizations would be covered by this paragraph only with the express consent of the ROK Government. As the Korean negotiators were fully aware, this was a very delicate problem which would have to be approached cautiously and which could only be solved by the mutual efforts of the Korean and U.S. authorities.

22. Mr. Whang stated that item (c) obviously referred to the invited contractors working for the U.S. armed

0256

forces. He asked if anyone else would be covered by this item. Mr. Habib replied that this item was intended to cover not only invited contractors of the U.S. armed forces but also contractors working for the United States Operations Mission under specific contracts. He said that no expansion in the range of such contracts was foreseen.

23. Mr. Whang thanked Mr. Habib for his explanation of the proposed Agreed Minute. Mr. Whang said the Korean negotiators would study the Agreed Minute and give their views at a subsequent meeting.

Customs

24. Turning to the Customs Article, Mr. Whang stated that the Korean negotiators were prepared to accept paragraph 2 of the U.S. draft, with the understanding that the word "organizations" was to be used instead of the word "activities", as agreed upon at the previous meeting. Mr. Habib confirmed that the word "organizations" was to be used throughout the Agreement wherever the phrase "non-appropriated fund organizations" appeared. He said the U.S. side assumed that the Korean negotiators were also agreeing to the previous U.S. proposal to place in parentheses the phrase "including their authorized procurement agencies and their non-appropriated fund organizations provided for in Article ". Mr. Whang asked if there was any special significance to the use of parentheses in this context. Mr. Habib replied that it was being proposed solely for the sake of grammatical clarity. Mr. Whang remarked that inasmuch as the use of parentheses did not change the substance of the paragraph, the Korean negotiators agreed to the placing of the phrase in question in parentheses.

25. Mr. Whang remarked that agreement had not yet

0257

been reached on subparagraph (b) of paragraph 3, subparagraphs (a), (b), and (c) of paragraph 5, and Agreed Minutes 2, and 3. He suggested that the negotiators take up paragraph 5(b) for discussion, noting that at the previous meeting the Korean negotiators had requested information regarding the size and markings of parcels mailed as first class mail.

26. Mr. Habib stated that the maximum weight limitation on parcels shipped by first class mail is 70 pounds. They are marked to indicate the class of mail being used. First class mail is handled separately from other classes of mail and and parcels sent by first class mail are shipped in separate mail bags and not mixed with first class letter mail. He pointed out that because of the greater cost of first class mail, the great bulk of parcels are shipped by parcel post. As an example of the cost differential, he cited the case of a 10 lb. parcel shipped by parcel post in Zone 8 (over 1800 miles). The cost of sending such a parcel would be $2.16. To ship the same parcel by first class mail would cost $8.00.

27. Mr. Whang stated that the Korean negotiators would like to have it agreed that Korean customs inspectors would function at the 17 main military post offices rather than at the 32 mail distribution centers mentioned by the U.S. negotiators at the previous meeting.

28. Mr. Habib replied that this was a detail which was not appropriate for inclusion in the SOFA but would have to be worked out by the Joint Committee. He said that the U.S. negotiators understood that if the Korean negotiators agreed to the revised text of paragraph 5(b) proposed by the U.S. negotiators at the previous meeting, it would be with the

0258

following understandings:

a. Examinations of parcels in the MPO mails in the ROK by ROK customs inspectors will be conducted so as not to damage the contents of the parcels inspected or delay delivery of the mail;

b. Such examinations will be conducted in U.S. MPO installations at designated points of mail distribution and in the presence of U.S. officials;

c. No parcel in the MPO mails will be removed from U.S. postal channels except as mutually agreed;

d. It is understood that the right of inspection will be exercised on a "spot check" basis so as not to unduly delay delivery or increase the administrative burden of the postal authorities.

With those understandings, Mr. Habib continued, the U.S. negotiators are prepared to agree to the principle of the right of the Korean authorities to inspect non-first class mail. The Korean authorities can be assured of the co-operation of the U.S. armed forces in implementing this provision of the SOFA.

29. Turning to paragraph 6, Mr. Whang stated that although the text of this paragraph had already been agreed upon, the Korean negotiators would like to spell out the fact that disposal of imported goods in contravention of the provisions of paragraph 6 shall be dealt with under Korean laws and customs regulations.

30. Mr. Habib replied by referring to Agreed Minutes #4 and #5. Colonel Fuller pointed out that obviously, if an illegal transaction occurred involving an unauthorized person, the Korean authorities would have jurisdiction over such a person. He added that in the case of any person

0259

caught disposing of goods illegally, the provisions of the Respect for Local Law Article, the Criminal Jurisdiction Article, and the U.S. armed forces' regulations would apply. Any exception to the foregoing would have to be spelled out in the Agreement.

31. Turning to paragraph 5(c), Mr. Whang pointed out that the phrase (including their authorized procurement agencies and their non-appropriated fund organizations provided for in Article was included both in 5(c) and in Agreed Minute 03, which related to 5(c). The Korean negotiators believed the appearance of the phrase in both places was redundant and suggested its deletion from paragraph 5(c). Mr. Habib replied that the U.S. negotiators would take this proposal under consideration.

32. At this point the meeting was adjourned. The next meeting wasscheduled for January 9, 1964 at 2:00 P.M.



0260

## 정/리/보/존/문/서/목/록

| 기록물종류 | 문서-일반공문서철 | 등록번호 | 919<br>9592 | 등록일자 | 2006-07-27 |
|---|---|---|---|---|---|
| 분류번호 | 741.12 | 국가코드 | US | 주제 | |
| 문서철명 | 한.미국 간의 상호방위조약 제4조에 의한 시설과 구역 및 한국에서의 미국군대의 지위에 관한 협정 (SOFA) 전59권. 1966.7.9 서울에서 서명 : 1967.2.9 발효 (조약 232호) *원본 | | | | |
| 생산과 | 미주과/조약과 | 생산년도 | 1952 - 1967 | 보존기간 | 영구 |
| 담당과(그룹) | 조약 | 조약 | 서가번호 | -- | |
| 참조분류 | | | | | |
| 권차명 | V.21 실무교섭회의, 제38-44차, 1964.1-2월 | | | | |
| 내용목차 | 1. 제38차 회의, 1.9 (p.2~55)<br>2. 제39차 회의, 1.17 (p.56~85)<br>3. 제40차 회의, 1.24 (p.86~139)<br>4. 제41차 회의, 2.6 (p.140~195)<br>5. 제42차 회의, 2.14 (p.196~271)<br>6. 제43차 회의, 2.20 (p.272~314)<br>7. 제44차 회의, 2.28 (p.315~380)<br><br>* 일지 :<br>1953.8.7 이승만 대통령-Dulles 미국 국무장관 공동성명<br>- 상호방위조약 발효 후 군대지위협정 교섭 약속<br>1954.12.2 정부, 주한 UN군의 관세업무협정 체결 제의<br>1955.1월, 5월 미국, 제의 거절<br>1955.4.28 정부, 군대지위협정 제의 (한국측 초안 제시)<br>1957.9.10 Hurter 미국 국무차관 방한 시 각서 수교 (한국측 제의 수락 요구)<br>1957.11.13, 26 정부, 개별 협정의 단계적 체결 제의<br>1958.9.18 Dawling 주한미국대사, 형사재판관할권 협정 제외 조건으로 행정협정 체결 의사 전달<br>1960.3.10 정부, 토지, 시설협정의 우선적 체결 강력 요구<br>1961.4.10 장면 국무총리-McConaughy 주한미국대사 공동성명으로 교섭 개시 합의<br>1961.4.15, 4.25 제1, 2차 한.미국 교섭회의 (서울)<br>1962.3.12 정부, 교섭 재개 촉구 공한 송부<br>1962.5.14 Burger 주한미국대사, 최규하 장관 면담 시 형사재판관할권 문제 제기 않는 조건으로 교섭 재개 통고<br>1962.9.6 한.미국 간 공동성명 발표 (9월 중 교섭 재개 합의)<br>1962.9.20~1965.6.7 제1-81차 실무 교섭회의 (서울)<br>1966.7.8 제82차 실무 교섭회의 (서울)<br>1966.7.9 서명<br>1967.2.9 발효 (조약 232호) | | | | |

**마/이/크/로/필/름/사/항**

| 촬영연도 | *롤 번호 | 화일 번호 | 후레임 번호 | 보관함 번호 |
|---|---|---|---|---|
| 2006-11-22 | I-06-0068 | 06 | 1-380 | |

0001

1. 제38차 회의, 1.9

0002

참석자 명단

| 성명 | 부처 | 직위 | 전화번호 |
| --- | --- | --- | --- |
| 金容海 | 労動庁 | 職業安定課長 | 1/5. ③-4651 미측 1부 |
| 李昌우 (少将) | 国防部 | 兵務局長 | |
| 許 信 | 援護処 | 管理局長 | 5/5 미측 1부 |
| 沈 尙燮 | 労動庁 | 職業安定局長 | 4/5 미측 1부 ③-5085 |
| 金 ○濟 | 労動庁 | 労政課長 | 3/5 미측 1부 ②-4295 |
| 李然憲 | 국방부 | 사무관 → 対外政策研究官 | 2/5 각 1부 미측 1부 한측 1부 |

노정국장 ③-5437

조용서 노동청직업안정과 ③-4651 / 1413

민성기 (비서) 대한해운공사 비서실 ②-1713.

0003

經濟企劃院

技術管理局

技術調查課

T 72-9705

林國軍

---

Col. Kenneth Charles Crawford

Judge Advocate General's Corps

United States Army

Tel: Yongsan Office 3628
2033

Home: 4863

0004

# 기 안 용 지

| 자체 통제 | | 기안처 | 미주과 강석재 | 전화번호 | 근거서류접수일자 |
|---|---|---|---|---|---|
| | 과장 | 국장 | 차관 | 장관 | |
| 관계관 서명 | | | | | |
| 기안 년월일 | 1964. 1. 8 | 시행 년월일 | | 보존 년한 | 정서기장 |
| 분류 기호 | | 전체 통제 | | 종결 | |
| 경유 수신 참조 | 건의 | | | 발신 | |
| 제목 | 제38차 주둔군지위협정 체결교섭회의에 임할 우리측 입장 | | | | |

1월 9일에 개최될 제38차 주둔군지위협정 체결을 위한 한미간 교섭회의에서는 관세업무, 비세출자금기관 및 군사우편에 관한 조문을 토의하도록 예정되고 있는바 이에 관하여 우리측 교섭 실무자는 1월7일 회합을 갖고 제38차회의에서 취할 태도를 별첨과 같이 결정하였아오니 재가하여 주시기 바랍니다.

유첨: 제38차 주둔군지위협정 체결교섭회의에 임할 우리측 태도 끝



승인서식 1-1-3 (11-00900-03) (195mm×265mm16절지)

0005

1. 교섭 촉진 요망사항

조문 토의에 들어가기전에 우리측은 협정체결을 위한 교섭 촉진을 목적으로 아래와 같은 요망사항을 피력하고 미국측의 협조를 요청하기로 한다.

가. 교섭 촉진을 위하여 형사재판 관할권 조문을 비롯한 기타 조문초안의 제출을 미국측에 촉구한다.

나. 실무자 교섭회의의 회의 소집빈도를 빨리하여 조속한 시일내에 전반적인 교섭을 종결토록 한다.

2. 관세조항

가. 우편물 검사 면제에 관한 미국측 초안 5 (b) 항에 있어서 미국측은 제 36 차 회의에서 " Official documents under official seal and First Class mail in United States military postal channels under official postal seal " 로 하자는 대안을 제의한바 있다. 그러나 미국측은 " first class mail " 에는 소포가 포함 될수 있다고 시사하고 그러한 소포에 적용되는 무게 표식 및 요금상의 제한에 관하여 제 37 차 회의에서 설명을 한바 있었다. 우리측은 공문서 및 사서한을 제외한 모든 소포에 대해서는 한국 세관 당국이 검사할 권한을 보유해야 한다는 입장에서 볼때 최저 70 파운드 까지의 소포가 포함될수 있는 미국측 대안인 "first class mail " 을 수락 할수 없음을 지적하고 미국측 주장을 "first class letter mail" 로 수정 할것을 제안하기로 한다.

나. 군사화물의 세관검사 면제에 관한 미국측 초안 5 (c) 항에 관련하여 우리측은 제 37 차 회의에서 조건 합의를 본바있는 미국측 초안 (6) 항 즉 무세로 수입된 물품은 상호 합의된 조건에 의거 한미 양 당국에 의하여 그 처분이 허가된 경우를 제외하고는 그러한 물품을 무세로 수입할 권한이 없는자에게 처분할수 없다는 규정에 위배하여 처분하였을 경우

1966.12.31.에 예고문에 의거 일반문서로 재분류됨

0006

한국 관세법에 적용 받는다는 것을 규제하기를 제의하였던바 한미 실무 교섭자는 그러한 물품을 무세로 수입할수 없는자는 당연히 한국의 관할권하에 속한다는 점에 있어서는 의견을 일치 한바 있으나 미국측은 그러한 물품을 불법적으로 처분한 미군인들은 접수 국법의 존중, 형사 재판 관할권 및 미군대 구정에 복종한다고 견해를 말한바 있다.

우리측은 미국측 초안 (6) 항은 단지 무세로 수입된 물품을 그러한 권한이 없는자에게 처분할수 없다고만 규제하고 있을뿐 만약 불법적으로 처분 하였을 경우에는 그러한 처분을 한 미국 군인에 대한 처벌이 규정되어 있지 않으며 또한 그러한 처벌 규정은 접수국 법의 존중에 관한 조문에서 규제 되어 있지 않으며 앞으로 교섭할 형사 재판관할권 조문에서는 구체적으로 규제되지 않을 것임으로 우리측으로서는 관세 조문에서 규제 함이 적절하며 타당하다고 생각한다고 계속 주장하기로 한다.

다. 미국측이 만약 전기한 우리측의 요구를 수락하지않을 경우에는 우리측은 계속 " 군사화물 " 에 관한 세관 검사 면제 규정인 5 ( c ) 항에 있어서 비세출 자금기관 앞으로 탁송되는 물품에 대해서는 (ㄱ) 현하 우리나라의 경제사정과 (ㄴ) 과거 및 현재에 있어서 많은 비세출 자금기관 물품이 한국 시장에서 암거래되고 있는 실정과 (ㄷ) 따라서 그러한 불법적 처분을 한 사람들에 대한 실질적인 처벌을 규정하지 않는한 그와 같은 불법적 거래가 계속되며 한국 경제를 저해할 가능성이 있음을 지적하고 우리 세관 당국이 검사만을 해야 하겠다는 입장을 설명한다.

라. 만약 미국측이 비세출자금기관에 탁송되는 물품에 대한 세관검사에 응하지 않을 경우에는 우리측은 최종적인 대안으로서 " 한국 정부가 비세출자금기관에 탁송되는 물품에 관하여 필요로 하는 정보를 요구하면 미국 당국은 신속히 그러한 정보를 제공해야한다 " 는 요지 양해사항을 합의 의사록에서 규제하도록 다음과 같이 제안한다.

0007

"

The Korean authorities may request the United States military authorities whatever information they deem necessary pertaining to all cargo consigned to the non-appropriated fund organizations and the United States military authorities shall promptly provide such information in the manner as is specified by the Korean authorities."

마. 관세 조문중 이외에 미합의된 조항은 차량 및 부속품의 무세 수입에 관한 미국측 초안 3 (b) 항과 한국에 출입하는 미군대 구성원에 대한 세관 검사 면제에 관한 5 (a) 항 및 합의 의사록 2 및 3 항인바 미국측이 우편물 및 군사화물에 대한 세관 검사 면제 규정에 관한 우리측 입장을 수락하여줄 경우에는 모두 미국측 안대로 수락하기로 한다.

3. 비세출 자금기관

가. 미국측 초안 (2) 항의 둘째 문장은 한국내에 있어서의 비세출 자금기관에 의한 상품및 보급품의 구매는 한국 조세에 따라야 할것을 규정하고 있으나 " to which other purchasers of such merchandises and supplies are subject and at rates no less favorable than those imposed on other purchasers

" 라는 부대적 구절을 삽입하고 있는바 이에 관하여 우리측은 계속 제 36 차 회의에서 제의한바와 같이 물품 구매에 관한 한국 조세 제도는 간접세를 채택하고 있으니 만큼 소비자에 따라 상외한 조세율이 적용되는 일이 없음을 지적하고 따라서 미국측 초안의 부대적 구절은 전혀 관계 없는 것임으로 삭제 할것을 주장한다.

만약 미국측이 이에 관한 우리입장에 동의하지 않을 경우에는 (ㄱ) " other purchasers " 란 말이 어떠한 내국인이나 혹은 한국에 체류하는 외국인을 지칭하는 것인지 (ㄴ) 또는 우리의 현 세제하에 미국측이 상정하는것 처럼 소비자에 따라 각각 상외한 조세율이 적용되는 일이 어떠한 경우에

0008

있다고 보는지를 미국측에 반문하여 부대적 구절을 삽입한 미국측의 저의가 무엇인지를 확인 하도록 한다.

나. 미국측 초안 (4) 항 및 우리측 초안 (5) 항은 다같이 " 비세출 자금기관이 한국 조세법에 의하여 필요로 하는 정보를 제공 할것 "을 규정하고 있으나 미국측 초안은 " after consultation between the representatives of the two Governments in the Joint Committee " 라는 구절을 첨가하고 있다. 우리측은 지난번 회의에서 동 구절을 삭제 할것을 주장한바 있고 미국측이 이에 불응하여 재차 "after consultation 을 " through consultation " 으로 변경하기를 제안한바 있었다. 우리측은 이 부대적 구절에 관하여 (ㄱ) 한국측으로서는 물론 불필요한 정보 제공을 요구하지 않을 것이나 (ㄴ) 꼭 필요한 정보는 정확히 그리고 필요한 시간에 제공 받아야 할 것이라고 생각함으로 제 1 대안으로 동 구절을 " upon request by the Korean authorities through the Joint Committee " 로 대치하도록 제의하며 이에 대한 합의를 얻지 못할 경우에는 제 2 안으로 "after consultation " 을 " upon consultation " 으로 변경하고 " provide " 란 단어 앞에 " immediately " 란 단어를 추가 시키도록 할것을 제의한다.

다. 미국측이 제 37 차 회의에서 (소위) 대안으로 제출한 합의 의사록에 관하여 우리측은 먼저 동 합의 의사록을 검토한 결과 (ㄱ) 일반 미국시민 을 제외한 미군대, 정부 및 각종단체와 관련을 갖고 한국에 체류하는 사람들은 실질적으로 대부분이 망라되어 있고 (ㄴ) 특히 주둔군 지위 협정에서 규제하는 대상외의 인원들 까지도 포함되고 있음을 지적하고 우리측으로서 만족할 만한 것이 못된다고 전제하고 나서 각 범주 별로 다음과 같이 우리측의 견해를 설명하기로 한다.

라. 범주 ( a) 및 (b ) 하에 포함되는 자 즉 통상 그러한 특권이 부여되는 미국정부 관리 및 인원과 미군대로 부터 병참 지원을 받는 유엔

0009

사령부 예하의 비 한국인 인원들에 의한 비세출 자금기관의 이용에 대하여서는 의의가 없으나 범주 (c) 에 관해서는 " 유솜 " 등 원조기관과의 계약관계로 한국에 체류하는 계약자들은 본 협정에서 규제 될것이 아니라 별도 원조 협정에서 규제될 성질의 것임으로 여기서는 제외되어야 한다. 범주 (d) 에 관하여서는 미국 적십자 및 USO 의 비한국인 인원뿐만아니라 그러한 기관 즉 " those organizations " 이 비세출 자금기관을 사용하도록 되어있는데 이 용어에 관한 미국측의 설명을 요구한다. 범주 (e) 에 관해서는 범주 (a), (b), (c) 및 (d) 에 포함되는자들의 가족을 일괄적으로 지칭하고 있는바 우리측은 군 계약자들의 가족과 같이 특정인들의 가족에게는 특권 및 면제를 일률적으로 허용하는데 의의를 갖고 있으므로 그와 같은 관계조문의 토의가 끝날때가지 우리측 입장을 보류한다. 범주 (f) 에 관해서는 (ㄱ) 본 협정 자체가 원칙적으로 미군대 구성원, 군속 및 그들의 가족에 대하여 규제하는 것이며 (ㄴ) 비록 과거 주한 외교관 기타 기관 및 인원들의 비세출 자금기관을 이용하여 왔다고 하지만 그러한 관례는 그간 주둔군지위 협정이 없었던 관계로 인한 비 정상적인 환경하의 일이며 따라서 본 협정이 체결된다면 그 규정에 따라야 할것이다. 우리정부로서는 앞으로 주한 외국인들이 필요로하는 물품을 구입할수 있도록 하며 또한 불편을 감소케 하기위하여 현재 운영중인 "Foreigner's commissary " 를 확대하며 필요하다면 외국인이 필요로하는 물품들을 무세로 충분한 양을 수입하며 적절한 가격으로 제공할 모든 편의를 도모할수 있음으로 본 협정규제 대상외의 인원들에 의한 비세출자금기관의 사용을 중지할것을 바라는 바이라고 설명하고 따라서 본 합의 의사록에서는 그러한 인원이나 기관들에 관하여 여하한 언급도 할 필요가 없다고 주장하고 범주 (f) 의 삭제를 요구한다.

4. 군사우편

미국측 초안 (2) 항은 통상 해외에서 그러한 특권이 부여된 미국 정부 관리 및 그들의 가족들도 군사 우편 시설을 이용할수 있도록 규정하고

0010

있는바 제 19 차 회의에서 양측은 본 규정은 예외적인 규정임으로 본문 대신에 합의 의사록에 넣도록 할것에 합의한바 있다. 우리측은 먼저 미국측 초안에 "their dependents " 란 구절을 포함시킨 이유를 묻기로 하고 미국측이 계속 동 구절의 삽입을 원할 경우에는 그들의 가족도 군사 우편을 이용할수 있다는 양해를 회의 기록에 남기도록 하고 본 문장에서는 삭제 할것을 주장한다.



0011

SOFA NEGOTIATION

Agenda for the 38th Session

15:30 January 9, 1963

1. Continuation of Discussions on:

    a. Customs Article

    b. Non-Appropriated Fund Organizations Article

    c. Military Post Offices Article

2. Other Business

3. Agenda and Date of the Next Meeting

4. Press Release

0012

Jan. 9 '64

2. No Korean tax shall be imposed on sales of merchandise or services by such organizations, except as provided in paragraph 1(b) of this article. Purchases within the Republic of Korea of merchandise and supplies by such organizations shall be subject to the Korean taxes to which other purchasers of such merchandise and supplies are subject unless otherwise agreed between the two Governments.

submitted by U.S. side on Jan. 9. '64

0013

ARTICLE

Non-Appropriated Fund Activities

1. Military exchanges, messes, social clubs, theaters, newspapers and other non-appropriated fund activities authorized and regulated by the United States military authorities may be established by the United States armed forces for the use of members of such forces, the civilian component, and their dependents. Except as otherwise provided in this Agreement, such activities shall not be subject to Korean regulations, licenses, fees, taxes, or similar controls.

2. No Korean tax shall be imposed on sales of merchandise or services by such activities. Purchases within Korea of merchandise and supplies by such activities shall be subject to the Korean taxes to which other purchasers of such merchandise and supplies are subject and at rates no less favorable than those imposed on other purchasers.

3. Except as such disposal may be permitted by the United States and Korean authorities in accordance with mutually agreed conditions, goods which are sold by such activities shall not be disposed of in Korea to persons not authorized to make purchases from such activities.

4. The activities referred to in this Article shall, (after consultation between the representatives of the two Governments in the Joint Committee,) provide such information to the Republic of Korea tax authorities as is required by Korean tax legislation.

0014

AGREED MINUTE

5. The United States Armed Forces may grant the use of the organizations referred to in paragraph 1 of Article to: (a) other officers or personnel of the United States Government ordinarily accorded such privileges; (b) those other non-Korean Armed Forces in Korea under the Unified Command which receive logistical support from the United States Armed Forces, and their members; (c) those non-Korean persons whose presence in the Republic of Korea is solely for the purpose of providing contract services financed by the United States Government; (d) those organizations which are present in the Republic of Korea primarily for the benefit and service of the United States Armed Forces, such as the American Red Cross and the United Service Organizations, and their non-Korean personnel; (e) dependents of the foregoing; and (f) other persons and organizations with the express consent of the Government of the Republic of Korea.

→ detailed category

가' AKF (America-Korea Foundation
UNKURK
UNTAB
Diplomatic Corps
Scandinavian Mission
etc

0015

5. The activities referred to in paragraph 1 may be used by other officers or personnel of the United States Government ordinarily accorded such privileges, by non-Korean persons whose presence in Korea is solely for the purpose of providing contract services financed by the United States Government, by the dependents of the foregoing, by organizations which are present in the Republic of Korea primarily for the benefit and service of the United States armed forces personnel, such as the American Red Cross and the United Service Organizations, and by the non-Korean personnel of such organizations and their dependents.

0016

## NON-APPROPRIATED FUND ACTIVITIES ARTICLE

Suggested Paragraph I (b):

(b) When a newspaper authorized and regulated by the United States military authorities is sold to the general public, it shall be subject to Korean regulations, licenses, fees, taxes or similar controls so far as such circulation is concerned.

0017

Jan 964

## Agreed Minute

The Korean authorities may request the United States military authorities whatever information they deem necessary pertaining to all cargo consigned to the non-appropriated fund organizations and the United States military authorities shall promptly provide such information in the manner as is specified by the Korean authorities.

.0018

Jan 9. '64

## Agreed Minute

7. It is understood that the duty free treatment provided in paragraph 2 shall apply to materials, supplies, and equipment imported for sale through commissaries and non-appropriated fund organizations, under such regulations as the United States armed forces may promulgate, to those individuals and organizations referred to in Article______and its Agreed Minute.

0019

AGREED MINUTES TO ARTICLE (Customs)

1. The quantity of goods imported under paragraph 2 by non-appropriated fund organizations of the United States armed forces for the use of the members of the United States armed forces, the civilian component, and their dependents shall be limited to the extent reasonably required for such use.

2. Paragraph 3(a) does not require concurrent shipment of goods with travel of owner nor does it require single loading or shipment. In this connection, members of the United States armed forces or civilian component and their dependents may import free of duty their personal and household effects during a period of six months from the date of their first arrival.

3. The term "military cargo" as used in paragraph 5(c) is not confined to arms and equipment but refers to all cargo consigned to the United States armed forces, including their authorized procurement agencies and their non-appropriated fund organizations provided for in Article .

4. The United States armed forces will take every practicable measure to ensure that goods will not be imported into the Republic of Korea by or for the members of the United States armed forces, the civilian component, or their dependents, the entry of which would be in violation of Korean customs laws and regulations. The United States armed forces will promptly notify the Korean customs authorities whenever the entry of such goods is discovered.

0020

5. The Korean customs authorities may, if they consider that there has been an abuse or infringement in connection with the entry of goods under Article , take up the matter with the appropriate authorities of the United States armed forces.

6. The words "The United States armed forces shall render all assistance within their power," etc., in paragraph 9(b) and (c) refer to reasonable and practicable measures by the United States armed forces authorized by United States law and service regulations.

0021

Importing components

ARTICLE (Customs)

2. All materials, supplies and equipment imported by the United States armed forces, including their authorized procurement agencies and their non-appropriated fund organizations provided for in Article , for the official use of the United States armed forces or for the use of forces logistically supported by the United States armed forces or for the use of the members of the United States armed forces, the civilian component, or their dependents shall be permitted entry into the Republic of Korea free from customs duties and other such charges. Similarly, materials, supplies and equipment which are imported by others than the United States armed forces but are to be used exclusively by the United States armed forces and/or forces logistically supported by the United States armed forces or are ultimately to be incorporated into articles or facilities to be used by such forces shall be permitted entry into the Republic of Korea free from customs duties and other such charges. Appropriate certification shall be made by the United States armed forces with respect to the importation of materials, supplies and equipment for the foregoing specified purposes.

will be provided in subsequent article

0022

ARTICLE VIII Joint Committee

1. A Joint Committee shall be established as the means for consultation between the Government of the United States and the Government of the Republic of Korea on all matters requiring mutual consultation regarding the implementation of this Agreement unless otherwise provided for. In particular, the Joint Committee shall serve as the means for consultation in determining the facilities and areas in the Republic of Korea which are required for the use of the United States in carrying out the purposes of this Agreement.

2. The Joint Committee shall be composed of a representative of the Government of the United States and a representative of the Government of the Republic of Korea, each of whom shall have one or more deputies and a staff. The Joint Committee shall determine its own procedures, and arrange for such auxiliary organs and administrative services as may be required. The Joint Committee shall be so organized that it may meet immediately at any time at the request of the representative of either the Government of the United States or the Government of the Republic of Korea.

3. If the Joint Committee is unable to resolve any matter, it shall refer that matter to the respective Governments for further consideration through appropriate channels.

OK

diplomatic channel 도 포함된다는 양해하에 합의.

for instance, Communication 에 올 별도로 취급하기 위한 것 등 기술적인 것을 별도로 다루기 위한 것.

B. 수 C

63. 2. 25

0023

October 19, 1962

ENTRY AND EXIT

1. The United States may bring into the Republic of Korea persons who are members of the United States armed forces, the civilian component, and their dependents, subject to the provisions of this Article. The Government of the Republic of Korea will be notified at regular intervals, in accordance with procedures to be agreed between the two Governments, of numbers and categories of persons entering and departing.

ok

2. Members of the United States armed forces shall be exempt from Korean passport and visa laws and regulations. Members of the United States armed forces, the civilian component, and their dependents shall be exempt from Korean laws and regulations on the registration and control of aliens, but shall not be considered as acquiring any right to permanent residence or domicile in the territory of the Republic of Korea.

ok

3. Upon entry into or departure from the Republic of Korea members of the United States armed forces shall be in possession of the following documents:

joint committee

(a) personal identity card showing name, date of birth, rank and service number, service, and photograph; and

(b) individual or collective travel order certifying to the status of the individual or group as a member or members of the United States armed forces and to the travel ordered.

ok

0024

For purposes of their identification while in the Republic of Korea, members of the United States armed forces shall be in possession of the foregoing personal identity card which must be presented on request to the appropriate Korean authorities.

4. Members of the civilian component, their dependents, and the dependents of members of the United States armed forces shall be in possession of appropriate documentation issued by the United States authorities so that their status may be verified by Korean authorities upon their entry into or departure from the Republic of Korea, or while in the Republic of Korea.

5. If the status of any person brought into the Republic of Korea under paragraph 1 of this Article is altered so that he would no longer be entitled to such admission, the United States authorities shall notify the Korean authorities and shall, if such person be required by the Korean authorities to leave the Republic of Korea, assure that transportation from the Republic of Korea will be provided within a reasonable time at no cost to the Government of the Republic of Korea.

6. If the Government of the Republic of Korea has requested the removal from its Territory of a member of the United States armed forces or civilian component or has made an expulsion order

0025

against an ex-member of the United States armed forces or the civilian component or against a dependent of a member or an ex-member, the authorities of the United States shall be responsible for receiving the person concerned into its own territory or otherwise disposing of him outside the Republic of Korea. This paragraph shall apply only to persons who are not nationals of the Republic of Korea ~~ordinarily resident in the Republic of Korea~~ and have entered the Republic of Korea as members of the United States armed forces or civilian component or for the purpose of becoming such members, and to the dependents of such persons.

## Agreed Minutes to Article

(Entry and Exit)

1. With regard to Paragraph 3(a), United States Armed Forces law enforcement personnel (such as MP, SP, AP, CID and CIC), who engage in military police activities in the Republic of Korea, will carry a bilingual identity card containing the bearer's name, position, and the fact that he is a member of a law enforcement agency. This card will be shown upon request to persons concerned when the bearer is in the performance of duty.

2. The United States Armed Forces will furnish, upon request, to Korean authorities the form of the identification cards of the members of the United States Armed Forces, the civilian component, and their dependents and descriptions of the various uniforms of the United States Armed Forces in the Republic of Korea.

3. The final sentence of Paragraph 3 means that members of the United States Armed Forces will display their identity cards upon request but will not be required to surrender them to Korean authorities.

4. Following a change of status pursuant to Paragraph 5, the responsibilities of the United States authorities under Paragraph 6 shall arise only if the expulsion order is issued within a reasonable time after the notice under Paragraph 5 has been communicated to the Korean authorities.

0027

# 기 안 용 지

| 자체통제 | 의무과장 | 기안처 | 미주과 강석재 | 전화번호 | 근거서류접수일자 |
|---|---|---|---|---|---|

| 과장 | 국장 | 차관 | 장관 |
|---|---|---|---|
| (서명) | (서명) | (서명) | (서명) |

| 관계관 서명 | |
|---|---|

| 기안년월일 | 1964. 1. 15 | 시행년월일 | | 보존년한 | | 정서 | 기장 |
|---|---|---|---|---|---|---|---|
| 분류기호 | 외구미722.2 | 전체통제 | 종결 | | | | |
| 경유 수신 참조 | 대통령 (참조: 비서실장) 국무총리 | | | 발신 | 장관 | | |
| 제목 | 주둔군지위협정 체결을 위한 제38차 교섭회의 보고 | | | | | | |

1. 1964. 1. 9. 하오 2시반부터 4시반까지 외무부장관 회의실에서 개최된 제38차 주둔군지위협정 체결교섭회의에서 토의된 내용을 별첨과 같이 보고합니다.

유첨: 제38차 교섭회의 보고서 1부. 끝

1966,12,31 에 예고문에 의거 일반문서로 재분류됨

승인서식 1-1-3 (11-00900-03) (195mm×265mm16절지)

0028

제 38 차

# 한미간 주둔군지위협정 체결 실무자회의

# 보 고 서

1. 일 시: 1964년 1월 9일 하오 2시반부터 4시반까지

2. 장 소: 외무부 장관 회의실

3. 토의사항:

우리측은 교섭촉진을 위하여 (가) 형사재판 관할권 및 기타조문 초안의 제출과 (나) 교섭회의를 매주 1회식 개최하기를 제의하였다. 미국측은 이에 동의하면서 교섭내용을 신문등에 보도할경우에는 상대방측과 사전에 협의하는것이 요망된다고 말하였다.

가. 비세출자금기관

비세출자금기관조문에 있어서 아직 합의를 못본 문제점은 합의의사록에서 미국측은 비세출자금기관을 이용할수 있는 대상을 군대 구성원, 군속 및 그들의 가족외에 주한 외교관 및 유엔 관계자만 (한국정부의 명시적 동의하에)에 까지도 확대하도록 규제할려고 하고 있다. 우리측은 앞으로 협정이 발효할시에는 이들 예외적인 사람들은 원칙적으로 비세출자금기관을 이용할수 없다는 입장을 취하고 있다. 이문제외에도 사소한 기술적 사항에 합의를 보지 못하고 있는 점이 있다.

나. 관세 업무

양측 입장에서 가장 문제가 되고 있는점은 첫째 우리측이 군사우편으로 들어오는 소포는 모두 한국세관 당국이 검사할 권한을 가질것을 요구하고 있는바 미국측은 " first class mail "로 들어오는 소포는 제외하자고 주장하고 있는점과 둘째로 우리측은 비세출자금기관앞으로 탁송되어 오는 물품에 대한 검사권한을 요구하고 있는데 대하여 미국측은 이는 군사화물임으로 검사할수 없는것이라는 입장을 취하고 있는점이다. 이외에도 몇가지 미합의사항이 있으나 위 두가지문제가 합의되면 쉽사리 해결되리라 전망된다.

1966.12.31, 에 예고문에 의거 일반문서로 재분류됨

4. 기타 사항: 차기회의 일자: 1964년 1월 17일 하오 2시

0029

0030

1. Mr. Habib opened the meeting by stating that the U.S. side was about to lose one of its original members, Captain Brownlie, who was being transferred out of Korea on completion of his assignment here. Mr. Habib stated that Captain Brownlie had made many significant contributions to the progress of the negotiations and it was with a great deal of regret that the U.S. negotiators regarded his departure. Mr. Habib then introduced Captain John Wayne, Captain Brownlie's successor as Assistant Chief of Staff, J-5, United Nations Command, and also his successor on the U.S. SOFA Negotiating team.

2. Mr. Chang expressed great regret at the departure of Captain Brownlie and welcomed Captain Wayne. Remarking that there was no ROK Navy representative on the Korean negotiating team, Mr. Chang predicted that Captain Wayne would make notable contributions to the negotiations.

3. Mr. Chang then remarked that this meeting was the first of the new year. He said the Korean negotiators began 1964 with renewed determination to achieve early completion of the negotiations. He pointed out that the negotiations had been in progress for one year and three months and that when they had begun it had been stated that entry into force of the SOFA would await the restoration of civilian government in the Republic of Korea. He stated that civilian government had now been restored and that the Korean negotiators wished to speed up the pace of the negotiations. He urged early tabling of drafts of the articles dealing with criminal jurisdiction and labor and suggested that negotiating meetings be held as often as possible, perhaps once a week instead of once every two weeks.

4. Mr. Habib replied that the U.S. negotiators shared the desire of their Korean counterparts to negotiate the Agreement as quickly as possible. He pointed out that the negotiations concerned exceedingly complicated matters to be covered by a complex Agreement which had to be negotiated line by line and sentence by sentence.

0031

He said the U.S. negotiators intended to table the remaining articles as soon as possible and had so informed Washington. They were also prepared to increase the frequency of meetings to four per month, provided progress continues to be made in the negotiations.

5. Mr. Habib went on to refer to the increased public attention being given to the negotiations. He said he wished to emphasize the view of the U.S. negotiators that the negotiations should not be conducted in the public press. To date, both sides have been able to maintain a united front with regard to press releases and public discussion of the negotiations. The U.S. side would like to see this united front maintained. The U.S. negotiators realize that the Prime Minister and the Foreign Minister from time to time are obliged to discuss with journalists the progress of the negotiations. The U.S. negotiators can have no objection to this. However, the U.S. negotiators do request that conscious and deliberate efforts continue to be made to avoid the appearance in the press of discussion of the substance of the negotiations. He pointed out that when such articles do appear, they are usually ill-informed. He expressed the hope that the Korean negotiators would discuss the problem in advance with the U.S. negotiators whenever they anticipated the need for discussion of the negotiations (which are classified) with the press, arising out of interpellations in the National Assembly or for other reasons.

6. Mr. Chang replied that he assumed Mr. Habib had been referring to recent articles appearing in the press. He said he felt that Mr. Habib's remarks were partially justified. He pointed out that questions had been posed concerning the SOFA negotiations during the recent press conferences held by the Prime Minister and the Foreign Minister. In those circumstances, he continued, the questions have to be answered and it did not appear that prior discussion with the U.S. negotiators was either feasible or justifiable.

7. Mr. Habib replied that the Prime Minister and Foreign Minister of course should answer questions concerning the progress of the negotiations. What he had been

0032

[redacted] referring to were newspaper articles which included discussion of the content of the negotiations. He reminded the Korean negotiators that the negotiations are classified and that it is not customary diplomatic practice to reveal details of classified matters under discussion. He said the U.S. negotiators had full confidence in the judgement of the Korean negotiators and that he had raised the question only because it was likely to become more of a problem for the Korean negotiators from now on.

Non-Appropriated Fund Organizations

8. Turning to the Non-Appropriated Fund Organizations article, Mr. Habib recalled that at the previous meeting the Korean negotiators had objected to the inclusion in the U.S. draft of paragraph 2 the phrase "at rates no less favorable than those imposed on other purchasers". The Korean negotiators had indicated that the ROK Government has no intention of imposing discriminatory taxes on non-appropriated fund organizations. Taking this into account, and in order to meet the objections of the Korean negotiators to the original language, the U.S. side wished to propose the following text for paragraph 2, in place of the original U.S. draft:

> "2. No Korean tax shall be imposed on sales of merchandise or services by such organizations, except as provided in paragraph 1(b) of this article. Purchases within the Republic of Korea of merchandise and supplies by such organizations shall be subject to the Korean taxes to which other purchasers of such merchandise and supplies are subject unless otherwise agreed between the two Governments."

In tabling this proposed language, Mr. Habib said the U.S. negotiators wished the record to clearly show that the ROK Government will levy taxes on purchases by the non-appropriated fund organizations at rates no less favorable than those imposed on other purchasers.

9. Mr. Chang replied that the Korean negotiators had made clear time after time that the ROK Government has no intention of imposing taxes on purchases made by the non-appropriated fund organizations at less favorable rates and therefore they had no objection to stating this in the record of negotiations. However, since the

0033

4

present system of taxation does not provide for the possibility of discriminatory rates, under what circumstances could such discriminatory rates be imposed? The Korean negotiators could foresee no such circumstances.

10. Mr. Habib replied that the U.S. side had met the request previously made by the Korean negotiators, by eliminating the phrase to which they had objected. Agreement had been reached on an understanding to be placed in the negotiating record. The Korean side had stated the intention of the ROK Government; the U.S. side had agreed to the Korean position. The proposed [new] language would ensure that any change in the Korean tax laws would not result in discriminatory taxes against the non-appropriated fund organizations.

11. Mr. Chang replied that the Korean negotiators appreciated the willingness of the U.S. negotiators to delete the phrase in question. However, the meaning of the new language was not yet clear. Was the U.S. side thinking of a situation in which taxes would be imposed on purchases by the military exchanges while other purchasers were not taxed?

12. Mr. Habib replied that this was a possibility; another would be a situation in which two or more tax rates existed. In either case, the military exchanges would be discriminated against. He reiterated that the U.S. negotiators had met the objections of the Korean negotiators. What difference of opinion regarding this paragraph remained?

13. Mr. Chang said the Korean negotiators believed the reference to "other purchasers" was unnecessary. He suggested that discussion of this point be resumed at the next meeting.

14. Mr. Habib said the U.S. negotiators could not agree to deletion of the reference to other purchasers but would be willing to discuss this point further at the next meeting. In reply to Mr. Chang's query whether "other purchasers" referred to foreign diplomats, Mr. Habib replied that it did not. Pointing out that diplomats

0034

5

are exempted from paying taxes under customary international practice, he said their status was totally irrelevant to the point at issue. The language of the paragraph states that purchases by the non-appropriated fund organizations "shall be subject" to Korean taxes, not "shall be exempt from" Korean taxes. Mr. Chang said the Korean negotiators would make their position clear at the next meeting.

15. Turning to paragraph 4, Mr. Habib recalled that at the previous meeting, the Korean negotiators had proposed the substitution of the word "through" for the word "after" immediately preceding the word "consultation". He said the U.S. negotiators agreed to this change. In so doing, they were agreeing that the Joint Committee was the channel through which the required information was to be passed to the Korean tax authorities. He also pointed out that in agreeing to this change, it was the understanding of the U.S. negotiators that the U.S. armed forces would not be required to provide information to the Korean tax authorities which is not relevant to tax administration or which is detrimental to the security interests of the United States Government. The implementation of this understanding would be left to the Joint Committee.

16. Mr. Chang replied that the Korean negotiators appreciated the agreement of the U.S. negotiators to the change in language. In this connection, the Korean negotiators wished the record to show that the information referred to in paragraph 4 included customs information and that the information required would be provided by the U.S. armed forces on a timely basis and without delay.

17. Mr. Habib replied that the Hoint Committee could be expected to work expeditiously and without delay. He pointed out that customs matters were dealt with in a separate article. ~~In discussing~~ Previous discussion of the customs article ~~the applicability of~~ had shown the relationship between that article ~~to~~ and the non-appropriated fund organizations article ~~has been adequately covered~~.

18. Mr. Chang replied that there seemed to be some difference of

0035

6

opinion regarding the scope of the information to be provided under paragraph 4. He suggested that this question be discussed further at the next meeting. Mr. Habib agreed and asked for the views of the Korean negotiators regarding the proposed Agreed Minute which had been tabled by the U.S. negotiators at the previous meeting to replace paragraph 5 of the U.S. draft.

19. Mr. Chang replied that the Korean negotiators had carefully studied the proposed Agreed Minute. They had concluded that if this language were agreed to, all Americans in the Republic of Korea except businessmen and missionaries would be covered by the Agreed Minute. In the view of the Korean negotiators, this language would provide coverage for people who should not be covered by the SOFA. He referred particularly to USOM contractors, who would be covered under category (c) and diplomats and UN personnel, who would be covered under category (f). He pointed out that the privileges of the USOM contractors are covered under other agreements with the ROK Government. With regard to the diplomats and other aliens, the ROK Government is making efforts to suit the convenience of such persons, through improving the Foreigners' Commissary and in other ways. Because of continuing discussions with various ministries of the ROK Government, the Korean negotiators wished to reserve their position regarding this point. With regard to category (d), Mr. Chang noted that provision was made for the use of non-appropriated fund organization facilities by "organizations" in addition to such use by their personnel. He asked if there were any circumstance under which use by organizations rather than by persons was possible.

20. Mr. Habib replied that this was indeed possible, since the USO and the Red Cross, as organizations, purchased equipment for the use of the troops visiting their facilities. The use of the word "organizations" in category (d), therefore, was accurate and necessary.

21. Regarding category (f), Mr. Habib reminded the negotiators that he had

0036

referred at the last meeting to mutual problems with regard to the persons to be included under this category. Under the terms of the proposed language, if the ROK Government does not wish diplomats and UN personnel to be granted the use of non-appropriated fund organization facilities, they will not be granted such use. Also, if the armed forces decide that they do not wish to grant the use of such facilities to these persons, they will not do so, even if the ROK Government should be willing. The language thus provides a framework for the granting of such facilities to such persons only if mutually agreed upon by the ROK Government and the U.S. armed forces.

22. With regard to contractors, Mr. Habib continued, the U.S. negotiators were not trying to establish any new privileges. The persons who would be covered by category (c) now generally enjoy these privileges under the terms of their present contracts. This language is merely an attempt to regularize the current procedures. If such privileges were granted in the individual contracts, the armed forces still would not have the right to grant the use of their facilities if specific permission to do so is not included in the SOFA.

23. Mr. Chang stated that the Korean negotiators would reserve detailed comment for a later meeting. However, they would prefer to list in the Agreed Minute all the types of persons who would be granted the use of non-appropriated fund organization facilities.

24. Mr. Habib replied that the U.S. negotiators would consider this proposal. However, the adoption of Mr. Chang's suggestion would undoubtedly create great problems for the ROK Ministry of Foreign Affairs. There would be a constant stream of visitors to the Foreign Ministry, complaining at having been left off the list. The retention of category (f) in the Agreed Minute would avoid many of these problems and would give both the armed forces and the ROK authorities greater flexibility in dealing with this extremely delicate problem, which involved United Nations agencies among other possibilities.

CUSTOMS

0037

8

Customs

25. In taking up consideration of the Customs Article, Mr. Habib stated that the U.S. negotiators wished to table an additional Agreed Minute, in order to make this article consistent with the Non-Appropriated Fund Organizations Article. While paragraph 2 of the Customs Article permits duty-free importation of goods, the language is inconsistent with the language of the Non-Appropriated Fund Organizations Article, as now proposed. Therefore, the U.S. negotiators proposed the following additional Agreed Minute:

"7. It is understood that the duty free treatment provided in paragraph 2 shall apply to materials, supplies, and equipment imported for sale through commissaries and non-appropriated fund organizations, under such regulations as the United States armed forces may promulgate, to those individuals and organizations referred to in Article ____ and its Agreed Minute."

26. Mr. Habib added that there was also need to modify the language of Agreed Minute #1, since the Non-Apppropriated Fund Organizations Article, as proposed, included more persons than just members of the armed forces, the civilian component, and their dependents. Therefore, the U.S. negotiators proposed the deletion from Agreed Minute #1 of the phrase "the members of the United States armed forces, the civilian component, and their dependents" and the insertion in its place of the phrase "persons authorized by Article ____ and its Agreed Minute".

27. Mr. Habib recalled that at the previous meeting, the Korean negotiators had proposed the deletion from paragraph 5(c) of the phrase "including their authorized procurement agencies and their non-appropriated fund organizations provided for in Article ____", on the grounds that this phrase was also included in Agreed Minute #3 and there was no need for repetition. Mr.Habib stated the U.S. negotiators agreed to the deletion of this phrase from paragraph 5(c).

28. With regard to the proposed Agreed Minute tabled by the U.S. negotiators and the change proposed by them in Agreed Minute #1, Mr. Chang said the

0038

Korean negotiators fully agreed with the necessity for consistency within the SOFA. He pointed out, however, that agreement had not yet been reached on what persons were to be covered by the provisions of the Non-Appropriated Fund Organizations Article. The Korean negotiators agreed to the deletion of the phrase in question from paragraph 5(c), with the understanding that final agreement had not yet been reached with regard to the text of Agreed Minute #3. Mr. Habib agreed.

29. Turning to paragraph 5(b), Mr. Chang stated the understanding of the Korean negotiators that both sides had agreed at previous meetings to the right of the ROKG authorities to inspect parcels. The U.S. negotiators had proposed that this subparagraph read as follows: "Official documents under official seal and First Class mail in United States military postal channels under official postal seal". The U.S. negotiators had explained that parcels can be included in First Class mail but are kept separate from letter mail. They had also pointed out that the rates for sending parcels by First Class mail are very high and therefore most parcels are sent by parcel post rather than as First Class mail. He said the Korean authorities wished to inspect the parcels which are sent as First Class mail. What was being suggested was not a postal inspection but a customs inspection. The Korean negotiators, therefore, suggested that paragraph 5(b) read as follows:

> "5(b). Official documents under official seal and First Class letter mail in United States military postal channels under official postal seal."

30. Mr. Habib stated that the U.S. negotiators would consider the Korean proposal.

31. Turning to paragraph 5(c), Mr. Chang stated that in the past and currently goods imported for the Non-Appropriated Fund Organizations have been the subject of illegal transactions in the black market, to the great detriment of the Korean economy. The ROK Government has been trying to prevent such abuses, without much success. Therefore, the Korean negotiators wish to retain, in this paragraph, the right of customs inspection of such goods. If the U.S. negotiators did not find this acceptable, Mr. Chang stated that the Korean negotiat[illegible]ve suggestions to make.

32. Mr. Habib replied that the Korean negotiators were confusing the administrative and police function with the purpose of this article. The provisions of this article do not affect punitive and preventive measures to be taken under the provisions of other articles of the SOFA and/or other agreements. The right of customs inspection has no bearing or relevancy on the disposal of these goods. Such goods constitute military cargo, as the U.S. negotiators have repeatedly pointed out. Stating that no purpose would be served in repeating the already oft-repeated U.S. position, Mr. Habib asked the Korean negotiators to present their alternative proposals.

33. Mr. Ku stated that the U.S. negotiators had previously explained that persons guilty of illegally disposing of these goods would be dealt with under the provisions of the Respect for Local Law Article, the Criminal Jurisdiction Article, and the regulations of the U.S. armed forces. Paragraph #6 provides that these goods shall not be disposed of to persons not entitled to import such goods free of duty. He said this provision was too general. The provisions of the Respect for Local Law Article also were quite general. The Korean negotiators did not foresee that the Criminal Jurisdiction Article would contain detailed provisions on this matter. Therefore, methods of preventing such illegal transactions should be provided for in some other way. The right to inspect such goods on their entry into the Republic of Korea must be provided for.

34. Mr. Habib replied that Mr. Ku had not mentioned paragraphs 8 and 9 of this article, which were also relevant. Mr. Habib said the SOFA will establish the principle that there should not be abuses. The implementation of that principle will be left to the Joint Committee. The U.S. negotiators anticipated that both sides would provide cooperation of the highest order to provide for the maximum effective prevention of abuses. He asked if the Korean negotiators had any specific suggestions to make.

35. Mr. Ku replied that the Korean negotiators had explained why the

0040

ROKG authorities wished to have the right of inspection. In order to solve this problem, the Korean negotiators wished to table the following proposed additional Agreed Minute:

> "4. The Korean authorities may request from the United States military authorities whatever information they deem necessary pertaining to all cargo consigned to the non-appropriated fund organizations and the United States military authorities shall promptly provide such information in the manner as is specified by the Korean authorities."

Inasmuch as Agreed Minute #3 refers to military cargo, Mr. Ku explained, the Korean authorities wished to propose the above Agreed Minute as Agreed Minute #4.

36. Mr. Habib said the U.S. negotiators would consider the Korean proposal.

37. The next meeting was scheduled for January 17 at 2:00 p.m.

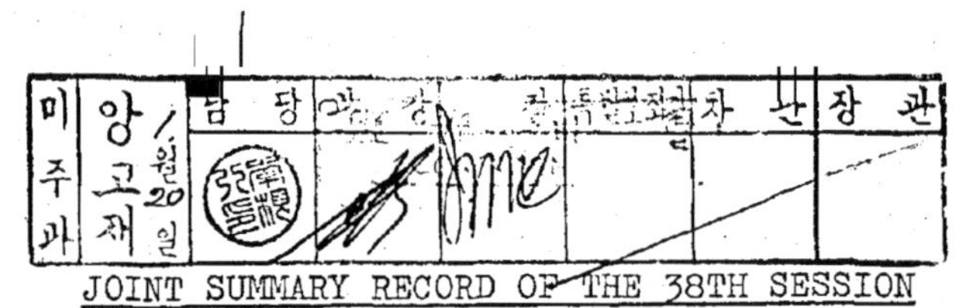

JOINT SUMMARY RECORD OF THE 38TH SESSION

1/3

1. Time and Place: 3:30 - 4:30 P.M. January 9, 1964 at the Foreign Ministry's Conference Room

2. Attendants:

ROK Side:

| | |
|---|---|
| Mr. Chang, Sang Moon | Director<br>European and American Affairs Bureau<br>Ministry of Foreign Affairs |
| Mr. Shin Kwan Sup | Director<br>Bureau of Customs Duty<br>Ministry of Finance |
| Mr. Koo, Choong Whay | Chief, American Section<br>Ministry of Foreign Affairs |
| Mr. Choo, Moon Ki | Chief, Legal Affairs Section<br>Ministry of Justice |
| Col. Kim, Won Kil | Chief, Military Affairs Section<br>Ministry of National Defence |
| Mr. Oh, Jae Hee | Chief, Treaty Section<br>Ministry of Foreign Affairs |
| Mr. Kang, Suk Jae (Rapporteur and Interpreter) | 2nd Secretary<br>Ministry of Foreign Affairs |
| Mr. Lee, Chung Bin | 3rd Secretary<br>Ministry of Foreign Affairs |
| Mr. Lee, Keun Pal | 3rd Secretary<br>Ministry of Foreign Affairs |

U.S. Side:

| | |
|---|---|
| Mr. Philip C. Habib | Counselor for Political Affairs<br>American Embassy |
| Col. Howard Smigelow | Deputy Chief of Staff<br>8th U.S. Army |
| Col. L.J. Fuller | Staff Judge Advocate<br>United Nations Command |
| Capt. R.M. Brownlie | Assistant Chief of Staff<br>USN/K |
| Capt. John Wayne | Assistant Chief of Staff<br>USN/K |

0042

| | |
|---|---|
| Mr. Benjamin A. Fleck (Rapporteur and Press Officer) | First Secretary American Embassy |
| Mr. James Sartorius | 2nd Secretary American Embassy |
| Mr. Robert A. Lewis | 2nd Secretary and Consul American Embassy |
| Mr. Robert A. Kinney | J-5 8th U.S. Army |
| Maj. Robert D. Peckham | Staff Officer, JAG 8th U.S. Army |
| Mr. Kenneth Campen | Interpreter |

1. Mr. Habib opened the meeting by stating that the U.S. side was about to lose one of its original members, Captain Brownlie, who was being transferred out of Korea on completion of his assignment here. Mr. Habib stated that Captain Brownlie had made many significant contributions to the progress of the negotiations and it was with a great deal of regret that the U.S. negotiators regarded his departure. Mr. Habib then introduced Captain John Wayne, Captain Brownlie's successor as Assistant Chief of Staff, J-5, United Nations Command, and also his successor on the U.S. SOFA negotiating team.

2. Mr. Chang expressed great regret at the departure of Captain Brownlie and welcomed Captain Wayne. Remarking that there was no ROK Navy representative on the Korean negotiating team, Mr. Chang predicted that Captain Wayne would make notable contributions to the negotiations.

3. Mr. Chang then remarked that this meeting was the first of the new year. He said the Korean negotiators began 1964 with renewed determination to achieve early completion of the negotiations. He pointed out that the negotiations had been in progress for one year and three months and that when they had begun it had been

0043

stated that entry into force of the SOFA would await the restoration of civilian government in the Republic of Korea. He stated that civilian government had now been restored and that the Korean negotiators wished to speed up the pace of the negotiations. He urged early tabling of drafts of the articles dealing with criminal jurisdiction and labor and suggested that negotiating meetings be held as often as possible, perhaps once a week instead of once every two weeks.

4. Mr. Habib replied that the U.S. negotiators shared the desire of their Korean counterparts to negotiate the Agreement as quickly as possible. He pointed out that the negotiations concerned exceedingly complicated matters to be covered by a complex Agreement which had to be negotiated line by line and sentence by sentence. He said the U.S. negotiators intended to table the remaining articles as soon as possible and had so informed Washington. They were also prepared to increase the frequency of meetings to four per month, provided progress continues to be made in the negotiations.

5. Mr. Habib went on to refer to the increased public attention being given to the negotiations. He said he wished to emphasize the view of the U.S. negotiators that the negotiations should not be conducted in the public press. To date, both sides have been able to maintain a united front with regard to press releases and public discussion of the negotiations. The U.S. side would like to see this united front maintained. The U.S. negotiators realize that the Prime Minister and the Foreign Minister from time to time are obliged to discuss with journalists

0044

the progress of the negotiations. The U.S. negotiators can have no objection to this. However, the U.S. negotiators do request that conscious and deliberate efforts continue to be made to avoid the appearance in the press of discussion of the substance of the negotiations. He pointed out that when such articles do appear, they are usually ill-informed. He expressed the hope that the Korean negotiators would discuss the problem in advance with the U.S. negotiators whenever they anticipated the need for discussion of the negotiations, which are classified, with the press, arising out of interpellations in the National Assembly or for other reasons.

6. Mr. Chang replied that he assumed Mr. Habib had been referring to recent articles appearing in the press. He said he felt that Mr. Habib's remarks were partially justified. He pointed out that questions had been posed concerning the SOFA negotiations during the recent press conferences held by the Prime Minister and the Foreign Minister. In those circumstances, he continued, the questions have to be answered and it did not appear that prior discussion with the U.S. negotiators was either feasible or justifiable.

7. Mr. Habib replied that the Prime Minister and Foreign Minister of course should answer questions concerning the progress of the negotiations. What he had been referring to were newspaper articles which included discussion of the content of the negotiations. He reminded the Korean negotiators that the negotiations are classified and that it is not customary diplomatic

practice to reveal details of classified matters under discussion. He said the U.S. negotiators had full confidence in the judgement of the Korean negotiators and that he had raised the question only because it was likely to become more of a problem for the Korean negotiators from now on.

Non-Appropriated Fund Organizations

8. Turning to the Non-Appropriated Fund Organizations article, Mr. Habib recalled that at the previous meeting the Korean negotiators had objected to the inclusion in the U.S. draft of paragraph 2 the phrase "at rates no less favorable than those imposed on other purchasers". The Korean negotiators had indicated that the ROK Government has no intention of imposing discriminatory taxes on non-appropriated fund organizations. Taking this into account, and in order to meet the objections of the Korean negotiators to the original language, the U.S. side wished to propose the following text for paragraph 2, in place of the original U.S. draft:

> "2. No Korean tax shall be imposed on sales of merchandise or services by such organizations, except as provided in paragraph 1(b) of this article. Purchases within the Republic of Korea of merchandise and supplies by such organizations shall be subject to the Korean taxes to which other purchasers of such merchandise and supplies are subject unless otherwise agreed between the two Governments."

In tabling this proposed language, Mr. Habib said the U.S. negotiators wished the record to clearly show that the ROK Government will levy taxes on purchases by the non-appropriated fund organizations at rates no less favorable than those imposed on other purchasers.

0046

9. Mr. Chang replied that the Korean negotiators had made clear time after time that the ROK Government has no intention of imposing taxes at less favorable rates on purchases made by the non-appropriated fund organizations and therefore they had no objection to stating this in the record of negotiations. However, since the present system of taxation does not provide for the possibility of discriminatory rates, under what circumstances could such discriminatory rates be imposed? The Korean negotiators could foresee no such circumstances.

10. Mr. Habib replied that the U.S. side had met the request previously made by the Korean negotiators, by eliminating the phrase to which they had objected. Agreement had been reached on an understanding to be placed in the negotiating record. The Korean side had stated the intention of the ROK Government; the U.S. side had agreed to the Korean position. The proposed new language would ensure that any change in the Korean tax laws would not result in discriminatory taxes against the non-appropriated fund organizations.

11. Mr. Chang replied that the Korean negotiators appreciated the willingness of the U.S. negotiators to delete the phrase in question. However, the meaning of the new language was not yet clear. Was the U.S. side thinking of a situation in which taxes would be imposed on purchases by the military exchanges while other purchasers were not taxed?

12. Mr. Habib replied that this was a possibility; another would be a situation in which two or more tax rates existed. In either case, the military exchanges would

0047

be discriminated against. He reiterated that the U.S. negotiators had met the objections of the Korean negotiators. What difference of opinion regarding this paragraph remained?

13. Mr. Chang said the Korean negotiators believed the reference to "other purchasers" was unnecessary. He suggested that discussion of this point be resumed at the next meeting.

14. Mr. Habib said the U.S. negotiators could not agree to deletion of the reference to other purchasers but would be willing to discuss this point further at the next meeting. In reply to Mr. Chang's query whether "other purchasers" referred to foreign diplomats, Mr. Habib replied that it did not. Pointing out that diplomats are exempted from paying taxes under customary international practice, he said their status was totally irrelevant to the point at issue. The language of the paragraph states that purchases by the non-appropriated fund organizations "shall be subject" to Korean taxes, not "shall be exempt from" Korean taxes. Mr. Chang said the Korean negotiators would make their position clear at the next meeting.

15. Turning to paragraph 4, Mr. Habib recalled that at the previous meeting, the Korean negotiators had proposed the substitution of the word "through" for the word "after" immediately preceding the word "consultation". He said the U.S. negotiators agreed to this change. In so doing, they were agreeing that the Joint Committee was the channel through which the required information was to be passed to the Korean tax authorities. He also pointed out that in agreeing to this change, it was the understanding of the U.S.

0048

negotiators that the U.S. armed forces would not be required to provide information to the Korean tax authorities which is not relevant to tax administration or which is detrimental to the security interests of the United States Government. The implementation of this understanding would be left to the Joint Committee.

16. Mr. Chang replied that the Korean negotiators appreciated the agreement of the U.S. negotiators to the change in language. In this connection, the Korean negotiators wished the record to show that the information referred to in paragraph 4 included customs information and that the information required would be provided by the U.S. armed forces on a timely basis and without delay.

17. Mr. Habib replied that the Joint Committee could be expected to work expeditiously and without delay. He pointed out that customs matters were dealt with in a separate article. Previous discussion of the customs article had shown the relationship between that article and the non-appropriated fund organizations article.

18. Mr. Chang replied that there seemed to be some difference of opinion regarding the scope of the information to be provided under paragraph 4. He suggested that this question be discussed further at the next meeting. Mr. Habib agreed and asked for the views of the Korean negotiators regarding the proposed Agreed Minute which had been tabled by the U.S. negotiators at the previous meeting to replace paragraph 5 of the U.S. draft.

19. Mr. Chang replied that the Korean negotiators had carefully studied the proposed Agreed Minute. They

0049

had concluded that if this language were agreed to, all Americans in the Republic of Korea except businessmen and missionaries would be covered by the Agreed Minute. In the view of the Korean negotiators, this language would provide coverage for people who should not be covered by the SOFA. He referred particularly to USOM contractors, who would be covered under category (c) and diplomats and UN personnel, who would be covered under category (f). He pointed out that the privileges of the USOM contractors are covered under other agreements with the ROK Government. with regard to the diplomats and other aliens, the ROK Government is making efforts to suit the convenience of such persons, through improving the Foreigners' Commissary and in other ways. Because of continuing discussions with various ministries of the ROK Government, the Korean negotiators wished to reserve their position regarding this point. With regard to category (d), Mr. Chang noted that provision was made for the use of non-appropriated fund organization facilities by "organizations" in addition to such use by their personnel, He asked if there were any circumstance under which use by organizations rather than by persons was possible.

20. Mr. Habib replied that this was indeed possible, since the USO and the Red Cross, as organizations, purchased equipment for the use of the troops visiting their facilities. The use of the word "organizations" in category (d), therefore, was accurate and necessary.

21. Regarding category (f), Mr. Habib reminded the negotiators that he had referred at the last meeting to mutual problems with regard to the persons to be

0050

included under this category. Under the terms of the proposed language, if the ROK Government does not wish diplomats and UN personnel to be granted the use of non-appropriated fund organization facilities, they will not be granted such use. Also, if the armed forces decide that they do not wish to grant the use of such facilities to these persons, they will not do so, even if the ROK Government should be willing. The language thus provides a framework for the granting of such facilities to such persons only if mutually agreed upon by the ROK Government and the U.S. armed forces.

22. With regard to contractors, Mr. Habib continued, the U.S. negotiators were not trying to establish any new privileges. The persons who would be covered by category (c) now generally enjoy these privileges under the terms of their present contracts. This language is merely an attempt to regularize the current procedures. If such privileges were granted in the individual contracts, the armed forces still would not have the right to grant the use of their facilities if specific permission to do so is not included in the SOFA.

23. Mr. Chang stated that the Korean negotiators would reserve detailed comment for a later meeting. However, they would prefer to list in the Agreed Minute all the types of persons who would be granted the use of non-appropriated fund organization facilities.

24. Mr. Habib replied that the U.S. negotiators would consider this proposal. However, the adoption of Mr. Chang's suggestion would undoubtedly create great problems for the ROK Ministry of Foreign Affairs. There

0051

would be a constant stream of visitors to the Foreign Ministry, complaining at having been left off the list. The retention of category (f) in the Agreed Minute would avoid many of these problems and would give both the armed forces and the ROK authorities greater flexibility in dealing with this extremely delicate problem, which involved United Nations agencies among other possibilities.

Customs 25. In taking up consideration of the Customs Article, Mr. Habib stated that the U.S. negotiators wished to table an additional Agreed Minute, in order to make this article consistent with the Non-Appropriated Fund Organizations Article. While paragraph 2 of the Customs Article permits duty-free importation of goods, the language is inconsistent with the language of the Non-Appropriated Fund Organizations Article, as now proposed. Therefore, the U.S. negotiators proposed the following additional Agreed Minute:

> "7. It is understood that the duty free treatment provided in paragraph 2 shall apply to materials, supplies, and equipment imported for sale through commissaries and non-appropriated fund organizations, under such regulations as the United States armed forces may promulgate, to those individuals and organizations referred to in Article ______ and its Agreed Minute."

26. Mr. Habib added that there was also need to modify the language of Agreed Minute #1, since the Non-Appropriated Fund Organizations Article, as proposed, included more persons than just members of the armed forces, the civilian component, and their dependents. Therefore, the U.S. negotiators proposed the deletion from Agreed Minute #1 of the phrase "the members of the United States armed forces, the civilian component, and their dependents"

0052

and the insertion in its place of the phrase "persons authorized by Article _______ and its Agreed Minute."

27. Mr. Habib recalled that at the previous meeting, the Korean negotiators had proposed the deletion from paragraph 5(c) of the phrase "including their authorized procurement agencies and their non-appropriated fund organizations provided for in Article _____", on the grounds that this phrase was also included in Agreed Minute #3 and there was no need for repetition. Mr. Habib stated the U.S. negotiators agreed to the deletion of this phrase from paragraph 5(c).

28. With regard to the proposed Agreed Minute tabled by the U.S. negotiators and the change proposed by them in Agreed Minute #1, Mr. Chang said the Korean negotiators fully agreed with the necessity for consistency within the SOFA. He pointed out, however, that agreement had not yet been reached on what persons were to be covered by the provisions of the Non-Appropriated Fund Organizations Article. The Korean negotiators agreed to the deletion of the phrase in question from paragraph 5(c), with the understanding that final agreement had not yet been reached with regard to the text of Agreed Minute #3. Mr. Habib agreed.

29. Turning to paragraph 5(b), Mr. Chang stated the understanding of the Korean negotiators that both sides had agreed at previous meetings to the right of the ROKG authorities to inspect parcels. The U.S. negotiators had proposed that this subparagraph read as follows:

0053

"Official documents under official seal and First Class mail in United States military postal channels under official postal seal". The U.S. negotiators had explained that parcels can be included in First Class mail but are kept separate from letter mail. They had also pointed out that the rates for sending parcels by First Class mail are very high and therefore most parcels are sent by parcel post rather than as First Class mail. He said the Korean authorities wished to inspect the parcels which are sent as First Class mail. What was being suggested was not a postal inspection but a customs inspection. The Korean negotiators, therefore, suggested that paragraph 5(b) read as follows:

> "5(b). Official documents under official seal and First Class letter mail in United States military postal channels under official postal seal."

30. Mr. Habib stated that the U.S. negotiators would consider the Korean proposal.

31. Turning to paragraph 5(c), Mr. Chang stated that in the past and currently goods imported for the Non-Appropriated Fund Organizations have been the subject of illegal transactions in the black market, to the great detriment of the Korean economy. The ROK Government has been trying to prevent such abuses, without much success. Therefore, the Korean negotiators wish to retain, in this paragraph, the right of customs inspection of such goods. If the U.S. negotiators did not find this acceptable, Mr. Chang stated that the Korean negotiators had some alternative suggestions to make.

32. Mr. Habib replied that the Korean negotiators were confusing the administrative and police function with the purpose of this article. The provisions of this

0054

article do not affect punitive and preventive measures to be taken under the provisions of other articles of the SOFA and/or other agreements. The right of customs inspection has no bearing or relevancy on the disposal of these goods. Such goods constitute military cargo, as the U.S. negotiators have repeatedly pointed out. Stating that no purpose would be served in repeating the already oft-repeated U.S. position, Mr. Habib asked the Korean negotiators to present their alternative proposals.

33. Mr. Ku stated that the U.S. negotiators had previously explained that persons guilty of illegally disposing of these goods would be dealt with under the provisions of the Respect for Local Law Article, the Criminal Jurisdiction Article, and the regulations of the U.S. armed forces. Paragraph #6 provides that these goods shall not be disposed of to persons not entitled to import such goods free of duty. He said this provision was too general. The provisions of the Respect for Local Law Article also were quite general. The Korean negotiators did not foresee that the Criminal Jurisdiction Article would contain detailed provisions on this matter. Therefore, methods of preventing such illegal transactions should be provided for in some other way. The right to inspect such goods on their entry into the Republic of Korea must be provided for.

34. Mr. Habib replied that Mr. Ku had not mentioned paragraphs 8 and 9 of this article, which were also relevant. Mr. Habib said the SOFA will establish the principle that

0055

there should not be abuses. The implementation of that principle will be left to the Joint Committee. The U.S. negotiators anticipated that both sides would provide cooperation of the highest order to provide for the maximum effective prevention of abuses. He asked if the Korean negotiators had any specific suggestions to make.

35. Mr. Ku replied that the Korean negotiators had explained why the ROKG authorities wished to have the right of inspection. In order to solve this problem, the Korean negotiators wished to table the following proposed additional Agreed Minute:

> "4. The Korean authorities may request from the United States military authorities whatever information they deem necessary pertaining to all cargo consigned to the non-appropriated fund organizations and the United States military authorities shall promptly provide such informatinn in the manner as is specified by the Korean authorities."

Inasmuch as Agreed Minute #3 refers to military cargo, Mr. Ku explained, the Korean authorities wished to propose the above Agreed Minute as Agreed Minute #4.

36. Mr. Habib said the U.S. negotiators would consider the Korean proposal.

37. The next meeting was scheduled for January 17 at 2:00 p.m.

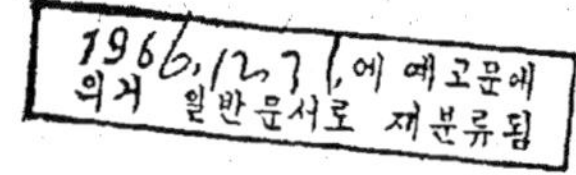


0056

2. 제39차 회의, 1.17

0057

# 기 안 용 지

| 자체통제 | | 기안처 | 미주과 이근팔 | 전화번호 | 근거서류접수일자 |
|---|---|---|---|---|---|
| | 과장 | 국장 | 차관 | 장관 | |
| 관계관 서명 | | | | | |
| 기안년월일 | 1964. 1. 16. | 시행년월일 | | 보존년한 | 정서기장 |
| 분류기호 | | 전체통제 | | 종결 | |
| 경유 수신 참조 | 건 의 | 발신 | | | |
| 제목 | 제39차 주둔군지위협정 체결교섭회의에 임할 우리측 입장 | | | | |

1월 17일에 개최될 제39차 주둔군지위협정 체결을 위한 한미간 교섭회의에서는 관세업무, 공익물 및 용역, 및 군사우편에 관한 조문을 토의하도록 예정되고 있는바 이에 대하여 우리측 교섭실무자는 1월 14, 15 양일간 회합을 갖고 제39차 회의에서 취할 태도를 별첨과 같이 결정하였아오니 재가하여 주시기 바랍니다.

유첨: 제39차 주둔군지위협정 체결교섭회의에 임할 우리측 태도.

196 . 12. 31 예고문에 의거 일반문서로 재분류됨

승인양식 1-1-3 (1112-040-016-018) (190mm×260mm16절지)

0058

1. 관세조항

가. 우편물 감사 면제에 관한 미국측 초안 5 (b) 항에 있어서 미국측은 제 36차 회의에서 "Official documents under official seal and First Class mail in United States military postal channels under official postal seal" 로 하자는 대안을 제의한바 있다. 그러나 미국측은 "First Class mail" 에는 소포가 포함될수 있다고 시사하고 제 37차 회의에서 소포에 적용되는 무게 표식 및 요금상의 제안에 관하여 설명한바 있다. 이에 대하여 우리측은 공문서 및 사서신을 제외한 모든 소포에 대하여서는 First Class로 송부되는 소포까지도 한국세관당국이 검사할 권한을 보유한다는 입장에서 미국측 대안인 "First Class mail" 을 수락할수 없음을 지적하고 미국측 주장을 "First Class letter mail로 수정할 것을 제 38차 회의에서 제안한바 있으므로 금차 회의에서 아측 안에 대한 미국측 태도를 보아 만약 미국측이 아측안을 수락하지 않을 경우에는 1) 우편물 검사에 있어서 우편물 배달을 지연 시키지 않을 것과 2) 모든 우편물을 검사하는 것은 아니고 단지 검사권을 보유한다는데 의의가 있다는 점 및 3) 사실상 가격면에서 제한을 받게 됨으로 이용가능성이 희박하다는 미측의 설명으로 보아 우리측이 검사권을 보유하여도 별다른 지장이 없을 것이라는 점을 들어 계속 우리측 수정안을 주장하기로 한다.

나. 우리측은 제 38차 회의에서 군사화물의 세관검사 면제에 관한 미국측 초안 5 (c) 항에 관련하여

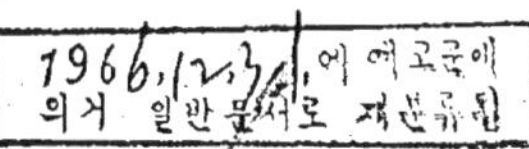


39

0059

미국측 초안 (6)항 즉 무세로 수입된 물품은 상호 합의된 조건에 의거 한미 양당국에 의하여 그 처분이 허가된 경우를 제외하고는 그러한 물품을 무세로 수입할 권한이 없는 자에게 처분할수 없다는 규정에 위배하여 처분하였을 경우 그러한 처분을 한 미국군인에 대한 처벌이 규정되어 있지 않으므로 관세 조문에서 규제함이 타당하다고 주장하였으나 미국측에서 수락하지 않으므로 우리측에서는 "군사화물"에 관한 세관검사 면제 규정인 5 (c)항에 있어서 비세출자금기관 앞으로 탁송되는 물품에 대하여서는 우리 세관당국이 검사권 만을 보유해야 하겠다고 주장한바 있음.

다. 그러나 미국측에서는 비세출기관 앞으로 탁송되는 화물도 군사화물의 일부이며 세관검사권 만으로서는 물품의 불법 처분에 대처할수는 없다 하여 아국측 제안을 수락하지 않은바 있음.

라. 우리측은 검사권 보유 주장에 대한 최종적인 대안으로서 "한국정부가 비세출자금 기관에 탁송되는 물품에 관하여 필요로 하는 정보를 요구하면 미국당국은 신속히 그러한 정보를 제공해야한다"는 요지 양해사항을 합의 의사록에서 규정하도록 다음과 같이 제안하고 금차 회의에서 미국측 견해를 듣기로 하였다.

" The Korean authorities may request from the United States military authorities whatever information they deem necessary pertaining to all cargo consigned to the non-appropriated fund organizations and the United States military authorities shall promptly provide such information in the manner as is specified by the Korean authorities."

0060

마. 제 39차 회의에서 만약 미국측이 우리측 제안을 대폭 수정하라고 할 경우에는 1) 과거 및 현재에 있어서 많은 비세출자금기관 물품이 한국시장에서 불법거래되고 있는 실정과 2) 따라서 그러한 불법적 거래를 한 사람들에 대한 실질적인 처벌을 규정하지 않는 한 그와 같은 불법적 거래가 계속될 것이며 3) 현하 우리나라 경제를 저해할 가능성이 있음을 지적하여 세관 당국이 검사권을 보유해야 하겠다는 입장으로 복귀한다.

바. 관세 조문중 이외에 미합이 된 조항은 차량 및 부속품의 무세수입에 관한 미국측 초안 3(b) 항과 한국에 출입하는 미군대 구성원에 대한 세관검사 면제에 관한 5(a) 항 및 합의 의사록 2 및 3항인바 미국측이 우편물 소모 및 군사화물에 대한 세관검사 면제에 관한 우리측 입장을 수락하여 줄 경우에는 모두 미국측 안대로 수락하기로 한다.

사. 미국측의 관세조항 제 1항은 비세출 기관이 미군구성원, 민간구성원 및 그들의 가족의 사용을 위하여 수입하는 물품에 대한 관세면제를 규정하고 있는바 제 38차 회의에서 미측은 비세출기관 조항과의 균형을 마치기 위하여 "the members of the United States armed forces, the civilian component, and their dependents 를 "persons authorized by Article _ and its Agreed Minute" 로 수정하여 줄것을 제의하였다. 미측 수정 제안에 대하여 아국측은 비세출기관의 사용대상자에 관해서는 동조문에 대한 합의를 조건으로 미측 수정안을 수락하기로 한다.

0061

아. 미측에서 제 38 차 회의에서 제안한 합의의사록 제 7 항 " It is understood that the duty free treatment provided in paragraph 2 shall apply to materials, supplies, and equipment imported for sale through commissaries and non-appropriated fund organizations, under such regulations as the United States armed forces may promulgate, to those individuals and organizations referred to in Article ______ and its Agreed Minute."

에 대하여서는 만약 미국측의 의도가 관세조문에 언급이 없는Commissary 를 합의의사록에서 모함규정하기 위한 것이라면 (1) Commissary 를 관세조항 제 2 항에 삽입하고 합의의사록 제 7 항을 삭제할 것을 주장한다. (2) 만약 미측의 의도가 Commissary 의 사용 대상 범위를 비세출기관의 사용대상 범위와 같이 확대시키기 위한 것이라면 Commissary 는 세출자금 기관임으로 그사용은 미군대 구성원, 군속 및 그들의 가족에게만 한정되어야 한다고 주장하고 따라서 합의의사록 7항을 다음과 같이 수정할 것을 제의한다.

" It is understood that the duty free treatment provided in paragraph 2 shall apply to materials, supplies, and equipment imported for sale through commissaries for the official use of the members of the United States armed forces, the civilian component, and their dependents."

0062

2. 군사우편

미국측 초안 (2) 항은 통상 해외에서 그러한 특권이 부여된 미국정부 관리 및 그들의 가족들도 군사 우편 시설을 이용할수 있도록 규정하고 있는바 제 19 차 회의에서 양측은 본규정은 예외적인 규정 임으로 본문대신에 합의의사록에 넣도록 할것에 합의한바 있다. 우리측은 먼저 미국측 초안에 their dependents 란 구절을 모함시킨 이유를 묻기로 하고 미국측이 동구절의 삽입을 원할 경우에는 그들의 가족도 군사우편을 이용할수 있다는 양해를 회의기록에 남기도록 하고 본 문장에서는 삭제할 것을 주장한다.



0063

3. 공익물 및 용역

가. 제 39 차 본회의의 의사 진행을 촉진시키기 위하여 1월 15일 한미간 실무자들이 회합을 갖고 공익물에 관한 미국측 초안을 중심으로 하여 협의된바에 따라 우리측에서는 다음과 같이 제안한다.

(1) 공익물에 관한 미국측 초안 3 (a) 항에서 우리측은

(가) 공익물 및 용역의 정의에 관한 둘째 문장에 있는 "however produced" 라는 구절은 공익물 및 용역의 생산방법에만 제한 관련되고 정부냐 개인이냐에 대한 생산자 여하에는 관계가 없으며 특히 개인경영으로 생산되는 공익물과 용역과는 관련이 없다는 것을 기록에 남기기로 하고 수락한다.

삭제함

나. 미국측 초안 3 (b) 항 둘째 문장은 비상시 작전상의 필요가 있을시 대한민국은 공익물 및 용역의 제공을 보장하기 위한 조치를 취할 것을 규정하고 있는바 우리측에서는 미국측이나 또는 한국측에서 비상시 작전상의 필요가 있다고 인정하는 경우는 제반 조치를 다취할 용의가 있는바이나 미군측의 일방적인 통고에 만 의할 것이 아니라 우리정부에서도 검토하여 적절하다고 인정할 때에 적당안 조치를 취할수 있기 위하여

(가) "upon notification thereon"를 "after consultation thereon"으로

(나) "take all measures"를 " take appropriate measures" 로 각각 수정할 것과 (다) 3 (b) 항 둘째 문장을 합의 의사록 제 3 항으로 규정할 것을 제의한다. 그러므로 동문장은 다음과 같다.

0064

" Should the emergency operating needs of the United States armed forces so require, the Republic of Korea shall, after consultation thereon, take appropriate measures to assure provision of utilities and services necessary to meet these needs."

(X) 다. 미국측 초안 제4항에 대하여서는 미국측에서 본 조항은 공익물 및 용역 조항에 관련되어 있기 보다 토지 시설문제에서 일어나는 요금청산 또는 본협정 전반에서 일어나는 금전거래에 적용될 청산조치에 관하여 규정하고 있다 함으로 우리측에서는 본 조항을 우선 공익물 및 용역 조항에서 삭제하여 차후 적당한 조항으로 신설 하자고 주장한다. 또한 토지시설 조항과 공익물 및 용역 조항과의 통합여부는 차후에 다시 토의키로 한다.

라. 합의의사록 제1항은 미군에 적용되는 공익물 및 용역의 사용우선권 또는 사용료의 변경이 있을 경우에는 합동위원회에서 사전에 협의해야 한다고 규정하고 있는바 (1) 공익물 및 용역의 사용우선권 또는 사용료의 변경문제는 중요한 문제임으로 우리나라 정부에서는 신중히 처리하는 문제이며 합동위원회의 협의에 구해될 수는 없는 문제이다. 또한 다음과 같은 수정안을 제시 하면서 1) 합동위원회에서의 토의는 미국측의 의견을 듣는데에 한하며 동의가 필요한 것은 아니며 2) 동료금책정에는 공공요금위원회와 국무회의를 거쳐야 발효됨으로 미국측과의 상의결과와 반드시 동일하지 않을수도 있다는 것을 기록에 남기다.

" The Joint Committee may be given the opportunities of discussing any changes ~~in~~ [of] [determined by the Korean Government] priority or rates applicable to the United States armed forces prior to their effective date."

0065

마. 합의의사록 초안 2항은 1958.12.18자 한미 양국이 체결한 공익물에 관한 청구권 청산 협정의 효력을 존속시키도록 한 규정인바 우리측은 상기협정의 개정 가능성을 유보하기 위하여 동 2항에 "unless otherwise agreed between the two Governments"을 추가할 것을 제의한다. 따라서 제2항은 다음과 같이 된다.

"Paragraph ___ of Article ___ will not be construed as in any way abrogating the Utilities and Claims Settlement Agreement of December 18, 1958 which continues in full force and effect unless otherwise agreed ~~between~~ by the two Governments."

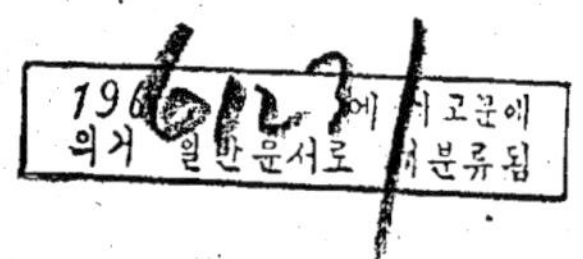


0066

SOFA NEGOTIATION

Agenda for the 39th Session

14:00 January 17, 1964

1. Continuation of Discussions on:

   a. Customs Article

   b. Military Post Offices Article

   c. Utilities and Services Article

2. Other Business

3. Agenda and Date of the Next Meeting

4. Press Release

0067

# 기 안 용 지

| 자체 통제 | 외무사무관 손일종 | 기안처 | 미주과 강석재 | 전화번호 | 근거서류접수일자 |
|---|---|---|---|---|---|
| | 과장 | 국장 | 차관 | 장관 | |
| | | | 전결 | | |
| 관계관 서명 | | | | | |
| 기안 년월일 | 1964. 1. 20 | 시행 년월일 | | 보존 년한 | 정서기장 |
| 분류 기호 | 외구미722.2 | 전체 통제 | 1964. 종결 | | |
| 경유 수신 참조 | 대통령 참조: 비서실장 국무총리 | | | 발신 | |
| 제목 | 주둔군지위협정체결을 위한 제39차 교섭회의 보고 | | | | |

1964. 1. 17. 하오 2시부터 3시15분까지 외무부장관 회의실에서 개최된 제39차 주둔군지위협정 체결교섭회의에서 토의된 내용을 별첨과 같이 보고합니다.

유첨: 제39차 교섭회의 보고서 1부 끝

1966.12.31에 예고문에 의거 일반문서로 재분류됨

승인서식 1-1-3 (11-00900-03) (195mm×265mm16절지)

0068

제 39 차

한미간 주둔군지위협정 체결실무자회의

보 고 서

1. 일 시: 1964년 1월 16일 하오 2시부터 3시15분까지

2. 장 소: 외무부 장관 회의실

3. 토의사항:

가. 관세업무

(1) 세관검사에 관련하여 우리측은 군사우편으로 들어오는 소포는 " first class mail "이건 일반 " parcel post "이건 모두 한국세관당국이 검사해야한다는 입장인바 미국측은확실히 상품이 아닌 경우에는 검사를 하지못하도록 " Official documents under official seal and first class mail in United States military postal channels obviously not containing merchandise "라는 대안을 제출하여 합의를 보지 못하였다.

(2) 우리측은 비세출자금기관앞으로 탁송되어 오는 물품에 관하여 근본적으로 검사권한을 해야한다는 입장을 취하고 있으나 "미국측은 한국세관당국이 요구하는 정보를 제공해야한다"라는 대안을 제시한바있다. 미국측은 이에관한 논평을 보류하기 때문에 상금 합의를 못보고 있다.

나. 공의물 및 용역

본 조문에 있어서는 용어 및 기타 기술적 사항만이 미합의로 남아 있는바 우리측은 이를 조정하여 본조문 및 합의의사록을 수정한 대안을 제출하였는바 미국측은 이를 본국정부에 조회하겠다고 답변하였다.

다. 군사우편

본조문에 대해서는 완전합의를 보았으나 합의의사록에서 미국측안은 통상 해외에서 군사우편을 사용할 특권이 부여된 미국정부 관리 및 직원과 그들의 가족들도 군사우편을 이용토록 규제하고 있음으로

0069

64-3-3(2) 미국무 109-9(2)

0070

우리측은 미일협정에는 그들의 가족이 포함되어 있지 않음을 지적하고 실제운영은 어떠냐고 반문하였는바 미국측은 실제 그들도 이용하고 있으며 만약 협정에서 규제않는다 하더라도 사실은 남편 기타 보호자 명의로 이용하기 때문에 위법적인 상태를 조성하게 된다는 설명이 있었으나 다음회의에서 계속 토의하기로 하였다.

4. 기타 사항

차기회의 일자: 1964년 1월 24일 하오 2시



0071

64-3-8

64-3-3(2) 미국.문 109-9(2)

0072

January 17, 1964

Customs

1. Mr. Chang opened the 39th meeting by asking whether the U.S. negotiators had any further comment to make on paragraph 5(b) of the Customs Article.

2. Mr. Habib replied that, before responding to Mr. Chang's question, he wished to review the course of previous discussion of this subparagraph. At previous meetings, the Korean negotiators had indicated that what they were seeking was a deterrent to the illegal use of the military postal channels. They had expressed primary interest in the right to inspect parcels coming into Korea through those channels. The U.S. negotiators, for their part, had expressed concern over the possibility that inspection might cause delays in the delivery of the mail, which would result in a lowering of the morale of the troops.

3. Mr. Habib said he wished to remind the Korean negotiators that at the 37th negotiating meeting on December 27, the U.S. negotiators had offered to agree to the principle of the right of the Korean authorities to inspect non-first class mail, provided the Korean negotiators would agree to four understandings. Those understandings were as follows:

a. Examination of parcels in the MPO mails in the ROK by ROK customs inspectors will be conducted so as not to damage the contents of the parcels inspected or delay delivery of the mail;

b. Such examinations will be conducted in U.S. MPO installations at designated points of mail distribution and in the presence of U.S. officials;

c. No parcel in the MPO mails will be removed from U.S. postal channels except as mutually agreed;

d. It is understood that the right of inspection will be exercised on a "spot check" basis so as not to unduly delay delivery or increase the administrative burden of the postal authorities.

4. Mr. Habib stated that the understandings which he had just read from the record of the 37th meeting had grown out of assurances given by the ROK negotiators in prior discussions of this subject. With those understandings, he continued, the U.S. negotiators were now prepared to agree to the principle of the right of the Korean

authorities to inspect parcel mail, regardless of class. The Korean negotiators had indicated that their interest was in inspecting parcels coming into Korea through the MPO mails. The Korean negotiators could be assured of the full cooperation of the U.S. armed forces in implementing whatever provision was finally agreed upon. If the Korean negotiators agreed to the four understandings which he had just read, the U.S. negotiators wished to propose the following revised language for this subparagraph:

> "(b) Official documents under official seal and First Class mail in the United States military postal channels obviously not containing merchandise;".

5. Mr. Habib pointed out that the proposed revised language would grant the right to inspect parcels in all classes of mail, including First Class and Air Parcel Post. He said the language suggested by the Korean negotiators ("First Class letter mail") was not satisfactory because it would not cover two special types of parcels which the U.S. negotiators believed should be exempted from inspection. The first of these consists of tapes containing recordings of personal messages which the troops send to, and receive from, their families in the United States. The second consists of photographic film being returned after having been sent to the United States for processing. Both types of parcel are individually and clearly marked. They do not contain merchandise and have only personal value. The U.S. negotiators equate them with letter mail.

6. Summing up the position of the U.S. negotiators with regard to paragraph 5(b), Mr. Habib stated that the revised language just tabled by the U.S. side would meet the needs of the Korean negotiators and would be acceptable to the U.S. negotiators, provided the Korean side accepted the four understandings which he had read from the record of the 37th meeting. He said the U.S. armed forces would extend all possible cooperation in the implementation of this provision.

7. In reply, Mr. Chang expressed the appreciation of the Korean negotiators that the U.S. side had obviously taken their previous proposal under consideration. He said that the Korean negotiators had been requesting the right to inspect parcels and that

0074

this right had been agreed upon in principle. He said the understandings read by Mr. Habib were fully understood by the Korean side and no further comment regarding them was necessary. Of course, it was agreed that delivery of the mail should not be unduly delayed but there might be delays which were unavoidable. He said the Korean side would present its views at the next meeting on the new language proposed by the U.S. negotiators. He asked whether the packages containing tape recordings and films were included in First Class letter mail. Also, the Korean negotiators wondered who would interpret the meaning of the word "obviously" in the implementation of the proposed new language.

8. With regard to Mr. Chang's remarks concerning unavoidable delays, Mr. Habib stated that what was really at issue was the definition of the word "unduly". He said it means that there will be no delay which is not warranted by the rights being exercised by the inspectors. He said on-the-spot decisions would be required and that if the U.S. armed forces believed that undue delays were occurring, the matter would be raised by the U.S. authorities in the Joint Committee. However, the U.S. negotiators looked forward to mutual cooperative efforts to ensure that no undue delays would occur. In response to Mr. Chang's question concerning packages containing tape recordings and films, Mr. Habib replied that such packages were included in Air Mail or First Class letter mail pouches, if postage was paid for such handling.

9. Mr. Chang stated that the Korean negotiators would give their views on the U.S. proposals at the next meeting. He then asked whether the U.S. side wished to comment on the proposal made at the previous meeting by the Korean negotiators to adopt a new Agreed Minute #4 in connection with paragraph 5(c). Mr. Habib replied that the U.S. negotiators had no comment to make on that proposal at that time.

10. Mr. Chang stated that there were some remaining minor points still unresolved in this article but suggested that the negotiators move on to the next item on the agenda. Mr. Habib said the U.S. negotiators would like to hear at the next meeting the views of the Korean negotiators regarding paragraph 3(b). Mr. Chang agreed.

0075

11. Mr. Habib referred to the proposed change in Agreed Minute #1 and the proposed new Agreed Minute #7 which the U.S. negotiators had tabled at the last meeting. Mr. Chang replied that the Korean negotiators had studied the U.S. proposals but were not yet prepared to comment on them. He said the Korean side did not believe that the only reason for proposing them was to insure consistency between the Customs Article and the Non-Appropriated Fund Organizations Article. He referred to the mention in the proposed Agreed Minute #7 of commissaries, which were not mentioned elsewhere in the customs article or the non-appropriated fund Organizations article.

12. Mr. Habib replied that he did not understand the first point which Mr. Chang appeared to be trying to make. In point of fact, the commissaries operated by the U.S. armed forces are appropriated fund activities and not non-appropriated fund activities. Therefore, mention has to be made of them in this article in order to make the text fully consistent with the administrative facts.

13. Mr. Chang asked what categories of personnel utilize the commissaries. Mr. Habib replied that at present personnel of the Embassy and USOM, as well as of UNCURK and some of the other personnel who would fall under category (f) of the proposed Agreed Minute to the non-appropriated fund organizations article used the commissaries. He pointed out, however, that military personnel without resident dependents were not permitted to use these facilities. In addition, there were also other controls on their use, such as a limitation on the amount of supplies that can be purchased in a month.

14. Mr. Chang then asked whether, with the exception of military personnel lacking resident dependents, the persons permitted to use the commissaries were identical with the persons permitted to use the non-appropriated fund organizations. Mr. Habib replied that they were not identical. Colonel Fuller pointed out that the negotiators were not so much concerned with the question of who is entitled to use the commissaries at present but with the question of who will be authorized to use such facilities by the Status of Forces Agreement. He added that this proposed Agreed Minute had been designed to make the conditions of use of the commissaries consistent with

0076

those pertaining to the non-appropriated fund organizations.

15. Mr. Chang stated that the tone of the proposed Agreed Minute #7 implied that non-appropriated fund organization users could automatically use the commissaries. Mr. Habib stated that it would not be automatic. The U.S. armed forces have to be willing to permit such use and the ROK Government would have to agree with respect to persons falling under category (f).

16. Mr. Chang said that the proposed Agreed Minute #7 would permit the U.S. armed forces to extend commissary privileges to the users of non-appropriated fund organizations. Mr. Habib confirmed Mr. Chang's interpretation. Mr. Chang stated that this was of concern to the ROK negotiators. He asked whether the categories of persons who might be authorized to use the commissaries were identical with the categories listed in the proposed Agreed Minute to the non-appropriated fund organizations article. Mr. Habib replied that the decision as to who could use the commissaries was based upon the regulations of the U.S. armed forces.

17. Mr. Chang stated that the Korean negotiators would like to have more specific information about who would be permitted to use the commissaries and the non-appropriated fund organizations under the provisions of the U.S. proposals. He said the Korean negotiators would present their views regarding the proposed Agreed Minute #7 at the next meeting.

Utilities and Services

18. Turning to the article on utilities and services, Mr. Chang reported that a subcommittee of negotiators from both sides had met and discussed this article. On the basis of that discussion, the Korean negotiators wished to table a proposed revision of the article. In tabling the revision, he pointed out that the Korean negotiators had deleted from paragraph 3 the term "however produced". As the Korean negotiators had previously pointed out, this phrase had no meaning for them and they did not understand why it should be included in the text when other qualifying phrases such as "by whomever produced" were not included. In the proposed new Agreed Minute #1, he added, the Korean

negotiators had included the term "changes determined by the Korean authorities", since both sides had previously agreed that the Korean authorities would make the final decision on changes in utilities rates or priorities.

19. Mr. Habib said that the U.S. negotiators would take the Korean proposed revision under consideration and comment thereon at a later meeting.

Military Post Offices

20. Turning to the Military Post Offices Article, Mr. Chang stated that the only point still unresolved was the inclusion of the phrase "and their dependents" in the U.S. draft of the Agreed Minute. He said this created difficulties for the ROK negotiators. There was no such provision in the Status of Forces Agreement with Japan; did dependents have the use of military post offices in Japan?

21. Mr. Habib replied that the phrase was included for the sake of clarity. Dependents did have the use of military post offices in Japan; in fact, this was true throughout the world. Although it was not mentioned in the SOFA with Japan, it was spelled out in other Status of Forces Agreements.

22. Mr. Chang noted that agreement had already been reached to convert paragraph 2 into an Agreed Minute. Mr. Habib confirmed this. Mr. Chang then stated that the ROK negotiators would consider the explanation given by the U.S. negotiators and would present their views at the next meeting.

23. The next meeting was scheduled for January 24 at 2:00 p.m.

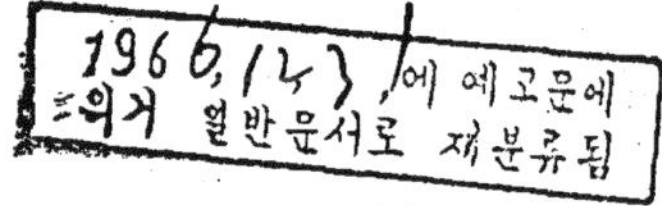


0078

## JOINT SUMMARY RECORD OF THE 39TH SESSION

1. Time and Place: 2:00-3:15 P.M. January 17, 1964 at the Foreign Ministry's Conference Room

| 미주과 | 양고재 | 담당 | 과장 | 국장 | 특별보좌관 | 차관 | 장관 |
|---|---|---|---|---|---|---|---|

2. Attendants:

ROK Side:

| | |
|---|---|
| Mr. Chang, Sang Moon | Director<br>European and American Affairs Bureau<br>Ministry of Foreign Affairs |
| Mr. Shin, Kwan Sup | Director<br>Bureau of Customs Duty<br>Ministry of Finance |
| Mr. Koo, Choong Whay | Chief, American Section<br>Ministry of Foreign Affairs |
| Mr. Choo, Moon Ki | Chief, Legal Affairs Section<br>Ministry of Justice |
| Mr. Oh, Jae Hee | Chief, Treaty Section<br>Ministry of Foreign Affairs |
| Mr. Kang, Suk Jae (Rapporteur and Interpreter) | 2nd Secretary<br>Ministry of Foreign Affairs |
| Mr. Lee, Chung Bin | 3rd Secretary<br>Ministry of Foreign Affairs |
| Mr. Lee, Keun Pal | 3rd Secretary<br>Ministry of Foreign Affairs |

U.S. Side:

| | |
|---|---|
| Mr. Philip C. Habib | Counselor for Political Affairs<br>American Embassy |
| Col. Howard Smigelow | Deputy Chief of Staff<br>8th U.S. Army |
| Col. L.J. Fuller | Staff Judge Advocate<br>United Nations Command |
| Capt. John Wayne | Assistant Chief of Staff<br>USN/K |
| Mr. Benjamin A. Fleck (Rapporteur and Press Officer) | First Secretary<br>American Embassy |

1/3

0079

| | |
|---|---|
| Mr. James Sartorius | 2nd Secretary<br>American Embassy |
| Mr. Robert A. Lewis | 2nd Secretary and Consul<br>American Embassy |
| Mr. Robert A. Kinney | J-5<br>8th U.S. Army |
| Maj.Robert D. Peckham | Staff Officer, JAG<br>8th U.S. Army |
| Mr. Kenneth Campen | Interpreter |

1. Mr. Chang opened the 39th meeting by asking whether the U.S. negotiators had any further comment to make on paragraph 5(b) of the Customs Article.

2. Mr. Habib replied that, before responding to Mr. Chang's question, he wished to review the course of previous discussion of this sub-paragraph. At previous meetings, the Korean negotiators had indicated that what they were seeking was a deterrent to the illegal use of the military postal channels. They had expressed primary interest in the right to inspect parcels coming into Korea through those channels. The U.S. negotiators, for their part, had expressed concern over the possibility that inspection might cause delays in the delivery of the mail, which would result in a lowering of the morale of the troops.

3. Mr. Habib said he wished to remind the Korean negotiators that at the 37th negotiating meeting on December 27, the U.S. negotiators had offered to agree to the principle of the right of the Korean authorities to inspect non-first class mail, provided the Korean negotiators would agree to four understandings. Those understandings were as follows:

0080

a. Examination of parcels in the MPO mails in the ROK by ROK customs inspectors will be conducted so as not to damage the contents of the parcels inspected or delay delivery of the mail;

b. Such examinations will be conducted in U.S. MPO installations at designated points of mail distribution and in the presence of U.S. officials;

c. No parcel in the MPO mails will be removed from U.S. postal channels except as mutually agreed;

d. It is understood that the right of inspection will be exercised on a "spot check" basis so as not to unduly delay delivery or increase the administrative burden of the postal authorities.

4. Mr. Habib stated that the understandings which he had just read from the record of the 37th meeting had grown out of assurances given by the ROK negotiators in prior discussions of this subject. With those understandings, he continued, the U.S. negotiators were now prepared to agree to the principle of the right of the Korean authorities to inspect parcel mail, regardless of class. The Korean negotiators had indicated that their interest was in inspecting parcels coming into Korea through the MPO mails. The Korean negotiators could be assured of the full cooperation of the U.S. armed forces in implementing whatever provision was finally agreed upon. If the Korean negotiators agreed to the four understandings which he had just read, the U.S. negotiators wished to propose the following revised language for this subparagraph:

"(b) Official documents under official seal and First Class mail in the United States military postal channels obviously not containing merchandise;"

5. Mr. Habib pointed out that the proposed revised language would grant the right to inspect parcels in all classes of mail, including First Class and Air Parcel Post. He said the language suggested by the Korean negotiators ("First Class letter mail") was not satisfactory

0081

because it would not cover two special types of parcels which the U.S. negotiators believed should be exempted from inspection. The first of these consists of tapes containing recordings of personal messages which the troops send to, and receive from, their families in the United States. The second consists of photographic film being returned after having been sent to the United States for processing. Both types of parcels are individually and clearly marked. They do not contain merchandise and have only personal value. The U.S. negotiators equate them with letter mail.

6. Summing up the position of the U.S. negotiators with regard to paragraph 5(b), Mr. Habib stated that the revised language just tabled by the U.S. side would meet the needs of the Korean negotiators and would be acceptable to the U.S. negotiators, provided the Korean side accepted the four understandings which he had read from the record of the 37th meeting. He said the U.S. armed forces would extend all possible cooperation in the implementation of this provision.

7. In reply, Mr. Chang expressed the appreciation of the Korean negotiators that the U.S. side had obviously taken their previous proposal under consideratinn. He said that the Korean negotiators had been requesting the right to inspect parcels and that this right had been agreed upon in principle. He said the understandings read by Mr. Habib were fully understood by the Korean side and no further comment regarding them was necessary. Of course, it was agreed that delivery of the mail should not be unduly delayed but there might be delays which were

0082

unavoidable. He said the Korean side would present its views at the next meeting on the new language proposed by the U.S. negotiators. He asked whether the packages containing tape recordings and films were included in First Class letter mail. Also, the Korean negotiators wondered who would interpret the meaning of the word "obviously" in the implementation of the proposed new language.

8. With regard to Mr. Chang's remarks concerning unavoidable delays, Mr. Habib stated that what was really at issue was the definition of the word "unduly". He said it means that there will be no delay which is not warranted by the rights being exercised by the inspectors. He said on-the-spot decisions would be required and that if the U.S. armed forces believed that undue delays were occurring, the matter would be raised by the U.S. authorities in the Joint Committee. However, the U.S. negotiators looked forward to mutual cooperative efforts to ensure that no undue delays would occur. In response to Mr. Chang's question concerning packages containing tape recordings and films, Mr. Habib replied that such packages were included in Air Mail or First Class letter mail pouches, if postage was paid for such handling,

9. Mr. Chang stated that the Korean negotiators would give their views on the U.S. proposals at the next meeting. He then asked whether the U.S. side wished to comment on the proposal made at the previous meeting by the Korean negotiators to adopt a new Agreed Minute #4 in connection with paragraph 5(c). Mr. Habib replied that the U.S. negotiators had no comment to make on that proposal at that time.

0083

10. Mr. Chang stated that there were some remaining major points still unresolved in this article but suggested that the negotiators move on to the next item on the agenda. Mr. Habib said the U.S. negotiators would like to hear at the next meeting the views of the Korean negotiators regarding paragraph 3(b). Mr. Chang agreed.

11. Mr. Habib referred to the proposed change in Agreed Minute #1 and the proposed new Agreed Minute #7 which the U.S. negotiators had tabled at the last meeting. Mr. Chang replied that the Korean negotiators had studied the U.S. proposals but were not yet prepared to comment on them. He said the Korean side did not believe that the only reason for proposing them was to insure consistency between the Customs Article and the Non-Appropriated Fund Organizations Article. He referred to the mention in the proposed Agreed Minute #7 of commissaries, which were not mentioned elsewhere in the customs article or the non-appropriated fund organizations article.

12. Mr. Habib replied that he did not understand the first point which Mr. Chang appeared to be trying to make. In point of fact, the commissaries operated by the U.S. armed forces are appropriated fund activities and not non-appropriated fund activities. Therefore, mention has to be made of them in this article in order to make the text fully consistent with the administrative facts.

13. Mr. Chang asked what categories of personnel utilize the commissaries. Mr. Habib replied that at present personnel of the Embassy and USOM, as well as

0084

of UNCURK and some of the other personnel who would fall under category (f) of the proposed Agreed Minute to the non-appropriated fund organizations article used the commissaries. He pointed out, however, that military personnel without resident dependents were not permitted to use these facilities. In addition, there were also other controls on their use, such as a limitation on the amount of supplies that can be purchased in a month.

14. Mr. Chang then asked whether, with the exception of military personnel lacking resident dependents, the persons permitted to use the commissaries were identical with the persons permitted to use the non-appropriated fund organizations. Mr. Habib replied that they were not identical. Colonel Fuller pointed out that the negotiators were not so much concerned with the question of who is entitled to use the commissaries at present but with the question of who will be authorized to use such facilities by the Status of Forces Agreement. He added that this proposed Agreed Minute had been designed to make the conditions of use of the commissaries consistent with those pertaining to the non-appropriated fund organizations.

15. Mr. Chang stated that the tone of the proposed Agreed Minute #7 implied that non-appropriated fund organization users could automatically use the commissaries. Mr. Habib stated that it would not be automatic. The U.S. armed forces have to be willing to permit such use and the ROK Government would have to agree with respect to persons falling under category (f).

16. Mr. Chang said that the proposed Agreed Minute #7 would permit the U.S. armed forces to extend commissary

0085

privileges to the users of non-appropriated fund organizations. Mr. Habib confirmed Mr. Chang's interpretation. Mr. Chang stated that this was of concern to the ROK negotiators. He asked whether the categories of persons who might be authorized to use the commissaries were identical with the categories listed in the proposed Agreed Minute to the non-appropriated fund organizations article. Mr. Habib replied that the decision as to who could use the commissaries was based upon the regulations of the U.S. armed forces.

17. Mr. Chang stated that the Korean negotiators would like to have more specific information about who would be permitted to use the commissaries and the non-appropriated fund organizations under the provisions of the U.S. proposals. He said the Korean negotiators would present their views regarding the proposed Agreed Minute #7 at the next meeting.

Utilities and Services

18. Turning to the article on utilities and services, Mr. Chang reported that a subcommittee of negotiators from both sides had met and discussed this article. On the basis of that discussion, the Korean negotiators wished to table a proposed revision of the article. In tabling the revision, he pointed out that the Korean negotiators had deleted from paragraph 3 the term "however produced". As the Korean negotiators had previously pointed out, this phrase had no meaning for them. Mr. Chang said the Korean negotiators understood from the remarks of the U.S. negotiators at the previous meetings that the qualifying phrase refers only to the

0086

method and process of production. Therefore, the Korean negotiators did not understand why it should be included in the text when other qualifying phrases as to time (season), location and producers, such as "by whomever produced" were not included. In the proposed new Agreed Minute #1, he added, the Korean negotiators had included the term "changes determined by the Korean authorities", since both sides had previously agreed that the Korean authorities would make the final decision on changes in utilities rates or priorities.

19. Mr. Habib said that the U.S. negotiators would take the Korean proposed revision under consideration and comment thereon at a later meeting.

Military Post Offices

20. Turning to the Military Post Offices Article, Mr. Chang stated that the only point still unresolved was the inclusion of the phrase "and their dependents" in the U.S. draft of the Agreed Minute. He said this created difficulties for the ROK negotiators. There was no such provision in the Status of Forces Agreement with Japan; did dependents have the use of military post offices in Japan?

21. Mr. Habib replied that the phrase was included for the sake of clarity. Dependents did have the use of military post offices in Japan; in fact, this was true throughout the world. Although it was not mentioned in the SOFA with Japan, it was spelled out in other Status of Forces Agreements.

22. Mr. Chang noted that agreement had already been reached to convert paragraph 2 into an Agreed Minute.

0087

Mr. Habib confirmed this. Mr. Chang then stated that the ROK negotiators would consider the explanation given by the U.S. negotiators and would present their views at the next meeting.

23. The next meeting was scheduled for January 24 at 2:00 p.m.

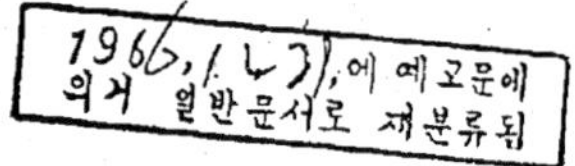


0088

3. 제40차, 1.24

0089

# 기 안 용 지

| 자체<br>통제 | | 기안처 | 미주과<br>이근팔 | 전화번호 | 근거서류접수일자 |
|---|---|---|---|---|---|
| | 과장 | 국장 | 차관 | 장관 | |
| | (서명) | (서명) | (서명) | 후열 (서명) | |
| 관계관<br>서명 | | | | | |
| 기안<br>년월일 | 1964. 1. 23. | 시행<br>년월일 | | 보존<br>년한 | 정서 / 기장 |
| 분류<br>기호 | | 전체<br>통제 | | 종결 | |
| 경유<br>수신<br>참조 | 건의 | | 발신 | | |
| 제목 | 제 40 차 주둔군지위협정 체결교섭회의에 임할 우리측 입장 | | | | |

1 월 24 일에 개최될 제 40 차 주둔군지위협정 체결을 위한 한미간 교섭회의에서는 관세업무, 군사우편 및 비세출자금기관에 관한 조문을 토의하도록 예정되고 있는바 이에 대하여 우리측 교섭실무자는 1 월 22 일 회합을 갖고 제 40 차회의에서 취할 태도를 별첨과 같이 결정하였아오니 재가하여 주시기 바랍니다.

유 첨: 제40차 주둔군지위협정 체결교섭회의에 임할 우리측 태도. 끝.

1966,12,31 에 예고문에 의거 일반문서로 재분류됨

승인양식 1-1-3 (1112-040-016-018) (190mm×260mm16절지)

0090

1. 군사우편

가. 문제점은 "and their dependents" 구절인바 미측이 미일협정에서 규정하고 있지 않으나 사실상 사용하고 있으므로 성문화한 것이라고 설명한 것에 감하여

(1) 비세출자금기관, 군계약자등에서 규정하고 있는 "their dependents" 라는 부분에 관련이 없다는 것을 명백히 하고,

(2) 가족의 군사우편 사용을 금할지라도 세대주 명을 통하여 사실상 사용할 것이라는 것을 고려하여 미국측 안을 수락한다.

2. 관세조항

가. 미측초안 3 (b) 항은 수락하고 5 (b), 및 5 (a) 항에 대한 미측의 양보를 촉구한다.

나. 미측안 5 (b) 항에서 우리측안 대로 "First Class letter mail"을 계속 주장한다.

(1) 미국측 대안이 "obviously not containing merchandise" 로 되어 있으나 명백히 상품이냐 아니냐의 판단과정에 있어서 양국관계자 간에 분쟁이 생길 가능성이 농후하며,

(2) 판단은 검사권한을 갖고 있는 한국세관 당국이 보유해야 할 문제이며

(3) 명백히 표식된 녹음테이프 및 현상을 위한 필림에 대하여서는 미국측 주장대로 사서신과 같은 개인적인 가치만을 가진 것으로 간주하여 검사에서 제외시킬 용의가 있다는 점등을 들어 우리측 입장을 주장한다.

다. 미국측이 상기 대안의 전제조건으로 들고 있는 4개 양해사항중

(1) (b) 항 : 세관검사원의 소포검사에 관하여 "in U.S. MPO installations at designated points of mail distribution" 으로 한것을 제시한데 대하여 우리측은 "Such examinations will be conducted in U.S. military post offices in the presence of U.S. officials" 로 주장하고

(2) (d) 항 : 미측이 주장하는 세관검사의 "spot check basis"에 대하여서는 우리측은 우리측이 원하는 군사우편국에 세관검사원을 상주케 하여 부당한 지연 또는 행정적 부담을 증가시키지 않도록 하겠으며

(가) 검사는 2개의 "스탬프"를 사용하되 수상하다고 생각하는 소포만 검사하고 "검사필"스탬프를 찍으며 기타 모든 소포에는"검사생략"스탬프를 찍을 것이라고 주장하여 미측의 우리입장에 대한 의의유무를 확인한다.

라. 미측 5 (a) 항 : "Members of the United States armed forces" 를 "Units of the United States armed forces" 로 계속 주장한다.

마. 합의의사록 3항 : Military cargo 에 비세출자금기관 앞으로 송부되는 화물이 포함되는가의 문제로서 미일협정에서

(1) 비세출자금기관 앞 화물이 포함되는 것으로 되어 있는가

(2) 세관검사를 여하히 받고 있는가

를 질문하여 우리측 주장을 뒷받침토록 한다.

바. 합의의사록 1항의 자구수정안 "persons authorized by Article _____ and its Agreed Minute" 은 수락한다.

0092

사. 우리측이 합의의사록 4항으로 삽입코저 제의한 비세출자금기관 앞으로 탁송되어 오는 화물에 관한 정보요청에 대한 미측의 반향을 듣는다.

아. 합의의사록 7항은 "commissary" 의 사용대상자에 관한 미국측 견해를 듣기로 한다.

자. 미측 합의의사록 2항은 5(b)항에 대한 우리측 입장을 받아줄 경우에는 수락하기로 한다.

3. 비세출자금기관

가. 미국측안 2항의 "other purchasers" 를 "other ordinary purchasers" 이라는 양해하에 수락한다.

나. 4항: 수락한다.

다. 미국측 합의의사록 초안 5항 비세출자금기관 사용대상자 규정: 우리측 입장이 결정될 때까지 토의를 보류한다.

1966,12,31,에 예고문에 의거 일반문서로 재분류됨

0093

SOFA NEGOTIATION

Agenda for the 40th Session

14:00 January 24, 1964

1. Continuation of Discussions on:
   a. Military Post Offices Article
   b. Customs Article
   c. Non-Appropriated Fund Organizations Article
2. Other Business
3. Agenda and Date of the Next Meeting
4. Press Release

0094

Submitted by U.S. side on Jan. 24.

Proposed additional sentence, Agreed Minute #3:

"Pertinent information on cargo consigned to non-appropriated fund organizations will be furnished authorities of the Republic of Korea upon request through the Joint Committee."

0095

AGREED MINUTES TO ARTICLE (CUSTOMS)

1. The quantity of goods imported under paragraph 2 by non-appropriated fund organizations of the United States armed fources for the use of the members of the UnitedStates armed forces, ~~for~~ the ~~use of the~~ civilian component, and their dependents shall be limited to the extent reasonablu required for such use.

2. Paragraph 3 (a) does not require concurrent shipment of goods with travel of owner nor does ~~not~~ it require single loading or shipment. In this connection, members of the United States armed forces or civilian component and their dependents may import free of duty tieir personal and household effects during a period of six months from the date of their first arrival.

3. The term "military cargo" as used in parargraph 5 (c) is not confined to arms and equipment but refers to all cargo consigne ed to the United States armed forces, including their authorized procurement agencies and their non-appropriated fund organizations / provided for in Article .

4. The United States armed forces will take every practicable measure to ensure that goods will not be imported into the Republic of Korea by or for the members of the United States armed forces, the civilian component, or their dependents, the entry of which would be in violation of Korean customs laws and regulations. The

0096

United States armed forces will promptly notify the Korean customs authorities whenever the entry of such goods is discovered.

5. The Korean customs authorities may, if they consider that there has been an abuse or infringement in connectionwith the entry of goods under Article , take up the matter with the appropriate authorities of the United States armed forces.

6. The words "The United States armed forces shall render all assistance within their power," etc., in paragraph 9(b) and (c) refer to reasonable and practicable measures by the UNited States armed forces authorized by United States law and service regulationns.

0096-1

ARTICLE (Customs)

2. All materials, supplies and equipment importedly by the United States armed forces, including their authorized procedrement agencies and their non-appropriated fund organizations provided for in Article , for the official use of the United States armed fo forces or for the use of forces logistically supported by the Unite Sdates armed forces or for the use of the members of the United States armed forces, the civilian component, or their dependents shall be permitted entry into the Republic of Korea free from customs duties and other such charges. Similarly, materials, supplies and equipment which are imported by others than the United States armed forces but are to be used exclusively by the United States armed forces and/ or forces logistically supported by the United States armed forces or are ultimately to be incorated into articles or facilities to be used by such forces shall be permitted entry into the Republic of Korea free from customs duties and other such charges. Appropriate certification shall be made by the United States armed forces with respect to the importation of materials, supplies and equipment for the foregoing specified purposes.

0097

ARTICLE [illegible]

1. A Joint Committee shall be established as the means for consultation between the Government of the United States and the Government of the Republic of Korea on all matters requiring mutual consultation regarding the implementation of this Agreement unless otherwise provided for. In particular, the Joint Committee shall serve as the means for consultation in determining the facilities and areas in the Republic of Korea which are required for the use of the United States in carrying out the purposes of this Agreement.

2. The Joint Committee shall be composed of a representative of the Government of the United States and a representative of the Government of the Republic of Korea, each of whom shall have one or more deputies and a staff. The Joint Committee shall determine its own procedures, and arrange for such auxiliary organs and administrative services as may be required. The Joint Committee shall be so organized that it may meet immediately at any time at the request of the representative of either the Government of the United States or the Government of the Republic of Korea.

3. If the Joint Committee is unable to resolve any matter, it shall refer that matter to the respective Governments for further consideration through appropriate channels.

0098

ENTRY AND EXIT

1. The United States may bring into the Republic of Korea persons who are members of the United States armed forces, the civilian component, and their dependents, subject to the provisions of this Article. The Government of the Republic of Korea will be notified at regular intervals, in accordance with procedures to be agreed between the two Governments, of numbers and categories of persons entering and departing.

2. Members of the United States armed forces shall be exempt from Korean passport and visa laws and regulations. Members of the United States armed forces, the civilian component, and their dependents shall be exempt from Korean laws and regulations on the registration and control of aliens, but shall not be considered as acquiring any right to parmanent residence or domicile in the territory of the Republic of Korea.

3. Upon entry into or departure from the Republic of Korea members of the United States armed forces shall be in possession of the following documents:

(a) personal identity card showing name, date of birth, rank and service number, service, and photograph; and

0099

(b) individual or collective travel order certifying to the status of the individual or group as a member or members of the United States armed forces and to the travel ordered.

For purposes of their identification while in the Republic of Korea, members of the United States armed forces shall be in possession of the foregoing personal identity card which must be presented on request to the appropriate Korean authorities.

4. Members of the civilian component, their dependents, and the dependents of members of the United States armed forces shall be in possession of appropriate documentation issued by the United States authorities so that their status may be verified by Korean authorities upon their entry into or departure from the Republic of Korea, or while in the Republic of Korea.

5. If the status of any person brought into the Republic of Korea under paragraph 1 of this Article is altered so that he would no longer be entitled to such admission, the United States authorities shall notify the Korean authorities and shall, if such person be required by the Korean authorities to leave the Republic of Korea, assure that transportation from the Republic of Korea will be provided within a reasonable time at no cost to the Government of the Republic of Korea.

0100

6. If the Government of the Republic of Korea has requested the removal from its Territory of a member of the United States armed forces or civilian component or has made an expulsion order against an ex-member of the United States armed forces or the civilian component or against a dependent of a member or an ex-member, the authorities of the United States shall be responsible for receiving the person concerned into its own territory or otherwise disposing of him outside the Republic of Korea. This paragraph shall apply only to persons who are not ordinarily resident in the Republic of Korea and have entered the Republic of Korea as members of the United States armed forces or civilian component or for the purpose of becoming such members, and to the dependents of such persons.

0101

## Agreed Minutes to Article
(Entry and Exit)

1. With regard to Paragraph 3(a), United States Armed Forces law enforcement personnel (such as MP, SP, AP, CID and CIC), who engage in military police activities in the Republic of Korea, will carry a bilingual identity card containing the bearer's name, position, and the fact that he is a member of a law enforcement agency. This card will be shown upon request to persons concerned when the bearer is in the performance of duty.

2. The United States Armed Forces will furnish, upon request, to Korean authorities the form of the identification cards of the members of the United States Armed Forces, the civilian component, and their dependents and descriptions of the various uniforms of the United States Armed Forces in the Republic of Korea.

3. The final sentence of Paragraph 3 means that members of the United States Armed Forces will display their identity cards upon request but will not be required to surrender them to Korean authorities.

4. Following a change of status pursuant to Paragraph 5, the responsibilities of the United States authorities under Paragraph 6 shall arise only if the expulsion order is issued within a reasonable time after the notice under Paragraph 5 has been communicated to the Korean authorities.

0102

Definition

In this Agreement the expression--

(a) "members of the United States forces" means the personnel on active duty belonging to the land, sea or air armed services of the United States of America when in the territory of the Republic of Korea.

(b) "civilian component" means the civilian persons of United States nationality who are in the employ of, serving with, or accompanying the United States forces in the Republic of Korea, but excludes persons who are ordinarily resident in the Republic of Korea or who are mentioned in Article XVIII. For the purposes of this agreement only, dual nationals, Korean and United States, who are brought to theRepublic of Korea by the United States shall be considered as United States nationals.

(c) "dependents" means

(i) Spouse, and children under 2I;

(ii) Parents, and children over 2I, if dependent for over half their support upon a member of the United States forces or civilian component.

0103

DEFINITIONS ARTICLE

PROPOSED ADDITIONAL SENTENCE TO SUBPARAGRAPH (b)

For the purposes of the Agreement only, dual nationals, i.e. persons having both United States and Korean nationality, who are brought into the Republic of Korea by the United States shall be considered as United States nationals.

0104

DEFINITIONS ARTICLE

Agreed Minute:

"The personnel referred to in subparagraph (a) for whom status has otherwise been provided include personnel of the United States armed forces attached to the United States Emabassy and personnel for whom status has been provided in the Military Advisory Group Agreement of January 26, 1950 as amended."

0105

DEFINITIONS ARTICLE

AGREED MINUTE

With regard to Article 1(a), the expression "members of the United States armed forces" does not include personnel on active duty belonging to the United States land, sea or air armed services for whom status has otherwise been provided such as personnel for whom status is provided in the Military Advisory Group Agreement signed on January 26, 1950, and personnel of service attache offices in the Embassy of the United States of America.

0106

DEFINITIONS ARTICLE

AGREED MINUTE

With regard to subparagraph (b), it is recognized that persons possessing certain skills, not readily available from United States or Korean sources, who are nationals of third states may be brought into Korea by the United States armed forces solely for employment by the United States armed forces. Such persons, and third state nationals who are employed by, serving with, or accompanying the United States armed forces in Korea when this agreement becomes effective, shall be considered as members of the civilian component.

0107

# 기 안 용 지

| 자체 통제 | | 기안처 | 미주과 강석재 | 전화번호 | 근거서류접수일자 |
|---|---|---|---|---|---|
| | 과장 | 국장 | 차관 | 장관 | |
| 관계관 서명 | | | | | |
| 기안 년월일 | 1964. 1. 29 | 시행 년월일 | | 보존 년한 | 정서기장 |
| 분류 기호 | 외구미722.2 | 전체 통제 | 종결 | | |
| 경유 수신 참조 | 대통령 (참조: 비서실장) 국무총리 | | | 발신 | 장관 |
| 제목 | 주둔군 지위협정체결을 위한 제40차 교섭회의 보고 | | | | |

1964. 1. 24. 하오 2시부터 하오 4시까지 외무부장관 회의실에서 개최된 제40차주둔군 지위협정 체결 교섭회의에서 토의된 내용을 별첨과 같이 보고합니다.

유 첨: 제40차 교섭회의 보고서 1부 끝

1966.12.31. 에 예고문에 의거 일반문서로 재분류됨

승인서식 1-1-3 (11-00900-03) (195mm×265mm16절지)

0108

제 40 차

한미간 주둔군지위협정 체결실무자회의

보 고 서

1. 일 시: 1964년 1월 24일 하오 2시부터 하오 4시까지

2. 장 소: 외무부 장관 회의실

3. 토의사항:

가. 군사우편

양측은 본조문의 예외적 규정으로 군사우편의 사용을 미국정부 관리 및 직원과 그들의 가족에게 허용하는 합의의사록에 대하여 합의보았다. 이로서 군사우편의 본조문과 합의의사록에 완전 합의를 본것이다.

나. 관세 업무

(1) 양측은 미국군대 구성원 및 군속의 사용을 위하여 수입하는 자동차 및 부속품에 대한 통관세 면제에 합의를 보았다.

(2) 그러나 군대 구성원, 군사우편 및 비세출자금기관앞으로 탁송되어 오는 물품에 대한 세관검사 여부에 관하여서는 합의를 보지 못하고 있다.

(3) 우리측은 출입국시의 세관검사 는 "부대"로 출입할경우에만 면제하고 구성원에 대하여서는 검사를 실시할 권한은 한국세관 당국이 보유해야 한다고 주장하였다. 군사우편물에 대하여서는 letter mail ( 녹음을 위한 테이프 및 현상을 위한 필림 포함) 만을 제외하고 모든 소포에 대한 검사 권한을 요구하며 또한 비세출자금기관에 탁송되는 물품은 현하 우리의 경제사정으로 비추어 볼때 비록 다른 국가에서는 검사를 면제하는 경우가 있다 할지라도 우리로서는 검사할 권한을보유 해야한다는 실정을 설명하고 강조하였다.

(4) 이외 commissary 의 사용대상범위에 관한 합의 의사록은 아직 검토가 완료되지 못하였음으로 당분간 토의를 보류하기로 하였다.

0109

64-1-8

64-3-4 (2)　　　　미국·북 105-8(2)

0110

다. 비세출자금기관

비세출자금기관 조문에서 가장 문제가 되고 있는점은 군대 구성원, 군속 및 그들의 가족외의 기타사람들의 비세출자금기관 사용허용의 대상범위인바 이에 관한 토의는 당분간 보류하였다. 그외의 미합 의사항은 비세출자금기관에 의한 물품구매에 대한 한국조세의 부과에 관한 것인바 양측은 원측적으로 이에 합의하였으나 다만 양해사항에 있어서 약간의 의견이개재하고 있을 뿐이다.

5. 기타사항: 차기회의 일자: 1964년 2월 6일 하오 2시



0111

0112

1. Brig General G. G. O'Connor, Deputy Chief of Staff, Eighth United States Army, served as Chief Negotiator for the U.S. Government, in the absence of Mr. Habib. Mr. Chang introduced Mr. LEE JAE SUP, who was substituting for Mr. Sin Kwan-sop.

Military Post Offices

2. Mr. Chang, the ROK Chief Negotiator, indicated that the ROK side had considered the explanation of the US side for the reasons the phrase "and their dependents" was included in the US draft of the Agreed Minute. In view of the fact that ~~Since~~ the dependents of US Government personnel in Japan ~~Korea~~ are actually ~~now~~ using MPO mails, although they are not specifically so provided for in the Agreed Minute, Mr. Chang indicated that the Korean negotiators are prepared to agree to the inclusion of the phrase in the Agreed Minute. ~~the US draft of the Agreed Minute is acceptable to the ROK side~~. However, in accepting the US draft of the Agreed Minute ~~MPO Article~~, the ROK Government negotiators desired to have the joint minute clearly show the ~~do so with the~~ understanding that such acceptance does not prejudice the ROK Government position with regard to the same phrase "their dependents" referred to in the U.S draft article dealing with customs and invited contractors. ~~in other articles, such as para 5(b) of the Customs Article, in which differences relating to [illegible] are still~~ (military post offices) ~~unresolved.~~ General O'Connor stated

0113

that neither side, in agreeing on the MPO Article, automatically commits itself in any way on related subjects in other articles. On this basis, it was agreed that the US draft of the MPO Article including both article and Agreed Minute was accepted by both sides.

Customs

3. General O'Connor referred to the new US draft of para 5(b), tabled on January, which exempted from ROK customs inspection US official documents under official seal and First Class mail "obviously not containing merchandise." He indicated that the proposal takes into consideration the expressed ROK desire for the right to inspect all categories of parcels in MPO channels in Korea, and asked if the ROK negotiators found the proposal acceptable. Chang replied that the ROK side had considered the proposed new para 5(b) and had found it unacceptable. Mr. Chang stated that the phrase that First Class mail "obviously not containing merchandise" was very vague and could be a source of much dispute. Mr. Chang emphasized that it had been agreed that the ROK side was to have the right in principle to inspect non-official parcels entering Korea in MPO channels. Therefore, the proposed para 5(b) tabled by the ROK on January, which would exempt from customs inspection "official documents under official seal and First Class letter mail in United States military channels," should be accepted. Regarding the two items brought up by the US side at the January meeting, photos and personal recording tapes, the ROK side would accept the US proposal that inspection of such types of goods be waived by the ROK Goverment.

4. General O'Connor indicated that the US side had previously expressed objection to this proposed para 5(b) and had proposed a suitable substitute. The US side does not yet understand fully why the ROK side finds the US draft of

0114

para 5(b) of 17 January unacceptable. Mr. Chang reiterated that if the US side accepted the ROK-proposed para 5(b), the right of customs examination would be waived for such special types of articles as personal recording tapes and films in APO mail. The ROK side agreed that such a mutual understanding should be included in the Joint Agreed Summary. General O'Connor indicated the US side would take the ROK proposal and statements under consideration and would reply at the next meeting.

5. General O'Connor noted that the ROK negotiators had not as yet given a specific response to the four understandings regarding ROKG customs inspection of MPO parcels, as read into Joint Agreed Summary by the US side on 27 December, 1963, and 17 January, 1964. Mr. Chang discussed the four points and indicated general concurrence in them, except for two proposed changes. (1) In the second understanding, (2) he desired deletion of words "at designated points of mail distribution and". Mr. Chang indicated that if the designated points of inspection were too many, it would be beyond the capacity of the ROK Government to administer and that the ROK Government has grave concern in this regard. The ROK Government desires that the number of inspection sites be as few as possible, for inspection at designated points of mail distribution would be an extremely heavy burden on the ROK customs administration. Mr. Chang again proposed deletion of the phrase and suggested that the two sides should let arrangements regarding mail inspection sites be worked out by the Joint Committee. General O'Connor stated, that as explained at a previous negotiating session (Agreed Summary, 35th meeting, November 14, 1963, para 4 and 5), it is not practical to have customs inspection of MPO parcels at ports of entry, such as Inchon and Kimpo. MPO parcel mail arrives in Korea in large sealed metal containers, which are each sent, unopened, directly to one of the 17 main military post offices which are located in various parts of the ROK. These facts have been clearly explained, in pointing out why any inspection would impose heavy administrative burden on the MPO system unless they were conducted at points of mail distribution.

0115

General O'Connor agreed that the Joint Committee, considering all relevant factors, could designate appropriate points of parcel inspection and, therefore, deletion of the phrase (the second understanding,) as proposed by the ROK side, would be agreeable.

7. Mr. Chang indicated that the second point of difference was in the fourth understanding, in which the ROK Government felt that it should be stated that the right of inspection would be on a "sample check" basis, rather than a "spot check" basis. Mr. Chang indicated that customs inspections should be at sites mutually agreed upon, and on the basis of sampling checks, so as to impose no great administrative burden or delay the mail. General O'Connor emphasized that any attempt to inspect all the parcel mail would certainly result in considerable delay of the mail. The terms "spot check" or "sample check" appear to have somewhat similar meanings, and it was mutually agreed that inspections should be at sites decided through the Joint Committee, and implemented so as not to delay the mail. Mr. Chang indicated that the ROK Government, in agreeing to sample checking at specified sites, does not prejudice its right in principle to inspect all parcels. General O'Connor replied the US Government conceded to the ROK the right to inspect all APO parcels, but agreed with the ROKG that actual inspections would be as indicated by the foregoing US-ROK agreed understandings.

8. Regarding para 5(a), General O'Connor explained that the US draft of this paragraph stipulates that members of the United States armed forces shall not be subject to ROK customs examination when entering or leaving the Republic of Korea under military orders. He explained how, with the personnel rotation system in effect in Korea, the ROK desire to substitute the word "units" for "members" would subject almost all United States armed forces personnel to ROK customs examinations when entering or leaving Korea. General O'Connor asked if this is what the ROK side wanted. Mr. Chang replied that the ROK negotiators proposed the use of the word "units" rather than the US-proposed word "members" because they did desire all individuals in the U.S. armed forces to be subject to Korean customs inspection when entering and leaving Korea. Mr. Chang stated that in view of past abuses, the ROKG felt that all members of the US forces entering and leaving

0116

Korea, except those which may move as "units," should be subject to ROK customs examinations. General O'Connor indicated that the United States was not asking for anything new in para 5(a), and that it has been the practice for both Japanese and ROK custom authorities to waive customs examinations for members of the US armed forces in Japan and Korea respectively. He pointed out that this exemption from customs inspection was to be applied only to members of the US armed forces, and not to the civilian component or to American dependents. Mr. Chang stated again that there had been abuses in the past, and the ROK Government desired to have the right of customs inspection. He indicated that even though the ROK Government not actually subject all members of the US armed forces entering and leaving Korea to customs examinatio it wanted the SOFA to give them the right to do so. It was agreed to continue discussion of this subject at a subsequent meeting.

9. Regarding para 5(c) and Agreed Minute No. 3, Mr. Chang indicated he wanted to explain the reasons the ROK negotiators did not want the term "military cargo" to include cargo for non-appropriated funds organizations. Mr. Chang emphasized that the situations in Japan and Korea were different, and that the illegal disposal of goods brought into Korea duty-free through non-appropriated funds channels adversely effected the growth of the Korean economy. Mr. Chang emphasized that the impact of NAF imports was different in Korea than in Japan, and that the ROK Government could not agree to the same arrangements were in effect in Japan. He stated that the ROK Government must have the right of customs inspection of NAF goods.

10. Mr. Chang asked if the term "military cargo" in the US-Japan SOFA covered goods for non-appropriated funds organizations, and how the inspection of such goods is accomplished in Japan. General O'Connor replied by reading para 3 of the US-Japan SOFA Customs Article which states that the term "military cargo" in the does refer to goods imported for NAF organizations. He indicated that Japanese customs does not inspect such imports, and that the US authorities furnish the Japanese authorities with information on such imports from Government bills of lading, as indicated in the US-Japan SOFA. General O'Connor indicated that a similar

0117

procedure could be established in the ROK ~~and~~ on that basis he tabled the following proposed sentence, to be added to the US draft of Agreed Minute No. 3:

"Pertinent information on cargo consigned to non-appropriated fund organizations will be furnished authorities of the Republic of Korea upon request through the Joint Committee."

11. General O'Connor stated that the US side would cooperate in supplying pertinent information to ROK authorities. The Joint Committee machinery could be used to screen requests and appropriate information, not involving the security of United States forces, would be furnished to ROK authorities. Mr. Chang indicated the ROK negotiators would take this proposed addition to Agreed Minute No. 3 under consideration.

12. Mr. Chang requested additional information about US Government bills of lading relating to NAF goods, including whether all such goods were imported into Korea on government bills of lading. He also asked about any formal agreements relating to the subject of NAF goods being designated as "military cargo." General O'Connor indicated military shipping is usually on government bills of lading, and thus NAF fund imports usually would be on U.S. Government bills of lading. Regarding the questions of agreements and procedures related to NAF imports, General O'Connor stated the subject would be investigated further and the US side would report its findings at the next negotiating session.

13. Mr. Chang thanked the US side for its explanations and for the copies of the US Army Regulations regarding commissaries, which had been supplied to them. The ROK negotiators are studying these materials and would explain the ROK position on the US draft of Agreed Minute No. 7 at the next meeting. In response to questions, General O'Connor explained that all personnel who had commissary privileges also have NAF privileges. However, many persons have NAF privileges

and not commissary privileges. In general, unless USFK personnel maintain a household in Korea, they do not have commissary privileges. The basis on which USFK personnel are eligible for commissary privileges, therefore, is related to whether they have dependents and a household in Korea. Of course, relatively few of the total USFK personnel qualify for commissary privileges under this criteria.

14. Mr. Chang thanked General O'Connor for his explanations and indicated he would be ready to reply for the ROK Government on the commissary question at the next meeting.

15. Mr. Chang indicated that the ROK negotiators had studied the revised US draft of Agreed Minute No. 1, and that it was acceptable to the ROK Government.

16. Mr. Chang stated that the ROK side was also willing to accept the US draft of para 3(b), thus demonstrating ROK cooperation in order to complete the SOF-K negotiations as soon as possible. General O'Connor noted the US-ROK agreement on Agreed Minute No. 1 and para 3(b), and expressed the hope that steady progress on the negotiations continue to be realized through a spirit of mutual cooperation.

17. Mr. Chang noted that agreement had now be reached on all provisions of the Customs Article, except paras 5(a) and 5(b), and Agreed Minutes 2, 3, and 7.

Non-Appropriated Funds

18. Mr. Chang stated that the ROK negotiators would prefer that the phrase relating to "other purchasers" in para 2 be deleted, but the US side had continuously insisted on such phraseology. The ROK side would be willing to accept the US draft of para 2, with the understanding that the NAF organizations would be subject

0119

to the same taxes as "other purchasers", except as the ROKG may decide in the future to exempt certain foreign organizations from certain taxes under specific arrangements. Mr. Chang explained that although the ROK negotiators do not perceive any necessity for the phraseology at present, in the future the ROK Government might desire to exempt from taxation some foreign agency which would come to Korea to help the economy. Although this was a hypothetical example, in such an event, the US might request similar exemption for NAF organizations. It was for this reason that the ROK side proposed that para 2 be accepted with the foregoing understanding. General O'Connor replied that the US side would take the ROK statements under consideration, and would discuss the subject again at the next meeting.

19. It was agreed to defer disuussion of the only other two points still at issue in the Non-Appropriated Funds Article, in para 4 and the Agreed Minute, until the next meeting.

20. The next meeting was scheduled for Thursday, 6 February 1964, at 2:00 PM.

CONFIDENTIAL

1. Brig. General G. G. O'Connor, Deputy Chief of Staff, Eighth United States Army, served as Chief Negotiator for the U.S. Government, in the absence of Mr. Habib. Mr. Chang introduced Mr. Lee Nam Sup, who was substituting for Mr. Kim [illegible].

Military Post Offices

2. Mr. Chang, the ROK Chief Negotiator, stated that the ROK side had considered the explanation of the US side for the reasons the phrase "and their dependents" was included in the US draft of the Agreed Minute and that the US draft of the Agreed Minute was acceptable to the ROK side. However, in accepting the US draft of the MPO Article, the ROK Government negotiators desired to have the joint [illegible] clearly show the understanding that such acceptance does not prejudice the ROK Government position with regard to the phrase "their dependents" referred to in [illegible] articles dealing with [illegible] and Invited Contractors. Mr. Chang emphasized that the acceptance by the Korean negotiators of the phrase, despite the fact that dependents of U.S. Government personnel are not specifically provided with MPO privileges in U.S.-Japan Status of Forces Agreement, constituted a major concession on their part and expressed their hope that the U.S. negotiators would favorably consider the position of the Korean side on other relevant matters, namely, paragraph 5(a) of the Customs Article which deals with the exemption of customs inspection of mail. General O'Connor stated

0121

stated that neither side, in agreeing on the MPO Article, automatically committed itself in any way on related subjects in other articles. On this basis, it was agreed that the US draft of the MPO Article, including both the article and Agreed Minute, was accepted by both sides.

<u>Customs</u>

1. General O'Connor referred to the new US draft of para 3(b), tabled on January 17, which exempted from ROK customs inspection US official documents under official seal and First Class mail "obviously not containing merchandise." He indicated that the proposal takes into consideration the expressed ROK desire for the right to inspect all categories of parcels in MPO channels in Korea, and asked if the ROK negotiators found the proposal acceptable. Mr. Chang replied that the ROK side had considered the proposed new para 3(b) and had found it unacceptable. Mr. Chang stated that the phrase "First Class mail obviously not containing merchandise" would not only impair the right of inspection by the Korean authorities but also could be a source of much dispute. Mr. Chang emphasized that it had been agreed in principle that the ROK side was to have the right to inspect all parcels entering Korea through MPO channels. Therefore, the Korean negotiators felt that the authority to determine whether certain parcels contain merchandise or not should rest with the Korean customs inspectors engaging in the inspection, rather than with [illegible] and that the [illegible] should be subject to the inspection for verification. [illegible] the proposed para 3(b) tabled by the ROK negotiators on January 9, which would exempt from customs inspection "official documents under official seal

0122

seal and First Class letter mail in United States military channels," should be accepted. However, he stated that mentioned by the US side at the January 17 meeting, the ROK side would be prepared to waive customs inspection of the two special type of goods, namely, recorded tapes and photographic films which are of personal value and are individually and clearly so marked.

4. General O'Connor indicated that the US side had previously expressed objection to this para 5(b) tabled by the Korean negotiators and had proposed a suitable substitute. The US side does not yet understand fully why the ROK side finds the US draft of para 5(b) of January 17 unacceptable. Mr. Chang reiterated that if the US side accepted the ROK-proposed para 5(b), the right of customs examination would be waived for such special types of articles as personal recorded tapes and films in MPO mail. The ROK side agreed that such a mutual understanding should be included in the Joint Agreed Summary. Mr. Chang stated that by so doing the Korean negotiators met the U.S. demand and, therefore, would see no difficulties on the part of the U.S. side in accepting the Korean proposal. General O'Connor indicated the US side would take the ROK proposal and statements under consideration and would reply at the next meeting.

0123

para 5(b) of 17 January unacceptable. Mr. Chang reiterated that if the US side accepted the ROK-proposed para 5(b), the right of customs examination would be waived for such special types of articles as personal recording tapes and films in APO mail. The ROK side agreed that such a mutual understanding should be included in the Joint Agreed Summary. General O'Connor indicated the US side would take the ROK proposal and statements under consideration and would reply at the next meeting.

5. General O'Connor noted that the ROK negotiators had not as yet given a specific response to the four understandings regarding ROKG customs inspection of MPO parcels, as read into the Joint Agreed Summary by the US side on 27 December, 1963, and 17 January, 1964. Mr. Chang discussed the four points and indicated general concurrence in them, except for two proposed changes. In the second understanding, he desired deletion of the words "at designated points of mail distribution and". Mr. Chang indicated that if the designated points of inspection were too many, it would be beyond the capacity of the ROK Government to administer and that the ROK Government has grave concern in this regard. The ROK Government desires that the number of inspection sites be as few as possible, for inspection at designated points of mail distribution would be an extremely heavy burden on the ROK customs administration. Mr. Chang again proposed deletion of the phrase and suggested that the two sides should let arrangements regarding mail inspection sites be worked out by the Joint Committee. General O'Connor stated, that as explained at a previous negotiating session (Agreed Summary, 35th meeting, November 14, 1963, para 4 and 5), it is not practical to have customs inspection of MPO parcels at ports of entry, such as Inchon and Kimpo. MPO parcel mail in Korea arrives in large sealed metal containers which are each sent, unopened, directly to one of the 17 main military post offices which are located in various parts of the ROK. These facts have been clearly explained, in pointing out why any inspections would impose a heavy administrative burden on the MPO system unless they were conducted at points of mail distribution.

0124

General O'Connor agreed that the Joint Committee, considering all relevant factors, could designate appropriate points of parcel inspection and, therefore, deletion of the phrase (the second understanding) as proposed by the ROK side, would be agreeable.

7. Mr. Chang indicated that the second point of difference was in the fourth understanding, in which the ROK Government felt that the right of inspection would be on a "sample check" basis, rather than a "spot check" basis. Mr. Chang indicated that the Korean Government intends to send customs inspectors at all mutually agreed upon inspection site to examine parcels and on the basis of sampling checks, so as to impose no administrative burden or delay the mail. He asked whether the U.S. negotiators understood the words "spot check" in the same sense as the Korean side's understanding of them. General O'Connor emphasized that any attempt to inspect all the parcel mail would certainly result in considerable delay of the mail. The terms "spot check" or "sample check" appear to have somewhat similar meanings, and it was mutually agreed that inspections should be at sites decided through the Joint Committee, and implemented so as not to delay the mail. Mr. Chang indicated that the ROK Government, in agreeing to sample checking at specified sites, does not prejudice its right in principle to inspect all parcels. General O'Connor replied the US Government conceded to the ROK the right to inspect all APO parcels, but agreed with the ROKG that actual inspections would be as indicated by the foregoing US-ROK agreed understandings.

8. Regarding para 5(a), General O'Connor explained that the US draft of this paragraph stipulates that members of the United States armed forces shall not be subject to ROK customs examination when entering or leaving the Republic of Korea under military orders. He explained how, with the personnel rotation system in effect in Korea, the ROK desire to substitute the word "units" for "members" would subject almost all United States armed forces personnel to ROK customs examinations when entering or leaving Korea. General O'Connor asked if this is what the ROK side wanted. Mr. Chang replied that the ROK negotiators proposed the use of the word "units" rather than the US-proposed word "members" because they did desire all individuals in the U.S. armed forces to be subject to Korean customs inspection when entering and leaving Korea. Mr. Chang stated that in view of past abuses, the ROKG felt that all members of the US armed forces entering and leaving

4

0125

Korea, except those which may move as "units," should be subject to ROK customs examinations. General O'Connor indicated that the United States was not asking for anything new in para 5(a), and that it has been the practice for both Japanese and ROK custom authorities to waive customs examinations for members of the US armed forces in Japan and Korea respectively. He pointed out that this exemption from customs inspection was to be applied only to members of the US armed forces, and not to the civilian component or to American dependents. Mr. Chang said that it was conceivable that there are many types of troop movements such as movements as units on order or as an individual or group for solely leave purpose or for official purposes. He stated that the Korean customs authorities are concerned with the inspection individual members entering or leaving Korea for solely leave purposes. The ROK Government, therefore, desired to have the right of customs inspection for individual members rather than units. He indicated that even though the ROK Government might not actually subject all members of the US armed forces entering and leaving Korea to customs examination it wanted the SOFA to give it the right to do so. It was agreed to continue discussion of this subject at a subsequent meeting.

9. Regarding para 5(c) and Agreed Minute No. 3, Mr. Chang indicated he wanted to explain the reasons why the ROK negotiators did not want the term "military cargo" to include cargo for non-appropriated funds organizations. Mr. Chang emphasized that the present economic situations in Japan and Korea were much different, and that the illegal disposal in the past of goods brought into Korea duty-free through non-appropriated funds channels adversely affected the growth of certain segments of the Korean economy. Mr. Chang emphasized that the impact upon the Korean economy that might be effected by illegal disposal of NAF imports would be much greater than that on the Japanese economy, and that the ROK would not agree to the

0126

same arrangements as were in effect in Japan. He stated that since Korean industries have already suffered much from the abuses of NAF goods, the ROK Government must have the right of custom inspection of NAF imports.

0127

Korea, except those which move as "units," should be subject to ROK customs examinations. General O'Connor indicated that the United States was not asking for anything new in para 5(a), and that it has been the practice for both Japanese and ROK custom authorities to waive customs examinations for members of the US armed forces in Japan and Korea. He pointed out that this exemption from customs inspection was to be applied only to members of the US armed forces, and not to the civilian component or to dependents. Mr. Chang stated that there had been abuses in the past and the ROK Government desired to have the right of customs inspection. He indicated that even though the ROK Government not actually subject all members of the US armed forces to customs examination it wanted the SOFA to give them the right to do so. It was agreed to continue discussion of this subject at a subsequent meeting.

Regarding para 5(c) and Agreed Minute No. 3, Mr. Chang indicated he wanted to explain the reasons the ROK negotiators did not want the term "military cargo" to include cargo for non-appropriated funds organizations. Mr. Chang emphasized that the situations in Japan and Korea were different, and that the illegal disposal of goods brought into Korea duty-free through non-appropriated funds channels adversely effected the growth of the Korean economy. Mr. Chang emphasized the impact of NAF imports, and that the ROK could not agree to the same arrangements as in effect in Japan. He stated that the ROK Government must have the right of customs inspection of NAF goods.

Mr. Chang asked if the term "military cargo" in the US-Japan SOFA covered goods for non-appropriated funds organizations, and how the inspection of such goods is accomplished in Japan. General O'Connor replied that the term "military cargo" does include goods imported for NAF organizations. He indicated that Japanese customs does not inspect such imports, and that the US authorities furnish the Japanese authorities with information on such imports from Government bills of lading. General O'Connor indicated that a similar



0128

procedure could be established in the ROK and on that basis he tabled the following proposed sentence, to be added to the US draft of Agreed Minute No. 3:

"Pertinent information on cargo consigned to non-appropriated fund organizations will be furnished authorities of the Republic of Korea upon request through the Joint Committee."

11. General O'Connor stated that the US side would cooperate in supplying pertinent information to ROK authorities. The Joint Committee machinery could be used to screen requests and appropriate information, not involving the security of United States forces, would be furnished to ROK authorities. Mr. Chang indicated the ROK negotiators would take this proposed addition to Agreed Minute No. 3 under consideration.

12. Mr. Chang requested additional information about US Government bills of lading relating to NAF goods, including whether all such goods imported into Korea were on government bills of lading. He also asked about any formal agreements relating to the subject of NAF goods being designated as "military cargo." General O'Connor indicated military shipping is usually on government bills of lading, and thus NAF fund imports usually would be on U.S. Government bills of lading. Regarding the questions of agreements and procedures related to NAF imports, General O'Connor stated the subject would be investigated further and the US side would report its findings at the next negotiating session.

13. Mr. Chang thanked the US side for its explanations and for the copies of the US Army Regulations regarding commissaries, which had been supplied to them. The ROK negotiators are studying these materials and would explain the ROK position on the US draft of Agreed Minute No. 7 at the next meeting. In response to questions, General O'Connor explained that all personnel who had commissary privileges also have NAF privileges. However, many persons have NAF privileges

6

0129

and not commissary privileges. In general, unless USFK personnel maintains a household in Korea, they do not have commissary privileges. The basis on which USFK personnel are eligible for commissary privileges, therefore, is related to whether they have dependents and a household in Korea. Of course, relatively few of the USFK personnel qualify for commissary privileges under this criteria.

14. Mr. Chang thanked General O'Connor for his explanations and indicated he would be ready to reply for the ROK Government on the commissary question at the next meeting.

15. Mr. Chang indicated that the ROK negotiators had studied the revised US draft of Agreed Minute No. 1, and that it was acceptable to the ROK Government.

16. Mr. Chang stated that the ROK side was also willing to accept the US draft of para 3(b), thus demonstrating ROK cooperation in order to complete the SOF-K negotiations as soon as possible. General O'Connor noted the US-ROK agreement on Agreed Minute No. 1 and para 3(b), and expressed the hope that progress on the negotiations could be realized through a spirit of mutual cooperation.

17. Mr. Chang noted that agreement had now be reached on all the Customs Article, except paras 5(a), 5(b) and Agreed Minutes 2, 3, and 7.

Non-Appropriated Funds

18. Mr. Chang stated that the ROK negotiators would prefer that the phrase relating to "other purchasers" in para 2 be deleted, but US side has continuously insisted on such phraseology. The ROK side would be willing to accept the US draft of para 2, with the understanding that the NAF organizations ... subject

0130

15. Mr. Chang indicated that the ROK negotiators had studied the revised US draft of Agreed Minute No. 1, and that it was acceptable to the ROK Government.

16. Mr. Chang stated that the ROK side was also willing to accept the US draft of para 3(b), thus demonstrating ROK cooperation in order to complete the SOFA negotiations as soon as possible. Mr. Chang asked that the U.S. negotiators [illegible] reconsider the Korean position with regard to those points still unresolved in the Customs Article and [illegible] reciprocate with the same spirit of cooperation. General O'Connor noted the US-ROK agreement on Agreed Minute No. 1 and para 3(b), and expressed the hope that steady progress in the negotiations would continue to be realized through a spirit of mutual cooperation.

17. Mr. Chang noted that agreement had now been reached on all provisions of the Customs Article, except paras 3(a), 5(b) and 5(c), and Agreed Minutes 2, 3, and 7.

Non-Appropriated Funds

18. Mr. Chang stated that the ROK negotiators would prefer that the phrase relating to "other purchasers" in para 2 be deleted, but the US side had continuously insisted on such phraseology. The ROK side, believing the phrase of little significance, would be willing to accept the US draft of para 2, with the understanding that "other purchasers" referred to in the NAF organizations article should not be construed as being either applicable to or relevant to [illegible] other purchasers such as certain foreign organizations or persons [illegible] whom the Korean Government may in the future exempt from certain taxes under specific arrangements with them. Mr. Chang explained that although the ROK negotiat[illegible] necessity for the phraseology at present, [illegible]rnment might desire to

0131

construed as either applicable to or relevant with other purchasers such as certain foreign organizations or persons for whom the Korean Government may in the future exempt

~~to the same taxes as "other purchasers", except as the ROK may decide in the future to exempt certain foreign organizations~~ from certain taxes under specific arrangements. Mr. Chang explained that although the ROK negotiators do not perceive any necessity for the phraseology at present, in the future the ROK Government might desire to exempt from taxation some foreign agency which would come to Korea to help the economy. Although this was a hypothetical example, in such an event, the US might request similar exemption for NAF organizations "in accordance with the phrase" unless otherwise agreed between the two governments". It was for this reason that the ROK side proposed that para 2 be accepted with the foregoing understanding. General O'Connor replied that the US side would take the ROK statements under consideration, and would discuss the subject again at the next meeting.

19. It was agreed to defer discussion of the only other two points still at issue in the Non-Appropriated Funds Article, in para 4 and the Agreed Minute, until the next meeting.

20. The next meeting was scheduled for Thursday, 6 February 1964, at 2:00 PM.

0132

JOINT SUMMARY RECORD OF THE 40TH SESSION

1. Time and Place: 2:00-4:00 P.M. January 24, 1964 at the Foreign Ministry's Conference Room

2. Attendants:

| 미주과 | 양 고 재 | 1월 29일 | 담 당 | 과 장 | 국 장 | 차관보 | 차 관 | 장 관 |
|---|---|---|---|---|---|---|---|---|

ROK Side:

| | |
|---|---|
| Mr. Chang, Sang Moon | Director<br>European and American Affairs Bureau<br>Ministry of Foreign Affairs |
| Mr. Koo, Choong Whay | Chief, American Section<br>Ministry of Foreign Affairs |
| Mr. Choo, Moon Ki | Chief, Legal Affairs Section<br>Ministry of Justice |
| Col. Kim, Won Kil | Chief, Military Affairs Section<br>Ministry of National Defense |
| Mr. Oh, Jae Hee | Chief, Treaty Section<br>Ministry of Foreign Affairs |
| Mr. Kang, Suk Jae (Rapporteur and Interpreter) | 2nd Secretary<br>Ministry of Foreign Affairs |
| Mr. Lee, Chung Bin | 3rd Secretary<br>Ministry of Foreign Affairs |
| Mr. Lee, Keun Pal | 3rd Secretary<br>Ministry of Foreign Affairs |
| Mr. Lee, Jae Sup | Bureau of Customs Duty<br>Ministry of Finance |

U.S. Side:

| | |
|---|---|
| Col. Howard Smigelow | Deputy Chief of Staff<br>8th U.S. Army |
| Col. L.J. Fuller | Staff Judge Advocate<br>United Nations Command |
| Capt. John Wayne | Assistant Chief of Staff<br>USN/K |
| Mr. Benjamin A. Fleck (Rapporteur and Press Officer) | First Secretary<br>American Embassy |
| Mr. James Sartorius | 2nd Secretary<br>American Embassy |

0133

| | |
|---|---|
| Mr. Robert A. Lewis | 2nd Secretary and Consul<br>American Embassy |
| Mr. Robert A. Kinney | J-5<br>8th U.S. Army |
| Maj. Robert D. Peckham | Staff Officer, JAG<br>8th U.S. Army |
| Mr. Kenneth Campen | Interpreter |

1. Brig. General G. G. O'Connor, Deputy Chief of Staff, Eighth United States Army, served as Chief Negotiator for the U.S. Government, in the absence of Mr. Habib. Mr. Chang introduced Mr. Lee Jae Sup, who was substituting for Mr. Sin Kwan-sop.

Military Post Offices

2. Mr. Chang, the ROK Chief Negotiator, stated that the ROK side had considered the explanation of the US side for the reasons the phrase "and their dependents" was included in the US draft of the Agreed Minute and that the US draft of the Agreed Minute was acceptable to the ROK side. However, in accepting the US draft of the MPO Article, the ROK Government negotiators desired to have the joint summary record clearly show the understanding that such acceptance does not projudice the ROK Government position with regard to the inclusion of the phrase "and their dependents" referred to in other articles of the agreement, including those dealing with Customs and Invited Contractors. Mr. Chang emphasized that the acceptance by the Korean negotiators of the phrase, despite the fact that the dependnnts of U.S. Government personnel are not specifically provided with MPO privileges in the U.S.-Japan Status of Forces Agreement, constitutes a major concession on their part and expressed their hope that the U.S. negotiators would favorably consider the position of the Korean side on relevant matters, namely, paragraph 5(b) of the Customs Article

0134

which deals with the exemption of customs inspection of mail. General O'Connor stated that neither side, in agreeing on the MPO Article, automatically committed itself in any way on related subjects in other articles. On this basis, it was agreed that the US draft of the MPO Article, including both the article and Agreed Minute, was accepted by both sides.

Customs

3. General O'Connor referred to the new U.S. draft of para. 5(b), tabled on January 17, which exempted from ROK customs inspection US official documents under official seal and First Class mail "obviously not containing merchandies." He indicated that the proposal takes into consideration the expressed ROK desire for the right to inspect all categories of parcels in MPO channels in Korea, and asked if the ROK negotiators found the proposal acceptable. Mr. Chang replied that the ROK side had considered the proposed new para. 5(b) and had found it unacceptable. Mr. Chang stated that the phrase "First Class mail obviously not containing merchandise" would not only impair the exercise of the right of inspection by the Korean authorities but also could be a source of much dispute. Mr. Chang emphasized that it had been agreed in principle that the ROK side was to have the right to inspect all parcels entering Korea through MPO channels. Therefore, the Korean negotiators felt that the authority to determine whether certain parcels contain merchandise or not should rest solely with the Korean customs inspectors engaging in the inspection, rather than the U.S. side, and that the packages ostensibly not containing merchandise should be

0135

subject to the inspection for verification. Therefore, the proposed para. 5(b) tabled by the ROK negotiators on January 9, which would exempt from customs inspection "official documents' under official seal and First Class letter mail in United States military channels," should be accepted. However, he stated that the ROK side would be prepared to waive customs inspection of the two special type of goods mentioned by the US side at the January 17 meeting, namely, recorded tapes and photographic films which are of personal velue and are individually and clearly so marked.

4. General O'Connor indicated that the US side had previously expressed objection to this para. 5(b) tabled by the Korean negotiators and had proposed a suitable substitute. The US side does not yet understand fully why the ROK side finds the US draft of para. 5(b) of January 17 unacceptable. Mr. Chang reiterated that if the US side accepted the ROK-proposed para. 5(b), the right of customs examination would be waived for such special types of articles as personal recorded tapes and films in MPO mail. The ROK side agreed that such a mutual understanding should be included in the Joint Agreed Summary. Mr. Chang stated that by so doing the Korean negotiators met the U.S. demand and, therefore, would see no difficulties on the part of the U.S. side in accepting the Korean proposal. General O'Connor indicated the US side would take the ROK proposal and statements under consideration and would reply at the next meeting.

5. General O'Connor noted that the ROK negotiators had not as yet given a specific response to the four understandings regarding ROKG customs inspection of MPO

0136

parcels, as read into the joint Agreed Summary by the US side on December 27, 1963, and January 17, 1964. Mr. Chang discussed the four points and indicated general concurrence in them, except for two proposed changes.

6. In the second understanding he desired deletion of the words "at designated points of mail distribution and". Mr. Chang indicated that if the designated points of inspection were too many, it would be beyond the capacity of the ROK Government to administer and that the ROK Government has grave concern in this regard. The ROK Government desires that the number of inspection sites be as few as possible, for inspection at designated points of mail distribution would be an extremely heavy burden on the ROK customs administration. Mr. Chang again proposed deletion of the phrase and suggested that the two sides should let arrangements regarding mail inspection sites be worked out by the Joint Committee. General O'Connor stated that as explained at a previous negotiating session (Agreed Summary, 35th meeting, November 14, 1963, para. 4 and 5), it is not practical to have customs inspection of MPO parcels at ports of entry, such as Inchon and Kimpo. MPO parcel mail arrives in Korea in large sealed metal containers, which are each sent, unopened, directly to one of the 17 main military post offices which are located in various parts of the ROK. These facts have been clearly explained, in pointing out why any inspections would impose a heavy administrative burden on the MPO system unless they were conducted at points of mail distribution. General O'Connor agreed that the Joint Committee, considering all relevant factors, could designate appropriate points of parcel inspection and, therefore,

0137

deletion of the phrase in ~~as~~ the second understanding, as proposed by the ROK side, would be agreeable.

7. Mr. Chang indicated that the second point of difference was in the fourth understanding, in which the ROK Government felt that the right of inspection would be on a "sample check" basis, rather than a "spot check" basis. Mr. Chang indicated that the Korean Government intends to send customs inspectors at all mutually agreed upon inspection site, and to examine parcels on the basis of sampling checks, so as to impose no great administrative burden or delay the mail. He asked whether the U.S. negotiators understood the words "spot check" in the same sense as the Korean side understood them. General O'Connor emphasized that any attempt to inspect all the parcel mail would certainly result in considerable delay of the mail. The terms "spot check" or "sample check" appear to have somewhat similar meanings, and it was mutually agreed that inspections should be at sites decided through the Joint Committee, and implemented so as not to delay the mail. Mr. Chang indicated that the ROK Government, in agreeing to sample checking at specified sites, does not prejudice its right in principle to inspect all parcels. General O'Connor replied the US Government conceded to the ROK the right to inspect all MPO parcels, but agreed with the ROKG that actual inspections would be as indicated by the foregoing US-ROK agreed understandings.

8. Regarding para. 5(a), General O'Connor explained that the US draft of this paragraph stipulates that members of the United States armed forces shall not be subject to ROK customs examination when entering or leaving the Republic of Korea under military orders. He explained how,

with the personnel rotation system in effect in Korea, the ROK desire to substitute the word "units" for "members" would subject almost all United States armed forces personnel to ROK customs examinations when entering or leaving Korea. General O'Connor asked if this is what the ROK side wanted. Mr. Chang replied that the ROK negotiators proposed the use of the word "units" rather than the US-proposed word "members" because they did desire all individuals in the U.S. armed forces to be subject to Korean customs inspection when entering and leaving Korea. Mr. Chang stated that in view of past abuses, the ROKG felt that all members of the U.S. armed forces entering and leaving Korea, except those which may move as "units," should be subject to ROK customs examinations. General O'Connor indicated that the United States was not asking for anything new in para. 5(a), and that it has been the practice for both Japanese and ROK custom authorities to waive customs examinations for members of the US armed forces in Japan and Korea respectively. He pointed out that this exemption from customs inspection was to be applied only to members of the US armed forces, and not to the civilian component or to American dependents. Mr. Chang said that it was conceivable that there are many types of troop movements such as movements as units on order or as an individual or group solely for leave purpose or for official purposes. He stated that the Korean customs authorities are concerned with the inspection of individual members entering or leaving Korea solely for leave purposes. The ROK Government, therefore, desired to have the right of customs inspection for individual members rather than units. He indicated that even though the ROK Government might not actually subject all members of the US armed forces entering and leaving Korea to customs examination it wanted the SOFA to give it the

0139

right to do so. It was agreed to continue discussion of this subject at a subsequent meeting.

9. Regarding para. 5(c) and Agreed Minute No.3, Mr. Chang indicated he wanted to explain the reasons why the ROK negotiators did not want the term "military cargo" to include cargo for non-appropriated funds organizations. Mr. Chang emphasized that the present economic situations in Japan and Korea were much different, and that the illegal disposal in the past of goods brought into Korea duty-free through non-appropriated funds channels adversely effected the growth of certain segments of the Korean economy. Mr. Chang emphasized that the impact upon the Korean economy that might be effected by illegal disposal of NAF imports would be much greater than that on the Japanese economy, and that the ROK Government, therefore, could not agree to the same arrangements as were in effect in Japan. He stated that since Korean industries have already suffered much from the abuses of NAF goods, the ROK Government must have the right of custom inspection of NAF imports.

10. Mr. Chang asked if the term "military cargo" in the US-Japan SOFA covered goods for non-appropriated funds organizations, and how the inspection of such goods is accomplished in Japan. General O'Connor replied by reading para 3 of the customs Article which states US-Japan SOFA that the term "military cargo" does refer to goods imported for NAF organizations. He indicated that Japanese customs does not inspect such imports, and that the US authorities furnish the Japanese authorities with information on such imports from Government bills of lading, as indicated in the US-Japan SOFA. General O'Connor indicated that a similar procedure could be

0140

established in the ROK and on that basis he tabled the following proposed sentence, to be added to the US draft of Agreed Minute No.3:

"Pertinent information on cargo consigned to non-appropriated fund organizations will be furnished authorities of the Republic of Korea upon request through the Joint Committee."

11. General O'Connor stated that the US side would cooperate in supplying pertinent information to ROK authorities. The Joint Committee machinery could be used to screen requests and appropriate information, not involving the security of United States forces, would be furnished to ROK authorities. Mr. Chang indicated the ROK negotiators would take this proposed addition to Agreed Minute No.3 under consideration.

12. Mr. Chang requested additional information about US Government bills of lading relating to NAF goods, including whether all such goods were imported into Korea on government bills of lading. He also asked about any formal agreements relating to the subject of NAF goods being designated as "military cargo." General O'Connor indicated military shipping is usually on government bills of lading, and thus NAF fund imports usually would be on U.S. Government bills of lading. Regarding the questions on agreements and procedures related to NAF imports, General O'Connor stated the subject would be investigated further and the US side would report its findings at the next negotiating session.

13. Mr. Chang thanked the US side for its explanations and for the copies of the US Army Regulations regarding commissaries, which had been supplied to them. The ROK

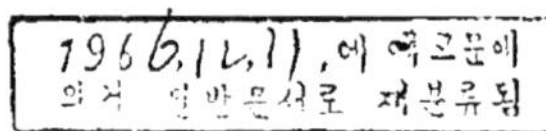


0141

negotiators are studying these materials and would explain the ROK position on the US draft of Agreed Minute No.7 at the next meeting. In response to questions, General O'Connor explained that all personnel who had commissary privileges also have NAF privileges. However, many persons have NAF privileges and not commissary privileges/ In general, unless USFK personnel maintain a household in Korea, they do not have commissary privileges. The basis on which USFK personnel are eligible for commissary privileges, therefore, is related to whether they have dependents and a household in Korea. Of course, relatively few of the total USFK personnel qualify for commissary privileges under this criteria.

14. Mr. Chang thanked General O'Connor for his explanations and indicated he would be ready to reply for the ROK Government on the commissary question at the next meeting.

15. Mr. Chang indicated that the ROK negotiators had studied the revised US draft of Agreed Minute No.1, and that it was acceptable to the ROK Government.

16. Mr. Chang stated that the ROK side was also willing to accept the US draft of para 3(b), thus demonstrating ROK cooperation in order to complete the SOFA negotiations as soon as possible. Mr. Chang asked that the U.S. negotiators reconsider the Korean position with regard to those points still unresolved in the Customs Article and reciprocate with the same spirit of cooperation. General O'Connor noted the US-ROK agreement on Agreed Minute No.1 and para 3(b), and expressed the hope that steady progress on the negotiations could continue to be realized through a spirit of mutual cooperation.

0142

17. Mr. Chang noted that agreement had now been reached on all provisions of the Customs Article, except para 5(a), 5(b) and 5(c), and Agreed Minutes 2, 3 and 7.

18. Mr. Chang stated that the ROK negotiators would prefer that the phrase relating to "other purchasers" in para 2 be deleted, but the US side had continuously insisted on such phraseology. The ROK side, believing the phrase of little significance, would be willing to accept the US draft of para 2, with the understanding that "other purchasers" referred to in the NAF organizations article should not be construed as being either applicable to or relevant to <u>other purchasers</u> such as certain foreign organizations or persons whom the Korean Government may in the future exempt from payment of certain taxes under specific arrangements with them. Mr. Chang explained that although the ROK negotiators do not perceive any necessity for the phraseology at present, in the future the ROK Government might desire to exempt from taxation some foreign agency which would come to Korea to help the economy. Although this was a hypothetical example, in such an event, the US might request similar exemption for NAF organizations in accordance with the phrase "unless otherwise agreed between the two governments." It was for this reason that the ROK side proposed that para 2 be accepted with the foregoing understanding. General O'Connor replied that the US side would take the ROK statements under consideration, and would discuss the subject again at the next meeting.

19. It was agreed to defer discussion of the only other two points still at issue in the Non-Appropriated Funds Article, in para 4 and the Agreed Minute, until the next meeting.

20. The next meeting was scheduled for Thursday, February 6, 1964, at 2:00 PM.

0143

4. 제41차 회의, 2.6

0144

노 동 청

노정노 735-2 1964. 2. 3

수신 외무부장관

제목 한미 행정 협정 초안 (노동관계)에 관한 의견

지난 1. 31 일자 귀부에서 주최한 한미 행정협정 실무자 회의에서 합의된 초안 내용에 대하여는 이를 전적으로 동의하오며 동 협정에 반영되도록 조치하여 주시기 바랍니다.

유첨: 미군 관계 노무자 실태 1통. 끝.

청 장 이

1966.12.31 에 예고문에 의거 일반문서로 재분류됨

0145

美軍機関 従業員 実態

一、全国外国機関 労動組合関係、

1. 直属労務者 34,000名 { 労務係 54%
事務係 46%

"内訳" 政府予算 27,000名
非予算 7,000 "

2. 下請労務者 P.X. 3,100名
美国人請負 3,000 "
合計 40,100 "

3. 其他 警備員 { 直属 1,000名
請負 1,500 "

(参考) 美国人請負会社名
1. Vinnel
2. Trans-Asia Engn.
3. Pacific Architecture Engn
4. Trans-American Engn
5. International Industrial

二、全国埠頭労動組合関係 (下請労務者)

1. 仁川地域 1,035名
2. 釜山 " 802 "
合計 1,837 "

總計 44,437名

공통서식 1-2 (을) (16절지)

0146

수신 외무부장관

제목 주한 미국군권의 지위에 관한 협정 초안에 관한 건

대호의 건에 관하여 동 협정안중 당부와 관련되는 사항을 검토한 결과 대체로 당부의 의견과 대동소이한것으로 사료되며 별도 지적한 2개 사항에 대한 당부 의견을 다음과 같이 회보하오니 참고하여 주시기 바랍니다.

기

1. 노동경쟁의 처리방법 (특히 해고와 관련하여) 현행 노동 쟁의 조정법에 의거 노동 쟁의는 반듯이 행정관청에 보고된후 일정기간의 냉각기를 두고 행정관청의 알선 또는 노동 위원회의 조정 중재를 통하여 그 해결을 모색하게 되는것이며, 동 기간중 해결이 불가능한 경우에 한하여 쟁의 행위가 인정되는것임. 또한 근로 기준법상 해고는 반듯이 정당한 이유가 있어야 가능한것임. 따라서 여상의 문제도 현존 노동법회의 취지에 의하여 해결될것이며 해고된자의 이의에 대하여는 귀 협정 초안 제 16조 6항 각호의 순서에 따라 처리되어도 가 할것임.

2. 미군 기관의 노역 조달 문제

동 협정 초안 제 17조 2에 표시된바와 같이 미군 및 관계기관의 요청에 따라 융통성 있게 노무를 조달하는 방법을 취하는것이 가 할것으로 사료됨.

0147

제 16 조

1. 가. 미 합중국 군 당국이 허가하고 규제하는 해군 판매소, 피엑스, 식당, 보급소, 사교클럽, 극장, 및 기타의 세출외 자금에 의한 제 기관을 미 합중국 군대 구성원, 군속 및 그 가족의 독점적 이용에 공하기 위하여 미 합중국 군대가 사용하고 있는 시설 및 구역내에 설치할수 있다. 본 협정에 규정이 있는 경우를 제외하고 이러한 제 기관은 한국의 규제, 면허수수료, 조세 또는 유사한 통제에 복종하지 않는다.

나. 미 합중국 군당국이 허가하고 또한 규제하는 신문이 일반공중에 판매되는 경우에는 당해 신문은 그 반포에 관한한 한국의 규제, 면허, 수수료, 조세, 또는 유사한 통제에 복종한다.

다. 미 합중국 군대가 사용하고 있는 시설 및 구역의 외부에서 전기 제 기관이 운용하는 역무는 양 정부간의 합의에 따른다. 단, 이러한 역무는 전기 (가)에 말한 면제규정을 적용받지 않는다.

2. 전기 제 기관에 의한 상품 및 역무의 판매에 대하여는 1항(나) 및 (다)에 규정한 경우를 제외하고 한국의 조세를 과하지 않으나 한국내에서의 전기 제 기관에 의한 상품 및 공급품의 구입에 대하여는 양 정부간에 별단의 합의가 없는한 한국의 조세를 과 한다.

3. 전기 제 기관이 판매하는 상품은 전기 제 기관으로 부터의 구입이 허용되지 않는자에 대하여 한국내에서 처분할수 없다.
미 합중국 당국은 전기의 처분을 방지하기 위하여 행정적 조치를 취하여야 한다.

4. 미 합중국 군대, 구성원, 군속 및 그 가족의 사용을 위하여 전기 제 기관이 수입하는 상품의 양은 그러한 사용을 위하여 필요한 합리적인 범위에 국한한다.

0148

5. 본조에서 말한 제 기관은 한국제법에 의하여 요구되는 자료를 한국 당국에 제공 한다.

0149

제 17 조

1. 미 합중국 군대 구성원, 군속 및 그 가족은 대한민국 국민과 동일한 조건하에 그들 자체의 소비를 위하여 필요한 물품과 그들이 필요로 하는 역무를 현지에서 구입할수 있다.
2. 현지에서 공급되는 미 합중국 군대의 유지를 위하여 필요한 자재, 공급품, 비품 및 역무로서, 그 조달이 한국 경제에 불리한 영향을 미칠 우려가 있는것은 대한민국 관계 당국과의 협조하에 그리고 의망되는 경우에는 대한민국 관계당국을 통하여 또는 원조를 받아 조달 한다.
3. 미 합중국 군대 구성원, 군속이나 또는 그 가족은 한국내에서 상품 및 역무의 개인적 구매에 관하여 조세 또는 유사한 과징금의 면제를 받지 못한다.
4. 미 합중국 군대 및 제 16조에서 규정된 제 기관의 현지 노무에 대한 수요는 한국 당국의 원조를 얻어 충족된다. 소득세 및 사회보장을 위한 납부금을 원천 징수하여 납부하는 의무 및 상호간 별단의 합의를 하는 경우를 제외하고 임금 및 제 수당에 관한것과 같은 고용 및 노동의 조건, 노동자 보호를 위한 조건및 노동 관계에 관한 노동자의 권미는 대한민국의 법률이 정하는바에 따라야 한다.
5. 미 합중국 군대는 한국 노동자의 고용을 저해하지 않도록 하기 위하여 제 삼국의 국민을 한국에서 고용하지 못한다.
6. 미 합중국 군대 또는 제 16조에서 규정한 기관이 노동자를 해고하고 대한민국 법정 또는 관계당국이 고용 계약이 종료되지 않았다는 결정을 한 경우에는 하기 절차를 적용한다.

0150

가. 미합중국 군대 또는 전기의 기관은 대한민국 정부로 부터 그 법정 또는 당국의 결정에 관하여 통고를 받는다.

나. 미 합중국 군대 또는 전기의 기관이 그 노동자를 다시 취로 시킬것을 원하지 않는 경우에는 미 합중 국 군대 또는 전기의 기관은 대한민국 정부로부터 법원 또는 당 국의 결정에 관하여 통보를 받은지 10일 이내에 그 뜻을 대한민국 정부에 통고하고 노동자를 잠정적으로 취로시키지 않을수 있다.

다. 대한민국 정부와 미합중국 군대 그리고 전기의 기관은 전기의 통고가 행하여진 경우에 그 사건의 실제적인 해결 방법을 발견하기 위하여 지체없이 협의하여야 한다.

타. (다)의 규정에 의한 협의 개시일로 부터 30일의 기간내에 그러한 해결에 도달하지 못한 경우에는 당해 노동자는 취로 하지 못한다. 그러한 경우에는 미 합중국 정부는 대한민국 정부에 대하여 합동 위원회를 통하여 양정부간에 합의된 기간의 당해 노동자의 고용 비용과 동일한 금액을 지불하여야 한다.



0151

① 外務部会議室
② 1964. 1. 31. 下午 2時
③ 参事 転便

Lobon

0151-1

Article

1. The United States armed forces and the organizations provided for in Article may employ civilian personnel under this Agreement. Such civilian personnel shall be nationals of the Republic of Korea.

2. Local labour requirements of the United States armed forces and of the said organizations ~~referred to in Paragraph 1 of this Article~~ shall be satisfied with the assistance of the Korean authorities. The obligations for the withholding and payment of income tax and social security contributions, and, unless otherwise agreed upon in this article, the conditions of employment and work, such as those relating to wages and supplementary payments, the conditions for the protection of workers, and the rights of workers concerning labour relations shall be those laid down by the legislation of the Republic of Korea.

3. Should the United States armed forces dismiss a worker and a decision of a court or a Labour Commission of the Republic of Korea to the effect that the contract of employment has not terminated become final, the following procedures shall apply:

(a) The United States armed forces shall be informed by the Government of the Republic of Korea of the decision of the court or ~~such authorities~~ Commission;

(b) Should the United States armed forces not desire to return the worker to duty, they shall so notify the Government of the Republic of Korea within ten days after being informed by the latter of the decision of the court or Commission, and may temporarily withhold the worker from duty;

(c) Upon such notification, the Government of the Republic of Korea and the United States armed forces shall consult together without delay with a view to finding a

0152

practical solution of the case;

(d) Should such a solution not be reached within a period of thirty days from the date of commencement of the consultations under (c) above, the worker will not be entitled to return to duty. In such case, the Government of the United States shall pay to the Government of the Republic of Korea an amount equal to the cost of employment of the worker for a period of time to be agreed between the two Governments through ~~out~~ the Joint Committee.

4. The United States Government shall ensure that the contractors referred to in Article ___ employ the Korean ~~civilian~~ personnel to the maximum extent practicable in connection with their activities under this Agreement. The provisions of Paragraph 2 of this Article shall be applied to the employment by the contractors of ~~such those~~ Korean ~~employees~~ personnel. ~~Korean nationals employed by the contractors referred to in Article~~ ___.

AGREED MINUTES

1. It is understood that the Government of the Republic of Korea shall be reimbursed for costs incurred under relevant contracts between appropriate authorities of the Korean Government and the United States armed forces or the organizations provided for in Article ___ in connection with the employment of workers to be provided for the United States armed forces or such organizations.

2. It is understood that the term " the legislation of the Republic of Korea " mentioned in Paragraph 2, Article ___ includes decisions of the courts and the Labour Commissions of the Republic of Korea, subject to the provisions of Paragraph 3, Article ___.

3. It is understood that the provisions of Article ___, Paragraph 3 shall only apply to discharges for security reasons including disturbing the maintenance of military

0153

discipline within the facilities and areas used by the United States armed forces.

0154

( alternative)

Article

1. The United States armed forces and the organizations provided for in Article ~~may~~ may employ civilian personnel under this Agreement. Such civilian personnel shall be nationals of the Republic of Korea.

2. Local labour requirements of the United States armed forces and of the said organizations ~~referred to in Paragraph 1 of this Article~~ shall be satisfied with the assistance of the Korean authorities. The obligations for the withholding and payment of income tax and social security contributions, and, unless otherwise agreed upon in this article, the conditions of employment and work, such as those relating to wages and supplementary payments, the conditions for the protection of workers, and the rights of workers concerning labour relations shall be those laid down by the legislation of the Republic of Korea.

3. Should the United States armed forces or, as appropriate, the said organizations dismiss a worker and a decision of a court or a Labour Commission of the Republic of Korea to the effect that the contract of employment has not terminated become final, the following procedures shall apply:

(a) The United States armed forces or the said organizations shall be informed by the Government of the Republic of Korea of the decision of the court or ~~such authorities,~~ Commission;

(b) Should the United States armed forces or the said organizations not desire to return the worker to duty, they shall so notify the Government of the Republic of Korea within ten days after being informed by the latter of the decision of the court or ~~the Labour~~ Commission, and may temporarily withhold the worker from duty;

(c) Upon such notification, the Government of the

0155

Republic of Korea ~~and the United~~ States armed forces or the said organizations shall consult together without delay with a view to finding a practical solution of the case;

(d) Should such a solution not be reached within a period of thirty days from the date of commencement of the consultations under (c) above, the worker will not be entitled to return to duty. In such case, the Government of the United States shall pay to the Government of the Republic of Korea an amount equal to the cost of employment of the worker for a period of time to be agreed between the two Governments through the Joint Committee.

4. The United States Government shall ensure that the contractors referred to in Article ___ employ the Korean ~~civilian~~ personnel to the maximum extent practicable in connection with their activities under this Agreement. The provisions of Paragraph 2 of this Article shall be applied to the employment by ~~the Korean nationals employed by~~ the contractors ~~referred to in Article~~ of the said Korean personnel.

AGREED MINUTES

1. It is understood that the Government of the Republic of Korea shall be reimbursed for costs incurred under relevant contracts between appropriate authorities of the Korean Government and ("U.S. armed forces" deleted) the organizations provided for in Article___ in connection with the employment of workers to be provided for ("U.S. armed forces or" deleted) such organizations.

따라 불필요

2. It is understood that the term " the legislation of the Republic of Korea " mentioned in Paragraph 2, Article__ includes decisions of the courts and the Labour Commission of the Republicof Korea, subject to the provisions of Paragraph 3, Article_____.

3. It is understood that the provisions of Article___ ,Paragraph 3 shall only apply to discharges for security reasons including disturbing the maintenance of military discipline

0156

within the facilities and areas used by the United States armed forces.

4. It is understood that the organizations referred to in Article_____ will be subject to the procedures of Paragraph 3 on the basis of mutual agreement between the appropriate authorities.

5. It is understood that the Government of the United States shall ensure that, in case the Korean personnel employed by the contractors referred to in Article are dismissed for security reasons before termination of employment contract, the contractors shall pay to the Government of the Republic of Korea an amount equal to the cost of employment of such personnel for a period of time to be agreed between the Government of the Republic of Korea and the said contractors.

0157

ARTICLE

1. The United States armed forces, the organizations provided for in Article _____, and the contractors provided for in Article ______, may employ civilian personnel under this Agreement. Such civilian personnel shall be nationals of the Republic of Korea.

2. Local labor requirements of the United States armed forces and the organizations or contractors referred to in Paragraph 1 of this Article shall be satisfied with the assistance of the Korean authorities. The obligations for the withholding and payment of income tax and of social security contributions, and, except as may be provided for in this article, the conditions of employment and work, such as those relating to wages and supplementary payments, the conditions for the protection of workers, and the rights of workers concerning labor relations shall be those laid down by the legislation of the Republic of Korea.

3. Should the United States armed forces or the organizations provided for in Article ______ dismiss a worker and a court or competent authorities of the Republic of Korea decide to the effect that the contract of employment has not terminated, the following procedures shall apply:

(a) The United States armed forces or the said organizations shall be informed by the Government of the Republic of Korea of the decision of the court or such authorities;

(b) Should the United States armed forces or the said organizations not desire to return the worker to duty,

0158

they shall so notify the Government of the Republic of Korea within ten days after being informed by the latter of the decision of the court or the authorities, and may temporarily withhold the worker from duty;

(c) Upon such notification, the Government of the Republic of Korea and the United States armed forces or the said organizations shall consult together without delay with a view to finding a practical solution of the cade;

(d) Should such a solution not be reached within a period of thirty days from the date of commencement of the consultations under (c) above, the worker will not be entitled to return to duty. In such case, the Government of the United States shall pay to the Government of the Republic of Korea an amount equal to the cost of employment of the worker for a period of time to be agreed between the two Governments through the Joint Committee.

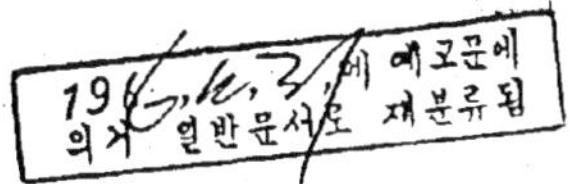

0159

# 기 안 용 지

| 자체 통제 | | 기안처 | 미주과 이근팔 | 전화번호 | 근거서류접수일자 |
|---|---|---|---|---|---|
| | 과장 | 국장 | 차관 | 장관 | |
| 관계관 서명 | | | | | |
| 기안 년월일 | 1964. 2. 4. | 시행 년월일 | | 보존 년한 | 정서 기장 |
| 분류 기호 | 외구미 722.2 | 전체 통제 | | 종결 | |
| 경유 수신 참조 | 건의 | | 발신 | | |
| 제목 | 제 41 차 주둔군지위협정 체결교섭회의에 임할 우리측 입장 | | | | |

2 월 6 일에 개최될 제 41차 주둔군지위협정 체결을 위한 한.미간 교섭회의에서는 관세업무, 비세출자금기관,및 군계약자 조항들의 및 노무에 관한 상방의 조문을 제시하도록 예정하고 있는바 이에 대하여 우리측 교섭실무자는 1 월 31 일 및 2 월 1일 회합을 갖고 제 41 차회의에서 취할 태도를 별첨과 같이 결정하였아오니 재가하여 주시기 바랍니다.

유 첨: 제 41차 주둔군지위협정 체결교섭회의에 임할 우리측 태도. 끝

승인양식 1-1-3 (1112-040-016-018) (190mm×260mm16절지)

196 , , 에 예고문에 의거 일반문서로 재분류됨

0160

1. 관세조항

가. 미측 5(b)항에 대하여 "First Class letter Mail "을 계속 주장하는 우리측안에 대한 미국측의 견해를 청취한다.

나. 미측안 5(a)항이 Members 를 주장하는데 대하여 우리측은 Units 를 계속 주장한다.

다. 미국측이 초안 5(c)항 및 합의의사록 3항에서 군사화물에 비세출자금기관 앞으로 탁송되는 화물을 포함시키려는데 대하여 40차 회의에 계속하여 미.일간의 양해사항에 관한 미국측 설명을 듣는다.

라. 미측 합의의사록 7항이 Commissary 앞으로 탁송되는 화물에 대하여서도 비세출자금기관 앞 화물과 같이 관세를 면제할 것을 주장하고 있는바

(1) 비세출기관을 사용할 수 있는 가족이라 할지라도 Commissary 사용에 있어서는 세대주 또는 세대주가 지정하는 가족의 일원 이외에는 Commissary 를 사용할 수 없는 것으로 알고 있는데 미측 견해는 어떠한가?

(2) 미군 Commissary 규정 265항의 Commissary 사용 대상자인 Other individuals, organizations and activities 는 미국인 또는 기관을 지롱하는 것으로 보는데 비세출자금기관조항 합의의사록 (f)항에 의하여 허가될 수 있는 외국인에게도 확장 적용 될 수 있는 것으로 보는가?

를 확인한 후 차기회의에서 토의하기로 한다.

2. 비세출자금기관

가. 미측 초안 2항의 "other purchasers "에 관하여 우리측이 40차 회의에서 유보한 사항에 대한 미국측 ~~견해를 청취하고~~ 의 양해가 있으면 2항을 수락한다.

나. 미측안 제 4항에서 세금에 관한 정보를 우리 나라 사세당국에 제공할 것을 규정한 것은 수락한다.

다. 합의의사록의 비세출자금기관 사용대상자의 범위에 관하여 c, d, e, f, 각항 해당자의 수를 묻고 비세출자금기관 특히 피.엑스 운영에 관한 미측의 자료 제공을 요청한다.

0161

3. 군계약자

가. 군계약자의 정의에 있어서 "미국법에 따라 조직된 법인체를 포함한 사람과 고용자로서 통상 미국에서 거주하는 자"를 그 범위로 규정하고 그들의 가족을 제외하는 우리측 안을 계속 주장하되. 우선 미국측의 우리 안 검토 결과를 청취한다.

나. 군계약자에 부여될 면제 및 특혜문제에 관한 미국측 초안 3(i)항이 운전면허 및 등록에 관한 특혜를 규정하고 있으나 우리측은 이들이 일반외국인과 동일하게 취급되어야 할 것으로 봄으로 3(i)항의 삭제를 주장한다. (BG.1311)

다. 미측이 제안한 군계약자조항에 관한 합의의사록 (1)항에 우리측이 소득세 면제의 적용을 배제하기 위하여 추가적용어 "except paragraph 7"을 제의한 우리측안을 계속 주장한다.

라. 미국측이 상금 제시하지 않고 있는 군계약자에 대한 대한민국의 재판관할권에 관한 안 (우리측 초안 제 7항에 해당)을 조속 제시할 것을 요구한다.

4. 노무조항

가. 우리측은 다음과 같은 노무에 관한 초안을 제시한다.

0162

1. The United States armed forces and the organizations provided for in Article ______ may employ civilian personnel under this Agreement. Such civilian personnel shall be nationals of the Republic of Korea.

2. Local labour requirements of the United States armed forces and of the said organizations shall be satisfied with the assistance of the Korean authorities. The obligations for the withholding and payment of income tax and social security contributions, and, unless otherwise agreed upon in this article, the conditions of employment and work, such as those relating to wages and supplementary payments, the conditions for the protection of workers, and the rights of workers concerning labour relations shall be those laid down by the legislation of the Republic of Korea.

3. Should the United States armed forces dismiss a worker and a decision of a court or a Labour Commission of the Republic of Korea to the effect that the contract of employment has not terminated become final, the following procedures shall apply:

(a) The United States armed forces shall be informed by the Government of the Republic of Korea of

0163

the decision of the court or Commission;

(b) Should the United States armed forces not desire to return the worker to duty, they shall so notify the Government of the Republic of Korea within ten days after being informed by the latter of the decision of the court or Commission, and may temporarily withhold the worker from duty;

(c) Upon such notification, the Government of the Republic of Korea and the United States armed forces shall consult together without delay with a view to finding a practical solution of the case;

(d) Should such a solution not be reached within a period of thirty days from the date of commencement of the consultations under (c) above, the worker will not be entitled to return to duty. In such case, the Government of the United States shall pay to the Government of the Republic of Korea an amount equal to the cost of employment of the worker for a period of time to be agreed between the two Governments through the Joint Committee.

4. The United States Government shall ensure that the contractors referred to in Article ______ employ the Korean personnel to the maximum extent practicable in connection with their activities under this Agreement.

0164

The provisions of ~~paragraph~~ this Article shall be applied to the employment by the contractors of the said Korean personnel.

AGREED MINUTES

1. It is understood that the Government of the Republic of Korea shall be reimbursed for costs incurred under relevant contracts between appropriate authorities of the Korean Government and the United States armed forces or the organizations provided for in Article _____ in connection with the employment of workers to be provided for the United States armed forces or such organizations.

2. It is understood that the term "the legislation of the Republic of Korea" mentioned in Paragraph 2, Article _____ includes decisions of the courts and the Labour Commissions of the Republic of Korea, subject to the provisions of Paragraph 3, Article _______.

3. It is understood that the provisions of Article_____, Paragraph 3 shall only apply to discharges for security reasons including disturbing the maintenance of military discipline within the facilities and areas used by the United States armed forces.

0165

POSITION PAPER

For the 41st SOFA Negotiating Meeting

Customs

1. Paragraph 5(b)

At last meeting, the Korean negotiators stated that the Korean side would be willing, in order to meet your particular concern regarding the two special types of articles, namely, the recorded tapes and photographic films which are of personal value, to waive customs inspection of such items individually and clearly so marked. At the same time, the Korean negotiators clearly pointed out the reasons why the revised draft of paragraph 5(b) tabled by your side which reads "official documents under official seal and First Class mail obviously not containing merchandise" is not acceptable.

Inasmuch as the both sides have agreed in principle that all parcels regardless of class, except special types of articles such as recorded tapes and films, would be subject to the Korean customs inspection, the Korean negotiators maintain that the both sides agree to the proposed paragraph 5(b) tabled by the Korean side on January 9 which exempt from customs inspection "official documents under official seal and First Class letter mail in the United States military postal channels". We would like to listen to your view if you care to make on our proposed draft.

2. Paragraph 5(a)

The Korean negotiators have noted the explnation of the U.S. side to the effect that the United States troops in Korea are rotated on individual basis. It is the belief of the Korean negotiators that the question posed in this paragraph is the matter of principle as to whether or not the Korean authorities should be given the right to exercise inspection of members of the U.S. armed forces entering and leaving Korea. However, as we have explained many times at the previous meetings, the Korean side is not attempting to inspect every individual member. We can assure that in actual administration of the Agreement,

0166

customs inspection for members would be almost for all cases waived unless the Korean customs authorities feels it absolutely necessary to exercise inspection right for certain members of the United States armed forces. In this connection, the Korean negotiators continue to request that the United States negotiators, taking into account the primary concern we have in this regard, would be able to accept our position.

3. <u>Paragraph 5(c) and related Agreed Minute No.3</u>

a. The Korean negotiators raised certain questions at last meeting regarding agreements between the U.S. and Japan and procedures related to NAF imports. Your side responded to further investigate and answer your findings at today's meeting. We would appreciate if you would give further explanation.

b. In this connection, the Korean negotiators would like to ask a few more questions:

(1) Under the provisions of the U.S.-Japan agreement, the Korean negotiators understand that cargo which are not shipped on the U.S. Government bill of lading does not come under the category of military cargo and also are not exempted from customs inspection. Is our understanding correct?

(2) And we have noted that in paragraph 2 of the Customs Article of the U.S.-Japan Agreement, the NAF organizations is specifically spelled out besides the United States armed forces as an independent entity to import materials, supplies and equipment. However, the NAF organizations is not spelled out in the Agreed Minute. In other words, military cargo is termed, in the Agree Minute No.3, to refer to all cargoes shipped on the U.S. Government bill of lading to the United States armed forces without any

mention of the NAF organizations. There exist no consistency between the text and related Agreed Minute as far as the NAF organization goods are concerned. Furthermore, due to ambuiguity of the structure of both the text and related Agreed Minute as indicated above, it is very questionable whether or not cargo shipped to the NAF organizations comes under the category of military cargo defined under the provisions of the said Agreed Minute. The Korean negotiators, therefore, would appreciate it very much if your side clarify the point under question.

4. Agreed Minute No.7

a. The Korean negotiators have considered the previous discussions in regard with Agreed Minute No.7 and have also taken into account the reasons you had proposed this Agreed Minute. In order to meet your requirement to provide for duty-free importation by the commissary, we would like to suggest that the word "commissaries" be included after the phrase "their authorized procurement agencies", and that persons who would be granted commissary privileges be agreed in the Joint Committee.

b. The Korean negotiators understand that under the provisions of the United States AR 31-200, commissary privileges in case of an individual foruse of his dependents is granted only to the individual who is the head of the household and an adult member designated as his agent for the purpose of making purchases on his behalf. If this understanding is correct, there is no consistency between users of NAF organizations and commissaries as far as dependents are concerned. Does the U.S. side believe that the provisions of Item 265 of the said AR could be extended to apply to those persons referred to under category (f) of the Agreed Minute related to the NAF organizations?

NAF Organizations

1. Paragraph 2

At last meeting, the Korean negotiators expressed their agreement to paragraph 2 of the U.S. draft with the understanding that

0168

"other purchases" referred to in the U.S. draft should not be construed as either applicable to or relevant with other purchasers such as foreign organizations and persons for whom the Korean Government may in the future exempt from certain Korean taxes under specific arrangements with them. We would like to know if your side agree to our understanding.

2. Paragraph 4

We accept paragraph 4 of the draft article tabled by yours side.

3. Agreed Minute

With regard to the Agreed Minute relating to the NAF organizations, the Korean negotiators are not yet ready to make any comment on our position. However, for our further study, we would like to know approximate number of persons who would be authorized to use the NAF organizations under each category and also would like to ask for materials such as army regulation concerning operation of the NAF organizations.

Invited Contractors

1. Sincer there has been developed much discrepency between position of the both sides regarding the Contractors article. The Korean negotiators have maintained that contractors who should be regularized under the Article should be limited only to persons, including corporations organized under the laws of the United States, and their employees, who are ordinarily resident in the United States and whose presence in the Republic of Korea is solely for the purpose of executing contracts with the United States armed forces. We have also made it quite clear that the Korean Government does not preclude the United States armed forces bringing into Korea employees of the third country nationals. The Korean negotiators believe that our position to this effect has been fully apprehended by your side.

2. However, having considered the previous discussion of the both sides on this Article and also in order to meet concern and difficulties indicated by your side regarding employees who are third country nationals, the Korean negotiators would like to make a suggestion.

3. The suggestion is this. Persons to be regularized and those

0169

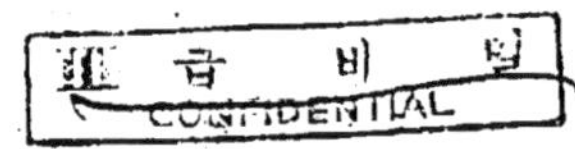

privileges to be accorded under this Article be divided into, let's say, two groups.

Under one group, we would like to have persons, including corporation organized under the laws of the United States, and their employees who are ordinarily resident in the United States as well as those benefits accorded them regulated, and under the other group those employees who are third country nationals and those benefits to be accorded them regulated separately. To be precise, the Korean negotiators would be prepared to accord those employees who would come under latter group such benefits as are:

(1) Accession and movement, as provided for in Article ____, paragraph 2;

(2) If authorized by the Government of the United States, the use of the service of the organizations provided for in Article N/S/E;

(3) Those provided in Article 외환, paragraph 2, for members of the United States armed forces, the civilian component, and their dependents;

(4) If authorized by the Government of the United States, the use of military payment certificates, as provided for in Article ____;

(5) The use of postal facilities provided for in Article ___.

4. Those employees who would come under latter group should be liable to pay income tax to the Government of the Republic of Korea on income derived from their service with or employment by the Contractors.

5. Neither persons nor employees under the both groups should be entitled to those benefits relatingto driving permit and registration of vehicles and fees and charges relating to the operation of vehicles.

6. Dependents of those persons and employees under the both groups should be excluded from application of this Article.

7. The Korean negotiators would like to request your consideration on our suggestion as indicated above.



0170

## SOFA NEGOTIATION

Agenda for the 41st Session

14:00 Feb. 6, 1964

1. Continuation of Discussions on:
    a. Customs Article
    b. Non-Appropriated Fund Organizations Article
    c. Contractors Article
    d. Labor Article
2. Other Business
3. Agenda and Date of the Next Meeting
4. Press Release

0171

# 기 안 용 지

| 자체 통제 | 외무사무관 손일홍 | 기안처 | 미주과 이근팔 | 전화번호 | 근거서류접수일자 |
|---|---|---|---|---|---|
| | 과장 | 국장 | 차관 | 장관 | |

| 관계관 서명 | | | | | |
|---|---|---|---|---|---|
| 기안 년월일 | 1964. 2. 11. | 시행 년월일 | | 보존 년한 | 정서 기장 |
| 분류 기호 | 외구미722.2 | 전체 통제 | 종결 | | |
| 경유 수신 참조 | 대통령 (참조: 비서실장) 국무총리 | | 발신 | 장관 | |
| 제목 | 주둔군 지위협정 체결을 위한 제41차 교섭회의 보고 | | | | |

1964. 2. 6. 하오 2시부터 하오 4시 까지 외무부장관 회의실에서 개최된 제41차 주둔군 지위협정 체결 교섭회의에서 토의된 내용을 별첨과 같이 보고합니다.

유첨: 제41차 교섭회의 보고서 1부. 끝.

승인양식 1-1-3 (1112-040-016-018) (190mm×260mm16절지)

0172

제 41 차

한미간 주둔군지위협정 체결실무자회의

보 고 서

1. 일 시: 1964 년 2 월 6 일 하오 2 시 부터 동 4 시 까지.

2. 장 소: 외무부장관 회의실

3. 토의사항:

가. 관세업무

(1) 미측초안 5(b)항: 양측은 한국세관이 공문서 및 first class letter mail 을 제외한 모든 소포에 대한 검사권을 행사할 수 있다는데 합의를 보았다.

(2) 미측초안 5(a)항: 출입국하는 미군대에 대한 세관검사는 미측으로 부터 미군이 unit 단위로 이동하는 경우는 이미 없어졌다는 설명에 따라 휴가 기타 사적용무로 출입국하는 경우를 제외하고 공무차 이동하는 미군대 구성원에 대하여서 세관검사를 면제할 수 있다는 우리측 태도를 밝히고 이에 대한 미측의 입장 재검토를 촉구하였다.

(3) 미측초안 5(c)항: 미측이 군사화물의 정의 속에 비세출자금기관 앞으로 탁송되어 오는 화물까지 포함시키려는데 대하여 비세출자금기관 앞 화물에 대하여서는 세관검사를 하겠다는 우리측 입장을 뒷바침하기 위하여 미측으로 부터 미.일간 주둔군지위협정에서 규정한 군사화물의 정의와 비세출자금기관 앞 화물에 대한 세관검사에 관한 미.일간 양해사항에 관하여 설명을 청취하였다.

(4) 미측합의의사록 7항: 미군 Commissary 사용 대상자의 범위 규정은 그와 연관성이 있는 비세출자금기관의 사용대상자의 범위 토의 때 같이 검토하기로 합의하였다.

나. 비세출자금기관

(1) 미측초안 2항: 비세출자금기관에 대한 과세에 있어서" other purchasers "를 " other ordinary purchasers "로 지음 한다는 우리측 요보사항을 미측이 양해하고 합의하였다.

(2) 미측초안 4항: 양측은 비세출자금기관이 한국조세법령에 따라 한국세관당국에 필요한 정보를 제공한다는데 합의하였다.

(41) -11

0173

0174

다. 군계약자

(1) 우리측은 군계약자의 범위를 우리안대로 " Persons, including corporations organized under the laws of the United States, and their employees, who are ordinarily resident in the United States" 로 규정하되

(가) 필수불가결한 제 3국인의 고용을 막지는 않겠으며,

(나) 군계약자의 가족과 제 3 국인 및 그들의 가족에 대하여서는 군표, 군사우편, 및 비세출자금기관 사용권만을 부여한다는 대두리 안에서 미측에게 그가 제시한 초안을 재검토하여 차기회의에 임하여 줄 것을 요청하였다.

다. 노무조항

(1) 양측은 2 월 7 일 노무에 관한 초안을 교환하고 차기 회의에서 토의하기로 하였다.

4. 기타 사항: 차기 회의 일자: 1964 년 2 월 14 일 하오 2 시.

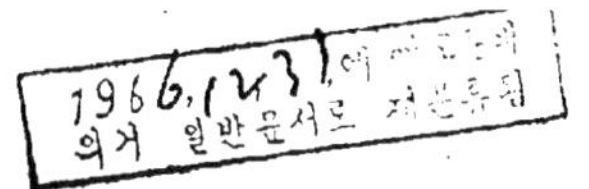


0175

64-3-5 (2)

미국모 129-7 (2)

0176

February 6, 1964

1. Mr. Chang opened the meeting by welcoming Mr. Habib back to the negotiating table following the latter's visit to Washington on consultation. Mr. Chang expressed the hope that as a result of Mr. Habib's consultation in Washington, the negotiations would now move rapidly to a successful conclusion.

2. Mr. Chang then introduced Mr. Chung Wu-yong, who was attending the meeting in place of Mr. Cho Kwang-che.

3. Mr. Habib stated that the Korean negotiators had previously asked when the U.S. negotiators would table the U.S. drafts of the articles dealing with labor and criminal jurisdiction. As they were aware, the U.S. negotiators were prepared to table the draft of the Labor Procurement Article at this meeting. Based on his conversations in Washington, he predicted that the draft of the Criminal Jurisdiction Article would also be available for tabling very soon.

4. Mr. Chang replied that the Korean negotiators welcomed Mr. Habib's statement regarding the Criminal Jurisdiction Article and hoped that it would be tabled within two or three weeks.

Customs

5. Taking up the Customs Article, Mr. Chang stated that the Korean position with regard to the points still at issue had been fully explained. With regard to paragraph 5(b), the Korean negotiators, in order to meet the concern of the U.S. negotiators, had stated the willingness of the ROK Government to waive customs inspection of photographic films and recorded tapes. At the same time, the Korean negotiators had stated that the latest version of paragraph 5(b) proposed by the U.S. negotiators was unacceptable to the Korean negotiators. He asked whether the U.S. negotiators wished to make any further comment regarding this subparagraph.

6. Mr. Habib replied by referring to the four understandings which the U.S. negotiators had twice read into the Joint Agreed Summary. He said the U.S. negotiators were prepared to agree to the latest version of paragraph 5(b) proposed by the Korean

0177

negotiators, provided the Korean negotiators accepted those understandings, which had been designed to forestall any delay in the delivery of mail. Mr. Chang, at the previous meeting, had suggested two minor changes in these understandings. The U.S. negotiators did not take exception to those changes. The purpose of reading the understandings into the record was to indicate to the Joint Committee the intentions of the negotiators. The Joint Committee would implement the provisions of this subparagraph. Referring to previous references to "spot checks" and "sampling checks", Mr. Habib stated that there was no need to debate the meaning of the two terms, so long as both sides were talking about the same process. The U.S. negotiators appreciated the concern of the Korean negotiators over having the right of inspection, which the Korean negotiators had previously discussed largely in terms of its effect as a deterrent to abuses. The U.S. negotiators, therefore, were willing to accept the latest Korean draft, provided the Korean negotiators agreed to the four understandings, thereby leaving the implementation of the subparagraph to the Joint Committee with guidance as to the intent of the negotiators.

7. Mr. Chang replied that at the previous meeting the remarks of the Korean negotiators had been incorporated in the Joint Agreed Summary. The Korean negotiators had also indicated that the ROK authorities had no intention of inspecting every parcel in the MPO mail. He asked whether the U.S. negotiators agreed to the Korean draft of paragraph 5(b) in the light of these statements at the previous meeting.

8. Mr. Habib replied in the affirmative. He said the subparagraph gave the Korean authorities the right to inspect parcels and left implementation to the Joint Committee, which would take into account as guidance the discussion of this subject by the negotiators, as recorded in the Joint Agreed Summary.

9. Full agreement was reached on the following text of paragraph 5(b):

0178

7. Mr. Chang welcomed the statement of the Chief U.S. negotiator accepting the Korean draft. He stated that at the previous meeting the Korean negotiators had stated their views with regard to the four understandings concerning the paragraph 5(b) and these views had been incorporated in the Joint Agreed Summary record of the 40th meeting. The Korean negotiators had also indicated that although the ROK authorities had no intention of inspecting every parcel in the MPO mail, should not be prejudiced their right to inspect all MPO parcels. He indicated concurrence of the Korean negotiators that the understandings written into the Joint Summary Record would serve as a guiding principle for the Joint Committee. However, he stated the Korean side took it that the U.S. negotiators agreed to the Korean draft of paragraph 5(b) in the light of the statements made by the Korean side regarding the four understandings at the previous meeting.

"5(b). Official documents under official seal and First Class letter mail in United States military postal channels under official postal seal."

10. Turning to paragraph 5(a), Mr. Habib noted that there was still a difference of view regarding the use of the word "units" or the word "members". He pointed out that the U.S. draft, in using the word "members", provides that dependents and members of the civilian component shall be subject to customs inspection. He noted that at the previous meeting the Korean negotiators had raised the subject of "past abuses". He said the U.S. negotiators were not aware of any past abuses and asked the Korean negotiators to explain their remark.

11. Mr. Chang replied that the Korean negotiators ~~possessed evidence of past abuses~~ evidence of such abuses would be prepared to make available to the U.S. negotiators outside of the formal negotiations. Mr. Habib ~~replied~~ stated that he was ~~not~~ talking about ~~postal abuses but was referring ... specifically to~~ Mr. Chang's statement at the previous meeting that in view of past abuses, the ROK Government believed that all members of the U.S. armed forces should be subject to ROKG customs inspection, except those moving as members of units.

12. Mr. Habib said the U.S. negotiators would be interested in a clarification of Mr. Chang's remark. He said that the provision desired by the Korean negotiators was not a normal provision in status of forces agreements and the U.S. negotiators did not see the necessity for it. He said that the use of the word "members" in the U.S. draft was based on the actual manner in which the personnel of the U.S. armed forces enter and leave Korea. It was intended, therefore, to be an accurate reflection of current practices. He remarked that there appeared to be a basic inconsistency in the position of the Korean negotiators. If they were willing to forego inspection for troops arriving as members of units, why were they not also willing to forego inspection of troops arriving as individuals? The U.S. negotiators had no objection to the inspection of non-members of the armed forces. This subparagraph applied to troops ar-

0180

riving under orders, and assigned to units already in place.

13. Mr. Chang replied that the Korean negotiators were aware of the circumstances under which the members of the U.S. armed forces arrived in Korea. What the Korean negotiators were seeking was the right to inspect U.S. military personnel entering or leaving Korea for purposes other than official business. Accordingly, the Korean negotiators wished to amend the languagex of the subparagraph to read as follows:

> "5(a). Members of the United States armed forces under orders entering or leaving the Republic of Korea for official duty purposes but not for leave or recreational purposes."

14. Mr. Habib replied that this proposal introduced a new element into the discussion of this subparagraph. The U.S. negotiators would study this proposal and give their views at the next meeting.

15. Turning to paragraph 5(c), Mr. Chang recalled that at the previous meeting, the Korean negotiators had queried the U.S. negotiators about procedures in Japan with regard to military cargo and cargo shipped to non-appropriated fund organizations.

16. Mr. Habib replied that other status of forces agreements have been written on the standard basic premise that all cargo shipped to the U.S. armed forces, including that shipped to non-appropriated fund organizations, is "military cargo". The Korean negotiators had also inquired concerning documentation of cargo. All military cargo, including cargo shipped to non-appropriated fund organizations, is shipped on government bills of lading or similar shipping documents. At the 40th meeting on January 24, the U.S. negotiators had indicated that the U.S. armed forces are prepared to cooperate with the Korean authorities by providing information concerning cargoes and had tabled a proposed additional sentence to Agreed Minute #3 which would provide for the furnishing of such information, upon the request of the Korean authorities through the Joint Committee. The U.S. negotiators

0181

believed that this proposed language would fully satisfy the needs of the Korean authorities.

17. Mr. Chang stated that, according to the explanation given by the U.S. negotiators, goods shipped to non-appropriated fund organizations in Japan are included in the category of military cargo. However, the Korean negotiators understood under the provisions of the U.S.-Japan Agreement that cargo not shipped on government bills of lading was not considered to be military cargo.

18. Mr.Habib replied that this was an incorrect interpretation of the situation. He explained that the U.S. Government no longer uses bills of lading for all military cargo. The important factor is the consignment of the goods. In other words, if the cargo is consigned to the U.S. armed forces it is considered to be military cargo. Equally important was the fact that the U.S. negotiators had proposed a provision which would provide information to the ROK authorities concerning the consignment of such cargoes.

19. Mr. Chang stated that the U.S. negotiators had previously stated that in actual practice the Japanese authorities waive customs examination of non-appropriated fund organization cargoes. However, a literal reading of the U.S.-Japan SOFA indicated that the Japanese authorities have the authority to make such examinations.

20. Mr. Habib replied that the negotiators were not engaged in negotiating the SOFA with Japan. He said the Korean negotiators had asked for information concerning the types of cargo being imported into Korea by the U.S. armed forces. In order to meet this request, the U.S. negotiators had proposed the additional sentence to Agreed Minute #3. He said the article should be drafted so as to reflect the existing situation with respect to cargo shipments. He asked if what the Korean negotiators were really saying was that they wanted the SOFA to grant the Korean authorities the right of customs inspection and the right to levy customs duties on military cargoes. The U.S. negotiators were not prepared

0182

to agree to any such provisions.

21. Mr. Chang stated that the Korean negotiators wanted the SOFA to give to the Korean authorities the right to conduct customs inspection of goods shipped to non-appropriated fund organizations. He said the Korean negotiators were confused by the statements of the U.S. negotiators regarding the implementation of the SOFA with Japan. The Korean negotiators believed that the SOFA with Japan did not include non-appropriated fund organization goods in the category of military cargo. The U.S. negotiators had said that such goods were shipped on bills of lading and then, later, had spoken of "similar documents". Were they or were they not shipped on bills of lading? What were the similar documents which had been mentioned. The U.S. negotiators had an obligation to tell the Korean negotiators how the SOFA with Japan is implemented.

22. Mr. Habib denied any such obligation. However, he said the U.S. negotiators were not indisposed to answer any specific questions which the Korean negotiators might wish to ask. He did not know whether or not it would be possible to obtain statistics on the amount or types of cargo shipped to U.S. armed forces in Korea on bills of lading but the U.S. negotiators would be glad to attempt to obtain such information if the Korean negotiators were really interested in it. He pointed out that a bill of lading is a specific type of document; there are also other types of shipping documents. With regard to the inspection of goods consigned to non-appropriated fund organizations, Mr. Habib informed the Korean negotiators that according to a supervisor currently employed by the U.S. armed forces in Korea, who had worked in Japan for eleven years as a cargo supervisor, cargoes consigned to non-appropriated fund organizations there were never inspected by Japanese customs authorities.

23. Mr. Chang replied that the Korean negotiators did not believe it necessary to verify the fact that goods are not inspected by Japanese customs

0183

authorities. The Korean negotiators did believe, however, that the SOFA with Japan gives the Japanese authorities the right to make such inspections. Mr. Habib replied that the U.S. negotiators do not agree with this interpretation of the SOFA with Japan.

24. Mr. Chang stated that in paragraph 2 of the Customs Article in the SOFA with Japan, non-appropriated fund organizations are spelled out as a separate entity from the U.S. armed forces but in the related Agreed Minute there is no mention of them. The Agreed Minute refers only to cargo shipped to the armed forces and does not refer to cargo shipped to the non-appropriated fund organizations. There is ambiguity, therefore, in the SOFA with Japan and the Korean negotiators would appreciate clarification by the U.S. negotiators. For example, what arrangements have been made with the Japanese authorities to exempt cargoes shipped to non-appropriated fund organizations from customs inspection?

25. Mr. Habib replied that the text which was under negotiation is not ambiguous. It makes no distinction between the U.S. armed forces and the non-appropriated fund organizations, which are an integral part of the armed forces. If the Korean negotiators find ambiguity in this draft, the U.S. negotiators are prepared to discuss the question. The U.S. negotiators believed that ambiguities in other status of forces agreements, if any existed, should not be carried over into this agreement. He stated that the Korean negotiators were engaging in fruitless discussion and wasting time. He proposed that further discussion of this subparagraph be postponed until the Korean negotiators could find the time to read the U.S. draft.

26. Mr. Chang replied that the Korean negotiators agreed that there was no ambiguity in the U.S. draft because it was an improvement over the SOFA with Japan. Would the U.S. negotiators please explain what the improvement was?

27. Mr. Habib replied that the improvement lay in the fact that the

0184

U.S. draft reflects actual current shipping practices. The definition of military cargo in this draft leaves no room for ambiguity.

28. Mr. Chang said that he would summarize the discussion as indicating that under the provisions of the SOFA with Japan, the Japanese authorities retain the right to conduct customs inspections of goods consigned to non-appropriated fund organizations, whereas the U.S. negotiators were demanding that the Korean negotiators give up this right. He suggested that further discussion of this sub-paragraph be postponed. He said the Korean negotiators would submit specific questions ~~xxxxxxxxxx~~ in writing concerning current practices in Japan.

29. Mr. Habib summarized the discussion by stating that the U.S. draft provides that all military cargoes will be exempt from customs inspection but that the U.S. armed forces will provide information regarding these cargoes, ~~xx~~ upon the request of the Korean authorities.

30. Turning to the proposed Agreed Minute #7, Mr. Chang referred to the inclusion of the word "commissaries", which had been discussed at previous meetings. He said the U.S. negotiators had indicated this Agreed Minute was necessary in order to make this article consistent with the article dealing with non-appropriated fund organizations. He said the Korean negotiators would like to suggest, in place of this Agreed Minute, the insertion of the word "commissaries" in paragraph 2 of this article. Agreement could be reached later on the persons who would be granted the use of the commissaries.

31. Mr. Habib pointed out that the granting of privileges is provided for in another article, not in this article. Furthermore, commissaries are already included in the language of paragraph 2. Insertion of the word "commissaries" there would not eliminate the need for the Agreed Minute. There really was no ~~xxxx~~ difference of opinion between the two sides regarding the need for this Agreed Minute and there was no need to delay agreement on it until after agreement was reached on the Non-Appropriated Fund Organizations ~~article~~

0185

32. Mr. Chang stated that the word "commissaries" should be inserted after the phrase "their procurement agencies" in paragraph 2. He suggested that further discussion of this point be deferred until a later meeting.

Non-Appropriated Fund Organizations

33. Mr. Chang recalled that at the previous meeting, the Korean negotiators had agreed to the new paragraph 2 proposed by the U.S. negotiators for the Non-Appropriated Fund Organizations Article, with the understanding that the phrase "other purchasers" should not be construed as being applicable or relevant to other purchasers such as foreign organizations or persons whom the ROK Government in the future might exempt from certain taxes under specific arrangements with them. Mr. Habib said the U.S. negotiators agreed to that understanding and that full agreement, therefore, had been reached on paragraph 2.

34. Mr. Chang stated that the Korean negotiators accepted Paragraph 4 of the U.S. draft, as revised. He said the Korean negotiators required more time for the study of the Agreed Minute proposed by the U.S. negotiators and therefore proposed that further discussion be deferred until a later meeting.

Invited Contractors

35. Mr. Chang stated that the Invited Contractors Article had been discussed at previous meetings and that there were still unresolved differences between the two drafts. In order to speed up the negotiations, the Korean negotiators wished to suggest an alternative proposal. Under the terms of this proposal, the persons covered by the provisions of this article would be divided into two groups. The first group would be comprised of contractors, including corporations organized under the laws of the United States, and employees ordinarily resident in the United States. The second group would comprise third couhtry national employees. Both the third country nationals and the dependents of contractors and the employees ordinarily resident in the U.S. in the first category would enjoy MPC, non-appropriated fund organization, [illegible] privileges. 0186

36. Mr. Habib stated that the proposal made by the Korean negotiators had opened up a new line of negotiation which would have to be considered. He said the U.S. negotiators would study this proposal and give their views at a later meeting. Mr. Chang suggested that this matter be discussed informally but Mr. Habib replied that the U.S. negotiators preferred to discuss it xxxxxx in the formal negotiating sessions.

Labor Procurement

37. Mr. Habib indicated that the U.S. side was prepared to table a draft of the Labor Procurement Article; Mr. Chang replied that the Korean side was not prepared to table its draft and suggested that the drafts be exchanged the next day. It was agreed that the Secretaries of the two negotiating teams should exchange the drafts of this article as soon as the Korean was ready.

38. The next meeting was scheduled for February 14 at 2:00 p.m.

0187

## JOINT SUMMARY RECORD OF THE 41ST SESSION

1. Time and Place: 2:00-4:00 P.M. February 6, 1964
   at the Foreign Ministry's Conference Room

| 미주과 | 양고재 | 일 | 담당 | 과장 | 국장 | 국방보좌관 | 차관 | 장관 |
|---|---|---|---|---|---|---|---|---|

2. Attendants:

ROK Side:

| | |
|---|---|
| Mr. Chang, Sang Moon | Director<br>European and American Affairs Bureau |
| Mr. Shin, Kwan Sup | Director<br>Bureau of Customs<br>Ministry of Finance |
| Mr. Koo, Chong Whay | Chief, American Section<br>Ministry of Foreign Affairs |
| Mr. Choo, Moon Ki | Chief, Legal Affairs Section<br>Ministry of Justice |
| Col. Kim, Won Kil | Chief, Military Affairs Section<br>Ministry of National Defense |
| Mr. Oh, Jae Hee | Chief, Treaty Section<br>Ministry of Foreign Affairs |
| Mr. Kang, Suk Jae (Rapporteur and Interpreter) | 2nd Secretary<br>Ministry of Foreign Affairs |
| Mr. Chung, Woo Yeun | 3rd Secretary<br>Ministry of Foreign Affairs |
| Mr. Lee, Chung Bin | 3rd Secretary<br>Ministry of Foreign Affairs |
| Mr. Lee, Keun Pal | 3rd Secretary<br>Ministry of Foreign Affairs |

U.S. Side:

| | |
|---|---|
| Mr. Philip C. Habib | Counselor<br>American Embassy |
| Col. Howard Smigelow | Deputy Chief of Staff<br>8th U.S. Army |
| Col. L.J. Fuller | Staff Judge Advocate<br>United Nations Command |
| Capt. John Wayne | Assistant Chief of Staff<br>USN/K |

0188

| | |
|---|---|
| Mr. Benjamin A. Fleck (Rapporteur and Press Officer) | First Secretary American Embassy |
| Mr. James Sartorius | 2nd Secretary American Embassy |
| Mr. Robert A. Lewis | 2nd Secretary and Consul American Embassy |
| Mr. Robert A. Kinney | J-5 8th U.S. Army |
| Maj. Robert D. Peckham | Staff Officer, JAG 8th U.S. Army |
| Mr. Kenneth Campen | Interpreter |

1. Mr. Chang opened the meeting by welcoming Mr. Habib back to the negotiating table following the latter's visit to Washington on consultation. Mr. Chang expressed the hope that as a result of Mr. Habib's consultation in Washington, the negotiations would now move rapidly to a successful conclusion.

2. Mr. Chang then introduced Mr. Chung Wu-yong, who was attending the meeting in place of Mr. Cho Kwang-che.

3. Mr. Habib stated that the Korean negotiators had previously asked when the U.S. negotiators would table the U.S. drafts of the articles dealing with labor and criminal jurisdiction. As they were aware, the U.S. negotiators were prepared to table the draft of the Labor Procurement Article at this meeting. Based on his conversations in Washington, he predicted that the draft of the Criminal Jurisdiction Article would also be available for tabling very soon.

4. Mr. Chang replied that the Korean negotiators welcomed Mr. Habib's statement regarding the Criminal Jurisdiction Article and hoped that it would be tabled within two or three weeks.

0189

Customs

5. Taking up the Customs Article, Mr. Chang stated that the Korean position with regard to the points still at issue had been fully explained. With regard to paragraph 5(b), the Korean negotiators, in order to meet the concern of the U.S. negotiators, had stated the willingness of the ROK Government to waive customs inspection of photographic films and recorded tapes. At the same time, the Korean negotiators had stated that the latest version of paragraph 5(b) proposed by the U.S. negotiators was unacceptable to the Korean negotiators. He asked whether the U.S. negotiators wished to make any further comment regarding this subparagraph.

6. Mr. Habib replied by referring to the four understandings which the U.S. negotiators had twice read into the Joint Agreed Summary. He said the U.S. negotiators were prepared to agree to the latest version of paragraph 5(b) proposed by the Korean negotiators, provided the Korean negotiators accepted those understandings, which had been designed to forestall any delay in the delivery of mail. Mr. Chang, at the previous meeting, had suggested two minor changes in these understandings. The U.S. negotiators did not take exception to those changes. The purpose of reading the understandings into the record was to indicate to the Joint Committee the intentions of the negotiators. The Joint Committee would implement the provisions of this subparagraph. Referring to previous references to "spot checks" and "sampling checks", Mr. Habib stated that there was no need to debate the meaning of the two terms, so long as both sides were talking about the same process. The U.S. negotiators appreciated

0190

the concern of the Korean negotiators over having the right of inspection, which the Korean negotiators had previously discussed largely in terms of its effect as a deterrent to abuses. The U.S. negotiators, therefore, were willing to accept the latest Korean draft, provided the Korean negotiators agreed to the four understandings, thereby leaving the implementation of the subparagraph to the Joint Committee with guidance as to the intent of the negotiators.

7. Mr. Chang welcomed the statement of the Chief U.S. negotiator accepting the Korean draft. He stated that at the previous meeting the Korean negotiators had stated their views with regard to the four understandings concerning the paragraph 5(b) and these views had been incorporated in the Joint Agreed Summary record of the 40th meeting. The Korean negotiators had also indicated that although the ROK authorities had no intention of inspecting every parcel in the MPO mail, their right to inspect all MPO parcels should not be prejudiced. He indicated concurrence of the Korean negotiators that the understandings written into the Joint Summary Record would serve as a guiding principle for the Joint Committee. However, he stated the Korean side took it that the U.S. negotiators agreed to the Korean draft of paragraph 5(b) in the light of the statements made by the Korean side regarding the four understandings at the previous meeting.

8. Mr. Habib replied in the affirmative. He said the subparagraph gave the Korean authorities the right to inspect parcels and left implementation to the Joint Committee, which would take into account as guidance the

0191

discussion of this subject by the negotiators, as recorded in the Joint Agreed Summary.

9. Full agreement was reached on the following text of paragraph 5(b):

> "5(b). Official documents under official seal and First Class letter mail in United States military postal channels under official postal seal."

10. Turning to paragraph 5(a), Mr. Habib noted that there was still a difference of view regarding the use of the word "units" or the word "members". He pointed out that the U.S. draft, in using the word "members", provides that dependents and members of the civilian component shall be subject to customs inspection. He noted that at the previous meeting the Korean negotiators had raised the subject of "past abuses". He said the U.S. negotiators were not aware of any past abuses and asked the Korean negotiators to explain their remark.

11. Mr. Chang replied that the Korean negotiators would be prepared to make evidence of such abuses available to the U.S. negotiators outside of the formal negotiations. Mr. Habib stated that he was not talking about postal abuses but was referring to specifically to Mr. Chang's statement at the previous meeting that in view of past abuses, the ROK Government believed that all members of the U.S. armed forces should be subject to ROKG customs inspection, except those moving as members of units.

12. Mr. Habib said the U.S. negotiators would be interested in a clarification of Mr. Chang's remark. He said that the provision desired by the Korean negotiators was not a normal provision in status of forces agreements and the U.S. negotiators did not see the necessity for it.

0192

He said that the use of the word "members" in the U.S. draft was based on the actual manner in which the personnel of the U.S. armed forces enter and leave Korea. It was intended, therefore, to be an accurate reflection of current practices. He remarked that there appeared to be a basic inconsistency in the position of the Korean negotiators. If they were willing to forego inspection for troops arriving as members of units, why were they not also willing to forego inspection of troops arriving as individuals? The U.S. negotiators had no objection to the inspection of non-members of the armed forces. This subparagraph applied to troops arriving under orders, and assigned to units already in place.

13. Mr. Chang replied that the Korean negotiators were aware of the circumstances under which the members of the U.S. armed forces arrived in Korea. What the Korean negotiators were seeking was the right to inspect U.S. military personnel entering or leaving Korea for purposes other than official business. Accordingly, the Korean negotiators wished to amend the language of the subparagraph to read as follows:

> "5(a). Members of the United States armed forces under orders entering or leaving the Republic of Korea for official duty purposes but not for leave or recreational purposes."

14. Mr. Habib replied that this proposal introduced a new element into the discussion of this subparagraph. The U.S. negotiators would study this proposal and give their views at the next meeting.

15. Turning to paragraph 5(c), Mr. Chang recalled that at the previous meeting, the Korean negotiators had queried the U.S. negotiators about procedures in Japan with regard to military cargo and cargo shipped to non-appropriated fund organizations.

0193

16. Mr. Habib replied that other status of forces agreements have been written on the standard basic premise that all cargo shipped to the U.S. armed forces, including that shipped to non-appropriated fund organizations, is "military cargo". The Korean negotiators had also inquired concerning documentation of cargo. All military cargo, including cargo shipped to non-appropriated fund organizations, is shipped on government bills of lading or similar shipping documents. At the 40th meeting on January 24, the U.S. negotiators had indicated that the U.S. armed forces are prepared to cooperate with the Korean authorities by providing information concerning cargoes and had tabled a proposed additional sentence to Agreed Minute #3 which would provided for the furnishing of such information, upon the request of the Korean authorities, through the Joint Committee. The U.S. negotiators believed that this proposed language would fully satisfy the needs of the Korean authorities.

17. Mr. Chang stated that, according to the explanation given by the U.S. negotiators, goods shipped to non-appropriated fund organizations in Japan are included in the category of military cargo. However, the Korean negotiators understood that under the provisions of the U.S.-Japan Agreement cargo not shipped on government bills of lading was not considered to be military cargo.

18. Mr. Habib replied that this was an incorrect interpretation of the situation. He explained that the U.S. Government no longer uses bills of lading for all military cargo. The important factor is the consignment of the goods. In other words, if the cargo is consigned to the U.S. armed forces it is considered to be military

0194

cargo. Equally important was the fact that the U.S. negotiators had proposed a provision which would provide information to the ROK authorities concerning the consignment of such cargoes.

19. Mr. Chang stated that the U.S. negotiators had previously stated that in actual practice the Japanese authorities waive customs examination of non-appropriated fund organization cargoes. However, a literal reading of the U.S.-Japan SOFA indicated that the Japanese authorities have the authority to make such examinations.

20. Mr. Habib replied that the negotiators were not engaged in negotiating the SOFA with Japan. He said the Korean negotiators had asked for information concerning the types of cargo being imported into Korea by the U.S. armed forces. In order to meet this request, the U.S. negotiators had proposed the additional sentence to Agreed Minute #3. He said the article should be drafted so as to reflect the existing situation with respect to cargo shipments. He asked if what the Korean negotiators were really saying was that they wanted the SOFA to grant the Korean authorities the right of customs inspection and the right to levy customs duties on military cargoes. He said the U.S. negotiators were not prepared to agree to any such provisions.

21. Mr. Chang stated that the Korean negotiators wanted the SOFA to give to the Korean authorities the right to conduct customs inspection of goods shipped to non-appropriated fund organizations. He said the Korean negotiators were confused by the statements of the U.S. negotiators regarding the implementation of the SOFA with Japan. The Korean negotiators believed that the SOFA

with Japan did not include non-appropriated fund organization goods in the category of military cargo. The U.S. negotiators had said that such goods were shipped on bills of lading and then, later, had spoken of "similar documents". Were they or were they not shipped on bills of lading? What were the similar documents which had been mentioned. The U.S. negotiators had an obligation to tell the Korean negotiators how the SOFA with Japan is implemented.

22. Mr. Habib denied any such obligation. However, he said the U.S. negotiators were not indisposed to answer any specific questions which the Korean negotiators might wish to ask. He did not know whether or not it would be possible to obtain statistics on the amount or types of cargo shipped to U.S. armed forces in Korea on bills of lading but the U.S. negotiators would be glad to attempt to obtain such information of the Korean negotiators were really interested in it. He pointed out that a bill of lading is a specific type of document; there are also other types of shipping documents. With regard to the inspection of goods consigned to non-appropriated fund organizations, Mr. Habib informed the Korean negotiators that according to a supervisor currently employed by the U.S. armed forcew in Korea, who had worked in Japan for eleven years as a cargo supervisor, cargoes consigned to non-appropriated fund organizations there were never inspected by Japanese customs authorities.

23. Mr. Chang replied that the Korean negotiators did not believe it necessary to verify the fact that such goods are not inspected by Japanese customs authorities. The Korean negotiators did believe, however, that the SOFA with Japan gives the Japanese authorities the right to make such inspections and this was one of main reasons

0196

why the Korean side was concerned with the U.S.-Japan Agreement and asked the U.S. side to clarify its provisions. Mr. Habib replied that the U.S. negotiators do not agree with this interpretation of the SOFA with Japan.

24. Mr. Chang stated that the Korean negotiators had also noted that in paragraph 2 of the Customs Article in the SOFA with Japan, non-appropriated fund organizations are spelled out as a separate entity from the U.S. armed forces but in the related Agreed Minute there is no mention of them. In other words, the Agreed Minute refers only to cargo shipped to the armed forces on U.S. Government bills of lading but does not refer to cargo shipped to the non-appropriated fund organizations. There is no consistency between the text and the related Agreed Minute as far as the NAF organizations goods are concerned. There is ambiguity, therefore, in the SOFA with Japan and the Korean negotiators would appreciate clarification by the U.S. negotiators. For example, what arrangements have been made with the Japanese authorities to exempt cargoes shipped to non-appropriated fund organizations from customs inspection?

25. Mr. Habib replied that the text of the U.S.-Korea Agreement which was under negotiation is not ambiguous. It makes no distinction between the U.S. armed forces and the non-appropriated fund organizations, which are an integral part of the armed forces. If the Korean negotiators find ambiguity in this draft, the U.S. negotiators are prepared to discuss the question. The U.S. negotiators believed that ambiguities in other status of forces agreements, if any existed, should not be carried over into this agreement. He stated that the

0197

Korean negotiators were engaging in fruitless discussion and wasting time. He proposed that further discussion of this subparagraph be postponed until the Korean negotiators could find the time to read the U.S. draft.

26. Mr. Chang replied that the Korean negotiators agreed that there was no ambiguity in the U.S. draft because an improvement had been made over the text of the SOFA with Japan.

27. Mr. Habib replied that the improvement lay in the fact that the U.S. draft reflects actual current shipping practices. The definition of military cargo in this draft leaves no room for ambiguity.

28. Mr. Chang said that he would summarize the discussion as indicating that under the provisions of the SOFA with Japan, the Japanese authorities retain the right to conduct customs inspections of goods consigned to non-appropriated fund organizations, whereas the U.S. negotiators were demanding that the Korean negotiators give up this right. He suggested that further discussion of this subparagraph be postponed. He said the Korean negotiators would submit specific questions in writing concerning current practices in Japan.

29. Mr. Habib summarized the discussion by stating that the U.S. draft provides that all military cargoes will be exempt from customs inspection but that the U.S. armed forces will provide information regarding these cargoes, upon the request of the Korean authorities.

30. Turning to the proposed Agreed Minute #7, Mr. Chang referred to the inclusion of the word "commissaries", which had been discussed at previous meetings. He said the U.S. negotiators had indicated this Agreed Minute

0198

was necessary in order to make this article consistent with the article dealing with non-appropriated fund organizations. He said the Korean negotiators would like to suggest, in place of this Agreed Minute, the insertion of the word "commissaries" in paragraph 2 of this article. Agreement could be reached later on the persons who would be granted the use of the commissaries.

31. Mr. Habib pointed out that the granting of privileges is provided for in another article, not in this article. Furthermore, commissaries are already included in the language of paragraph 2. Insertion of the word "commissaries" there would not eliminate the need for the Agreed Minute. There really was no difference of opinion between the two sides regarding the need for this Agreed Minute and there was no need to delay agreement on it until after agreement was reached on the Non-Appropriated Fund Organizations Article.

32. Mr. Chang stated that the word "commissaries" should be inserted after the phrase "their procurement agencies" in paragraph 2. He suggested that further discussion of this point be deferred until a later meeting.

Non-Appropriated Fund Organizations

33. Mr. Chang recalled that at the previous meeting, the Korean negotiators had agreed to the new paragraph 2 proposed by the U.S. negotiators for the Non-Appropriated Fund Organizations Article, with the understanding that the phrase "other purchasers" should not be construed as being applicable or relevant to other purchasers such as foreign organizations or persons whom the ROK Government in the future might exempt from certain taxes under specific arrangements with them. Mr. Habib said the U.S. negotiators

0199

agreed to that understanding and that full agreement, therefore, had been reached on paragraph 2.

34. Mr. Chang stated that the Korean negotiators accepted paragraph 4 of the U.S. draft, as revised. He said the Korean negotiators required more time for the study of the Agreed Minute proposed by the U.S. negotiators and therefore proposed that further discussion be deferred until a later meeting.

Invited Contractors

35. Mr. Chang stated that the Invited Contractors Article had been discussed at previous meetings and that there were still unresolved differences between the two drafts. In order to speed up the negotiations, the Korean negotiators wished to suggest an alternative proposal. Under the terms of this proposal, the persons covered by the provisions of this article would be divided into two groups. The first group would be comprised of contractors, including corporations organized under the laws of the United States, and employees ordinarily resident in the United States. The second group would comprise third country national employees. Both the third country nationals and the dependents of contractors and the employees ordinarily resident in the U.S. in the first category would enjoy MPC, non-appropriated fund organization, and MPO privileges.

36. Mr. Habib stated that the proposal made by the Korean negotiators had opened up a new line of negotiation which would have to be considered. He said the U.S. negotiators would study this proposal and give their views at a later meeting. Mr. Chang suggested that this matter be discussed informally but Mr. Habib replied that the

0200

U.S. negotiators preferred to discuss it in the formal negotiating sessions.

Labor Procurement

37. Mr. Habib indicated that the U.S. side was prepared to table a draft of the Labor Procurement Article. Mr. Chang replied that the Korean side was not prepared to table its draft and suggested that the drafts be exchanged the next day. It was agreed that the Secretaries of the two negotiating teams should exchange the drafts of this article as soon as the Korean was ready.

38. The next meeting was scheduled for February 14 at 2:00 p.m.

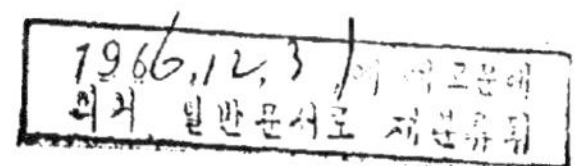

0201

5. 제42차 회의, 2.14

0202

# 기 안 용 지

| 자 체<br>통 제 | | 기안처 | 미주과<br>이 근 팔 | 전화번호 | 근거서류접수일자 |
|---|---|---|---|---|---|
| | 과장 | 국장 | 차관 | 장관 | |
| 관계관<br>서 명 | | | | | |
| 기 안<br>년월일 | 1964. 2. 14. | 시 행<br>년월일 | | 보존<br>년한 | 정 서 기 장 |
| 분 류<br>기 호 | 외구미722.2 | 전 체<br>통 제 | | 종결 | |
| 경 유<br>수 신<br>참 조 | 건 의 | | | 발 신 | |
| 제 목 | 제 42 차 주둔군지위협정 체결교섭회의에 임할 우리측 입장 | | | | |

2월 14일에 개최될 제 42 차 주둔군지위협정 체결을 위한 한.미간 교섭회의에서는 토지시설, 군계약자, 노무에 관한 조문 토의 및 형사재판관할권에 관한 쌍방의 조문초안을 제시하도록 예정하고 있는바 이에 대하여 우리측 교섭실무자는 2월 10일, 11일, 및 동 13일 회합을 갖고 제 42 차 회의에서 취할 태도를 별첨과 같이 결정하였아오니 재가하여 주시기 바랍니다.

유 첨: 제 42 차 주둔군지위협정 체결회의에 임할 우리측 태도. 끝.



승인양식 1-1-3 (1112-040-016-018) (190mm×260mm16절지)

0203

1. 토지시설

(가) 원상회복에 관한 우리 조안 13 항(미국측 조안 C조 1항)은 원칙적으로 미국의 원상 회복 의무를 면제하나 단지 미국의 사용으로 막심한 파손을 입은 사유재산에 대하여서는 우리 정부 요청에 의하여 원상복구 또는 이에 대한 보상에 관하여 규정하고 있는바 우리측 안을 계속 주장한다.

(나) 가동설비의 소유권 및 처분문제에 관한 미측조안 C 조 2항은 이러한 설비가 미국정부의 재산이며 따라서 한국외로 철거할 수 있다함은 당연한 것인바 우리측은

(1) " on behalf of the United States at its expenses" 라는 용어가 미국이 군사원조하에 우리 국군에 공급한 장비 및 물자를 포함하는가?를 질문하고 만약 그렇지 않다면

(2) 조약 본문에서 규정할 필요가 없으므로 본문에서 삭제하여 합의의사록에 넣도록 주장하고

(3) 한국정부는 여하한 경우에도 미군의 가동설비에 대한 보관 책임을 지지 않는다는 점을 기록에 남기도록 한다.

(다) 토지시설 개량에 대한 우리 정부의 보상의무문제에 관한 우리측 조안 14항중 제 33 차 회의에서 우리측이 제안한바에 따라 " supply or any other materials "용어를 삭제한 우리측 원안을 미측 조안 C조 2 항과 대체하도록 계속 주장한다.

2. 군계약자

(가) 우리측은 41차 실무자교섭회의에서 군계약자의 범위를 우리 안 대로 규정하되

(1) 필수불가결한 제 3 국인의 고용은 막지는 않겠으며

(2) 군계약자의 가족과 제 3 국인 및 그들의 가족에 대하여서는 군표, 군사우편, 및 비세출자금기관 사용권 만을 부여할 용의가 있다고 제안한바에 따라

(3) 미측의 재검토 결과를 청취하고 우리측은 별첨(1)과 같은 수정조안을 제시한다.

0204

3. 노무조항

(가) 우리측은 41 차 회의에서 양측이 교환한바 있는 초안을 검토하여 본 결과

(1) 우리초안이 노무자의 고용 및 처우, 기타 노사관계에 관하여 우리 나라 노동관계 법규의 적용을 규정하고,

(2) 미군의 " local labor requirements "는 한국 관계당국의 조력하에 충족되어야하며,

(3) 미군의 안전에 관한 해고라 할지라도 신중한 절차에 의하여 처리되어야 한다고

규정한데 반하여 미측안은 우리안과 현저한 차의점이 있으므로 우리측 초안에 따라 심의하여 나가자는 요지의 우리측 태도를 밝히고 다음 회의에서 토의하기로 한다.

4. 형사재판관할권

(1) 우리측은 형사재판관할권에 관한 별첨 ( 2)과 같은 우리측 초안을 제출하고 미측 초안과 교환할 것이며

(1) 다음 회의까지 우리측 초안에 관한 합의의사록를 제시할 것을 밝히고

(2) 차기 회의부터 심의할 것을 요청한다.



0205

별첨 (1)

ARTICLE

1. Persons, including corporations organized under the laws of the United States, and their employees, who are ordinarily resident in the United States and whose presence in the Republic of Korea is solely for the purpose of executing contracts with the United States for the benefit of the United States armed forces or other armed forces in Korea under the Unified Command receiving logistical support from the United States armed forces, who are designated by the Government of the United States in accordance with the provisions of the paragraph 2 below, shall, except as provided in this Article, be subject to the laws and regulations of the Republic of Korea.

2. The designation referred to in paragraph 1 above shall be made upon consultation with the Government of the Republic of Korea and shall be restricted to cases where open competitive bidding is not practicable due to security considerations, to the technical qualifications of the contractors involved, to the unavailability of materials or services required by United States standards, or to limitations of United States law. The designation shall be withdrawn by the Government of the United States:

0206

(a) Upon completion of contracts with the United States armed forces or other armed forces in Korea under the Unified Command receiving logistical support from the United States armed forces;

(b) Upon proof that such persons are engaged in business activities in Korea other than those pertaining to the United States armed forces or other armed forces in Korea under the Unified Command receiving logistical support from the United States armed forces;

(c) Upon proof that such persons are engaged in practices illegal in Korea.

3. Upon certification by appropriate United States authorities as to their identity, such persons shall be accorded the following benefits of this Agreement:

(a) Accession and movement, as provided for Article , paragraph 2;

(b) Entry into Korea in accordance with the provisions of Article ;

(c) The exemption from customs duties, and other such charges provided for in Article , paragraph 3, for members of the United States armed forces, the civilian component, and their dependents;

(d) If authorized by the Government of the United States, the use of the services of the organizations provided

0207

for in Article

(e) Those provided in Article , paragraph 2, for members of the United States armed forces, the civilian component, and their dependents;

(f) If authorized by the Government of the United States, the use of military payment certificates, as provided for in Article ;

(g) The use of postal facilities provided for in Article ;

(h) The use of utilities and services in accordance with those priorities, conditions, rates, or tariffs accorded the United States armed forces by Article paragraph 3, relating to utilities and services;

(i) Exemption from the laws and regulations of Korea with respect to licensing and registration of business and corporations.

4. The arrival, departure, and place of residence in Korea of such persons shall from time to time be notified by the United States armed forces to the Korean authorities.

5. Upon certification by an authorized representative of the United States armed forces, depreciable assets, except houses, held, used or transferred by such persons exclusively for the execution of contracts referred to in paragraph 1 shall not be subject to taxes or similar

0208

charges of Korea.

6. Upon certification by an authorized representative of the United States armed forces, such persons shall be exempt from taxation in Korea on the holding, use, transfer by death, or transfer to persons or agencies entitled to tax exemption under this Agreement, of movable property, tangible or intangible, the presence of which in Korea is due solely to the temporary presence of these persons in Korea, provided that such exemption shall not apply to property held for the purpose of investment or the conduct of other business than those executing contracts as described in paragraph 1 of this Article in Korea or to any intangible property registered in Korea.

7. The persons referred to in paragraph 1 shall not be liable to pay income or corporation taxes to the Government of Korea or to any other taxing agency in Korea on any income derived under a contract with the Government of the United States in connection with the construction, maintenance or operation of any of the facilities or areas covered by this Agreement. Persons in Korea in connection with the execution of such a contract with the United States shall not be liable to pay any Korean taxes to the Government of Korea or to any taxing agency in Korea on income derived from sources

0209

outside of Korea nor shall periods during which such persons are in Korea be considered periods of residence or domicile in Korea for the purposes of Korean taxation. The provisions of this paragraph do not exempt such persons from payment of income or corporation taxes on income derived from Korean sources, other than those sources referred to in the first sentence of this paragraph, nor do they exempt such persons who claim Korean residence for United States income tax purposes from payment of Korean taxes on income.

8. The Korean authorities shall have the primary right to exercise jurisdiction over the contractors and their employees referred to in paragraph 1 of this Article in relation to offences committed in the Republic of Korea and punishable by the law of the Republic of Korea. In those cases in which the Korean authorities decide not to exercise such jurisdiction they shall notify the military authorities of the United States as soon as possible. Upon such notification the military authorities of the United States shall have the right to exercise such jurisdiction over the persons referred to as is conferred on them by the law of the United States.

0210

## Agreed Minutes

1. This Article shall not prevent the persons referred to in paragraph 1 from employing third-country nationals who shall, except as provided in paragraph 2, and sub-paragraphs (a), (d), (e), (f), (g) of paragraph 3, be subject to the laws and regulations of the Republic of Korea.

2. The dependents of the persons and their employees, including third-country nationals, shall, except those benefits as provided in sub-paragraphs (d), (f) and (g), be subject to the laws and regulations of the Republic of Korea.

3. There is no obligation under this Article to grant exemption from taxes payable in respect of the use and ownership of private vehicles.

0211

별첨 (2)

CONFIDENTIAL

ARTICLE

Criminal Jurisdcition

1. Subject to the provisions of this Article:

(a) the military authorities of the United States shall have the right to exercise within the Republic of Korea criminal and disciplinary jurisdiction conferred on them by the law of the United States over the members of the United States armed forces and the civilian components.

(b) the authorities of the Republic of Korea shall have jurisdiction over the members of the United States armed forces, the civilian component, and their dependents with respect to offenses committed within the territory of the Republic of Korea and punishable by the law of the Republic of Korea.

2. (a) The military authorities of the United States shall have the right to exercise exclusive jurisdiction over members of the United States armed forces and the civilian components with respect to offenses, including offenses relating to its security, punishable by the law of the United States, but not by the law of the Republic of Korea.

(b) The authorities of the Republic of Korea shall have the right to exercise exclusive jurisdiction over members

0212

of the United States armed forces, the civilian component, and their dependents with respect to offenses, including offenses relating to the security of the Republic of Korea, punishable by its law but not by the law of the United States.

(c) For the purpose of this paragraph and of paragraph 3 of this Article a security offense against a State shall include:

(i) treason against the State;

(ii) sabotage, espionage or violation of any law relating to official secrets of that State, or secrets relating to the national defense of that State.

3. In cases where the right to exercise jurisdiction is concurrent the following rules shall apply;

(a) The military authorities of the United States shall have the primary right to exercise jurisdiction over members of the United States armed forces or the civilian component in relation to:

(i) offenses solely against the property or security of the United States, or offenses solely against the person or property of another member of the United States armed forces or the civilian component or of a dependent;

0213

(ii) offenses arising out of any act or omission done in the performance of official duty provided that such act or omission is directly related to the duty. The question as to whether offenses were committed in the performance of official duty shall be decided by a competent district public prosecutor of the Republic of Korea.

In case the offender's commanding officer finds otherwise, he may appeal from the prosecutor's decision to the Minister of Justice within ten days from the receipt of the decision of the prosecutor, and the decision of the Minister of Justice shall be final.

(b) In the case of any other offenses the authorities of the Republic of Korea shall have the primary right to exercise jurisdiction.

(c) If the State having the primary right decides not to exercise jurisdiction, it shall notify the authorities of the other State as soon as practicable. The authorities of the State having the primary right shall give sympathetic consideration to a request from the authorities of the other

0214

State for a waiver of its right in cases where that other State considers such waiver to be of particular importance.

4. The foregoing provisions of this Article shall not imply any right for the military authorities of the United States to exercise jurisdiction over persons who are nationals of or ordinarily resident in the Republic of Korea, unless they are members of the United States forces.

5. (a) The military authorities of the United States and the authorities of the Republic of Korea shall assist each other in the arrest of members of the United States armed forces, the civilian component, or their dependents in the territory of the Republic of Korea and in handing them over to the authorities which is to exercise jurisdiction in accordance with the above provisions.

(b) The authorities of the Republic of Korea shall notify the military authorities of the United States of the arrest of any member of the United States armed forces, the civilian component, or their dependents.

(c) The military authority of the United States shall immediately notify the authority of the Republic of Korea of the arrest of a member of the United States armed forces, the civilian component, or a dependent, unless the United States authority has the right to exercise exclusive jurisdiction

0215

over such a person.

(d) An accused member of the United States armed fo[illegible] the civilian component or a dependent over whom the Republic Korea is to exercise jurisdiction shall, if he is in the hand of the United States, be under the custody of the United State Upon presentation of a warrant issued by a judge of the Repub[illegible] Korea he shall be handed over immediately to the Korean Authorities.

6. (a) The authorities of the Republic of Korea and the military authorities of the United States shall assist each other in the carrying out of all necessary investigations into offenses, and in the collection and production of evidenc[illegible] including the seizure and, in proper case, the handing over of objects connected with an offense. The handing over of such objects may, however, be made subject to their return within the time specified by the authority delivering them.

(b) The authorities of the Republic of Korea and the military authorities of the United States shall notify each other of the disposition of all cases in which there are concurr[illegible] rights to exercise jurisdiction.

7. (a) A death sentence shall not be carried out in the Republic of Korea by the military authorities of the United States if the legislation of the Republic of Korea does not provide for such punishment in a similar case.

0216

(b) The authorities of the Republic of Korea shall give sympathetic consideration to a request from the military authorities of the United States for assistance in carrying out a sentence of imprisonment pronounced by the military authorities of the United States under the provisions of this Article within the territory of the Republic of Korea.

8. Where an accused has been tried in accordance with the provisions of this Article either by the authorities of the Republic of Korea or the military authorities of the United States and has been acquitted, or has been convicted and is serving, or has served, his sentence or has been pardoned, he may not be tried again for the same offense within the territory of the Republic of Korea by the authorities of the other State. However, nothing in this paragraph shall prevent the military authorities of the United States from trying a member of its forces for any violation of rules of discipline arising from an act or omission which constituted an offense for which he was tried by the authorities of the Republic of Korea.

9. Whenever a member of the United States armed forces, the civilian component or a dependent is prosecuted under the jurisdiction of the Republic of Korea he shall be entitled:

(a) to a prompt and speedy trial;

0217

(b) to be informed, in advance of trial, of the specific charge or charges made against him;

(c) to be confronted with the witnesses against him;

(d) to have compulsory process for obtaining witnesses in his favor, if they are within the jurisdiction of the Republic of Korea;

(e) to have legal representation of his own choice for his defense or to have free or assisted legal representation under the conditions prevailing in the Republic of Korea;

(f) If he considers it necessary, to be provided with the services of a competent interpreter; and

(g) to communicate with a representative of the Government of the United States and to have such a representative present at his trial.

10. (a) Regularly constituted military units or formation of the United States armed forces shall have the right to police any facilities or areas which they use under Article IV of this Agreement. The military police of such forces may take all appropriate measures to ensure the maintenance of order and security within such facilities and areas.

(b) Outside these facilities and areas such military police shall be employed only subject to arrangements with the authorities of the Republic of Korea and in liaison with those authorities and in so far as such employment is necessary

0218

to maintain discipline and order among the members of the United States armed forces.

POSITION PAPER

42ND MEETING OF THE SOFA NEGOTIATIONS

FACILITIES AND AREAS

1. The Korean negotiators would like to recall our discussions on the Facilities and Areas Article C at the previous meetings. During our discussions at the 31st meeting held on September 20, 1963, the Korean negotiators proposed that the U.S. side agree to the deletion of paragraph 2 of your draft or alternatively its conversion into an Agreed Minute in favor of paragraph 14 of our draft article minus the language "supplies or other materials". In this regard, we would like to listen if you have any comment to make on our latest proposal.

2. Regarding removable facilities referred to in paragraph 2 of your draft article, the Korean negotiators wish to know, for the sake of clarity, whether or not the phrase "all removable facilities erected or constructed by or on behalf of the United States at its expense" include those removable facilities, if any, erected or constructed with the United States military assistance funds to the Republic of Korea Army.

3. It is ~~also~~ recalled that at the 32nd meeting, the Korean negotiators requested to add to paragraph 1 of the U.S. draft the last sentence of paragraph 13 of the Korean draft which provides for restoration or compensation for private property extremely demolished by the use of the United States armed forces. Your side opposed payment of compensation for such cases and further proposed the deletion of the said sentence from this Article in favor of the article D of your draft on the basis of relevancy. The Korean negotiators responded to put aside the question until agreement would have been reached on your draft article D. The position

0220

of the Korean negotiators in this regard has since then not changed. We would like to listen to your view or comment if you have further to make on the question of compensation.

CONTRACTORS

1. At last meeting, the Korean negotiators made a new suggestion with a view to arriving at mutually agreeable solution of the Contractors Article. We have prepared the revised draft of the Article in line of our suggestion and are now ready to submit the draft for your consideration. In tabling the revised draft, the Korean negotiators would like to remark that we have made concession on our part as much as possible with full consideration given to your concern and difficulties you had expressed with regard to contractors, specifically, employees of third State nationals. As you would note in the revised draft, we have retreated from the position of what we had originally intended to regularize contractors and their employees, particularly, with respect to their nationality and number as well as benefits to be accorded them. In this connection, the Korean negotiators urge the U.S. side to study our revised draft and to find it acceptable reciprocating in turn the same spirit of mutual cooperation.

LABOR

1. First, the Korean negotiators would like to present general outline of the Korean draft dealing with labor. The fundamental principle set forth in the Korean draft is to uphold and assure the conditions of employment, protection and rights of Korean workers as are stipulated under the provisions of the applicable laws of the Republic of Korea.

It provides that, first, local labor requirements of the United States armed forces shall be satisfied with the

0221

assistance of the Korean authorities. Secondly, the conditions of employment, the conditions for the protection of workers and the rights of workers concerning labor relations etc. shall be those laid down by the Korean legislation. Thirdly, it provides for irrevocably detailed procedures, in order to cope with problems arising from possible ~~eliminate dispute which may prossibly arise between the ROK and U.S. authorities, which shall apply in case of~~ dismissal of a worker by the United States armed forces for security reasons.

2. The Korean negotiators studied the draft article tabled by your side in comparison of our draft. However, there are substantial difference on substance of the two drafts and that your draft, unfortunately, ~~being~~ far from being satisfiable in the light of our requirements, is not acceptable by us in many respect. The Korean negotiators, therefore, request (for the convenience's sake) that discussions on the subject of labor should be conducted on the basis of the Korean draft. (*U.S. concurrence to be sought)

3. In this connection, the Korean negotiators suggest to deffer the discussions of this Article to a subsequent meeting, and we also urge that in the meantime the U.S. negotiating members favorably consider our position regarding labor Article in an effort so as to enable to come to full agreement mutually satisfactory.

0222

CONTRACTOR

At last meeting, the Korean side made a new suggestion with a view to arriving at mutually agreeable solution on the Contractors' Article. Now we have prepared the revised draft of the Article in line with our suggestion. In tabling the revised draft, we would like to say that we have made concession on our part as much as possible.

The following is the main modifications in our new draft:

First: To permit persons including corporations organized under the laws of the United States to employ third-country nationals. The third-country nationals would be given such benefits as APO, MPC, PX etc., the details of which are laid down in the Agreed Minutes.

Secondly: To accord the dependents of the persons under the ~~Article Invited~~ Contractors, ~~includ-~~ ing employees of third-country nationals, such benefits as APO,MPC,PX etc., the details of which are laid down in the Agreed Minutes.

Thirdly: To delete paragraph 3, sub-paragraph(i) of your draft. We feel that as far as driving permits and registration of vehicles are concerned, they should be governed by the laws and regulations of Korea.

Forthly: In connection with the above, we included the following in the Agreed Minutes.

"There is no obligation under this Article to grant exemption from taxes payable in respect of the use and ownership of private vehicles"

0223

Finally: As for the Agreed Minute which your side proposed in the previous meeting, we are still studying with the Ministries concerned. That's why we excluded it tentatively in our new draft.

The Korean negotiators wish that the U.S. side would study our revised draft. At the same time, we hope that our new draft would be acceptable to you.



0224

SOFA NEGOTIATION

Agenda for the 42nd Session

14:00 Feb. 14, 1964

1. Continuation of Discussions on:
   a. Facilities and Areas Article - "C"
   b. Contractors Article
   c. Labor Article
   d. Criminal Jurisdiction Article
2. Agenda and Date of the Next Meeting
3. Press Release

0225

February 14, 1964
Submitted by
U.S. side

ARTICLE

1. Subject to the provisions of this Article,

(a) the authorities of the United States shall have the right to exercise within the Republic of Korea all criminal and disciplinary jurisdiction conferred on them by the law of the United States over members of the United States armed forces or civilian component, and their dependents.

(b) the civil authorities of the Republic of Korea shall have the right to exercise jurisdiction over the members of the United States armed forces or civilian component, and their dependents, with respect to offenses committed within the territory of the Republic of Korea and punishable by the law of the Republic of Korea.

2. (a) The authorities of the United States shall have the right to exercise exclusive jurisdiction over members of the United States armed forces or civilian component, and their dependents, with respect to offenses, including offenses relating to its security, punishable by the law of the United States, but not by the law of the Republic of Korea.

(b) The authorities of the Republic of Korea shall have the right to exercise exclusive jurisdiction over members of the United States armed forces or civilian component, and their dependents, with respect to offenses, including offenses relating to the security of the Republic of Korea, punishable by its law but not by the law of the United States.

(c) For the purpose of this paragraph and of paragraph 3 of this Article, a security offense against a State shall include:

(i) treason against the State;

0226

(ii) sabotage, espionage or violation of any law relating to official secrets of that State, or secrets relating to the national defense of that State.

3. In cases where the right to exercise jurisdiction is concurrent the following rules shall apply:

(a) The authorities of the United States shall have the primary right to exercise jurisdiction over members of the United States armed forces or civilian component, and their dependents, in relation to:

(i) offenses solely against the property or security of the United States, or offenses solely against the person or property of another member of the United States armed forces or civilian component or of a dependent;

(ii) offenses arising out of any act of omission done in the performance of official duty;

(b) In the case of any other offense, the authorities of the Republic of Korea shall have the primary right to exercise jurisdiction.

(c) If the State having the primary right decides not to exercise jurisdiction, it shall notify the authorities of the other State as soon as practicable. The authorities of the State having the primary right shall give sympathetic consideration to a request from the authorities of the other State for a waiver of its right in cases where that other State considers such waiver to be of particular importance.

0227

4. The foregoing provisions of this Article shall not imply any right for the authorities of the United States to exercise jurisdiction over persons who are nationals of or ordinary resident in the Republic of Korea, unless they are members of the United States armed forces.

5. (a) The authorities of the United States and the authorities of the Republic of Korea shall assist each other in the arrest of members of the United States armed forces, the civilian component, or their dependents in the territory of the Republic of Korea and in handing them over to the authority which is to have custody in accordance with the following provisions.

(b) The authorities of the Republic of Korea shall notify promptly the authorities of the United States of the arrest of any member of the United States armed forces, or civilian component, or a dependent.

(c) The custody of an accused member of the United States armed forces or civilian component, or of a dependent, over whom the Republic of Korea is to exercise jurisdiction shall, if he is in the hands of the United States, remain with the United States pending the conclusion of all judicial proceedings and until custody is requested by the authorities of the Republic of Korea. If he is in the hands of the Republic of Korea, he shall be promptly handed over to the authorities of the United States and remain in their custody pending completion of all judicial proceedings and until custody is requested by the authorities of the Republic of Korea. The United States authorities will make any such accused available to the authorities of the Republic of Korea upon their request for purposes of investigation and trial. The authorities of the Republic of Korea shall give sympathetic consideration to a request from the authorities of the United States

0228

for assistance in maintaining custody of an accused member of the United States armed forces, the civilian component, or a dependent.

6. (a) The authorities of the United States and the authorities of the Republic of Korea shall assist each other in the carrying out of all necessary investigations into offenses, and in the collection and production of evidence, including the seizure and, in proper cases, the handing over of objects connected with an offense. The handing over of such objects may, however, be made subject to their return within the time specified by the authority delivering them.

(b) The authorities of the United States and the authorities of the Republic of Korea shall notify each other of the disposition of all cases in which there are concurrent rights to exercise jurisdiction.

7. (a) A death sentence shall not be carried out in the Republic of Korea by the authorities of the United States if the legislation of the Republic of Korea does not provide for such punishment in a similar case.

(b) The authorities of the Republic of Korea shall give sympathetic consideration to a request from the authorities of the United States for assistance in carrying out a sentence of imprisonment pronounced by the authorities of the United States under the provisions of this Article within the territory of the Republic of Korea. The authorities of the Republic of Korea shall also give sympathetic consideration to a request from the authorities of the United States for the custody of any member of the United States armed forces or civilian component or a dependent, who is serving a sentence of confinement imposed by a court of the Republic of Korea. If such custody is released to the

0229

authorities of the United States, the United States shall be obligated to continue the confinement of the individual in an appropriate confinement facility of the United States until the sentence to confinement shall have been served in full or until release from such confinement shall be approved by competent Korean authority.

8. Where an accused has been tried in accordance with the provisions of this Article either by the authorities of the United States or the authorities of the Republic of Korea and has been acquitted, or has been convicted and is serving, or has served, his sentence, or his sentence has been remitted or suspended, or he has been pardoned, he may not be tried again for the same offense within the territory of the Republic of Korea by the authorities of the other State. However, nothing in this paragraph shall prevent the authorities of the United States from trying a member of its armed forces for any violation of rules of discipline arising from an act or omission which constituted an offense for which he was tried by the authorities of the Republic of Korea.

9. Whenever a member of the United States armed forces or civilian component or a dependent is prosecuted under the jurisdiction of the Republic of Korea he shall be entitled:

(a) to a prompt and speedy trial;

(b) to be informed, in advance of trial, of the specific charge or charges made against him;

(c) to be confronted with the witnesses against him;

(d) to have compulsory process for obtaining witnesses in his favor, if they are within the jurisdiction of the Republic of Korea;

(e) to have legal representation of his own choice for his defense or to have free or assisted legal representation under the conditions prevailing for the time being in the Republic of Korea;

(f) if he considers it necessary, to have the services of a competent interpreter; and

(g) to communicate with a representative of the Government of the United States and to have such a representative present at his trial.

10. (a) Regularly constituted military units or formations of the United States armed forces shall have the right to police any facilities or areas which they use under Article of this Agreement. The military police of such forces may take all appropriate measures to ensure the maintenance of order and security within such facilities and areas.

(b) Outside these facilities and areas, such military police shall be employed only subject to arrangements with the authorities of the Republic of Korea and in liaison with those authorities, and in so far as such employment is necessary to maintain discipline and order among the members of the United States armed forces, or ensure their security.

11. In the event of hostilities to which the provisions of Article II Of the Treaty of Mutual Defense apply, the provisions of this Agreement pertaining to criminal jurisdiction shall be immediately suspended and the authorities of the United States shall have the right to exercise exclusive jurisdiction over members of the United States armed forces, the civilian component, and their dependents.

0231

12. The provisions of this Article shall not apply to any offenses committed before the entry into force of this Agreement. Such cases shall be governed by the provisions of the Agreement between the United States of America and the Republic of Korea effected by an exchange of notes at Taejon, Korea on July 12, 1950.

AGREED MINUTES

The provisions of this Article shall not affect existing agreements, arrangements, or practices, relating to the exercise of jurisdiction over personnel of the United Nations forces present in Korea other than forces of the United States.

RE Paragraph 1(b)

1. The authorities of the United States shall have the right to exercise exclusive jurisdiction over members of the United States armed forces or civilian component, and their dependents, if any, in the combat zone. The extent of the combat zone shall be defined by the Joint Committee and shall include the area from the demilitarization zone to the rear boundaries of the United States corps (group) and the Republic of Korea army-size unit deployed in that zone.

2. In the event that martial law is declared by the Republic of Korea, the provisions of this Article shall be immediately suspended in the part of the Republic of Korea under martial law, and the authorities of the United States shall have the right to exercise exclusive jurisdiction over members of the United States armed forces or civilian component, and their dependents, in such part until martial law is ended.

0232

3. The jurisdiction of the authorities of the Republic of Korea over members of the United States armed forces or civilian component, and their dependents, shall not extend to any offenses committed outside the Republic of Korea.

RE Paragraph 2

The Republic of Korea, recognizing the effectiveness in appropriate cases of the administrative and disciplinary sanctions which may be imposed by the United States authorities over members of the United States armed forces or civilian component, and their dependents, will give sympathetic consideration in such cases to requests in the Joint Committee for waivers of its right to exercise jurisdiction under paragraph 2.

RE Paragraph 2 (c)

Each Government shall inform the other of the details of all security offenses mentioned in this subparagraph, and of the provisions regarding such offenses in its legislation.

RE Paragraph 3

The Republic of Korea, recognizing that it is theprimary responsibility of the United States authorities to maintain good order and discipline among the members of the United States Armed Forces and civilian component, and their dependents, waives the right of the authorities of the Republic of Korea to exercise jurisdiction under paragraph 3. The United States authorities shall notify the competent authorities of the Republic of Korea of individual cases falling under the waiver thus provided. If, by reason of special circumstances in a specific case, the authorities of the Republic of Korea consider that it is

0233

of particular importance that jurisdiction be exercised by the Republic of Korea in that case, they shall, within 15 days of receipt of the notification envisaged above, seek agreement of the Joint Committee to recall the waiver for that particular case.

Subject to the foregoing, the waiver granted by the Republic of Korea shall be unconditional and final for all purposes and shall bar both the authorities and the nationals of the Republic of Korea from instituting criminal proceedings.

To facilitate the expeditious disposal of offenses of minor importance, arrangements may be made between United States authorities and the competent authorities of the Republic of Korea to dispense with notification.

RE Paragraph 3 (a)

1. The authorities of the United States shall have the primary right to exercise juridiction over members of the United States armed forces in relation to offenses which, if committed by a member of the armed forces of the Republic of Korea, would be tried by court-martial rather than by a civilian court.

2. Where a member of the United States armed forces or civilian component is charged with an offense, a certificate issued by or on behalf of his commanding officer stating that the alleged offense, if committed by him, arose out of an act or omission done in the performance of official duty, shall be conclusive for the purpose of determining primary jurisdiction.

RE Paragraph 6

1. The authorities of the United States and the authorities of the Republic of Korea shall assist each other in obtaining the appearance of witnesses

necessary for the proceedings conducted by such authorities within the Republic of Korea.

When a member of the United States armed forces in Korea is summoned to appear before a Korean court, as a witness or as a defendant, United States authorities shall, unless military exigency requires otherwise, secure his attendance provided such attendance is compulsory under Korean law. If military exigency prevents such attendance, the authorities of the United States shall furnish a certificate stating the estimated duration of such disability.

Service of process upon a member of the United States armed forces or civilian component, or a dependent required as a witness or a defendant must be personal service in the English language. Where the service of process is to be effected by a Korean process server upon any person who is inside a military installation or area, the authorities of the United States shall take all measures necessary to enable the Korean process server to effect such service.

In addition, the Korean authorities shall promptly give copies of all criminal writs (including warrants, summonses, indictments, and subpoenas) to an agent designated by the United States authorities to receive them in all cases of Korean criminal proceedings involving a member of the United States armed forces or civilian component, or a dependent.

When citizens or residents of the Republic of Korea are required as witnesses or experts by the authorities of the United States, the courts and authorities of the Republic of Korea shall, in accordance with Korean law, secure the attendance of such persons. In these cases the authorities of the United States shall act through the Attorney General of the Republic of Korea, or such other agency as is designated by the authorities of the Republic of Korea.

Fees and other payments for witnesses shall be determined by the Joint Committee established under Article

2. The privileges and immunities of witnesses shall be those accorded by the law of the court, tribunal or authority before which they appear. In no event shall a witness be required to provide testimony which may tend to incriminate him.

3. If, in the course of criminal proceedings before authorities of the United States or the Republic of Korea, the disclosure of an official secret of either of these States or the disclosure of any information which may prejudice the security of either appears necessary for the just disposition of the proceedings, the authorities concerned shall seek written permission to make such disclosure from the appropriate authority of the State concerned.

RE Paragraph 9 (a)

The right to a prompt and speedy trial by the courts of the Republic of Korea shall include public trial by an impartial tribunal composed exclusively of judges who have completed their probationary period. A member of the United States armed forces or civilian component, or a dependent, shall not be tried by a military tribunal of the Republic of Korea.

RE Paragraph 9 (b)

A member of the United States armed forces or civilian component, or a dependent, shall not be arrested or detained by the authorities of the Republic of Korea without adequate cause, and he shall be entitled to an immediate

0236

hearing at which such cause must be shown in open court in his presence and the presence of his counsel. His immediate release shall be ordered if adequate cause is not shown. Immediately upon arrest or detention he shall be informed of the charges against him in a language which he understands.

He shall also be informed a reasonable time prior to trial of the nature of the evidence that is to be used against him. Counsel for the accused shall, upon request, be afforded the opportunity before trial to examine and copy the statements of witnesses obtained by authorities of the Republic of Korea which are included in the file forwarded to the court of the Republic of Korea scheduled to try the case.

RE Paragraph 9 (c) and (d)

A member of the United States armed forces or civilian component, or a dependent, who is prosecuted by the authorities of the Republic of Korea shall have the right to be present throughout the testimony of all witnesses, for and against him, in all judicial examinations, pretrial hearings, the trial itself, and subsequent proceedings, and shall be permitted full opportunity to examine the witnesses.

RE Paragraph 9 (e)

The right to legal representation shall exist from the moment of arrest or detention and shall include the right to have counsel present, and to consult confidentially with such counsel, at all preliminary investigations, examinations, pretrial hearings, the trial itself, and subsequent proceedings, at which the accused is present.

0237

RE Paragraph 9 (f)

The right to have the services of a competent interpreter shall exist from the moment of arrest or detention.

RE Paragraph 9 (g)

The right to communicate with a representative of the Government of the United States shall exist from the moment of arrest or detention, and no statement of the accused taken in the absence of such a representative shall be admissible as evidence in support of the guilt of the accused. Such representative shall be entitled to be present at all preliminary investigations, examinations, pretrial hearings, the trial itself, and subsequent proceedings, at which the accused is present.

RE Paragraph 9

A member of the United States armed forces or civilian component, or a dependent, tried by the authorities of the Republic of Korea shall be accorded every procedural and substantive right granted by law to the citizens of the Republic of Korea. If it should appear that an accused has been, or is likely to be, denied any procedural or substantive right granted by law to the citizens of the Republic of Korea, representatives of the two Governments shall consult in the Joint Committee on the measures necessary to prevent or cure such denial of rights.

In addition to the rights enumerated in items (a) through (g) of paragraph 9 of this Article, a member of the United States armed forces or civilian component, or a dependent, who is prosecuted by the authorities of the Republic of Korea:

(a) shall be furnished a verbatim record of his trial in English;

(b) shall have the right to appeal a conviction or sentence; in addition, he shall be informed by the court at the time of conviction or sentencing of his right to appeal and of the time limit within which that right must be exercised;

(c) shall have credited to any sentence of confinement his period of pretrial confinement in a United States or Korean confinement facility;

(d) shall not be held guilty of a criminal offense on account of any act or omission which did not constitute a criminal offense under the law of the Republic of Korea at the time it was committed;

(e) shall not be subject to a heavier penalty than the one that was applicable at the time the alleged criminal offense was committed or was adjudged by the court of first instance as the original sentence;

(f) shall not be held guilty of an offense on the basis of rules of evidence or requirements of proof which have been altered to his prejudice since the date of the commission of the offense.

(g) shall not be compelled to testify against or otherwise incriminate himself;

(h) shall not be subject to cruel or unusual punishment;

(i) shall not be subject to prosecution or punishment by legislative or executive act;

(j) shall not be prosecuted or punished more than once for the same offense.

(k) shall not be required to stand trial if he is physically or mentally unfit to stand trial and participate in his defense;

0239

(l) shall not be subjected to trial except under conditions consonant with the dignity of the United States armed forces, including appearing in appropriate military or civilian attire and unmanacled.

No confession, admission, or other statement, or real evidence, obtained by illegal or improper means will be considered by courts of the Republic of Korea in prosecutions under this Article.

In any case prosecuted by the authorities of the Republic of Korea under this Article no appeal will be taken by the prosecution from a judgment of not guilty or an acquittal nor will an appeal be taken by the prosecution from any judgment which the accused does not appeal, except upon grounds of errors of law.

The authorities of the United States shall have the right to inspect any Korean confinement facility in which a member of the United States armed forces, civilian component, or dependent is confined, or in which it is proposed to confine such an individual.

In the event of hostilities, the Republic of Korea will take all possible measures to safeguard mrembers of the United States armed forces, members of the civilian component, and their dependents who are confined in Korean confinement facilities, whether awaiting trial or serving a sentence imposed by the courts of the Republic of Korea. The Republic of Korea shall give sympathetic consideration to requests for release of these persons to the custody of responsible United States authorities. Necessary implementing provisions shall be agreed upon between the two governments through the Joint Committee.

Facilities utilized for the execution of a sentence to death or a period of confinement, imprisonment, or penal servitude, o r for the detention of members of the United States armed forces or civilian component or dependents, will

0240

meet minimum standards as agreed by the Joint Committee. The United States authorities shall have the right upon request to have access at any time to members of the United States armed forces, the civilian component, or their dependents who are confined or detained by authorities of the Republic of Korea. During the visit of these persons at Korean confinement facilities, United States authorities shall be authorized to provide supplementary care and provisions for such persons, such as clothing, food, bedding, and medical and dental treatment.

RE Paragraph 10 (a) and 10 (b)

The United States authorities will normally make all arrests within facilities and areas in use by the United States armed forces. The Korean authorities will normally not exercise the right of search, seizure, or inspection with respect to any person or property within facilities and areas in use by the authorities of the United States or with respect to property of the United States wherever situated, except in cases where the competent authorities of the United States consent to such search, seizure, or inspection by the Korean authorities of such persons or property.

Where search, seizure, or inspection with respect to persons or property within facilities and areas in use by the United States or with respect to property of the United States in Korea is desired by the Korean authorities, the United States authorities will undertake, upon request, to make such search, seizure, or inspection. In the event of a judgment concerning such property, except property owned or utilized by the United States Government or its instrumentalities, the United States will in accordance with its laws turn over such property to the

Korean authorities for disposition in accordance with the judgment.

The United States authorities may arrest or detain in the vicinity of a facility or area any person in the commission or attempted commission of an offense against the security of that facility or area. Any such person who is not a member of the United States armed forces or civilian component or a dependent shall immediately be turned over to the Korean authorities.

ARTICLE____

Labor Procurement

1. In this Article the expression:

(a) "employer" refers to the United States armed forces (including nonappropriated fund activities) and the persons referred to in the first paragraph of Article________.

(b) "employee" refers to any civilian (other than a member of the civilian component) employed by an employer, except (1) a member of the Korean Service Corps, (who is an employee of the Government of Korea,) and (2) a domestic employed by an individual member of the United States armed forces, civilian component or dependent thereof.

2. Employers may accomplish the recruitment, employment and management of employees directly. upon the request of the authorities of the R.O.K.

3. The condition of employment, the compensation, and the labor-management practices shall be established by the United States armed forces for their employees in general conformity with the labor laws, customs and practices of the Republic of Korea; (provided however, that an employer may terminate employment whenever the continuation of such employment would materially impair the accomplishment of the mission of the United States armed forces).

4. (a) An employee shall have the same right to strike as an employee in a comparable position in the employment of the armed forces of the Republic of Korea. Such an employee may voluntarily organize and join a union or other employee group whose objectives are not inimical to the interests of the United States. Membership or nonmembership in such groups shall not be a cause for discharge or non-employment.

0243

(b) Employers will maintain procedures designed to assure the just and timely resolution of employee grievances.

5. (a) Should the Republic of Korea adopt measures allocating labor, the United States armed forces shall be accorded employment privileges no less favorable than those enjoyed by the armed forces of the Republic of Korea.

(b) In the event of a national emergency, employees who have acquired skills essential to the mission of the United States armed forces shall be exempt from Republic of Korea military service or other compulsory service. The United States armed forces shall furnish to the Republic of Korea lists of those employees deemed essential.

6. Members of the civilian component shall not be subject to Korean laws or regulations with respect to their terms and conditions of employment.

AGREED MINUTES

1. The Republic of Korea will make available, at designated induction points, qualified personnel for Korean Service Corps units in numbers sufficient to meet the requirements of United States armed forces. The employment of a domestic by an individual member of the United States armed forces, civilian component or dependent thereof shall be governed by applicable Korean law and in addition by wage scales and control measures promulgated by the United States armed forces.

2. The undertaking of the United States Government to conform to Korean labor laws, customs, and practices, does not imply any waiver by the United States Government of its immunities under international law.

0244

# 기 안 용 지

| 자체 통제 | 외무사무관 손일금 | 기안처 | 미주과 이근팔 | 전화번호 | 근거서류접수일자 |
|---|---|---|---|---|---|
| | 과장 | 국장 | 차관 | 장관 | |
| 관계관 서명 | | | | | |
| 기안 년월일 | 1964. 2. 18. | 시행 년월일 | 검열 1964.2.21 통제관 | 보존 년한 | 정서기장 |
| 분류 기호 | 외무미 722.2 | 전체 통제 | 종결 | | |
| 경유 수신 참조 | 대통령 (참조: 비서실장) 국무총리 | 발신 | 장관 | | |
| 제목 | 주둔군 지위협정 체결을 위한 제 42 차 교섭회의 보고 | | | | |

1964. 2. 14. 하오 2 시 부터 하오 4 시 40 분 까지 외무부장관 회의실에서 개최된 제 42 차 주둔군지위협정 체결 교섭회의에서 토의된 내용을 별첨과 같이 보고합니다.

유 첨: 제 42 차 교섭회의 보고서 1 부. 끝.

1966.12.31. 에 예고문에 의거 일반문서로 재분류됨

발송 1964. 2. 21

승인양식 1-1-3 (1112-040-016-018) (190mm×260mm16절지)

0245

제 42 차

한미간 주둔군지위협정 체결교섭실무자회의

보 고 서

1. 일 시: 1964 년 2 월 14 일 하오 2 시 부터 동 4 시 40 분 까지.

2. 장 소: 외무부장관 회의실

3. 토의사항

가. 토지시설

(1) 우리측 초안 13 항(미측초안 C조 1 항): 우리초안은 원칙적으로 미국의 원상회복의 의무를 면제하나 막심한 파손을 입은 사유재산에 대하여서는 원상복구 또는 보상할 것을 규정한바 미국측은 이 미측초안 C조 1항으로 부터 삭제하고,

(2) 미측초안 C 조 2 항: 미군의 가동설비가 미국정부의 재산이며 한국외로 철거할 수 있다는 것을 규정한 본조항은 우리측 주장대로 본문에서 삭제하여 합의의사록에 삽입할 것과

(3) 우리측 초안 14항: 미군의 토지시설 개량에 대한 우리정부의 보상의무를 면제하는 우리초안은 우리측이 동의한바에 따라 " supply or any other materials "용어를 삭제한 본문을 미측초안 C조 2 항과 대체하는데 각각 동의할 용의가 있다는 태도를 표명하여 온바 우리측은 미국측으로 부터 (ㄱ) 미초안 C 조 2 항중 "on behalf of the United States at its expenses "라는 용어가 미국이 군사원조 하에 우리 국군에 공급한 장비 및 물자를 포함하는 것이 안이라는 것, (ㄴ) 미군의 잔류 가동설비에 대하여 우리 정부가 보관책임을 지지안는 다는 것 및 (ㄷ) 사유재산에 대한 보상을 규정한 우리초안 13항은 만일 우리측이 본조항에서 삭제하는데 동의하는 경우에도 후일 반듯이 본조항이 토의되어야하고 또 한국측 (주장이 충분히 고료되어야 한다는 미측의 양해가 필요하다고 주장한데 대하여 미측은 한국측이 후일) 보상문제 토의를 제안하는 것은 좋으나 미측으로서는 보상을 할 입장에 있지 않다는 태도를 되풀이하였으므로 한국측은 다음회의에서 입장을 밝히겠다고 하였다.

64-3-13

0246

0247

나. 군계약자

(1) 우리측은 제 41 차 교섭회의에서 제안한바에 따라 군계약자에 관한 수정조안을 제시하고 수정된 부분에 대한 설명을 하고 미측은 이에 대하여 검토 후 다음 회의에서 견해를 표명 하겠다고 제의하였다.

다. 노무조항

(1) 미측으로 부터 미측조안에 대하여 (ㄱ) 한국법률에 부합 하도록 하였으며 (ㄴ) 노무자는 노동조합에 가입할 수 있으며 (ㄷ) 한국군의 고용원에 허용된 범위내에서 파업에 관한 권리가 인정된다는 요지의 제안설명이 있은 다음 미측조안에 의하여 검토하기를 제의한데 대하여

(2) 우리측은 (ㄱ) 미군의 노무자 수요는 한국관계당국의 조력에 의하여 이루어져야 하며 (ㄴ) 우리조안의 근본방침은 노무자는 한국법에 의하여 보호되어야 하며 (ㄷ) 안전을 이유로 한 해고 일지라도 신중하게 취급되어야 한다는 제안설명을 하고 우리측 조안을 근거로 하여 토의할 것을 요구하였다.

라. 형사재판관할권

(1) 쌍방은 현안이면 형사재판관할권에 관한 조안을 교환하고 검토가 끝나는 대로 토의하기로 합의하였다.

4. 기타 사항: 차기회의 일자: 1964 년 2 월 20 일 하오 2 시 부터. 끝.

1966,12,31,에 예고문에 의거 일반문서로 재분류됨

0248

64-3-14

1. Mr. Chang opened the meeting by introducing: Mr. Shin Kang-sup, Director of the Employment Security Bureau, Office of Labor Affairs, who was attending the meeting in lieu of Mr. Shin Kwan-sop; Mr. Yoon Doo-suk, Director, Prosecutor's Bureau, Ministry of Justice; and Mr. Chung Tai-kyun, Chief of the Prosecutor's Section, Ministry of Justice. Messrs. Shin and Yoon were attending as negotiators and Mr. Chung as an observer.

2. Mr. Habib welcomed these gentlemen to the negotiations and then introduced Colonel Kenneth C. Crawford, of the Staff Judge Advocate's Office, Eighth United States Army. Mr. Habib announced that Colonel Crawford was joining the U.S. negotiating team and would eventually serve as a replacement for Colonel Fuller, who would be attending a few more meetings before his expected transfer from Korea. Mr. Habib then introduced Mr. O. C. Reed, Director of the EUSA Office of Civilian Personnel, and Mr. Julio Hernandez, Labor Adviser, who would attend those negotiating meetings at which the Labor Procurement Article would be discussed and advise the U.S. negotiators as necessary.

3. Mr. Chang welcomed Colonel Crawford, Mr. Reed, and Mr. Hernandez and expressed regret at the news of Colonel Fuller's imminent departure. Referring to the many contributions which Colonel Fuller had made to the negotiations, Mr. Chang said the Korean negotiators would be sorry to see him go.

Facilities and Areas

4. Turning to Facilities and Areas Article "C", Mr. Habib noted that the negotiators had been discussing the general subject of facilities and areas in separate articles as tabled by the U.S. negotiators. In this fashion, agreement had been reached on major portions of the subject. With regard to Article "C", only minor differences remained between the U.S. and Korean drafts. The Korean negotiators had previously made certain proposals regarding this

0250

ARTICLE. The U.S. negotiators wished to respond to those proposals. At the same time, they wished to expedite agreement on all of the facilities and areas provisions and to eliminate instances of overlapping in the several articles dealing with this general subject. It was in this spirit that the U.S. negotiators wished to respond to the following proposals made previously by the Korean negotiators: (a) convert paragraph 14 of the Korean draft into a new paragraph 2 of the U.S. draft, deleting the words "supply or any other materials"; (b) convert the existing paragraph 2 of the U.S. draft into an Agreed Minute.

5. Mr. Habib said the U.S. negotiators were prepared to agree to these Korean proposals but also wished to reach agreement on the article as a whole. He pointed out that the final sentence of paragraph 13 of the Korean draft referred to the subject of compensation. It was the view of the U.S. negotiators that this subject should be dealt with in only one article and since Article "D" dealt with that subject, it would be logical to concentrate discussion of compensation in Article "D", omitting it from Article "C". He reminded the negotiators that the general Korean position was in favor of compensation while the U.S. position was opposed to the payment of any compensation. Rather than debate this general question in discussion dealing with Article "C", the U.S. negotiators proposed deletion of the final sentence of paragraph 13 of the Korean draft, with no prejudice to the overall Korean or U.S. position on compensation.

6. Mr. Habib pointed out that full agreement on this article would be achieved if the Korean negotiators accepted the deletion of the final sentence of paragraph 13. With Articles "A" and "B" already agreed to, if agreement were reached on Article "C", the only remaining point at issue with regard to facilities and areas would be the question of compensation. The U.S. negotiators proposed that Article "D", which dealt with this subject, be placed on the agenda for discussion at an early meeting.

7. Mr. Chang stated [illegible] an answer to the U.S. proposal,

0251

the Korean negotiators wished to point out that full agreement had not yet been reached on the text of paragraph 2 of the U.S. draft. Mr. Habib replied that at the 31st negotiating meeting on September 20, 1963, the Korean negotiators had proposed the conversion of the existing paragraph 2 of the U.S. draft into an Agreed Minute. He pointed out that if the U.S. understanding that this proposal indicated agreement with the text was incorrect, the negotiators would have to begin negotiating this paragraph all over again.

8. Mr. Chang replied that the Korean proposal had been to delete paragraph 2 from the U.S. draft or convert it into an Agreed Minute. He said the Korean negotiators still had some question regarding the substance of this paragraph. While they had agreed to the deletion of the words "supply or any other materials" from paragraph 14 of the Korean draft, they had done so only in anticipation that agreement could be reached on the text of paragraph 2 of the U.S. draft. The Korean negotiators welcomed the agreement of the U.S. negotiators to substitute paragraph 14 for paragraph 2 of the U.S. draft. However, they still believed that private property extremely demolished should be compensated for. They had no objection to discussing the subject of compensation with reference to Article "D" but they believed that any such discussion should include the question of property extremely demolished.

9. Mr. Habib replied that the Korean negotiators certainly had the right to raise that question and the U.S. negotiators would expect them to do so. He reiterated the U.S. position against the payment of compensation and recalled that the Korean position favored such payment.

10. Mr. Chang replied that the Korean negotiators regretted to hear that the U.S. negotiators were not prepared to agree to the payment of compensation. He characterized Mr. Habib's statement as a unilateral declaration which would act as a deterrent to the negotiations. He said that unless the U.S. negotiators were pre-

0252

pared to discuss the subject and give due consideration to the Korean position, the Korean negotiators were not prepared to agree to the deletion of the final sentence of paragraph 13 of the Korean draft.

11. Mr. Chang asked whether the term "removable facilities" in paragraph 2 of the U.S. draft included facilities constructed as part of the military aid given to the ROK armed forces by the U.S. Government. Mr. Habib replied that such inclusion would be unreasonable and that the title to all facilities constructed as part of the military aid program was transferred to the ROK armed forces.

12. In response to Mr. Chang's previous remark regarding the U.S. position on compensation, Mr. Habib said that the U.S. negotiators had not indicated unwillingness to discuss the issue. They had merely suggested that such discussion be concentrated under one article (Article "D") in order to permit full agreement on Article "C". The U.S. negotiators had discussed the issue of compensation in the past and would continue to do so. He had stated that the U.S. Government was unwilling to pay compensation. The U.S. negotiators were prepared to discuss the reasons underlying this position, as well as the innumerable precedents which supported it. The U.S. negotiators had proposed deletion of the final sentence of paragraph 13 of the Korean draft, indicating that such deletion would in no way prejudice the Korean position in support of compensation or the U.S. position in opposition to it.

13. Mr. Chang thanked Mr. Habib for his clarification of the matter of removable facilities. He noted that there had been no change in the position of either side regarding the payment of compensation. He also noted that disagreement over the final sentence of paragraph 13 of the Korean draft was all that stood in the way of full agreement on Article "C". He said the Korean negotiators would give further consideration to this matter and give their views at a subsequent meeting.

0253

14. Mr. Ku remarked that there was still a question with regard to removable facilities, and the loss or damage which might occur to materials left behind by the U.S. armed forces in facilities returned to the Republic of Korea. If all such materials were evacuated by the U.S. armed forces, there would be no problem. However, if they were not all removed, the Korean negotiators would like to ensure that the ROK Government would not be held responsible for loss or damage to those left behind.

15. Mr. Habib replied that there was nothing in the text of the Agreement which said that the ROK Government would be liable for such loss or damage. The Joint Committee would supervise the transfer of such facilities and there was no need for the negotiators to involve themselves in this question. Property introduced into Korea under the Military Assistance Program was governed by separate agreements which will continue in effect after the SOFA goes into effect. He pointed out that there is no provision in the SOFA which dealt with MAP property, which had been transferred to the Republic of Korea.

16. Mr. Chang said that the Korean negotiators would discuss the question of MAP property with the ministries concerned and would then discuss the question further at a subsequent negotiating meeting. Mr. Habib replied that this question had no relevance to the SOFA negotiations.

Invited Contractors

17. Turning to the article on Invited Contractors, Mr. Habib recalled that at the previous meeting, the Korean negotiators had made a general proposal which seemed to the U.S. negotiators to suggest the possibility of making a distinction between U.S. contractors and their employees and other contractors and their employees. The U.S. negotiators would like to have an explanation in greater detail of the privileges which these groups would enjoy under the terms of the Korean proposal. Noting that the U.S. draft provided certain privi[illegible]aragraphs 3, 5, 6, 7, and 8 (not

0254

yet tabled), he asked how the Korean negotiators proposed to deal with third country nationals. Specifically, what did the Korean negotiators have in mind with regard to taxes, customs, foreign exchange, driving permits, licenses, and similar privileges, with regard to third country nationals and dependents? He noted that the U.S. armed forces are currently engaged in a program to replace gradually all third country nationals with Koreans, as soon as a sufficient number of trained Koreans is available.

18. Mr. Chang replied that at the last meeting the Korean negotiators had made a new proposal with a view to arriving at a mutually agreeable text of this article. They had presented briefly the framework of this proposal and had suggested an informal meeting for further discussion. Since the U.S. negotiators had rejected an informal meeting, the Korean negotiators had revised their original draft of the article and wished to table a new draft at this time. He said that Mr. Chung would explain the main features of the new draft.

19. Mr. Chung summarized the main features of the revised Korean draft of the article in the following terms. It would permit persons, including corporations organized under the laws of the United States, to employ third country nationals, who would be given the use of non-appropriated fund organizations, military post offices, and military payment certificates, under the terms of Agreed Minute #1. It would also extend those privileges to dependents, including the dependents of third country nationals, under the terms of Agreed Minute #2. Mr. Chung noted that the revised draft omitted the provisions of paragraph 3(i) of the U.S. draft, pertaining to driving permits and registration of vehicles, since the Korean negotiators believed that invited contractors should be subject to Korean laws and regulations in regard to these matters. He also noted that the revised draft did not provide for an exemption from payment of taxes arising out of the use and ownership. Nor did it include the provisions

0255

of the Agreed Minute of the U.S. draft. Finally, the Korean revision deletes the provisions of paragraph 3(j) of the U.S. draft, which would provide exemption from the laws and regulations of Korea with respect to terms and conditions of employment. Mr. Chung pointed out that the Korean draft of the Labor Procurement Article provides that the terms and conditions of employment in so far as they apply to Korean persons should be ~~prescribed by the ROK Government~~ those laid down by Korean legislation.

20. Mr. Habib thanked Mr. Chung for his explanation of the revised Korean draft. He said the U.S. negotiators would study it and comment at a subsequent meeting.

Criminal Jurisdiction

21. The negotiators then exchanged drafts of the article dealing with criminal jurisdiction. Mr. Chang stated that, in his capacity as Chief Negotiator for the Korean side, he wished to express great satisfaction that these drafts had finally been tabled. The Korean negotiators looked forward to a mutually satisfactory agreement on this subject, based on mutual cooperation by both negotiating teams. Mr. Habib replied that the U.S. negotiators had indicated in December that they hoped to be able to table the U.S. draft at about this time and were glad that their prediction had proved accurate. The U.S. negotiators looked forward to quiet, systematic, and fruitful discussion of this subject.

Labor Procurement

22. Turning to the article on labor procurement, Mr. Habib said that it would be helpful to both sides to have a presentation of general views on this subject. He then asked Colonel Fuller to present the views of the U.S. negotiators.

23. Colonel Fuller stated that it is the intention of the U.S. armed forces to continue to act as a good and enlightened local employer and in general to conform to Korean practices, customs, and Korean labor laws, consistent with the ROK-US defense mission. The U.S. armed forces intended to permit their employees to join voluntarily unions or [illegible] have the same right to strike

0256

as the U.S. draft reflected current labor practice and the result of fifteen years of U.S. employment practice, Colonel Fuller suggested that

as employees in comparable positions of employment with the armed forces of the ROK. Stating that the U.S. draft serve as the basis for negotiation, he asked whether the Korean negotiators had any questions regarding the content of the U.S. draft.

24. Mr. Chang replied that before asking questions, he would like to sum up the basic differences between the two drafts, as the Korean negotiators saw them. The three fundamental differences were as follows: (a) The basic principle embodied in the Korean draft is to uphold and protect the rights of the Korean workers, as stipulated under the provisions of the applicable Korean laws. Therefore, the Korean draft provides that local labor requirements of the U.S. armed forces "shall be satisfied with the assistance of the Korean authorities". (b) The Korean draft provides that the conditions of employment and work shall be laid down by ROK legislation, whereas the U.S. draft provides only for "general conformity" with Korean labor legislation, customs and practices. He remarked that there was, in this respect, a wide gap between the two drafts. (c) The Korean draft included detailed and fundamental provisions in order to cope with problems arising from possible dismissal of a worker by the U.S. armed forces for security reasons than did the U.S. draft. Inasmuch as there are these substantial differences between the two drafts, the Korean negotiators believed that it would be more useful and more fruitful to use the Korean draft as the basis for negotiation.

25. Mr. Chang stated that the identification, in the U.S. draft, of Korean Service Corps members as employees of the ROK Government posed a difficult problem to the Korean negotiators. They wondered what the basis of this statement in the U.S. draft was, since they had been unable to find any evidence that would support it.

26. Colonel Fuller asked Mr. Chang to repeat the three basic differences which the Korean negotiators had found in their study of the two drafts. Mr. Chang summarized the three differences as

0257

(a) The U.S. draft provides for direct hire, whereas the Korean draft provides that local labor requirements shall be satisfied with the assistance of the ROK Government;

(b) The U.S. draft provides only for "general conformity" with Korean laws and regulations, whereas the Korean draft provides that working conditions shall be those prescribed by ROK legislation;

(c) The Korean draft provides detailed provisions covering the discharge of employees for security reasons, whereas the U.S. draft is silent on this subject.

27. Colonel Fuller asked what the phrase "with the assistance of the Korean authorities" in the Korean draft meant. Mr. Chang replied that according to current practice, the U.S. armed forces hire their Korean employees directly, with certain exceptions. However, the Korean negotiators believed that in order to make the most effective and efficient use of Korean labor, all hiring should be done in coordination with the appropriate Korean agencies.

28. In response to Colonel Fuller's inquiry as to the nature of such agencies, Mr. Chang stated that there are currently in operation many employment offices and that in the future, many specialized employment offices will be established. In response to further questioning, Mr. Chang stated that the only agency referred to by the Korean draft was that which operates employment offices, which serves only as a labor recruiting service. As Mr. Chang had indicated that this service was currently used to some extent by the U.S. armed forces, Colonel Fuller asked how present practice would be changed under the provisions of the Korean draft. Mr. Chang said that in future it was planned to have all employment for the U.S. armed forces handled by this agency.

~~29. In reply to a series of questions by Colonel Fuller, Mr. Chang stated that it was the Korean intention to have this agency perform functions such as recruiting employees required by the armed forces. It would handle recruiting and not dismissals or promotions. When asked if it was intended that the agency should have a say in the~~

0258

29. In reply to a series of questions by Colonel Fuller, Mr. Chang stated that it was the Korean intention to have this agency handle only recruiting for the U.S. armed forces and that the agency would not hire or fire, promote, demote, discipline, or assign such employees. When asked how the agency would assist in recruiting, Mr. Chang said that if there were a requirement for 1 person, the agency would send 3 or 4 eligible persons to the armed forces. The armed forces would then make the final selection.

0259

assignment of employees to specific positions, Mr. Chang said that if there were a requirement for 1 person, the agency would send 3 or 4 eligible persons to the armed forces. The armed forces would then make the final selection.

30. In reply to questions by Colonel Fuller regarding the cost of such an employment service, Mr. Chang stated that the Korean draft provides that the U.S. armed forces shall reimburse the ROK Government. He said such reimbursement would only be for advertisement fees, travel expenses, and other costs incurred directly in the recruitment of labor for the U.S. armed forces. Inasmuch as the employment agency was run by the ROK Government, there would be no charge to the U.S. armed forces to cover the expenses of salaries, materials, and supplies.

31. In reply to further questioning by Colonel Fuller, Mr. Chang stated that there are currently about 40 branches of the employment agency scattered throughout the country, with one or two in every city having a population of 50,000 or over. The ROK Government obtains laborers for its public works and construction projects from this agency. However, government officials are recruited through the Ministry of ~~General Affairs~~ Government Administration.

32. Mr. Chang pointed out, in reply to a question, that the Korean draft would permit the U.S. armed forces to hire employees only with the assistance of ROK Government authorities, and ~~therefore~~ the U.S. forces would not be permitted to recruit employees from other sources. Colonel Fuller then asked why the Korean negotiators were offering the U.S. armed forces assistance which the armed forces had not asked for, ~~but~~ and did not need but would be obliged to pay for. Mr. Chang replied that reimbursement was being asked only for legitimate expenses incurred by the employment agency. He said the details could be worked out by the Joint Committee.

33. Colonel Fuller replied that the U.S. armed forces had not found any need for the type of assistance that was being offered. He pointed out that currently the armed forces were hiring employees from lists of persons who had previously lost

0260

their jobs with the armed forces as a result of reductions in force. The armed forces would no longer be able to rehire such people if they were forced to hire only those persons sent to them by a Korean employment agency.

34. Mr. Chang replied that he understood Colonel Fuller's remark. However, it was based on past experience and procedures. The Korean negotiators' position was that all future requirements of the U.S. armed forces were to be met with ROKG assistance. Since there currently existed in the ROK a surplus of labor, employees might have to accept employment under unfavorable conditions unless the situation were regularized by ROK Government supervision. To the ROK Government, it was important to see that Korean labor legislation was enforced. The U.S. negotiators had indicated that implementation of the provisions of the Korean draft would cause difficulties for the U.S. armed forces. If the U.S. negotiators would point out the difficulties and problems, the Korean negotiators would be glad to consider them and discuss the matter further at a subsequent meeting.

35. Colonel Fuller asked if all other employers in Korea were required to use the government employment service. If the U.S. armed forces were the only employer required to obtain all its employees from this service, how was that "regularizing" the situation?

36. Mr. Chang replied that the ROK Government met its requirements through the use of the employment service and the Ministry of ~~General Affairs~~ Government Administration. However, private employers were not compelled to use the employment service in all areas of the country.

37. Colonel Fuller pointed out that ~~under any scale of~~ no matter how small the costs, use of this employment service by the U.S. armed forces would ~~entail an~~ cause some increase over the present cost of hiring employees. Currently, the U.S. armed forces were under compulsion to reduce costs, yet the Korean proposal would cause an increase in their labor costs.

0261

38. ~~With regard~~ In answer to Mr. Chang's earlier question concerning the Korean Service Corps, Colonel Fuller stated that since 1950 these persons had been secured and hired for the U.S. armed forces by the ROK government, currently by the Ministry of Health and Social Affairs and the U.S. armed forces ~~therefore~~ have consistently considered them to be ROK Government employees and not U.S. government employees.

39. Mr. Chang commented that Colonel Fuller had indicated that one of the difficulties in implementing the Korean proposals would be increased cost to the U.S. armed forces. However, the Korean negotiators believed that the reimbursement costs would be only nominal and should cause the U.S. armed forces ~~no~~ little concern. The Korean negotiators could assure the U.S. negotiators that these costs would not impose unreasonable difficulties on the U.S. armed forces.

40. Regarding the Korean Service Corps, Mr. Chang said that the Korean negotiators had been unable to find anything in the relavant materials that would indicate any clear agreement on the status of KSC employees. They wondered, therefore, under what circumstances such an agreement had been reached. The KSC employees were paid by the U.S. armed forces and were not ROK Government employees. The ROK Government merely recruited them for the U.S. armed forces.

41. At this point, the meeting was adjourned. The next meeting was scheduled for February 20 at 2:00 p.m.

0262

JOINT SUMMARY RECORD OF THE 42nd SESSION

1/3

1. Time and Place: 2:00-4:40 P.M. February 14, 1964
at the Foreign Ministry's Conference
Room

2. Attendants:

ROK Side:

| | |
|---|---|
| Mr. Chang, Sang Moon | Director<br>European and American Affairs<br>Bureau |
| Mr. Yoon, Doo Sik | Director<br>Prosecutor's Bureau<br>Ministry of Justice |
| Mr. Shin, Kang Sup | Director<br>Employment Security Bureau<br>Office of Labor Affairs |
| Mr. Koo, Chong Whay | Chief, American Section<br>Ministry of Foreign Affairs |
| Mr. Choo, Moon Ki | Chief, Legal Affairs Section<br>Ministry of Justice |
| Col. Kim, Won Kil | Chief, Military Affairs Section<br>Ministry of National Defense |
| Mr. Oh, Jae Hee | Chief, Treaty Section<br>Ministry of Foreign Affairs |
| Mr. Chung, Tai Kyun | Chief, Prosecutor's Section<br>Ministry of Justice |
| Mr. Kang, Suk Jae<br>(Rapporteur and<br>Interpreter) | 2nd Secretary<br>Ministry of Foreign Affairs |
| Mr. Chung, Woo Young | 3rd Secretary<br>Ministry of Foreign Affairs |
| Mr. Lee, Chung Bin | 3rd Secretary<br>Ministry of Foreign Affairs |
| Mr. Lee, Keun Pal | 3rd Secretary<br>Ministry of Foreign Affairs |

U.S. Side:

| | |
|---|---|
| Mr. Philip C. Habib | Counselor<br>American Embassy |
| Col. Howard Smigelow | Deputy Chief of Staff<br>8th U.S. Army |
| Col. L.J. Fuller | Staff Judge Advocate<br>United Nations Command |

0263

| | |
|---|---|
| Col. Kenneth C. Crawford | Staff Judge Advocates Office 8th U.S. Army |
| Capt. John Wayne | Assistant Chief of Staff USN/K |
| Mr. Benjamin A. Fleck (Rapporteur and Press Officer) | First Secretary American Embassy |
| Mr. James Sartorius | 2nd Secretary American Embassy |
| Mr. Robert A. Lewis | 2nd Secretary and Consul American Embassy |
| Mr. Robert A. Kinney | J-5 8th U.S. Army |
| Maj. Robert D. Peckham | Staff Officer, JAG 8th U.S. Army |
| Mr. O. C. Reed | Director Office of Civil Personnel 8th U.S. Army |
| Mr. Kenneth Campen | Interpreter |
| Mr. Jurio Hernandez | Labor Adviser 8th U.S. Army |

1. Mr. Chang opened the meeting by introducing: Mr. Shin Kang-sup, Director of the Employment Security Bureau, Office of Labor Affairs, who was attending the meeting in lieu of Mr. Shin Kwan-sop; Mr. Yoon Doo-sik, Director, Prosecutor's Bureau, Ministry of Justice; and Mr. Chung Tai-kyun, Chief of the Prosecutor's Section, Ministry of Justice. Messrs. Shin and Yoon were attending as negotiators and Mr. Chung as an observer.

2. Mr. Habib welcomed these gentlemen to the negotiations and then introduced Colonel Kenneth C. Crawford, of the Staff Judge Advocate's Office, Eighth United States Army. Mr. Habib announced that Colonel Crawford was joining the U.S. negotiating team and would eventually serve as a replacement for Colonel Fuller, who would be attending a few more meetings before his expected transfer from Korea. Mr. Habib then introduced Mr. O.C. Reed, Director of the EUSA Office of Civilian Personnel,

0264

and Mr. Julio Hernandez, Labor Adviser, who would attend those negotiating meetings at which the Labor Procurement Article would be discussed and advise the U.S. negotiators as necessary.

3. Mr. Chang welcomed Colonel Crawford, Mr. Reed, and Mr. Hernandez and expressed regret at the news of Colonel Fuller's imminent departure. Referring to the many contributions which Colonel Fuller had made to the negotiations, Mr. Chang said the Korean negotiators would be sorry to see him go.

Facilities and Areas

4. Turning to Facilities and Areas Article "C", Mr. Habib noted that the negotiators had been discussing the general subject of facilities and areas in separate articles as tabled by the U.S. negotiators. In this fashion, agreement had been reached on major portions of the subject. With regard to Article "C", only minor differences remained between the U.S. and Korean drafts. The Korean negotiators had previously made certain proposals regarding this article. The U.S. negotiators wished to respond to those proposals. At the same time, they wished to expedite agreement on all of the facilities and areas provisions and to eliminate instances of overlapping in the several articles dealing with this general subject. It was in this spirit that the U.S. negotiators wished to respond to the following proposals made previously by the Korean negotiators: (a) convert paragraph 14 of the Korean draft into a new paragraph 2 of the U.S. draft, deleting the words "supply or any other materials"; (b) convert the existing paragraph 2 of the U.S. draft into an Agreed Minute.

0265

5. Mr. Habib said the U.S. negotiators were prepared to agree to these Korean proposals but also wished to reach agreement on the article as a whole. He pointed out that the final sentence of paragraph 13 of the Korean draft referred to the subject of compensation. It was the view of the U.S. negotiators that this subject should be dealt with in only one article and since Article "D" dealt with that subject, it would be logical to concentrate discussion of compensation in Article "D", omitting it from Article "C". He reminded the negotiators that the general Korean position was in favor of compensation while the U.S. position was opposed to the payment of any compensation. Rather than debate this general question in discussion dealing with Article "C", the U.S. negotiators proposed deletion of the final sentence of paragraph 13 of the Korean draft, with no prejudice to the overall Korean or U.S. position on compensation.

6. Mr. Habib pointed out that full agreement on this article would be achieved if the Korean negotiators accepted the deletion of the final sentence of paragraph 13. With Articles "A" and "B" already agreed to, if agreement were reached on Article "C", the only remaining point at issue with regard to facilities and areas would be the question of compensation. The U.S. negotiators proposed that Article "D", which dealt with this subject, be placed on the agenda for discussion at an early meeting.

7. Mr. Chang stated that before giving an answer to the U.S. proposal, the Korean negotiators wished to point out that full agreement had not yet been reached on the text of paragraph 2 of the U.S. draft. Mr. Habib replied that at the 31st negotiating meeting on September 20, 1963, the Korean negotiators had proposed the conversion of the existing paragraph 2 of the U.S. draft

0266

into an Agreed Minute. He pointed out that if the U.S. understanding that this proposal indicated agreement with the text was incorrect, the negotiators would have to begin negotiating this paragraph all over again.

8. Mr. Chang replied that the Korean proposal had been to delete paragraph 2 from the U.S. draft <u>or</u> convert it into an Agreed Minute. He said the Korean negotiators still had some question regarding the substance of this paragraph. While they had agreed to the deletion of the words "supply or any other materials" from paragraph 14 of the Korean draft, they had done so only in anticipation that agreement could be reached on the text of paragraph 2 of the U.S. draft. The Korean negotiators welcomed the agreement of the U.S. negotiators to substitute paragraph 14 for paragraph 2 of the U.S. draft. However, they still believed that private property extremely demolished should be compensated for. They had no objection to discussing the subject of compensation with reference to Article "D" but they believed that any such discussion should include the question of property extremely demolished.

9. Mr. Habib replied that the Korean negotiators certainly had the right to raise that question and the U.S. negotiators would expect them to do so. He reiterated the U.S. position against the payment of compensation and recalled that the Korean position favored such payment.

10. Mr. Chang replied that the Korean negotiators regretted to hear that the U.S. negotiators were not prepared to agree to the payment of compensation. He characterized Mr. Habib's statement as a unilateral declaration which would act as a deterrent to the

0267

negotiations. He said that unless the U.S. negotiators were prepared to discuss the subject and give due consideration to the Korean position, the Korean negotiators were not prepared to agree to the deletion of the final sentence of paragraph 13 of the Korean draft.

11. Mr. Chang asked whether the term "removable facilities" in paragraph 2 of the U.S. draft included facilities constructed as part of the military aid given to the ROK armed forces by the U.S. Government. Mr. Habib replied that such inclusion would be unreasonable and that the title to all facilities constructed as part of the military aid program was transferred to the ROK armed forces.

12. In response to Mr. Chang's previous remark regarding the U.S. position on compensation, Mr. Habib said that the U.S. negotiators had not indicated unwillingness to discuss the issue. They had merely suggested that such discussion be concentrated under one article (Article "D") in order to permit full agreement on Article "C". The U.S. negotiators had discussed the issue of compensation in the past and would continue to do so. He had stated that the U.S. Government was unwilling to pay compensation. The U.S. negotiators were prepared to discuss the reasons underlying this position, as well as the innumerable precedents which supported it. The U.S. negotiators had proposed deletion of the final sentence of paragraph 13 of the Korean draft, indicating that such deletion would in no way prejudice the Korean position in support of compensation or the U.S. position in opposition to it.

0268

13. Mr. Chang thanked Mr. Habib for his clarification of the matter of removable facilities. He noted that there had been no change in the position of either side regarding the payment of compensation. He also noted that disagreement over the final sentence of paragraph 13 of the Korean draft was all that stood in the way of full agreement on Article "C". He said the Korean negotiators would give further consideration to this matter and give their views at a subsequent meeting.

14. Mr. Ku remarked that there was still a question with regard to removable facilities, and the loss or damage which might occur to materials left behind by the U.S. armed forces in facilities returned to the Republic of Korea. If all such materials were evacuated by the U.S. armed forces, there would be no problem. However, if they were not all removed, the Korean negotiators would like to ensure that the ROK Government would not be held responsible for loss or damage to those left behind.

15. Mr. Habib replied that there was nothing in the text of the Agreement which said that the ROK Government would be liable for such loss or damage. The Joint Committee would supervise the transfer of such facilities and there was no need for the negotiators to involve themselves in this question. Property introduced into Korea under the Military Assistance Program was governed by separate agreements which will continue in effect after the SOFA goes into effect. He pointed out that there is no provision in the SOFA which dealt with MAP property, which had been transferred to the Republic of Korea.

0269

16. Mr. Chang said that the Korean negotiators would discuss the question of MAP property with the ministries concerned and would then discuss the question further at a subsequent negotiating meeting, Mr. Habib replied that this question had no relevance to the SOFA negotiations.

Invited Contractors

17. Turning to the article on Invited Contractors, Mr. Habib recalled that at the previous meeting, the Korean negotiators had made a general proposal which seemed to the U.S. negotiators to suggest the possibility of making a distinction between U.S. contractors and their employees and other contractors and their employees. The U.S. negotiators would like to have an explanation in greater detail of the privileges which these groups would enjoy under the terms of the Korean proposal. Noting that the U.S. draft provided certain privileges under paragraphs 3, 5, 6, 7 and 8 (not yet tabled), he asked how the Korean negotiators proposed to deal with third country nationals. Specifically, what did the Korean negotiators have in mind with regard to taxes, customs, foreign exchange, driving permits, license, and similar privileges, with regard to third country nationals and dependents? He noted that the U.S. armed forces are currently engaged in a program to replace gradually all third country nationals with Koreans, as soon as a sufficient number of trained Koreans is available.

18. Mr. Chang replied that at the last meeting the Korean negotiators had made a new proposal with a view

0270

to arriving at a mutually agreeable text of this article. They had presented briefly the framework of this proposal and had suggested an informal meeting for further discussion. Since the U.S. negotiators had rejected an informal meeting, the Korean negotiators had revised their original draft of the article and wished to table a new draft at this time. He said that Mr. Chung would explain the main features of the new draft.

19. Mr. Chung summarized the main features of the revised Korean draft of the article in the following terms. It would permit persons, including corporations organized under the laws of the United States, to employ third country nationals, who would be given the use of non-appropriated fund organizations, military post offices, and military payment certificates, under the terms of Agreed Minute #1. It would also extend those privileges to dependents, including the dependents of third country nationals, under the terms of Agreed Minute #2. Mr. Chung noted that the revised draft omitted the provisions of paragraph 3(i) of the U.S. draft, pertaining to driving permits and registration of vehicles, since the Korean negotiators believed that invited contractors should be subject to Korean laws and regulations in regard to these matters. He also noted that the revised draft did not provide for an exemption from payment of taxes arising out of the use and ownership of private vehicles. Nor did it include the provisions of the Agreed Minute of the U.S. draft. Finally, the Korean revision deletes the provisions of paragraph 3(j) of the U.S. draft, which would provide exemption from the laws and regulations of Korea with respect to terms and conditions of

employment. Mr. Chung pointed out that the Korean draft of the Labor Procurement Article provides that the terms and conditions of employment in so far as they apply to Korean persons should be those laid down by Korean legislation.

20. Mr. Habib thanked Mr. Chung for his explanation of the revised Korean draft. He said the U.S. negotiators would study it and comment at a subsequent meeting.

Criminal Jurisdiction

21. The negotiators then exchanged drafts of the Article dealing with criminal jurisdiction. Mr. Chang stated that, in his capacity as Chief Negotiator for the Korean side, he wished to express great satisfaction that these drafts had finally been tabled. The Korean negotiators looked forward to a mutually satisfactory agreement on this subject, based on mutual cooperation by both negotiating teams. Mr. Habib replied that the U.S. negotiators had indicated in December that they hoped to be able to table the U.S. draft at about this time and were glad that their prediction had proved accurate. The U.S. negotiators looked forward to quiet, systematic, and fruitful discussion of this subject.

Labor Procurement

22. Turning to the article on labor procurement, Mr. Habib said that it would be helpful to both sides to have a presentation of general views on this subject. He then asked Colonel Fuller to present the views of the U.S. negotiators.

23. Colonel Fuller stated that it is the intention of the U.S. armed forces to continue to act as a good and

0272

enlightened local employer and in general to conform to Korean practices, customs, and Korean labor laws, consistent with the ROK-US defense mission. The U.S. armed forces intended to permit their employees to join voluntarily unions or employee groups and to have the same right to strike as employees in comparable positions of employment with the armed forces of the ROK. Stating that as the U.S. draft reflected current Labor practice, and the result of fifteen years of U.S. employment practice, Colonel Fuller suggested that the U.S. draft serve as the basis for negotiation. He asked whether the Korean negotiators had any questions regarding the content of the U.S. draft.

24. Mr. Chang replied that before asking question, he would like to sum up the basic differences between the two drafts, as the Korean negotiators saw them. The three fundamental differences were as follows:

The basic principle embodied in the Korean draft is to uphold and protect the rights of the Korean workers, as stipulated under the provisions of the applicable Korean laws. Therefore, the Korean draft provides that (a) local labor requirements of the U.S. armed forces "shall be satisfied with the assistance of the Korean authorities". (b) The Korean draft provides that the conditions of employment and work shall be laid down by ROK legislation, whereas the U.S. draft provides only for "general conformity" with Korean labor legislation, customs and practices. He remarked that there was, in this respect, a wide gap between the two drafts. (c) The Korean draft included detailed and fundamental provisions in order to cope with problems arising from

0273

possible dismissal of a worker by the U.S. armed forces for security reasons. Inasmuch as there are these substantial differences between the two drafts, the Korean negotiators believed that it would be more useful and more fruitful to use the Korean draft as the basis for negotiation.

25. Mr. Chang stated that the identification, in the U.S. draft, of Korean Service Corps members as employees of the ROK Government posed a difficult problem to the Korean negotiators. They wondered what the basis of this statement in the U.S. draft was, since they had been unable to find any evidence that would support it.

26. Colonel Fuller asked Mr. Chang to repeat the three basic differences which the Korean negotiators had found in their study of the two drafts. Mr. Chang summarized the three differences as follows:

(a) The U.S. draft provides for direct hire, whereas the Korean draft provides that local labor requirements shall be satisfied with the assistance of the ROK Government;

(b) The U.S. draft provides only for "general conformity" with Korean laws and regulations, whereas the Korean draft provides that working conditions shall be those prescribed by ROK legislation;

(c) The Korean draft provides detailed provisions covering the discharge of employees for security reasons, whereas the U.S. draft is silent on this subject.

27. Colonel Fuller asked what the phrase "with the assistance of the Korean authorities" in the Korean draft meant. Mr. Chang replied that according to current practice, the U.S. armed forces with certain exceptions, hire their Korean employees directly.

0274

However, the Korean negotiators believed that in order to make the most effective and efficient use of Korean labor, all hiring should be done in coordination with the appropriate Korean agencies.

28. In response to Colonel Fuller's inquiry as to the nature of such agencies, Mr. Chang stated that there are currently in operation many employment offices and that in the future, many specialized employment offices will be established. In response to further questioning, Mr. Chang stated that the only agency referred to by the Korean draft was that which operates employment offices, which serves only as a labor recruiting service. As Mr. Chang had indicated that this service was currently used to some extent by the U.S. armed forces, Colonel Fuller asked how present practice would be changed under the provisions of the Korean draft. Mr. Chang said that in future it was planned to have all employment for the U.S. armed forces handled by this agency.

29. In reply to a series of questions by Colonel Fuller, Mr. Chang stated that it was the Korean intention to have this agency handle only recruiting for the U.S. armed forces and that the agency would not hire or fire, promote, demote, discipline, or assign such employees. When asked how the agency would assist in recruiting, Mr. Chang said that if there were a requirement for 1 person, the agency would send 3 or 4 eligible persons to the armed forces. The armed forces would then make the final selection.

30. In reply to questions by Colonel Fuller regarding the cost of such an employment service, Mr. Chang stated

0275

that the Korean draft provides that the U.S. armed forces shall reimburse the ROK Government. He said such reimbursement would only be for advertisement fees, travel expenses, and other costs incurred directly in the recruitment of labor for the U.S. armed forces. Inasmuch as the employment agency was run by the ROK Government, there would be no charge to the U.S. armed forces to cover the expenses of salaries, materials, and supplies.

31. In reply to further questioning by Colonel Fuller, Mr. Chang stated that there are currently about 40 branches of the employment agency scattered throughout the country, with one or two in every city having a population of 50,000 or over. The ROK Government obtains laborers for its public works and construction projects from this agency. However, government officials are recruited through the Ministry of Government Administration.

32. Mr. Chang pointed out, in reply to a question, that the Korean draft would permit the U.S. armed forces to hire employees only with the assistance of ROK Government authorities, and the U.S. forces would not be permitted to recruit employees from other sources. Colonel Fuller then asked why the Korean negotiators were offering the U.S. armed forces assistance which the armed forces had not asked for and did not need but would be obliged to pay for. Mr. Chang replied that reimbursement was being asked only for legitimate expenses incurred by the employment agency. He said the details could be worked out by the Joint Committee.

0276

33. Colonel Fuller replied that the U.S. armed forces had not found any need for the type of assistance that was being offered. He pointed out that currently the armed forces were hiring employees from lists of persons who had previously lost their jobs with the armed forces as a result of reductions in force. The armed forces would no longer be able to rehire such people if they were forced to hire only those persons sent to them by a Korean employment agendy.

34. Mr. Chang replied that he understood Colonel Fuller's remark. However, it was based on past experience and procedures. The Korean negotiators' position was that all future requirements of the U.S. armed forces were to be met with ROKG assistance. Since there currently existed in the ROK a surplus of labor, employees might have to accept employment under unfavorable conditions unless the situation were regularized by ROK Government supervision. To the ROK Government, it was important to see that Korean labor legislation was enforced. The U.S. negotiators had indicated that implementation of the provisions of the Korean draft would cause difficulties for the U.S. armed forces. If the U.S. negotiators would point out the difficulties and problems, the Korean negotiators would be glad to consider them and discuss the matter further at a subsequent meeting.

35. Colonel Fuller asked if all other employers in Korea were required to use the government employment service. If the U.S. armed forces were the only employer required to obtain all its employees from this service, how was that "regularizing" the situation?

0277

36. Mr. Chang replied that the ROK Government met its requirements through the use of the employment service and the Ministry of Government Administration. However, private employers were not compelled to use the employment service in all areas of the country.

37. Colonel Fuller pointed out that no matter how small the cost, use of this employment service by the U.S. armed forces would cause some increase over the present oost of hiring employees. Currently, the U.S. armed forces were under compulsion to reduce costs, yet the Korean proposal would cause in increase in their labor costs.

38. In answer to Mr. Chang's earlier question concerning the Korean Service Corps, Colonel Fuller stated that since 1950 these persons had been secured and hired for the U.S. armed forces by the ROK government, currently by the Ministry of Health and Social Affairs and the U.S. armed forces have consistently considered them to be ROK Government employees and not U.S. Government employees.

39. Mr. Chang commented that Colonel Fuller had indicated that one of the difficulties in implementing the Korean proposals would be increased cost to the U.S. armed forces. However, the Korean negotiators believed that the reimbursement costs would be only nominal and should cause the U.S. armed forces little concern. The Korean negotiators could assure the U.S. negotiators that these costs would not impose unreasonable difficulties on the U.S. armed forces.

0278

40. Regarding the Korean Service Corps, Mr. Chang said that the Korean negotiators had been unable to find anything in the relevant materials that would indicate any clear agreement on the status of KSC employees. They wondered, therefore, under what circumstances such an agreement had been reached. The KSC employees were paid by the U.S. armed forces and were not ROK Government employees. The ROK Government merely recruited them for the U.S. armed forces.

41. At this point, the meeting was adjourned. The next meeting was scheduled for February 20 at 2:00 p.m.

6. 제43차, 2.20

0280

43차회의 예비회담 참석자 명단 1964.2.18.

| 성명 | 부처 및 직위 | 연락처전화번호 |
| --- | --- | --- |
| 武秉鎬 | 内務部治安局情報課外事係長 | 2-1354 |
| 尹昇榮 | 法務部法務局法務官兼檢事 | 3-1461 1462 |
| 錢正鎬 | " | 8-3643 |
| 沈尙燮 | 勞動庁職業安定局長 | 38-5085 |
| 金台靖 | " 労政課長 | 2-4295 |
| 李啓薰 | 国防部 対外政策研究官 | 302-4116 |
| 韓甲石 | 治安局企劃審査課法制係長 | 2-1353 |
| 상공부 전기국 전정과 전기국장 | 오희석 박용건 | 74-3362 |

철도청 운수국화물과 계장

| | | |
| --- | --- | --- |
| 許成俊 | 労動庁労政局長 | ③ 5437 |
| 金容海 | 労動庁職業安定課長 | ~~5885~~ ③-4651 |

조용석 (남영) 약공장다- 5215.

# 참석자 명단

| 성명 | 직위 | 부처 |
| --- | --- | --- |
| 崔鍾文 | 財務部 | 財務部 外換課 |
| 南悳熙 | 商務課長 | 商工部 商易局 |
| 李啓薰 | 對外政策研究官 | 國防部 [illegible]局 |
| ~~金東[illegible]~~ 김혜택 | 國際觀光公社 [illegible] | |
| | Foreigners commissary 소장 | 정혜택 ④-2074 |
| 양회석 | 교통부 관광국 | ③-7464 |
| | 여행업과 | |
| | 교통부 관광국 여무과 | 김석종 담당 (Foreign C.) [illegible] |
| 朱文基 | ~~法務部~~ 法務課長 | 法務部 |
| 李廷彬 | 外務官 | 外務部 |
| 吳在熙 | 條約課長 | 〃 |
| 재무부 외환과 | | 72-4973 |
| 조광제 | | |
| 강석재 | (97대)(20대) | |
| 李錫桂 | 市警保安課 警衛 | 2-7595 경비-490 |
| 법무부 국내과-72-7952 | 서울시 교통운수국 차량과 | 2-4905 |

0282

Mr. Robert A. Lewis Ext. 229

Res. Ext. 657

Mr. James Sartorius

o 서울시 수도국 주계과(요금과) 과장 ⑦-1139 —

상공부 전기국장 교환상공부 74-2671/8 74-3454

전기국 電政課 (오희서) 74-3362

상공부 상역국상무과장 南 [illegible] 74-2671

교통부 육운국 감리과장 박진섭 교환 ④-0459

④-0420

한국전력 보급과 과장 8-4112

" 성도환

체신부 전무국 전신전화과 權 [illegible] ③-0653

②-0131

[illegible] — 몰배정

₩100,000 —

53,000 — 3[illegible]

0283

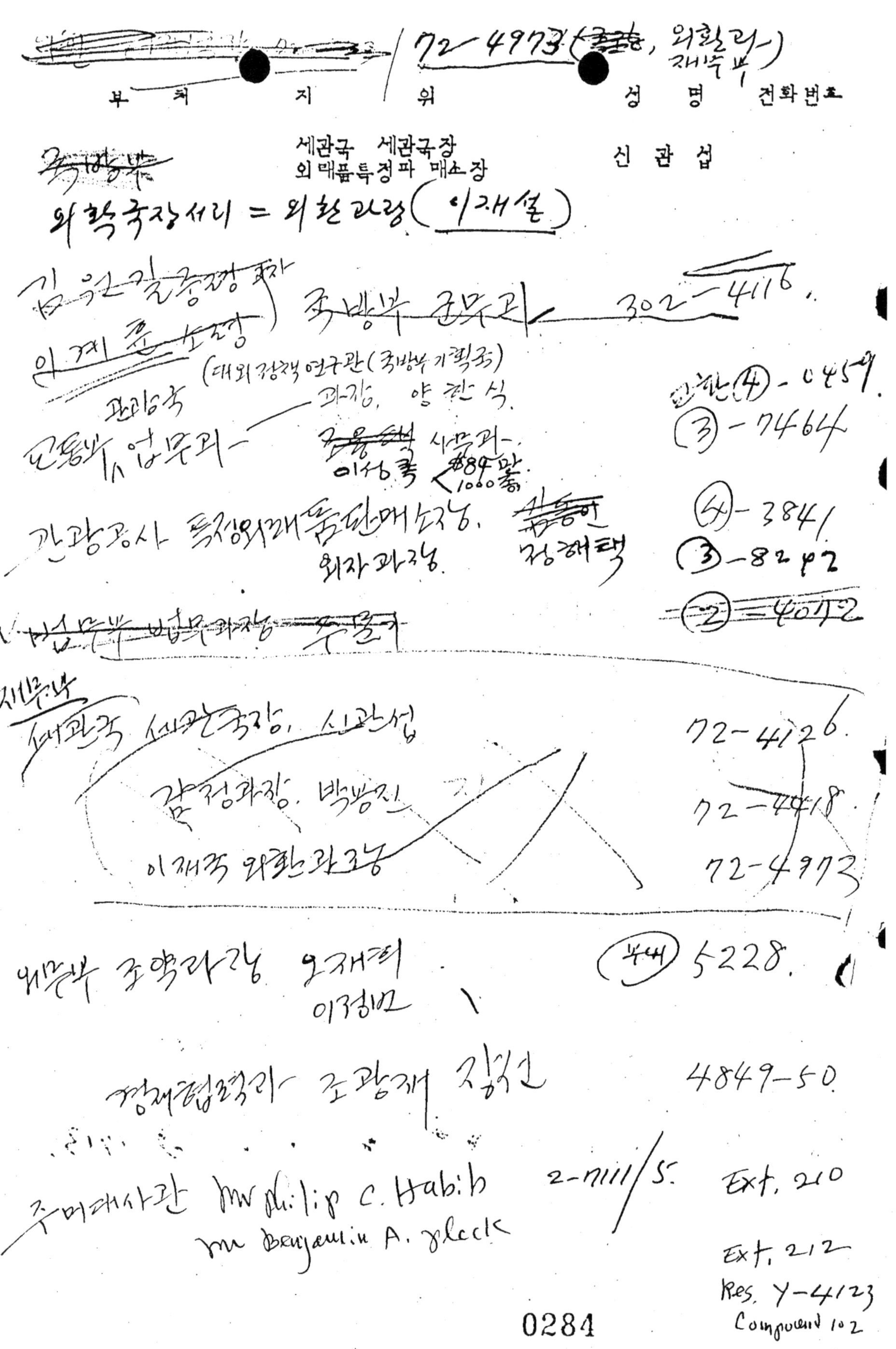

부 처 지 위 성 명 전화번호
세관국 세관국장
외래품특정판매소장
신 관 섭
72-4973
72-4126
72-4418
72-4973
5228
4849-50
주미대사관 Mr Philip C. Habib 2-7111/5 Ext. 210
Ext. 212
Res. Y-4123
Compound 102
0284

# 기 안 용 지

| 자 체<br>통 제 | | 기안처 | 미주과<br>이근팔 | 전화번호 | 근거서류접수일자 |
|---|---|---|---|---|---|
| | 과장 | 국장 | 차관 | 장관 | |
| 관계관<br>서 명 | | | | | |
| 기 안<br>년월일 | 1964. 2. 19. | 시 행<br>년월일 | | 보존<br>년한 | 정 서 / 기 장 |
| 분 류<br>기 호 | 외구미722.2 | 전 체<br>통 제 | | 종결 | |
| 경 유<br>수 신<br>참 조 | 건 의 | | | 발 신 | |
| 제 목 | 제 43 차 주둔군지위협정 체결교섭회의에 임할 우리측 입장 | | | | |

2 월 20 일 개최될 제 43 차 주둔군지위협정 체결을 위한 한.미간 교섭회의에서는 군계약자, 미군인 가족 및 재산의 안건, 및 노무에 관한 조문을 토의하도록 예정하고 있는바 이에 대하여 우리측 교섭실무자는 2 월 18 일 회합을 갖고 제 43 차 회의에서 취할 태도를 별첨과 같이 결정하였아오니 재가하여 주시기 바랍니다.

유 첨: 제 43 차 주둔군지위협정 체결교섭회의에 임할 우리측 태도. 끝.

1966,12,31,에 예고문에 의거 일반문서로 재분류

승인양식 1-1-3 (1112-040-016-018) (190mm×260mm16절지)

0285

1. 군계약자

가. 제 42 차 회의에서 우리측이 제시한 수정조안에 대하여 미측이 검토한 결과를 청취하고 우리측 입장을 계속 주장한다.

2. 미군의 군속 및 가족의 신체와 재산에 대한 안전조치

가. 우리측은 우리측이 제시한 조안대로 주장한다. 따라서 미측조안에서 안전조치를 취하는데 한국측에 협조를 요청하는 대상자에 군대, 그들의 구성원, 군속 및 그들의 가족과 재산이외에 우리측 조안에 없는 군계약자까지도 포함시키고 있는바 우리는 군계약자는 군속과 같이 취급할 수 없음으로 이를 삭제할 것을 주장한다.

나. 미국정부의 재산의 안전과 보호를 위하여서는 필요한 입법조치를 취할 것에 동의할 수 있다는 것이 우리측 입장이며 미측조안이 포함하고 있는 개인과 그들의 재산에 대하여서는 입법조치를 취할 수 없음으로 "of the persons referred to in this paragraph, and their property and "어구를 삭제할 것과 " to ensure "대신 우리안대로 " for "로 대체할 것을 요구한다.

3. 노무조항

가. 우리측 조안에 따라 우리측 입장을 계속 주장한다.

나. 미측조안 1(b)항: 본항에서 피고용자 대상에서 제외한 Korean Service Corps 는 한국정부에서 단지 모집에 협조하여 주고 있을 뿐 그들의 고용, 임금, 노무관리 및 해고를 미측에서 전담하고 있음으로 미측의 노무자이며 결코 한국정부의 노무자가 않임을 주장한다.

다. 미측조안 4(a)항: 미조안이 미측 노무자가 그와 동등한 위치에 있는 한국군 노무자와 같이 파업할 수 있다고 규정

0286

하고 있는바 " in a comparable position "이라는 용어와 관련하여 한국군에 근무하는 노무자와 동등한 직위에 있는 것으로 미측이 간주하는 미측 노무자의 부류를 열거토록 하여 미측이 의도하는바를 명백하게 한다. 끝.



0287

SOFA NEGOTIATION

Agenda for the 43rd Session

14:00 Feb. 20, 1964

1. Continuation of Discussions on:
   a. Contractors Article
   b. Security Measures Article

2. Other Business

3. Agenda and Date of the Next Meeting

4. Press Release

0288

ARTICLE ______

CONTRACTORS

who are ordinary residents in the United States (Feb 20 '64)

1. Persons, including corporations, their employees, and the dependents of such persons, present in Korea solely for the benefit of the United States armed forces or other armed forces in Korea under the Unified Command receiving logistical support from the United States armed forces, who are designated by the Government of the United States in accordance with the provisions of paragraph 2 below, shall, except as provided in this Article, be subject to the laws and regulations of Korea.

2. The designation referred to in paragraph 1 above shall be made upon consultation with the Government of Korea and shall be restricted to cases where open competitive bidding is not practicable due to security considerations, to the technical qualifications of the contractors involved, to the unavailability of materials or services required by United States standards, or to limitations of United States law. The designation shall be withdrawn by the Government of the United States:

(a) Upon completion of contracts with the United States for the United States armed forces or other armed forces in Korea under the Unified Command receiving ligistical support from the United States armed forces:

0289

(b) Upon proof that such persons are engaged in business activities in Korea other than those pertaining to the United States armed forces or other armed forces in Korea under the Unified Command receiving logistical support from the United States armed forces;

(c) Upon proof that such persons are engaged in practices illegal in Korea.

3. Upon certification by appropriate United States authorities as to their identity, such persons shall be accorded the following benefits of this Agreement:

(a) Rights of accession and movement, as provided for Article , paragraph 2;

(b) Entry into Korea in accordance with the provisions of Article ;

(c) The exemption from customs duties, and other such charges provided for in Article , paragraph 3, for members of the United States armed forces, the civilian component, and their dependents;

(d) If authorized by the Government of the United States, the right to use the services of the activities provided for in Article ;

(e) Those rights provided in Article , paragraph 2, for members of the United States armed forces, the civilian component, and their dependents;

0290

(f) If authorized by the Government of the United States, the right to use military payment certificates, as provided for in Article ;

(g) The use of postal facilities provided for in Article ;

(h) Those rights accorded the United States armed forces by Article , paragraph 3, relating to utilities and services;

(i) Those rights provided to members of the United States armed forces, the civilian component, and their dependents by Article , relating to driving permits and registration of vehicles;

(j) Exemption from the laws and regulations of Korea with respect to terms and conditions of employment, and licensing and registration of businesses and corporations.

4. The arrival, departure, and place of residence in Korea of such persons shall from time to time be notified by the United States armed forces to the Korean authorities.

5. Upon certification by an authorized representative of the United States armed forces, depreciable assets, except houses, held, used or transferred by such persons exclusively for the execution of contracts referred to in paragraph 1 shall not be subject to taxes or similar charges of Korea.

0201

Submitted by U.S on Feb. 20 '64

8. The persons referred to in paragraph 1 shall be subject to those provisions of Article and the Agreed Minutes thereto which pertain to members of the civilian component, and to dependents.

0292

7. The persons referred to in paragraph 1 shall not be liable to pay income or corporation taxes to the Government of Korea or to any other taxing agenty in Korea on any income derived under a contract with the Government of the United States in connection with the construction, maintenance or operation of any of the facilities or areas covered by this Agreement.

Persons in Korea in connection with the execution of such a contract with the United States shall not be liable to pay any Korean taxes to the Government of Korea or to any taxing agency in Korea on income derived from sources outside of Korea nor shall periods during which such persons are in Korea be considered periods of residence or domicile in Korea for the purposes of Korean taxation. The provisions of this paragraph do not exempt such persons from payment of income or corporation taxes on income derived from Korean sources, other than those sources referred to in the first sentence of this paragraph, nor do they exempt such persons who claim Korean residence for United States income tax purposes from payment of Korean taxes on income.

Agreed Minute:

1. The execution of contracts with the United States in addition to those specified in paragraph 1 of Article ____

0293

shall not exclude the persons provided for in Article ____ from the application of that Article.

0294

Submitted by U.S. on February 20, '64

## AGREED MINUTE

2. Contractor employees who are present in Korea on the effective date of this agreement and who would qualify for the privileges contained in Article ________ but for the fact that they are not ordinarily resident in the United States shall be entitled to enjoy such privileges so long as their presence is for the purpose stated in paragraph 1 of Article ________.

0295

ARTICLE ____

3. Upon certification by appropriate United States authorities as to their identity, such persons shall be accorded the following benefits of this Agreement:

(a) Accession and movement, as provided for in Article ____, paragraph 2;

(b) Entry into Korea in accordance with the provisions of Article ____;

(c) The exemption from customs duties and other such charges provided for in Article ____, paragraph 3, for members of the United States armed forces, the civilian component, and their dependents;

(d) If authorized by the Government of the United States, the use of the services of the activities provided for in Article ____;

(e) Those provided in Article ____, paragraph 2, for members of the United States armed forces, the civilian component, and their dependents;

(f) If authorized by the Government of the United States, the use of military paymebt certificates, as provided in Article ____;

(g) The use of postal faciliities provided for in Article ____;

(h) The use of utilities and services in accordance with those priorities, conditions, rates, or tariffs

0296

accorded the United States armed forces by Article ____, paragraph 3, relating to utilities and services;

(i) Those provided to members of the United States armed forces, the civilian component, and their dependents by Article ______, relating to driving permits and registration of vehicles;

(j) Exemption from the laws and regulations of Korea with respect to terms and conditions of employment, and licensing and registration of businesses and corporations.

0297

ARTICLE

MILITARY POST OFFICES

1. The United States may establish and operate, within the facilities and areas in use by the U.S. armed forces, United States military post offices for the use of members of the United States armed forces, the civilian component, and their dependents, for the transmission of mail between United States military post offices in Korea and between such military post offices and other United States post offices.

2. United States military post offices may be used by other officers and personnel of the United States Government, and ~~their dependents~~, ordinarily accorded such privileges abroad.

0298

ARTICLE

MILITARY PAYMENT CERTIFICATES

1. (a) United States military payment certificates denominated in dollars may be used by persons authorized by the United States for internal transactions. The Government of the United States will take appropriate action to insure that authorized personnel are prohibited from engaging in transactions involving military payment certificates except as authorized by United States regulations. The Government of Korea will take necessary action to prohibit unauthorized persons from engaging in transactions involving military payment certificates and with the aid of United States authorities will undertake to apprehend and punish any person or persons under its jurisdiction involved in the counterfeiting or uttering of counterfeit military payment certificates.

(b) It is agreed that the United States authorities will to the extent authorized by United States law, apprehend and punish members of the United States armed forces, the civilian component, or their dependents, who tender military payment certificates to unauthorized persons and that no obligation will be due to such unauthorized persons or to the Government of Korea or its agencies from the United States or any of its agencies as a result of any unauthorized use of military payment certificates within Korea.

0299

2. In order to exercise control of military payment certificates the United States may designate certain American financial institutions to maintain and operate, under United States supervision, facilities for the use of persons authorized by the United States to use military payments certificates. Institutions authorized to maintain military banking facilities will establish and maintain such facilities physically separated from their Korean commercial banking business, with personnel whose sole duty is to maintain and operate such facilities. Such facilities shall be permitted to maintain United States currency bank accounts and to perform all financial transactions in connection therewith including receipt and remission of funds to the extent provided by Article .... paragraph 2, of this Agreement.

0300

ARTICLE XIX - Military Payment Certificates

AGREED MINUTE

Inasmuch as United States Military Payment Certificates are property of the United States Government, any Military Payment Certificates which are in, or come into, the possession of the Government of the Republic of Korea shall be returned without compensation to the authorities of the United States armed forces as expeditiously as practicable.

0301

ARTICLE

1. Members of the United States armed forces, the civilian component and their dependents, shall be subject to the foreign exchange controls of the Government of the Republic of Korea.

2. The preceding paragraph shall not be construed to preclude the transmission into or out of Korea of United States dollars or dollar instruments representing the official funds of the United States or realized as a result of service or employment in connection with this Agreement by members of the United States armed forces and the civilian component, or realized by such persons and their dependents from sources outside Korea.

3. The United States authorities shall take suitable measures to preclude the abuse of the privileges stipulated in the preceding paragraphs or circumvention of the Korean foreign exchange controls.

0302

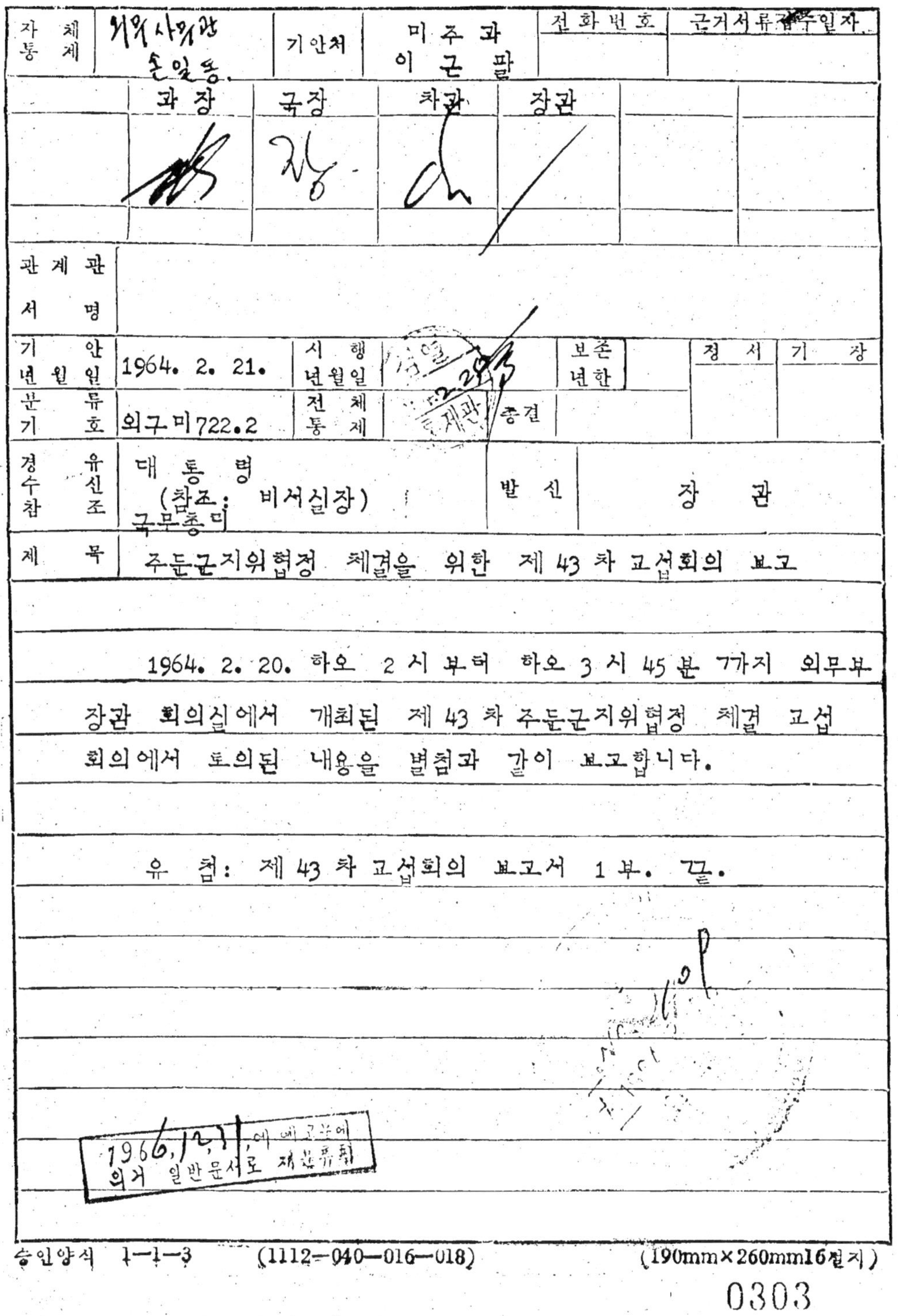

# 기 안 용 지

| 자체통제 | 외무사무관 손일동 | 기안처 | 미주과 이근팔 | 전화번호 | 근거서류접수일자 |
|---|---|---|---|---|---|
| | 과장 | 국장 | 차관 | 장관 | |
| 관계관 서명 | | | | | |
| 기안년월일 | 1964. 2. 21. | 시행년월일 | | 보존년한 | 정서 기장 |
| 분류기호 | 외구미722.2 | 전체통제 | | 종결 | |
| 경유 수신 참조 | 대통령 (참조: 비서실장) 국무총리 | | | 발신 | 장관 |
| 제목 | 주둔군지위협정 체결을 위한 제43차 교섭회의 보고 | | | | |

1964. 2. 20. 하오 2시부터 하오 3시 45분 까지 외무부 장관 회의실에서 개최된 제43차 주둔군지위협정 체결 교섭 회의에서 토의된 내용을 별첨과 같이 보고합니다.

유 첨: 제43차 교섭회의 보고서 1부. 끝.

1966, 12, 31, 에 예고문에 의거 일반문서로 재분류됨

승인양식 1-1-3 (1112-040-016-018) (190mm×260mm16절지)

0303

제 43 차

한미간 주둔군지위협정 체결교섭실무자회의

보 고 서

1. 일 시: 1964 년 2 월 20 일 하오 2 시 부터 동 3 시 45 분 까지.

2. 장 소: 외무부장관 회의실

3. 토의사항:

가. 군계약자

(1) 미측초안 1항: 미측은 군계약자가 미군의 군사명 수행을 위한 중요성에 있어서 미군구성원 및 군속과 하등의 차의점이 없다고 설명하고 제 3 국인을 배제하려는 우리측 주장의 일부를 받아드려 고용인에 한해서 " who are ordinarily resident in the United States"라는 구절을 삽입 한정할 것과,

(2). 미측초안 8항: 미측이 이미 제시한 형사재판관할권 초안에서 규정한 군속 및 동 가족에 관한 조항이 군계약자에게도 적용되는 것을 규정하는 8항초안을 제시하였다.

(3) 미측 초안 합의의사록 2항: 미측은 제 3 국인 고용인을 점차 한국인과 교체할 것을 고려하고 있으나 본 협정 체결 시 재직중인 제 3 국인에게 만은 잠정적 조치로서 특권을 부여할 것을 규정하는 초안을 제시하였다. 우리측은 미측의 수정안이 우리측 주장과 상당한 거리가 있음을 지적하고 검토 후 다음 회의에서 입장을 밝히기로 하였다.

나. 미군에 대한 안전조치

(1) 미측은 미.일간 주둔군지위협정에서 군계약자가 제외되고 있으나 사실상 보호를 받고 있으며 본 조항은 단순히 한국관계당국의 협력을 의뢰하고 있음에 불과함으로 그들을 보호대상자로 포함시켜 주기를 요청하였다. 우리측은 군계약자는 군인 군속과는 명백히 구별되어야 함으로 보호대상자에서 제외할 것을 주장하고 미국 정부 재산에 대하여서는

64-3-11

0304

14-3-7 (2)
미국.북 109-5 (2)
0305

보호를 위하여 입법조치까지도 취할 용의가 있으나 군인 군속의 사유재산에 대해서는 우리 나라 국내법상 충분한 보호를 받고 있음으로 삭제할 것을 주장하였다.

(2) 본 조항 후단에 관하여 미측으로 부터 형사재판관할권과 연관성을 갖고 가해자를 처벌할 수 있게 하기 위하여 필요하다는 보충설명이 있었다.

4. 기타 사항: 차기회의일자: 1964 년 2 월 28 일 하오 2 시 부터. 끝



(64) 7b

0306

1. Mr. Chang opened the meeting by introducing Mr. Yi Chae-sup of the Ministry of Finance, substituting for Mr. Sin Kwan-sup; Mr. Ham Chung-ho of the Ministry of Justice; Mr. Kim Nai-sung of the Foreign Ministry; and Mr. Chung U-young, who would serve from now on as interpreter for the Korean negotiators. Mr. Habib welcomed these gentlemen to the negotiating table.

Invited Contractors

2. Taking up the Invited Contractors Article, Mr. Habib remarked that the U.S. negotiators had considered carefully the various proposals previously made by the Korean negotiators. Before making counter-proposals, he said he wished to emphasize certain aspects of ~~a fact of life regarding~~ the way in which the U.S. armed forces fulfill their mission. The complicated organizational framework of the U.S. armed forces, which is sometimes confusing to a non-member of those forces, is a fact of life worldwide. Invited contractors are a very important part of that framework and are not just ordinary businessmen, as the Korean negotiators have claimed. These contractors are in Korea solely for the purpose of carrying out certain specific functions for the armed forces. They are a part of the overall military organization. Their role and functions are much the same as the role and functions of the civilian component. The services, privileges, and amenities which they enjoy are no different from those enjoyed by any other arm of the military establishment. For these reasons, the revised draft proposed by the Korean negotiators does not meet the needs of the situation.

3. At the same time, Mr. Habib continued, certain aspects of the U.S. draft had presented difficulties for the Korean negotiators. He recalled discussion of this article at the 22nd negotiating meeting and read the following paragraphs from the Agreed Joint Summary of that meeting:

> "9. Mr. Hwang reiterated the view of the Korean side that inasmuch as the SOFA would be an agreement between the United States Government and the ROK Government, this article should cover only United States corporations and residents of the United States. Although quite willing to extend the suggested privileges and immuni-

0308

"ties to such corprations and residents, the ROK Government would find it difficult to extend the same treatment to third-country nationls. He said if the U.S. side would agree to the ROK position, the Korean side was prepared to consider favorably the inclusion of dependents or residents of the United States under the provisions of this article.

"10. ..... Mr. Hwang remarked that the ROK draft was similar to the provisions of the SOFA with Japan, which made no mention of third-country nationals. He said if the U.S. side would accept the Korean side's language regarding this point, the Korean side would accept the U.S. side's language regarding dependents and 'other armed forces in Korea under the Unified Command'...."

4. Mr. Habib stated that he had read the above paragraphs into the record of this discussion for a special purpose. The U.S. negotiators had taken into account the Korean position as explained by Mr. Hwang and had tried to develop language which would meet it and still be in accord with the practical realities of the situation. The U.S. negotiators recognized that third-country nationals caused difficulties for the Korean negotiators. Therefore, the U.S. negotiators wished to propose some changes in the U.S. draft.

5. The first proposed change, Mr. Habib continued, was to insert in paragraph 1 following the word "employees" the words "who are ordinarily resident in the United States". He pointed out that this additional clause pertained only to "employees" and not to "persons, including corporations". This additional language would bar third-country national employees from the provisions of the SOFA, with the exception of those covered by a proposed Agreed Minute #2, which Mr. Habib thereupon tabled.

6. Mr. Habib pointed out that the proposed Agreed Minute #2 provided that any third-country national in the employment of the U.S. armed forces in Korea on the effective date of the Agreement will continue to enjoy whatever privileges he has enjoyed prior to that date, so long as he continues in the job which he holds on that date. Mr. Habib stated that this proposal took into account

0309

the concern of the Korean negotiators and at the same time was intended to serve as a transitional mechanism. The U.S. armed forces, he pointed out, have already begun a program of replacing third-country nationals with trained Koreans. This program will gradually [so] replace all of the third-country nationals but it would not be equitable to try to do this all at once.

7. Mr. Habib then tabled paragraph 8 of the Invited Contractors Article, saying that this paragraph had been held in abeyance until after the tabling of the draft of the Criminal Jurisdiction Article. He stated that this paragraph was self-explanatory.

8. Mr. Habib remarked that each side has now tabled drafts of all of the substantive articles of the Agreement. This constituted a milestone in the negotiations in which all could take satisfaction. He said the articles dealing with ratification and duration of the Agreement could be discussed after agreement had been reached on the substantive articles.

9. Mr. Chang thanked Mr. Habib for his explanation of the revisions proposed by the U.S. negotiators. He remarked that there was a big difference between these proposed changes and the revised draft which the Korean negotiators had tabled. He said the Korean negotiators would take the U.S. proposals under consideration and would comment on them at a subsequent meeting.

10. Mr. Chang said he wished to comment on the revised draft proposed by the Korean negotiators, who believed that the status of invited contractors was different from the status of civilian employees and dependents. The Korean negotiators understood the contributions made by the contractors and the importance of their work worldwide. Therefore, the ROK Government was prepared to give them some privileges not ordinarily accorded aliens. Mr. Chang said that the Korean negotiators would study the record to see whether their present position was different from the position previously taken by them, as the alleged. He said the fundamental

0310

objective of the Korean negotiators in proposing a revised draft had been to try to present language which took into account the concern of the U.S. negotiators. The Korean negotiators believed their revised draft constituted a great concession on their part.

11. Regarding the proposals just made by the U.S. negotiators, Mr. Chang said the Korean negotiators would like to ask a few questions. Mr. Habib had indicated that the proposed additional clause in paragraph 1 would modify only "employees". Did this mean that corporations could be third-country national corporations, under the terms of the U.S. draft as revised? Mr. Habib replied that this was a correct interpretation. He pointed out that there might be occasions when it would be necessary for the U.S. armed forces to invite a contractor from a third country to come to Korea to do a special job. However, the employees of such a contractor would have to be ordinarily resident in the United States in order to be covered by the provisions of this article.

12. Mr. Chang said the Korean negotiators welcomed Mr. Habib's explanation of the intention of the U.S. armed forces to replace third-country nationals. Mr. Habib reiterated that this program was already under way. Mr. Chang then asked if it was the intention of the U.S. armed forces to introduce additional third-country nationals after the SOFA went into effect, and if so, what privileges did the U.S. armed forces intend them to have? Mr. Habib replied that there was no intention to bring in any third-country nationals after the Agreement went into force, but if any were brought in, they would have no privileges under the terms of the U.S. draft article.

Security Measures

13. Turning to the article dealing with security measures, Mr. Habib recalled that each side had tabled a draft and explained its position on what the U.S. negotiators considered to [illegible] between the two drafts. The

0311

Korean negotiators had then urged that further discussion of this article be postponed until after the Invited Contractors Article had been tabled and discussed. The latter article had now been discussed and the U.S. negotiators presumed that the Korean negotiators now wished to make their views known regarding the Security Measures Article.

14. Mr. Chang replied that the position of the Korean negotiators regarding this article had not changed. He suggested that since discussion of the Invited Contractors Article had not yet been completed, discussion of the Security Measures Article be postponed.

15. Mr. Habib stated that the U.S. negotiators had no objection to such a postponement. However, they believed this to be an article expressing general intent. No matter what final wording was ultimately agreed upon for the Invited Contractors Article, it would have no effect on the wording of this article. In making additions to the language of the SOFA with Japan, the U.S. negotiators were attempting to improve upon the latter agreement. Invited contractors should be mentioned specifically in this article because of the provision in the Invited Contractors Article which stated that specific provisions of the SOFA would not apply to the contractors unless the pertinent articles specifically mentioned them. The U.S. negotiators believed this article to be non-controversial, since it calls for cooperation and the taking of necessary measures. There is no substantive difference between the positions of the two sides and the U.S. negotiators would like to reach agreement and get this article out of the way.

16. Mr. Chang replied that the reference in the first sentence of this article to contractors and employees should be deleted. He said that the security of such persons would be fully protected by existing Korean laws and regulations. He further stated that the Korean negotiators could not accept the phrase "of the persons referred to in this paragraph, and their property" in the second sentence of the U.S. draft. He said the ROK Government was

0312

seek legislation, if needed, for protection of
prepared to ~~protect~~ property belonging to the U.S. Government but not of property belonging to private individuals.

17. In response to Mr. Habib's question whether the ROK Government was prepared to protect only official property, Mr. Chang replied in the affirmative, adding that existing Korean laws and regulations provided adequate protection for private property. Mr. Habib stated that the U.S. negotiators understood the Korean position and would take it under consideration.

18. Mr. Chang stated that the Korean negotiators found the reference to the Criminal Jurisdiction Article in Paragraph 8 of the U.S. draft of the Invited Contractors Article, which the U.S. negotiators had just tabled, to be unacceptable. Similarly, they found the reference to the Criminal Jurisdiction Article in the last sentence of the U.S. draft of the Security Measures Article to be also unacceptable.

19. Mr. Habib explained that this reference was necessary in order to remove any possibility of this article infringing upon the Criminal Jurisdiction Article, particularly with regard to inter se offenses. He said that if this reference were not included, the ROK Government, under the terms of the Security Measures Article, might have a claim to jurisdiction over a member of the U.S. armed forces who had committed an offense involving destruction of the equipment or property of the U.S. Government. He pointed out that it was necessary to make the text of this article consistent with the text of the Criminal Jurisdiction Article and that this would be accomplished by the inclusion of the phrase in question, regardless of the final agreed text of the Criminal Jurisdiction Article.

20. Mr. Chang stated that the Korean negotiators had not fully understood the import of the phrase but they still believed that it should be deleted from the article. Mr. Habib urged the Korean negotiators to study the question from a legal standpoint. He pointed out that the phrase modifies the entire sentence, not just the immediately following clause. He suggested that each side consider the other's position and be ready to discuss this article again at a subsequent

0313

meeting.

21. At this point it was agreed to adjourn the meeting. The next meeting was scheduled for February 28 at 2:00 p.m.

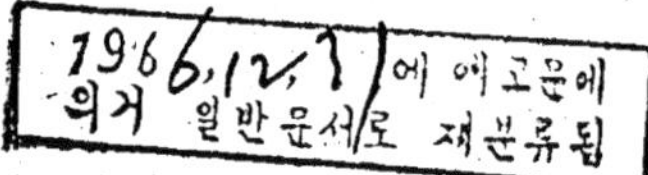


0314

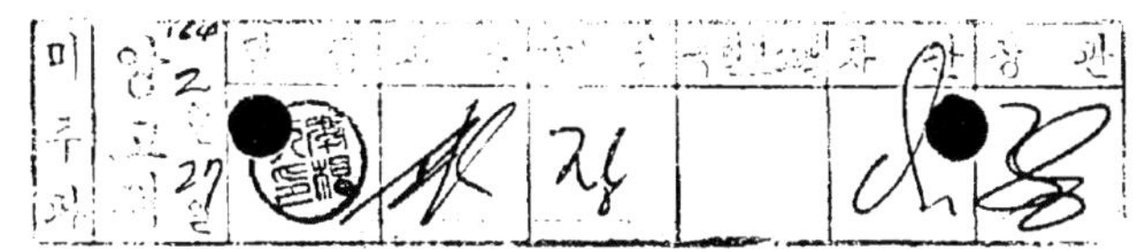

JOINT SUMMARY RECORD OF THE 43RD SESSION

1. Time and Place: 2:00-3:45 P.M. February 20, 1964 at the Foreign Ministry's Conference Room

2. Attendants:

ROK Side:

| | |
|---|---|
| Mr. Chang, Sang Moon | Director<br>European and American Affairs Bureau |
| Mr. Koo, Chong Whay | Chief, American Section<br>Ministry of Foreign Affairs |
| Mr. Lee, Chai Sup | Staff Officer<br>Customs Bureau<br>Ministry of Finance |
| Mr. Ham Chung Ho | Prosecutor<br>Ministry of Justice |
| Col. Kim, Won Kil | Chief, Ministry Affairs Section<br>Ministry of National Defense |
| Mr. Oh, Jae Hee | Chief, Treaty Section<br>Ministry of Foreign Affairs |
| Mr. Kang, Suk Jae (Rapporteur and Interpreter) | 2nd Secretary<br>Ministry of Foreign Affairs |
| Mr. Chung, Woo Young | 3rd Secretary<br>Ministry of Foreign Affairs |
| Mr. Lee, Chung Bin | 3rd Secretary<br>Ministry of Foreign Affairs |
| Mr. Lee, Keun Pal | 3rd Secretary<br>Ministry of Foreign Affairs |
| Mr. Kim, Nai Sung | Staff Officer<br>Europe Section<br>Ministry of Foreign Affairs |

U.S. Side:

| | |
|---|---|
| Mr. Philip C. Habib | Counselor<br>American Embassy |
| Brig. Gen. G. G. O'Connor | Deputy Chief of Staff<br>8th U.S. Army |
| Col. Howard Smigelow | Deputy Chief of Staff<br>8th U.S. Army |

0315

| | |
|---|---|
| Col. L. J. Fuller | Staff Judge Advocate<br>United Nations Command |
| Col. Kenneth C. Crawford | Staff Judge Advocates Office<br>8th U.S. Army |
| Capt. John Wayne | Assistant Chief of Staff<br>USN/K |
| Mr. Benjamin A. Fleck<br>(Rapporteur and<br>Press Officer) | First Secretary<br>American Embassy |
| Mr. James Sartorius | 2nd Secretary<br>American Embassy |
| Mr. Robert A. Lewis | 2nd Secretary and Consul<br>American Embassy |
| Mr. Robert A. Kinney | J-5<br>8th U.S. Army |
| Maj. Robert D. Peckham | Staff Officer, JAG<br>8th U.S. Army |
| Mr. O. C. Reed | Director<br>Office of Civil Personnel<br>8th U.S. Army |
| Mr. Kenneth Campen | Interpreter |
| Mr. Jurio Hernandez | Labor Adviser<br>8th U.S. Army |

1. Mr. Chang opened the meeting by introducing Mr. Yi Chae-sup of the Ministry of Finance, substituting for Mr. Sin Kwan-sup; Mr. Ham Chung-ho of the Ministry of Justice; Mr. Kim Nai-sung of the Foreign Ministry; and Mr. Chung U-young, who would serve from now on as interpreter for the Korean negotiators. Mr. Habib welcomed these gentlemen to the negotiating table.

Invited Contractors

2. Taking up the Invited Contractors Article, Mr. Habib remarked that the U.S. negotiators had considered carefully the various proposals previously made by the Korean negotiators. Before making counter-proposals, he said he wished to emphasize certain aspects of the way in which the U.S. armed forces fulfill their mission. The complicated organizational framework of the U.S. armed

0316

forces, which is sometimes confusing to a non-member of those forces, is a fact of life worldwide. Invited contractors are a very important part of that framework and are not just ordinary businessmen, as the Korean negotiators have claimed. These contractors are in Korea solely for the purpose of carrying out certain specific functions for the armed forces. They are a part of the overall military organization. Their role and functions are much the same as the role and functions of the civilian component. The services, privileges, and immunities which they enjoy are no different from those enjoyed by any other army of the military establishment. For these reasons, the revised draft proposed by the Korean negotiators does not meet the needs of the situation.

3. At the same time, Mr. Habib continued, certain aspects of the U.S. draft had presented difficulties for the Korean negotiators. He recalled discussion of this article at the 22nd negotiating meeting and read the following paragraphs from the Agreed Joint Summary of that meeting:

> "9. Mr. Hwang reiterated the view of the Korean side that inasmuch as the SOFA would be an agreement between the United States Government and the ROK Government, this article should cover only United States corporations and residents of the United States. Although quite willing to extend the suggested privileges and immunities to such corporations and residents, the ROK Government would find it difficult to extend the same treatment to third-country nationals. He said if the U.S. side would agree to the ROK position, the Korean side was prepared to consider favorably the inclusion of dependents or residents of the United States under the provisions of this article.
>
> "10. .... Mr. Hwang remarked that the ROK draft was similar to the provisions of the SOFA with Japan, which made no mention of third-country nationals. He said if the U.S. side would accept the Korean side's language regarding this point, the Korean side would accept the U.S. side's language regarding dependents and 'other armed forces in Korea under the Unified Command'... "

0317

4. Mr. Habib stated that he had read the above paragraphs into the record of this discussion for a special purpose. The U.S. negotiators had taken into account the Korean position as explained by Mr. Hwang and had tried to develop language which would meet it and still be in accord with the practical realities of the situation. The U.S. negotiators recognized that third-country nationals caused difficulties for the Korean negotiators. Therefore, the U.S. negotiators wished to propose some changes in the U.S. draft.

5. The first proposed change, Mr. Habib continued, was to insert in paragraph 1 following the word "employees" the words "who are ordinarily resident in the United States". He pointed out that this additional clause pertained only to "employees" and not to "persons, including corporations". This additional language would bar third-country national employees from the provisions of the SOFA, with the exception of those covered by a proposed Agreed Minute #2, which Mr. Habib thereupon tabled.

6. Mr. Habib pointed out that the proposed Agreed Minute #2 provided that any third-country national in the employment of the U.S. armed forces in Korea on the effective date of the Agreement will continue to enjoy whatever privileges he has enjoyed prior to that date, so long as he continues in the job which he holds on that date. Mr. Habib stated that this proposal took into account the concern of the Korean negotiators and at the same time was intended to serve as a transitional mechanism. The U.S. armed forces, he pointed out, have already begun a program of replacing third-country

0318

nationals with trained Koreans. This program will grandually so replace all of the third-country nationals but it would not be equitable to try to do this all at once.

7. Mr. Habib then tabled paragraph 8 of the Invited Contractors Article, saying that this paragraph had been held in abeyance until after the tabling of the draft of the Criminal Jurisdiction Article. He stated that this paragraph was self-explanatory.

8. Mr. Habib remarked that each side has now tabled drafts of all of the substantive articles of the Agreement. This constituted a milestone in the negotiations in which all could take satisfaction. He said the articles dealing with ratification and duration of the Agreement could be discussed after agreement had been reached on the substantive articles.

9. Mr. Chang thanked Mr. Habib for his explanation of the revisions proposed by the U.S. negotiators. He remarked that there was a big difference between these proposed changes and the revised draft which the Korean negotiators had tabled. He said the Korean negotiators would take the U.S. proposals under consideration and would comment on them at a subsequent meeting.

10. Mr. Chang said he wished to comment on the revised draft proposed by the Korean negotiators, who believed that the status of invited contractors was different from the status of civilian employees and dependents. He stated it was not correct to believe that the Korean negotiators had considered them as just ordinary aliens. The Korean negotiators understood the contributions made by the contractors and the importance of their work worldwide. Therefore, the ROK Government was prepared

0319

to give them some privileges not ordinarily accorded aliens. Mr. Chang said that the Korean negotiators would study the record to see whether their present position was different from the position previously taken by them, as the U.S. negotiators had alleged. He said the fundamental objective of the Korean negotiators in proposing a revised draft had been to try to present language which took into account the concern of the U.S. negotiators. The Korean negotiators believed their revised draft constituted a great concession on their part.

11. Regarding the proposals just made by the U.S. negotiators, Mr. Chang said the Korean negotiators would like to ask a few questions. Mr. Habib had indicated that the proposed additional clause in paragraph 1 would modify only "employees". Did this mean that corporations could be third-country national corporations, under the terms of the U.S. draft as revised? Mr. Habib replied that this was a correct interpretation. He pointed out that there might be occasions when it would be necessary for the U.S. armed forces to invite a contractor from a third country to come to Korea to do a special job. However, the employees of such a contractor would have to be ordinarily resident in the United States in order to be covered by the provisions of this article.

12. Mr. Chang said the Korean negotiators welcomed Mr. Habib's explanation of the intention of the U.S. armed forces to replace third-country nationals. Mr. Habib reiterated that this program was already under way. Mr. Chang then asked if it was the intention of the U.S.

0320

armed forces to introduce additional third-country nationals after the SOFA went into effect, and if so, what privileges did the U.S. armed forces intend them to have? Mr. Habib replied that there was no intention to bring in any third-country nationals after the Agreement went into force, but if any were brought in, they would have no privileges under the terms of the U.S. draft article.

Security Measures

13. Turning to the article dealing with security measures, Mr. Habib recalled that each side had tabled a draft and explained its position on what the U.S. negotiators considered to be minor, non-substantive differences between the two drafts. The Korean negotiators had then urged that further discussion of this article be post-poned until after the Invited Contractors Article had been tabled and discussed. The latter article had now been discussed and the U.S. negotiators presumed that the Korean negotiators now wished to make their views known regarding the Security Measures Article.

14. Mr. Chang replied that the position of the Korean negotiators regarding this article had not changed. He suggested that since discussion of the Invited Contractors Article had not yet been completed, discussion of the Security Measures Article be postponed.

15. Mr. Habib stated that the U.S. negotiators had no objection to such a postponement. However, they believed this to be an article expressing general intent. No matter what final wording was ultimately agreed upon for the Invited Contractors Article, it would have no effect on the

0321

wording of this article. In making additions to the language of the SOFA with Japan, the U.S. negotiators were attempting to improve upon the latter agreement. Invited contractors should be mentioned specifically in this article because of the provision in the Invited Contractors Article which stated that specific provisions of the SOFA would not apply to the contractors unless the pertinent articles specifically mentioned them. The U.S. negotiators believed this article to be non-controversial, since it calls for cooperation and the taking of necessary measures. There is no substantive difference between the positions of the two sides and the U.S. negotiators would like to reach agreement and get this article out of the way.

16. Mr. Chang replied that the reference in the first sentence of this article to contractors and employees should be deleted. He said that the security of such persons would be fully protected by existing Korean laws and regulations. He further stated that the Korean negotiators could not accept the phrase "of the persons referred to in this paragraph, and their property" in the second sentence of the U.S. draft. He said the ROK Government was prepared to seek legislation if needed, for protection of property belonging to the U.S. Government but not of property belonging to private individuals.

17. In response to Mr. Habib's question whether the ROK Government was prepared to protect only official property, Mr. Chang replied in the affirmative, adding that existing Korean laws and regulations provided adequate protection for private property. Mr. Habib stated that the U.S. negotiators understood the Korean position and would take it under consideration.

0322

18. Mr. Chang stated that the Korean negotiators found the reference to the Criminal Jurisdiction Article in Paragraph 8 of the U.S. draft of the Invited Contractors Article, which the U.S. negotiators had just tabled, to be unacceptable. Similarly, they found the reference to the Criminal Jurisdiction Article in the last sentence of the U.S. draft of the Security Measures Article to be also unacceptable.

19. Mr. Habib explained that this reference was necessary in order to remove any possibility of this article infringing upon the Criminal Jurisdiction Article, particularly with regard to inter se offenses. He said that if this reference were not included, the ROK Government, under the terms of the Security Measures Article, might have a claim to jurisdiction over a member of the U.S. armed forces who had committed an offense involving destruction of the equipment or property of the U.S. Government. He pointed out that it was necessary to make the text of this article consistent with the text of the Criminal Jurisdiction Article and that this would be accomplished by the inclusion of the phrase in question, regardless of the final agreed text of the Criminal Jurisdiction Article.

20. Mr. Chang stated that the Korean negotiators had not fully understood the import of the phrase but they still believed that it should be deleted from the article. Mr. Habib urged the Korean negotiators to study the question from a legal standpoint. He pointed out that the phrase modifies the entire sentence, not just the immediately following clause. He suggested that each side consider

0323

the other's position and be ready to discuss this article again at a subsequent meeting.

21. At this point it was agreed to adjourn the meeting. The next meeting was scheduled for February 28 at 2:00 p.m.



0324

7. 제44차 회의, 2.28

0325

44차 회의 예비회담

| 성 명 | 부처 및 직위 | 전화번호 |
| --- | --- | --- |
| ~~국방부~~ | | |
| 朴商[illegible] | 국방부 법제위원장 (陸軍大領) | 4-6246 |
| 金[illegible] | 국방부 법무과 (법무관보) 겸 [illegible] | 4-62[illegible] |

0326

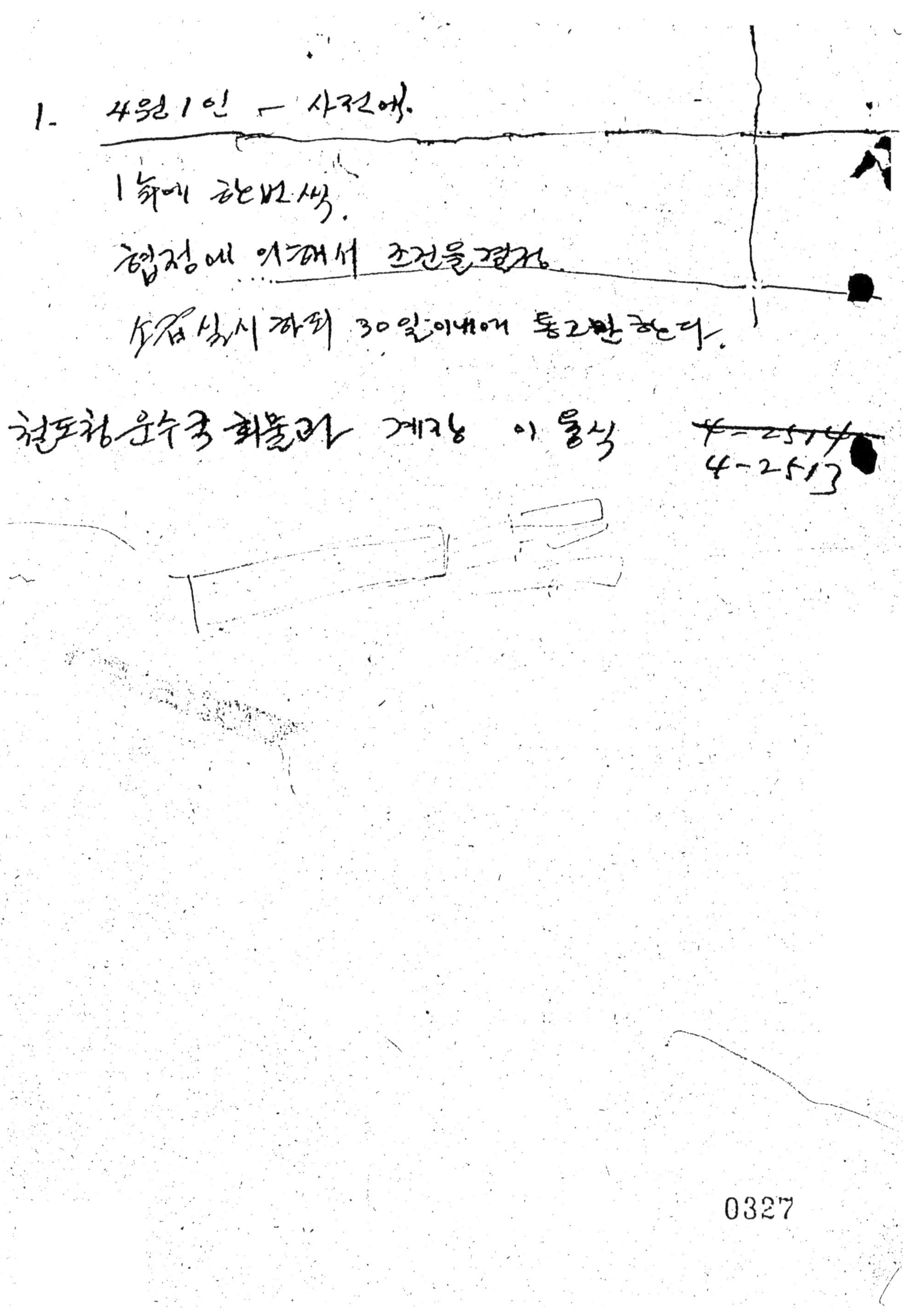

1. 4월1일 — 사전에.

1年에 한번씩.

협정에 의해서 조건을 결정.

소집 실시하되 30일 이내에 통고만 한다.

철도청 운수국 화물과 계장 이용식 ~~4-2514~~ 4-2513

0327

# 기 안 용 지

| 자체 통제 | | 기안처 | 미주과 이근팔 | 전화번호 | 근거서류접수일자 |
|---|---|---|---|---|---|
| | 과장 | 국장 | 차관 | 장관 | | |
| 관계관 서명 | | | | | | |
| 기안 년월일 | 1964. 2. 27. | 시행 년월일 | | 보존 년한 | | 정서기장 |
| 분류 기호 | 외구미722.2 | 전체 통제 | | 종결 | | |
| 경유 수신 참조 | 건의 | | | 발신 | | |
| 제목 | 제 44 차 주둔군지위협정 체결교섭회의에 임할 우리측 입장 | | | | | |

2 월 28 일 개최될 제 44 차 주둔군지위협정 체결을 위한 한.미간 교섭회의에서는 형사재판관할권, 공유물 및 용역에 관한 조항을 토의하도록 예정하고 있는바 이에 대하여 우리측 교섭실무자는 2 월 26 일 및 동 27 일 회합을 갖고 제 44 차 회의에서 취할 태도를 별첨과 같이 결정하였아오니 재가하여 주시기 바랍니다.

유 첨: 제 44 차 주둔군지위협정 체결교섭회의에 임할 우리측 태도. 끝

승인서식 1-1-3 (11 00900-03) (195mm×265mm16절지)

1966, 12, 31, 에 예고문에 의거 일반문서로 재분류됨

0328

1. 형사재판관할권

가. 미측이 제시한 형사재판관할권에 관한 초안에 대한 제안설명을 청취한 후,

나. 우리측은 미측초안을 검토한 바에 따라 우리측 입장을 다음과 같이 강조한다.

(1) 미측은 동 초안에서 우리 나라가 접수국으로서 의당히 행사하여야 할 형사재판관할권의 적용 범위를 인적 지역적 및 시간적으로 대폭 제한하였을 뿐만 아니라 범인의 체포 수사 재판 행형등 제반 절차에 걸쳐 우리 나라의 주권 행사를 배제 또는 포기할 것을 요구하였으며

(2) 우리측은 한.미양국이 1950년 7월 12일 비상사태 하에서 각서형식으로 교환한 대전협정의 적용을 지양하려는데 반하여 동 협정과 사실상 별 차의없는 초안을 제시하여

(3) 주둔군지위협정을 조속히 체결함으로서 양국간의 현안문제를 원만하게 해결하여 우호관계를 증진시키려는 우리 나라 입장과 거리가 멀어 실망을 금할 수 없는 초안을 제시하였음을 지적하고

(4) 미측이 본초안을 철회하고 우리측이 만족할 만한 새로운 초안을 제시함으로서 성실성있는 태도를 표명할 것을 촉구한다.

다. 우리측 초안에 대한 합의의사록(안)을 미측에 수교한다.

2. 공익물 및 용역

가. 제 39 차 실무자교섭회의에서 우리측이 제시한 바 있는 본문 및 합의의사록의 수정초안에 대한 미측 입장을 청취하고

나. 만일 대안이 나오면 검토 후 다음 회의에서 우리측 견해를 밝히기로 한다.



0329

## SOFA NEGOTIATION

Agenda for the 44th Session

14:00 Feb. 28, 1964

1. Continuation of Discussions on:

    a. Criminal Jurisdiction Article

    b. Utilities and Services Article

2. Other Business

3. Agenda and Date of the Next Meeting

4. Press Release

0330

It is the duty of members of the United States Armed Forces, the civilian component, the persons who are present in the Republic of Korea pursuant to Article ______, and their dependents, to respect the law of Korea and to abstain from any activity inconsistent with the spirit of this Agreement, and, in particular, from any political activity in Korea.

0331

ARTICLE

The United States may enroll in its reserve forces and train, in Korea, eligible United States citizens who are in the Republic of Korea.

0332

## Meteorological Services

## Article ___

The Government of Korea undertakes to furnish the United States armed forces with the following meteorological services in accordance with arrangements between the appropriate authorities of the two Governments:

(a) Meteorological observations from land and ocean areas including observations from ships;

(b) Climatological information including periodic summaries and historical data wherever available;

(c) Telecommunications service to disseminate meteorological information;

(d) Seismographic data.

0333

UTILITIES AND SERVICES

Proposed new third and fourth sentences, paragraph 3 (a)

Article "D"

The use of utilities and services as provided herein shall not prejudice the right of the United States to operate military transportation, communication, power and such other utilities and services deemed necessary for the operations of the United States armed forces. This right shall not be exercised in a manner inconsistent with the operation by the Government of the Republic of Korea of its utilities and services.

0334

A

우리 제1 1, 2, 3

ARTICLE

1, 2 項 (우리 草案)

1. (a) The United States is granted, under Article IV of the Mutual Defense Treaty, the use of facilities and areas in the Republic of Korea. Agreements as to specific facilities and areas shall be concluded by the two Governments through the Joint Committee provided for in Article ___ of this Agreement. "Facilities and Areas" include existing furnishings, equipment and fixtures, wherever located, used in the operation of such facilities and areas. (necessary)

(b) 3項 The facilities and areas of which the United States has the use at the effective date of this Agreement shall be considered as facilities and areas agreed upon between the two Governments in accordance with sub-paragraph (a) above.

O.K. 2. 6項 At the request of either Government, the Governments of the United States and the Republic of Korea shall review such arrangements and may agree that such facilities and areas or portions thereof shall be returned to the Republic of Korea or that additional facilities and areas may be provided.

3. 7項 The facilities and areas used by the United States shall be returned to the Republic of Korea under such conditions as may be agreed through the Joint Committee whenever they are no longer needed for the purposes of this Agreement and the United States agrees to keep the needs for facilities and areas under continual observation with a view toward such return.

1959 survey Oct 31 will be completed

0335

4. (a) When facilities and areas are temporarily not being used and the Government of the Republic of Korea is so advised, the Government of the Republic of Korea may make, or permit Korean nationals to make, interim use of such facilities and areas provided that it is agreed between the two Governments through the Joint Committee that such use would not be harmful to the purposes for which the facilities and areas are normally used by the United States armed forces.

(b) With respect to facilities and areas which are to be used by United States armed forces for limited periods of time, the Joint Committee shall specify in the agreements covering such facilities and areas the extent to which the provisions of this Agreement shall apply.

0336

## Facilities and Areas

### Article ____

3. (a) The United States armed forces shall have the use of all utilities and services, whether publicly or privately owned, which are controlled or regulated by the Government of the Republic of Korea or political subdivisions thereof. The term "utilities and services" shall include, but not be limited to, transportation and communications facilities and systems, electricity, gas, water, steam, heat, light, power, however produced, and sewage disposal. The use of utilities and services as provided herein shall not prejudice the right of the United States to operate military transportation, communication, power and such other services and facilities deemed necessary for the operations of the United States armed forces.

(b) The use of such utilities and services by the United States shall be in accordance with priorities, conditions, and rates or tariffs no less favorable than those accorded any other user, governmental or private. The Republic of Korea shall insure that, by reason of legislation or otherwise, there shall be no discrimination against the United States armed forces in the procurement of such utilities and services. Should the emergency operating needs of the United States armed forces so require, the Republic of Korea shall, upon notification thereof, take all measures to assure provision of utilities and services necessary to meet these needs.

0337

4. It is agreed that arrangements will be effected between the Governments of the United States and the Republic of Korea for accounting applicable to financial transactions arising out of this Agreement.

0338

Agreed Minutes to Article______

1. It is understood that any change in priority or increase in utility or service rates applicable to the United States armed forces shall be the subject of prior consultation in the Joint Committee.

2. Paragraph 3 of Article____ will not be construed as in any way abrogating the Utilities and Claims Settlement Agreement of December 18, 1958 which continues in full force and effect.

0339

Article II- Facilities and Areas(Grant of and Return)

I. .....

(b) The facilities and areas of which the United Statess armed fprces have have the use at the effectve date of this agreement together with those area and facilities which the United States armed forces gave returned to the Republic of Korea with the reserved right of re-entry, when these facilities and areas have been re-entered by U.S. forces, shall be considered as the facilities and areas agreed upon between the two Govefnments in accordance with wubparagraph (a) above. Records of facilities and areas of which the United States armed forces have the use or right of re-entry shall be maintained through the Joint Committee after this Agreement comes into force.

0340

B

ARTICLE

1. Within the facilities and areas, the United States may take all the measures necessary for their establishment, operation, safeguarding and control. In an emergency, measures necessary for their safeguarding and control may also be taken in the vicinity thereof. In order to provide access for the United States armed forces to the facilities and areas for their support, safeguarding and control, the Government of the Republic of Korea shall, at the request of the United States armed forces and upon consultation between the two Governments through the Joint Committee, take necessary measures within the scope of applicable laws and regulations over land, territorial waters and airspace adjacent to, or in the vicinities of the facilities and areas. The United States may also take necessary measures for such purposes upon consultation between the two Governments through the Joint Committee.

2. (a) The United States agrees not to take the measures referred to in paragraph 1 in such a manner as to interfere unnecessarily with navigation, aviation, communication, or land travel to or from or within the territories of the Republic of Korea.

(b) All questions relating to telecommunications, including radio frequencies for electromagnetic radiating devices, or like matters, shall continue to be resolved expeditiously in the utmost spirit of coordination and cooperation by arrangement between the designated military communications authorities of the two Governments.

(c) The Government of the Republic of Korea shall, within the scope of applicable laws, regulations and agreements, take all reasonable measures to avoid or eliminate interference with electromagnetic radiation sensitive devices, telecommunications devices, or other apparatus required by the United States armed forces.

0341

(12) 12次

3. Operations in the facilities and areas in use by the United States armed forces shall be carried on with due regard for the public safety.

0342

ARTICLE III - Facilities and Areas
(Security Measures In)

AGREED MINUTE

It is agreed that in the event of an emergency, the United States armed forces shall be authorized to take such measures in the vicinity of the areas and facilities as may be necessary to provide for their safeguarding and control.

0343

c

ARTICLE

13項

1. The United States is not obliged, when it returns facilities and areas to the Republic of Korea on the expiration of this Agreement or at an earlier date, to restore the facilities and areas to the condition in which they were at the time they became available to the United States armed forces, or to compensate the Republic of Korea in lieu of such restoration.

14項

2. All removable facilities erected or constructed by or on behalf of the United States at its expense and all equipment, materials and supplies brought into or procured in the Republic of Korea by or on behalf of the United States in connection with the construction, development, operation, maintenance, safeguarding and control of the facilities and areas will remain the property of the United States Government and may be removed from the Republic of Korea.

3. The foregoing provisions shall not apply to any construction which the Government of the United States may undertake under special arrangements with the Government of the Republic of Korea.

materials and supplies

0344

Feb. 28, 1964
Submitted
by U.S side

Agreed Minute #1

It is understood that any changes determined by the Korean authorities in priorities, conditions, and rates or tariffs, applicable to the United States armed forces shall be the subject of consultation in the Joint Committee prior to their effective date.

0345

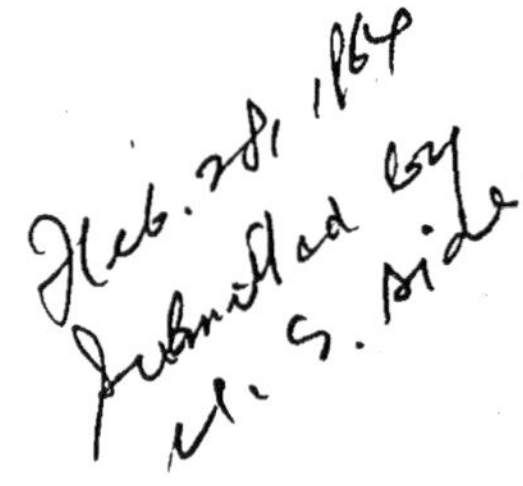

Agreed Minute #3

In an emergency the Republic of Korea agrees to take appropriate measures to assure provision of utilities and services necessary to meet the needs of the United States armed forces.

0343

Minutes:

This article will not be construed as in any way abrogating the Utilities and Claims Settlement Agreement of December 18, 1958 which continues in full force and effect. Existing arrangements under that Agreement for the use of utilities and services by the United States armed forces and the payment therefor continue in effect. Changes in priorities or rates applicable to the United States armed forces shall be the subject of prior consultation in the Joint Committee.

0347

Agreed Minutes to Article_____

1. It is understood that any change in priority or increase in utility or service rates applicable to the United States armed forces shall be the subject of prior consultation in the Joint Committee.

2. Paragraph 3 of Article____ will not be construed as in any way abrogating the Utilities and Claims Settlement Agreement of December 18, 1958 which continues in full force and effect.

0348

Article II - Facilities and Areas (Grant of and Return)

1. .....

(b) The facilities and areas of which the United States armed forces have the use at the effective date of this agreement together with those areas and facilities which the United States armed forces have returned to the Republic of Korea with the reserved right of re-entry, when these facilities and areas have been re-entered by U.S. forces, shall be considered as the facilities and areas agreed upon between the two Governments in accordance with subparagraph (a) above. Records of facilities and areas of which the United States armed forces have the use or right of re-entry shall be maintained through the Joint Committee after this Agreement comes into force.

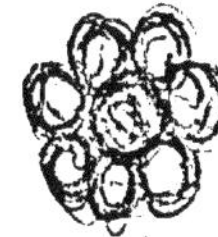

0349

ARTICLE III-Facilities and Areas

(Security Measures In)

AGREED MINUTE

It is agreed that in the event of an emergency, the United States armed forces shall be authorized to take such measures in the vicinity of the areas and facilities as may necessary to provide for their safeguarding and control.

0350

c

ARTICLE

1. The United States is not obliged, when it returns facilities and areas to the Republic of Korea on the expiration of this Agreement or at an earlier date, to restore the facilities and areas to the condition in which they were at the time they became available to the United States armed forces, or to compensate the Republic of Korea in lieu of such restoration.

2. All removable facilities erected or constructed by or on behalf of the United States at its expense and all equipment, materials and supplies brought into or procured in the Republic of Korea by or on behalf of the United States in connection with the construction, development, operation, maintenance, safeguarding and control of the facilities and areas will remain the property of the United States Government and may be removed from the Republic of Korea.

3. The foregoing provisions shall not apply to any construction which the Government of the United States may undertake under special arrangements with the Government of the Republic of Korea.

0351

AREAS AND FACILITIES ARTICLE PROPOSED ADDITIONAL PARAGRAPH TO AREAS AND FACILITIES ARTICLE PERTAINING TO RETURN OF FACILITIES AND AREAS

The Republic of Korea is not obligated to compensate the United States for improvements made in United States facilities and areas or for the buildings, structures, supplies or any other materials remaining thereon upon the returnof the facilities and areas.

0352

D

## ARTICLE

1. It is agreed that the United States will bear for the duration of the Agreement without cost to the Republic of Korea all expenditures incident to the maintenance of the United States armed forces in the Republic of Korea, except those to be borne by the Republic of Korea as provided in paragraph 2.

2. It is agreed that the Republic of Korea will furnish for the duration of this Agreement without cost to the United States and make compensation where appropriate to the owners and suppliers thereof all facilities and areas and rights of way, including facilities and areas jointly used such as those at airfields and ports as provided in Articles II and III. The Government of the Republic of Korea assures the use of such facilities and areas to the United States Government and will hold the United States Government as well as its agencies and employees harmless from any third party claims which may be advanced in connection with such use.

3. /Use of public utilities and services to be inserted later./

0353

ARTICLE

1. All civil and military air traffic control shall be developed in close coordination and shall be integrated to the extent necessary for the operation of this Agreement. Procedures, and any subsequent changes thereto, necessary to effect this coordination and integration will be established by arrangement between the appropriate authorities of the two Governments.

2. The United States is authorized to establish, construct and maintain aids to navigation for vessels and aircraft, both visual and electronic as required, throughout the Republic of Korea and in the territorial waters thereof. Such navigation aids shall conform generally to the system in use in Korea. The United States and Korean authorities which have established navigation aids shall duly notify each other of their positions and characteristics and shall give advance notification where practicable before making any changes in them or establishing additional navigation aids.

0354

NAVIGATIONAL AIDS ARTICLE

Agreed Minute:

"Installation by the United States Armed Forces of permanent navigational aids for vessels and aircraft outside of areas and facilities in use by the United States Armed Forces will be effected in accordance with the procedures established under paragraph I of Article      ."

0355

ARTICLE

1. United States and foreign vessels and aircraft operated by, for, or under the control of the United States for official purposes shall be accorded access to any port or airport of Korea free from toll or landing charges. When cargo or passengers not accorded the exemptions of this Agreement are carried on such vessels and aircraft, notification shall be given to the appropriate Korean authorities, and their entry into and departure from Korea shall be according to the laws and regulations of Korea.

2. The vessels and aircraft mentioned in paragraph 1, United States Government-owned vehicles including armor, and members of the United States armed forces, the civilian component, and their dependents shall be accorded access to and movement between facilities and areas in use by the United States armed forces and between such facilities and areas and the ports or airports of Korea. Such access to and movement between facilities and areas by United States military vehicles shall be free from toll and other charges.

3. When the vessels mentioned in paragraph 1 enter Korean ports, appropriate notification shall, under normal conditions, be made to the proper Korean authorities. Such vessels shall have freedom from compulsory pilotage, but if a pilot is taken pilotage shall be paid for at appropriate rates.

0356

## AGREED MINUTES TO ARTICLE

1. "United States and foreign vessels... operated by, for, or under the control of the United States for official purposes" mean United States public vessels and chartered vessels (bare boat charter, voyage charter and time charter). Space charter is not included. Commercial cargo and private passengers are carried by them only in exceptional cases.

2. The Korean ports mentioned herein will ordinarily mean "open ports".

3. An exception from making the "appropriate notification" referred to in paragraph 3 will apply only in unusual cases where such is required for security of the United States armed forces or similar reasons.

4. The laws and regulations of Korea will be applicable except as specifically provided otherwise in this Article.

0357

ARTICLE (Customs)

1. Save as provided in this Agreement, members of the United Satas armed forces, the civilian component, and their dependents shall be subject to the laws and regulations administere red by the customs authorities of the Republic of Korea.

2. All materials, supplies and equipment imported by the United States armed forces, including their authorized procurement agencies and their non-appropriated fund organizations provided for in Article , for the official use of the United States armed forces or for the use of the members of the United States armed forces, the civilian component, and their dependents, and materials, suplies and equipment which are to be used exclusive ely by the United States armed forces or are ultimately to be incorporated into articles or facilities used by such forces, shall be permitted entry into the Republic of Korea; such entry shall be free from customs duties and other such charges. Appropriated certification shall be made that such materials, supplies and equipment are being imported by the United States armed forces, (inclding their authrized procurement agencies and their non-appropriated fund organizations provided for in Article) , or, in the case of materials, supplies and equipment to be used exclusively by the United States armed forces or ultimately

0358

to be incorporated into articles or facilities used by such forces, that delivery thereof is to be taken by the United States armed forces for the purposes specified above. The exemptions provided in this paragraph shall extend to materials, and equipment imported by the United States armed forces for the use of other armed forces in Korea which receive logistical support from the UnitedStates armed forces.

3. Property consigned to and for the personal use of members of the United States armed forces, the civilian component, and their dependents, shall be subject to customs duties and other such charges, except that no duties or charges shall be paid with respect to:

(a) Furniture, household goods, and personal effects for their private use imported by the members of the United States armed forces or civilian component when they first arrive to serve in the Republic of Korea or by their dependents when they first arrive for reunion with members of such forces or civilian component;

(b) Vehicles and parts imported by members of the United States armed forces or civilian component for the private use of themselves or their dependents;

(c) Reasonable quantities of personal effects and household goods of a type which would ordinarily be purchased in the United

0359

5 (6). official documents under official seal and first class mail in United States military postal channels obviously containing not merchandise.

0360

States for the private use of members of the United States armed forces, civilian component, and their dependents, which are mailed into the Republic of Korea through United States military post offices.

4. The exemptions granted in paragraphs 2 and 3 shall apply only to cases of importation of goods and shall notbe interpreted as refunding customs duties and domestic excises collected by the customs authrities at the time of entry in cases of purchase of goods on which such duties and excises have already been collected.

5. Customs examination shall not be made in the following cases:

(a) Members of the United States armdd forces under orders entering or leaving the Rpublic ofKorea;

(b) Official documents under official seal and mail in United States military postal channels;

(c) Military cargo consigned to the United States armed forces, (including their authorized procurement agencies and their non-appropriated fund organizations provided for in Article)

6. Except as such disposal may be authorized by the United States and Korean authorities in accordance with mutually agreed conditions, goods imported into the Republic of Korea free

0361

of duty shall not be disposed of in the Republic of Korea to person ns not entitled to import such goods free of duty.

7. Goods imported into the Republic of Korea free from customs duties and other such charges pursuant to paragraphs 2 nd 3, may be re-exported free from customs duties and other such charges.

8. The United States armed forces, in cooperation with K Korean authorities, shall take such steps as are necessary to prevent abuse of privileges granted to the United States armed forces, members of such forces, the civilian component, and their dependents in accordance with this Article.

9. (a) In order to prevent offenses against laws and regulations administered by the customs authorities of the Government of the Republic of Korea, the Korean authorities and the United States armed forces shall assist each other in the conduct of inquiries and the collection of evidence.

(b) The United States armed forces shall render all assistance within their power to ensure that articles liable to seizure by, or on behalf of, the customs authorities of the Government of the Republic of Korea are handed to those authorities

(c) The United States armed forces shall render all assistance within their power to ensure the payment of duties, taxes, and penalties payable by members of such forces or of the civilian component, or their dependents.

0362

(d) Vehicles and articles belonging to the United States armed forces seized by the customs authorities of the Government of the Republic of Korea in connection with and offence against its customs or fiscal laws or regulations shall be handed over to the appropriate authorities of the forces concerned.

0363

# 기 안 용 지

| 자 체 통 제 | 외무사무관 손 일 봉 | 기안처 | 미 주 과 이 근 팔 | 전화번호 | 근거서류접수일자 |
|---|---|---|---|---|---|

| 과장 | 국장 | 차관 | 장관 |
|---|---|---|---|
| | | | |

| 관계관 서명 | |
|---|---|

| 기안년월일 | 1964. 3. 2. | 시행년월일 | | 보존년한 | | 정서 | 기장 |
|---|---|---|---|---|---|---|---|
| 분류기호 | 외구미 722.2 | 전체통제 | | | | | |

| 경유 수신 참조 | 대 통 령 (참조: 비서실장) 국 무 총 리 | 발 신 | 장 관 |
|---|---|---|---|

| 제 목 | 주둔군지위협정 체결을 위한 제 44 차 교섭회의 보고 |
|---|---|

1964. 2. 28. 하오 2 시 부터 동 4 시 까지 외무부장관 회의실에서 개최된 제 44 차 주둔군지위협정 체결 교섭회의에서 토의된 내용을 별첨과 같이 보고합니다.

유 첨: 제 44 차 교섭회의 보고서 1 부. 끝.

1966.12.31 에 예고문에 의거 일반문서로 재분류됨

승인서식 1-1-3 (11-00900-03) (195mm×265mm16절지)

0364

제 44 차

한미간 주둔군지위협정 체결교섭 실무자회의

보 고 서

1. 일 시: 1964 년 2 월 28 일 하오 2 시 부터 동 4 시 까지.

2. 장 소: 외무부장관 회의실

3. 토의사항:

가. 형사재판관할권

(1) 우리측은 미측이 제 42 차 회의에서 제시한 형사재판관할권에 관한 초안을 검토한 결과에 따라 미측초안이 우리측 주장과는 ~~상당한~~ 근본적이며 심원한 차의가 있음을 지적하고 앞으로 교섭함에 있어서 우리 정부나 국민이 납득할 수 있는 성실성있는 태도를 표명하여 주기를 촉구하였다.

(2) 미측은 미국회 및 행정부로 부터의 요망에 의하여 미측이 필요하다고 생각하는 입장을 표명한 것이며 한국에서는 독일에서와 같이 많은 미국군대가 주둔하고 있기 때문에 일본등 기타 국가와의 행정협정과는 상의한 문제가 고려되어야 할 것이다. 한국의 입장도 미국측 주장과는 상당한 거리가 있음은 마찬가지 이며 이러한 서로 상의한 입장은 앞으로 교섭에서 협의되어야 할 것이라고 미측의 태도를 밝히고 다음 회의에서 토의를 계속하기로 하였다.

나. 공익물 및 용역

(1) 우리측은 미군의 공익물 및 용역의 사용에 관한 3(a)항에서 "however produced "용어를 불필요한 것임으로 삭제할 것을 주장하였는데 미측은 한국측이 차별대우를 하지않을 것을 기록에 남기기로 하고 우리 주장을 수락하였다.

(2) 양측은 본 협정에 의한 금전거래의 청산에 관한 4 항은 협정 전반에 적용되는 것임으로 본조항에서 삭제하여 별개항목으로서 토의하는데 합의하였다.

0365

64-3-9 (2)
0365-1

(3) 양측은 기존협정의 효력 존속에 관한 합의의사록 2항에 우리측이 추가 삽입할 것을 주장한 " unless otherwise agreed by the two Governments "용어에 대하여 현재 별도로 합의할 의도가 없음을 밝히고 수락하였다.

(4) 합의의사록 1 항 및 3 항에 대하여서는 미측으로 부터 대안을 제시하였으며 우리측은 다음 기회에 태도를 표명하기로 하였다.

4. 기타 사항: 차기회의일자: 1964 년 3 월 6 일 하오 2 시 부터. 끝.



0365-2

64-3-30

64-3-9 (2)

미경.ㅂ 109-4-12

0366

4

February 28, 1964

1. Mr. Chang opened the meeting by extending the congratulations of the Korean negotiators to Brig. General Fuller, who had been promoted that very morning. Mr. Chang then introduced the following gentlemen: Mr. YUN Tu-sik, Director of the Prosecutor's ~~Office~~ Bureau, Ministry of Justice; Mr. CHUNG Tai-kyun, Chief of the Prosecutors' ~~Office~~ Section, Ministry of Justice; and Mr. YI Myung-hi, Prosecutor, from the same office. Mr. Habib welcomed these gentlemen to the negotiations.

<u>Criminal Jurisdiction</u>

2. Taking up the Criminal Jurisdiction Article, Mr. Chang stated that he wished to make some introductory remarks. He then made the following statement:

0367

We do not think it is necessary to emphasize the importance our people attach to the article dealing with criminal jurisdiction of the prospective Status of Forces Agreement now under negotiation between the two parties. However, I would like to reiterate that the successful and speedy conclusion of our present negotiations entirely depends upon how soon we can come to an agreement on this Article.

We have studied most carefully the draft tabled by the U.S. negotiators at the 42nd meeting. To our great disappointment, however, the Korean negotiators have found that fundamental differences are wide between the two sides' drafts on the subject matter.

Aside from various differences of major or minor nature, we believe that there is a fundamental difference in the approach of both sides. While the Korean side is trying to replace the Taejon Agreement, concluded "in view of prevailing conditions of warfare", with a new one based on the spirit of mutual respect and under totally different conditions, it seems that the basic position of your side is to modify the already existing agreement.

We noted with grave concern that the U.S. negotiators have incorporated in their draft article a totally irrelevant concept of geographical limitation in the application of our rights to exercise jurisdiction over the Korean territory. Under the provisions of the U.S. draft, the authorities of the Republic of Korea is precluded from exercising its jurisdiction in certain areas of Korean territory under the term of "combat zone". The concept of the combat zone may be useful for military operational purposes during war time but we believe this concept should have no room for consideration in negotiating this "criminal jurisdiction". Moreover, the extent of the so called "combat zone" you have suggested covers most of the area and zone where most of United States armed forces are currently stationed. According to our statistics and records, major offenses

0368

and accidents were committed or happened in that zone in the past. Without jurisdiction over that part of Korea, the agreement would have very little meaning to us.

Furthermore, your draft requests the Korean authorities to waive in cases where there are concurrent rights, except under special circumstances in the specific case, in recognition of the primary responsibility of the U.S. military authorities for maintaining good order and discipline among the members of the United States armed forces, civilian component and their dependents.

Your draft also requests us to give sympathetic consideration even in the exercise of exclusive jurisdiction in recognition of the effectiveness of administrative and disciplinary sanctions to be excercised by the U.S. Authorities. However, we believe that the right of exclusive jurisdiction of a State should not be waived in favour of administrative or disciplinary sanctions of the military authorities of another State.

We also noted your side's intention to have primary right to exercise jurisdiction over the members of the U.S. armed forces with respect to offenses which, if committed by the members of the armed forces of Korea, would be tried by court-martial. We do not know whether or not the U.S. negotiators before proposing this have studied the existing Korean Military Law. According to the said law, as far as the members of the Korean armed forces and civilian components are concerned, the court-martial has exclusive right to exercise jurisdiction with respect to all offenses no matter whether they are committed on or off duty and however minor they are in nature. Without waiting further explanation, it becomes quite clear that the U.S. Side is demanding exclusive jurisdiction over all members of the U.S. armed forces regardless of the nature and place of the offenses committed.

0369

As all of us know well, the problem of determining the scope of jurisdiction constitutes the backbone of the entire Article and consequently the agreement as a whole. The imposition of such conditions as indicated in your draft would be quite contrary to our bona fide intentions of negotiating this Status of Forces Agreement. Now, at this point, let us make assumption that we come to an agreement on the basis of your draft, what would be left for us then? We really wonder what sort of jurisdiction we are supposed to exercise, and over whom? It would have been simpler for your side only to provide for over what cases the Korean authorities could exercise their jurisdiction, instead of enumerating so many conditions under which our right to exercise jurisdiction is limited, in practice, to a degree of non-existence.

Your draft also requests that the U.S. military authorities should have primary right in the custody of an accused member of the United States armed forces or civilian component or of a dependent even if he is in the hands of the Republic of Korea. It further provides that the Korean authorities should give sympathetic consideration to the request of the U.S. authorities asking for turn-over of offenders who are serving a sentence of confinement imposed by a Korean court. The acceptance of this request would mean almost total waiver of our remaining token right.

What I mentioned above are but a few of the examples which make our two positions fundamentally and substantially different. As a whole, we are under a impression that the contents of your draft article are not much different from those of the Taejon Agreement, as far as the substance of the matter is concerned. We do hope that this is certainly not the desire of the U.S. negotiators. We want your side to understand that the people of Korea have been anxious for more than a decade to see the conclusion of the Status of Forces Agreement. Unfortunately, your draft does not meet the desire of the Korean people. The Korean negotiators, therefore, find it

0370

difficult to accept the draft tabled by the United States negotiators as a basis of our further discussions.

In view of the above explanation, we sincerely hope that your side would reconsider your position on the subject of criminal jurisdiction or accept our draft as a basis for conducting the negotiation. We will now table our draft Agreed Minutes.

0371

3. Mr. Habib stated that he wished to make a few general remarks in reply to those made by Mr. Chang. He said the U.S. negotiators had not expected that the Korean negotiators would accept the U.S. draft. Nor did the U.S. negotiators accept the Korean draft. The drafts had been exchanged in order to provide a basis for negotiation. The purpose of each draft was to set forward as clearly as possible the views of each side on the subject of criminal jurisdiction.

4. Mr. Habib said the purpose of the U.S. negotiators could be stated very simply. With regard to the judicial rights of the individual, the U.S. negotiators are bound by Congressional, moral, ethical, and personal desires to insure that the U.S. military and civilian personnel in the Republic of Korea pursuant to the terms of the Mutual Security Treaty receive judicial treatment according to standards acceptable to the United States. He said the U.S. negotiators believe that this purpose can be achieved through the adoption of provisions consonant with the large body of precedents which has been developed. If both sides are responsive to the Korean desires and the U.S. needs, the U.S. negotiators believe that a criminal jurisdiction article can be negotiated successfully.

5. Mr. Habib said the U.S. negotiators would like to call to the attention of the Korean negotiators the fact that the article which was about to be negotiated would be something quite unique among status of forces agreements. He pointed out that it would cover a very considerable number of U.S. troops. The only similar situation was that in the Federal Republic of Germany, where the United States also has large numbers of troops. Additional important factors in the situation in the Republic of Korea, which do not exist anywhere else in the world, include the facts that U.S. forces are in tactical, combat positions under a condition of armistice, and in fulfillment of special international obligations. This is a unique situation. It cannot be equated with the situation anywhere else in the world.

0372

6. The Korean negotiators, Mr. Habib continued, appear to have a tendency to want to equate the situation in the Republic of Korea with the situation in Japan. The draft of this article tabled by the Korean negotiators reflects that tendency. In Japan, the United States has only a few thousand support troops in special compounds. Furthermore, the Status of Forces Agreement with Japan was negotiated more than ten years ago. In the actual application of that agreement, procedures have developed which differ from the actual text of the agreement. The Korean negotiators tended to follow blindly the text of the agreement, while ignoring the practice.

7. Mr. Habib pointed out that a more suitable precedent than the SOFA with Japan would be the SOFA with the Federal Republic of Germany, or the SOFA with the West Indies, or perhaps the Australian or Netherlands Agreements, which are modifications of the NATO Agreement. He urged that the negotiators not attempt to pattern the ROK SOFA after one which is completely alien to the conditions existing in the Republic of Korea.

8. Mr. Habib said that the U.S. negotiators did not intend to reply immediately to the opening statement by the Korean negotiators, in view of the fact that the Agreed Minutes of the Korean draft had just been tabled. The U.S. negotiators would study carefully the remarks made by the Korean chief negotiator and would be prepared to discuss the various elements of the article in a logical fashion at a subsequent meeting. There should be no question in the minds of any of the negotiators that both sides are trying to reach agreement on a text which will meet the needs of both sides. The opening remarks of the Korean chief negotiator appeared to indicate that the Korean negotiators believed the intention of the U.S. negotiators to be invidious. This was not the case. The U.S. negotiators must see to it that the article provides that measure of judicial right to U.S. personnel to which they are entitled. How to accomplish this was a task that challenged the ingenuity of both sides. However, it could not be accomplished by taking the SOFA with Japan and adding three or four additional restrictions. Such a course would not be

0373

acceptable to the U.S. negotiators.

9. Mr. Habib asked the Korean negotiators to keep in mind the purpose of the U.S. negotiators. He reminded them that both drafts were subject to negotiation. The U.S. negotiators would study the Korean draft and present their sincere response at a subsequent meeting. Mr. Chang agreed that both sides should give further consideration to the subject and be prepared to discuss the article again at the next meeting.

Publicity Regarding the Negotiations

10. Mr. Habib stated that before leaving the Criminal Jurisdiction Article, he wished to call the attention of the Korean negotiators to an article appearing in that day's press (Chosun Ilbo and Taehan Ilbo) which was attributed to officials of the Foreign Ministry and which made invidious references to the U.S. draft of this article. The U.S. negotiators wished to suggest that Foreign Ministry officials not state their negotiating positions in the press and, above all, not state the negotiating positions of the U.S. negotiators. He reminded the Korean negotiators that at the outset of the negotiations, it had been agreed that the negotiations would not be discussed in detail with the press by either side. The U.S. negotiators, in accordance with that agreement, had declined to discuss the substance of the negotiations with reporters. However, the reporters had indicated to Mr. Habib that Foreign Office officials did not share this view.

11. Mr. Habib stated that the U.S. negotiators would not agree to negotiate in the press. If any further articles of the type he had cited appeared in the press, the U.S. negotiators would suspend the negotiations and take the matter up with high officials of the ROK Government. Continued appearance in the press of articles of this sort could only create trouble, since they were based on no facts or a very poor interpretation of the facts. If the Korean negotiators wished to arouse the emotions of the Korean people, for completely unwarranted

0374

reasons, this would be the way to do it. But the U.S. negotiators would not be parties to such a course of action. The U.S. negotiators were determined to negotiate a Status of Forces Agreement but they would not negotiate it in the public press. The U.S. negotiators would continue to refuse to discuss details of the negotiations with newsmen. They asked the Korean negotiators to adopt a similar stance.

12. Mr. Chang replied that the U.S. negotiators misunderstood the situation. They had implied that the Korean negotiators were conducting a press campaign. In the Republic of Korea, as in the United States, there is freedom of the press. When reporters write speculative articles concerning the negotiations, they cite Foreign Ministry officials as their sources. There was nothing which the Korean negotiators could do to stop such a practice. The Korean negotiators ~~would~~ did abide by the agreement made at the beginning of the negotiations and ~~would~~ did not carry out any press campaign to influence the course of the negotiations. However, the people of the Republic of Korea have an interest in these negotiations second only to their interest in the normalization negotiations with Japan. Consequently, the Korean press, unavoidably, would tend to produce considerable number of articles and commentaries on the negotiations, factual or speculative. The Korean negotiators found the remark ~~threat [illegible]~~ made by the U.S. negotiators to suspend negotiations to be quite regrettable.

13. Mr. Habib replied that the U.S. negotiators believed that discussion in the press of what occurs during the negotiating meetings ~~[illegible]~~ is equally regrettable. The U.S. negotiators believed that the least the Korean negotiators could do would be to have the newspapers publish retractions of speculative stories. He said he wished to discuss this matter further with the Korean negotiators outside of the negotiating sessions.

Utilities and Services

14. Turning to the article dealing with utilities and services, Mr. Habib stated that the Korean negotiators had made valuable suggestions for revising this article. The U.S. side was ~~[illegible]~~ principle to almost all of

0375

these suggestions.

15. In paragraph 3(a), Mr. Habib stated, the U.S. negotiators agreed to the deletion of the phrase "however produced", with the understanding that the negotiating record should clearly show that no discrimination based on type or manner of production of utilities or services will occur.

16. Mr. Habib stated that the U.S. negotiators accepted the proposal of the Korean negotiators that paragraph 4 of the U.S. draft be deleted from this article and be made a separate article.

17. With regard to Agreed Minute #2 of the revised Korean draft, the U.S. negotiators accepted the Korean text, including the phrase "unless otherwise agreed by the two governments", but stipulated that the negotiating record show that the U.S. Government has no current intention of agreeing otherwise.

18. Mr. Habib then tabled revised drafts of Agreed Minutes #1 and #3, which the U.S. negotiators believed to be consistent with the views of the Korean negotiators. The U.S. negotiators suggested that the Korean negotiators study these revisions and give their views at the next meeting.

19. The revision of Agreed Minute #1 tabled by the U.S. negotiators reads as follows:

> "It is understood that any changes determined by the Korean authorities in priorities, conditions, and rates or tariffs, applicable to the United States armed forces shall be the subject of consultation in the Joint Committee prior to their effective date."

20. The revision of Agreed Minute #3 tabled by the U.S. negotiators reads as follows:

> "In an emergency the Republic of Korea agrees to take appropriate measures to assure provision of utilities and services necessary to meet the needs of the United States armed forces."

0376

~~those suggestions.~~

~~In paragraph 3(a), Mr. Habib stated, the U.S. negotiators agreed to the deletion of the phrase "however produced", withthe understanding that the negotiating record should clearly show that no discrimination based on type or manner of production of utilities or services will occur.~~

~~Mr. Habib stated that the U.S. negotiators accepted the proposal of the Korean negotiators that paragraph 4 of the U.S. draft be deleted from this article and be made a separate article.~~

~~With regard to Agreed Minute #2 of the revised Korean draft, the U.S. negotiators accepted the Korean text, including the phrase "unless otherwise agreed by the two governments", provided that the negotiating record show that the U.S. Government has no current intention of agreeing otherwise.~~

~~Mr. Habib then tabled revised drafts of Agreed Minutes #1 and #3, which the U.S. negotiators believed to be consistent with the views of the Korean negotiators. The U.S. negotiators suggested that the Korean negotiators study these revisions and give their views at a subsequent meeting.~~

21. Mr. Chang stated that the Korean negotiators accepted the deletion of the phrase "however produced" with the understanding which Mr. Habib had mentioned. They also agreed to the placing of paragraph 4 elsewhere in the Agreement as a separate article. They understood the position of the U.S. negotiators with regard to Agreed Minute #2 and wished to state for the record that the ROK Government also had no immediate plans for agreeing otherwise. Mr. Chang stated that there appeared to be no difference in substance between the drafts of Agreed Minutes #1 and #3 tabled by the two sides. However, the Korean negotiators would study the U.S. revisions and give their views at a later meeting.

0377

22. At this point, it was agreed to hold the next meeting on March 6 at 2:00 p.m. and the meeting was adjourned.

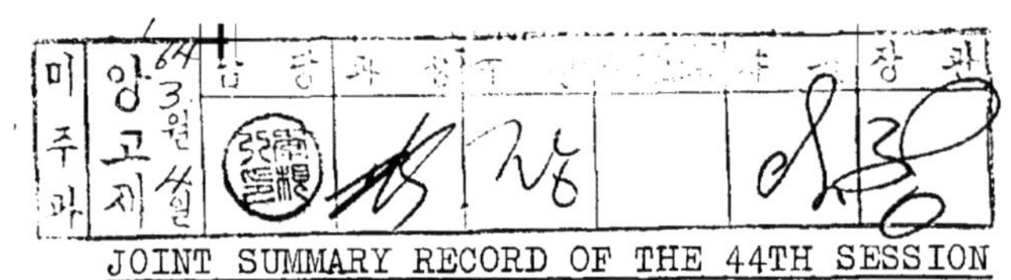

JOINT SUMMARY RECORD OF THE 44TH SESSION

1. Time and Place: 2:00-4:00 P.M. February 28, 1964 at the Foreign Ministry's Conference Room

2. Attendants:

ROK Side:

| | |
|---|---|
| Mr. Chang, Sang Moon | Director<br>European and American Affairs Bureau |
| Mr. Yoon, Doo Sik | Director<br>Prosecutor's Bureau<br>Ministry of Justice |
| Mr. Chung, Tai Kyun | Chief<br>Prosecutor's Section<br>Prosecutor's Bureau<br>Ministry of Justice |
| Mr. Lee, Myung Hi | Prosecutor<br>Prosecutor's Bureau<br>Ministry of Justice |
| Mr. Koo, Choong Whay | Chief, American Section<br>Ministry of Foreign Affairs |
| Mr. Lee, Chai Sup | Staff Officer<br>Customs Bureau<br>Ministry of Finance |
| Col. Kim, Won Kil | Chief, Ministry Affairs Section<br>Ministry of National Defense |
| Mr. Oh, Jae Hee | Chief, Treaty Section<br>Ministry of Foreign Affairs |
| Mr. Kang, Suk Jae<br>(Rapporteur and Interpreter) | 2nd Secretary<br>Ministry of Foreign Affairs |
| Mr. Chung, Woo Young | 3rd Secretary<br>Ministry of Foreign Affairs |
| Mr. Lee, Chung Bin | 3rd Secretary<br>Ministry of Foreign Affairs |
| Mr. Lee, Keun Pal | 3rd Secretary<br>Ministry of Foreign Affairs |
| Mr. Kim, Nai Sung | Staff Officer<br>Europe Section<br>Ministry of Foreign Affairs |

0378

U.S. Side:

| | |
|---|---|
| Mr. Philip C. Habib | Counselor<br>American Embassy |
| Brig. Gen. G.G. O'Connor | Deputy Chief of Staff<br>8th U.S. Army |
| Brig. Gen. L.J. Fuller | Staff Judge Advocate<br>United Nations Command |
| Col. Howard Smigelow | Deputy Chief of Staff<br>8th U.S. Army |
| Col. Kenneth C. Crawford | Staff Judge Advocates Office<br>8th U.S. Army |
| X Capt. John Wayne | Assistant Chief of Staff<br>USN/K |
| Mr. Benjamin A. Fleck (Rapporteur and Press Officer) | First Secretary<br>American Embassy |
| Mr. James Sartorius | 2nd Secretary<br>American Embassy |
| X Mr. Robert A. Lewis | 2nd Secretary and Consul<br>American Embassy |
| Mr. Robert A. Kinney | J-5<br>8th U.S. Army |
| Mr. Robert D. Peckham | Staff Officer, JAG<br>8th U.S. Army |
| Mr. Kenneth Campen | Interpreter |
| Mr. D. C. Reed | Director<br>Office of Civil Personnel<br>8th U.S. Army |

1. Mr. Chang opened the meeting by extending the congratulations of the Korean negotiators to Brig. General Fuller, who had been promoted that very morning. Mr. Chang then introduced the following gentlemen: Mr. YUN Tu-sik, Director of the Prosecutor's Bureau, Ministry of Justice; Mr. CHUNG Tai-kyun, Chief of the Prosecutor's Section, Ministry of Justice; and Mr. YI Myung-hi, Prosecutor, from the same office. Mr. Habib welcomed these gentlemen to the negotiations.

Criminal Jurisdiction

2. Taking up the Criminal Jurisdiction Article, Mr. Chang stated that he wished to make some introductory remarks. He then made the following statement:

0379

We do not think it is necessary to emphasize the importance our people attach to the article dealing with criminal jurisdiction of the prospective Status of Forces Agreement now under negotiation between the two parties. However, I would like to reiterate that the successful and speedy conclusion of our present negotiations entirely depends upon how soon we can come to an agreement on this Article.

We have studied most carefully the draft tabled by the U.S. negotiators at the 42nd meeting. To our great disappointment, however, the Korean negotiators have found that fundamental differences are wide between the two sides' drafts on the subject matter.

Aside from various differences of major or minor nature, we believe that there is a fundamental difference in the approach of both sides. While the Korean side is trying to replace the Taejon Agreement, concluded "in view of prevailing conditions of warfare", with a new one based on the spirit of mutual respect and under totally different conditions, it seems that the basic position of your side is to modify the already existing agreement.

We noted with grave concern that the U.S. negotiators have incorporated in their draft article a totally irrelevant concept of geographical limitation in the application of our rights to exercise jurisdiction over the Korean territory. Under the provisions of the U.S. draft, the authorities of the Republic of Korea is precluded from exercising its jurisdiction in certain areas of Korean territory under the term of "combat

0380

zone". The concept of the combat zone may be useful for military operational purposes during war time but we believe this concept should have no room for consideration in negotiating this "criminal jurisdiction". Moreover, the extent of the so called "combat zone" you have suggested covers most of the area and zone where most of United States armed forces are currently stationed. According to our statistics and records, major offenses and accidents were committed or happened in that zone in the past. Without jurisdiction over that part of Korea, the agreement would have very little meaning to us.

Furthermore, your draft requests the Korean authorities to waive in cases where there are concurrent rights, except under special circumstances in the specific case, in recognition of the primary responsibility of the U.S. military authorities for maintaining good order and discipline among the members of the United States armed forces, civilian component and their dependents.

Your draft also requests us to give sympathetic consideration even in the exercise of exclusive jurisdiction in recognition of the effectiveness of administrative and disciplinary sanctions to be exercised by the U.S. Authorities. However, we believe that the right of exclusive jurisdiction of a State should not be waived in favour of administrative or disciplinary sanctions of the military authorities of another State.

We also noted your side's intention to have primary right to exercise jurisdiction over the members of the U.S. armed forces with respect to offenses which, if committed by the members of the armed forces of Korea, would be tried by court-martial. We do not know whether or not the U.S. negotiators before proposing

0381

this have studied the existing Korean Military Law. According to the said law, as far as the members of the Korean armed forces and civilian components are concerned, the court-martial has exclusive right to exercise jurisdiction with respect to all offenses no matter whether they are committed on or off duty and however minor they are in nature. Without waiting further explanation, it becomes quite clear that the U.S. side is demanding exclusive jurisdiction over all members of the U.S. armed forces regardless of the nature and place of the offenses committed.

As all of us know well, the problem of determining the scope of jurisdiction constitutes the backbone of the entire Article and consequently the agreement as a whole. The imposition of such conditions as indicated in your draft would be quite contrary to our bona fide intentions of negotiating this Status of Forces Agreement. Now, at this point, let us make assumption that we come to an agreement on the basis of your draft, what would be left for us then? We really wonder what sort of jurisdiction we are supposed to exercise, and over whom? It would have been simpler for your side only to provide for over what cases the Korean authorities could exercise their jurisdiction, instead of enumerating so many conditions under which our right to exercise jurisdiction is limited, in practice, to a degree of non-existence.

Your draft also requests that the U.S. military authorities should have primary right in the custody of an accused member of the United States armed forces

0382

or civilian component or of a dependent even if he is in the hands of the Republic of Korea. It further provides that the Korean authorities should give sympathetic consideration to the request of the U.S. authorities asking for turn-over of offenders who are serving a sentence of confinement imposed by a Korean court. The acceptance of this request would mean almost total waiver of our remaining token right.

What I mentioned above are but a few of the examples which make our two positions fundamentally and substantially different. As a whole, we are under a impression that the contents of your draft article are not much different from those of the Taejon Agreement, as far as the substance of the matter is concerned. We do hope that this is certainly not the desire of the U.S. negotiators. We want your side to understand that the people of Korea have been anxious for more than a decade to see the conclusion of the Status of Forces Agreement. Unfortunately, your draft does not meet the desire of the Korean people. The Korean negotiators, therefore, find it difficult to accept the draft tabled by the United States negotiators as a basis of our further discussions.

In view of the above explanation, we sincerely hope that your side would reconsider your position on the subject of criminal jurisdiction or accept our draft as a basis for conducting the negotiation. We will now table our draft Agreed Minutes.

3. Mr. Habib stated that he wished to make a few general remarks in reply to those made by Mr. Chang.

0383

He said the U.S. negotiators had not expected that the Korean negotiators would accept the U.S. draft. Nor did the U.S. negotiators accept the Korean draft. The drafts had been exchanged in order to provide a basis for negotiation. The purpose of each draft was to set forward as clearly as possible the views of each side on the subject of criminal jurisdiction.

4. Mr. Habib said the purpose of the U.S. negotiators could be stated very simply. With regard to the judicial rights of the individual, the U.S. negotiators are bound by Congressional, moral, ethical, and personal desires to insure that the U.S. military and civilian personnel in the Republic of Korea pursuant to the terms of the Mutual Security Treaty receive judicial treatment according to standards acceptable to the United States. He said the U.S. negotiators believe that this purpose can be achieved through the adoption of provisions consonant with the large body of precedents which has been developed. If both sides are responsive to the Korean desires and the U.S. needs, the U.S. negotiators believe that a criminal jurisdiction article can be negotiated successfully.

5. Mr. Habib said the U.S. negotiators would like to call to the attention of the Korean negotiators the fact that the article which was about to be negotiated would be something quite unique among status of forces agreements. He pointed out that it would cover a very considerable number of U.S. troops. The only similar situation was that in the Federal Republic of Germany, where the United States also has large numbers of troops.

0384

Additional important factors in the situation in the Republic of Korea, which do not exist anywhere else in the world, include the facts that U.S. forces are in tactical, combat positions under a condition of armistice, and in fulfillment of special international obligations. This is a unique situation. It cannot be equated with the situation anywhere else in the world.

6. The Korean negotiators, Mr. Habib continued, appear to have a tendency to want to equate the situation in the Republic of Korea with the situation in Japan. The draft of this article tabled by the Korean negotiators reflects that tendency. In Japan, the United States has only a few thousand support troops in special compounds. Forthermore, the Status of Forces Agreement with Japan was negotiated more than ten years ago. In the actual application of that agreement, procedures have developed which differ from the actual text of the agreement. The Korean negotiators tended to follow blindly the text of the agreement, while ignoring the practice.

7. Mr. Habib pointed out that a more suitable precedent than the SOFA with Japan would be the SOFA with the Federal Republic of Germany, or the SOFA with the West Indies, or perhaps the Australian or Netherlands Agreements, which are modifications of the NATO Agreement. He urged that the negotiators not attempt to pattern the ROK SOFA after one which is completely alien to the conditions existing in the Republic of Korea.

8. Mr.Habib said that the U.S. negotiators did not intend to reply immediately to the opening statement by

the Korean negotiators, in view of the fact that the Agreed Minutes of the Korean draft had just been tabled. The U.S. negotiators would study carefully the remarks made by the Korean chief negotiator and would be prepared to discuss the various elements of the article in a logical fashion at a subsequent meeting. There should be no question in the minds of any of the negotiators that both sides are trying to reach agreement on a text which will meet the needs of both sides. The opening remarks of the Korean chief negotiator appeared to indicate that the Korean negotiators believed the intention of the U.S. negotiators to be invidious. This was not the case. The U.S. negotiators must see to it that the article provides that measure of judicial right to U.S. personnel to which they are entitled. How to accomplish this was a task that challenged the ingenuity of both sides. However, it could not be accomplished by taking the SOFA with Japan and adding three or four additional restrictions. Such a course would not be acceptable to the U.S. negotiators.

9. Mr. Habib asked the Korean negotiators to keep in mind the purpose of the U.S. negotiators. He reminded them that both drafts were subject to negotiation. The U.S. negotiators would study the Korean draft and present their sincere response at a subsequent meeting. Mr. Chang agreed that both sides should give further consideration to the subject and be prepared to discuss the article again at the next meeting.

<u>Publicity Regarding the Negotiations</u>

10. Mr. Habib stated that before leaving the Criminal Jurisdiction Article, he wished to call the attention

0386

of the Korean negotiators to an article appearing in that day's press (Chosun Ilbo and Taehan Ilbo) which was attributed to officials of the Foreign Ministry and which made invidious references to the U.S. draft of this article. The U.S. negotiators wished to suggest that Foreign Ministry officials not state their negotiating positions in the press and, above all, not state the negotiating positions of the U.S. negotiators. He reminded the Korean negotiators that at the outset of the negotiations, it had been agreed that the negotiations would not be discussed in detail with the press by either side. The U.S. negotiators, in accordance with that agreement, had declined to discuss the substance of the negotiations with reporters. However, the reporters had indicated to Mr. Habib that Foreign Office officials did not share this view.

11. Mr. Habib stated that the U.S. negotiators would not agree to negotiate in the press. If any further articles of the type he had cited appeared in the press, the U.S. negotiators would suspend the negotiations and take the matter up with high officials of the ROK Government. Continued appearance in the press of articles of this sort could only create trouble, since they were based on no facts or a very poor interpretation of the facts. If the Korean negotiators wished to arouse the emotions of the Korean people, for completely unwarranted reasons, this would be the way to do it. But the U.S. negotiators would not be parties to such a course of action. The U.S. negotiators were determined to negotiate a Status of Forces Agreement but they would not negotiate it in the public press. The U.S. negotiators would continue

0387

to refuse to discuss details of the negotiations with newsmen. They asked the Korean negotiators to adopt a similar stance.

12. Mr. Chang replied that the U.S. negotiators misunderstood the situation. They had implied that the Korean negotiators were conducting a press campaign. In the Republic of Korea, as in the United States, there is freedom of the press. When reporters write speculative articles concerning the negotiations, they cite Foreign Ministry officials as their sources. There was nothing which the Korean negotiators could do to stop such a practice. The Korean negotiators did abide by the agreement made at the beginning of the negotiations and did not carry out any press campaign to influence the course of the negotiations. However, the people of the Republic of Korea have an interest in these negotiations second only to their interest in the normalization negotiations with Japan. Consequently, the Korean press, unavoidably, would tend to produce a considerable number of articles and commentaries on the negotiations, factual or speculative. The Korean negotiators found the remark made by the U.S. negotiators to suspend negotiations to be quite regrettable.

13. Mr. Habib replied that the U.S. negotiators believed that discussion in the press of what occurs during the negotiating meetings is equally regrettable. The U.S. negotiators believed that the least the Korean negotiators could do would be to have the newspapers publish retractions of speculative stories. He said he wished to discuss this matter further with the Korean negotiators outside of the negotiating sessions.

0388

Utilities and Services

14. Turning to the article dealing with utilities and services, Mr. Habib stated that the Korean negotiators had made valuable suggestions for revising this article. The U.S. side was prepared to agree in principle to almost all of these suggestions.

15. In paragraph 3(a), Mr. Habib stated, the U.S. negotiators agreed to the deletion of the phrase "however produced", with the understanding that the negotiating record should clearly show that no discrimination based on type or manner of production of utilities or services will occur.

16. Mr. Habib stated that the U.S. negotiators accepted the proposal of the Korean negotiators that paragraph 4 of the U.S. draft be deleted from this article and be made a separate article.

17. With regard to Agreed Minute #2 of the revised Korean draft, the U.S. negotiators accepted the Korean text, including the phrase "unless otherwise agreed by the two governments", but stipulated that the negotiating record show that the U.S. Government has no current intention of agreeing otherwise.

18. Mr. Habib then tabled revised drafts of Agreed Minutes #1 and #3, which the U.S. negotiators believed to be consistent with the views on the Korean negotiators. The U.S. negotiatprs suggested that the Korean negotiators study these revisions and give their views at the next meeting.

19. The revision of Agreed Minute #1 tabled by the U.S. negotiators reads as follows:

0380

"It is understood that any changes determined by the Korean authorities in priorities, conditions, and rates or tariffs, applicable to the United States armed forces shall be the subject of consultation in the Joint Committee prior to their effective date."

20. The revision of Agreed Minute #3 tabled by the U.S. negotiators reads as follows:

"In an emergency the Republic of Korea agrees to take appropriate measures to assure provision of utilities and services necessary to meet the needs of the United States armed forces."

21. Mr. Chang stated that the Korean negotiators accepted the deletion of the phrase "however produced" with the understanding which Mr. Habib had mentioned. They also agreed to the placing of paragraph 4 elsewhere in the Agreement as a separate article. They understood the position of the U.S. negotiators with regard to Agreed Minute #2 and wished to state for the record that the ROK Government also had no immediate plans for agreeing otherwise. Mr. Chang stated that there appeared to be no difference in substance between the drafts of Agreed Minutes #1 and #3 tabled by the two sides. However, the Korean negotiators would study the U.S. revisions and give their views at a later meeting.

22. At this point, it was agreed to hold the next meeting on March 6 at 2:00 p.m. and the meeting was adjourned.

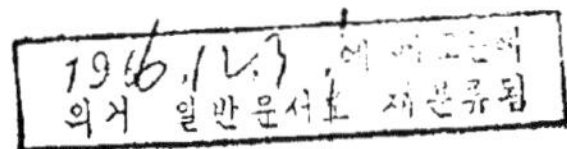

0390

외교문서 비밀해제: 주한미군지위협정(SOFA) 7
주한미군지위협정(SOFA) 서명 및 발효 7

초판인쇄 2024년 03월 15일
초판발행 2024년 03월 15일

지은이 한국학술정보(주)
펴낸이 채종준
펴낸곳 한국학술정보(주)
주 소 경기도 파주시 회동길 230(문발동)
전 화 031-908-3181(대표)
팩 스 031-908-3189
홈페이지 http://ebook.kstudy.com
E-mail 출판사업부 publish@kstudy.com
등 록 제일산-115호(2000. 6. 19)

ISBN 979-11-7217-018-9 94340
979-11-7217-011-0 94340 (set)


책에 대한 더 나은 생각, 끊임없는 고민, 독자를 생각하는 마음으로 보다 좋은 책을 만들어갑니다.